Intelligent Biosignal Analysis Methods

Intelligent Biosignal Analysis Methods

Editor

Alan Jović

MDPI • Basel • Beijing • Wuhan • Barcelona • Belgrade • Manchester • Tokyo • Cluj • Tianjin

Editor
Alan Jović
Faculty of Electrical Engineering
and Computing
University of Zagreb
Zagreb
Croatia

Editorial Office
MDPI
St. Alban-Anlage 66
4052 Basel, Switzerland

This is a reprint of articles from the Special Issue published online in the open access journal *Sensors* (ISSN 1424-8220) (available at: www.mdpi.com/journal/sensors/special_issues/Intelligent_Biosignal).

For citation purposes, cite each article independently as indicated on the article page online and as indicated below:

LastName, A.A.; LastName, B.B.; LastName, C.C. Article Title. *Journal Name* **Year**, *Volume Number*, Page Range.

ISBN 978-3-0365-1692-9 (Hbk)
ISBN 978-3-0365-1691-2 (PDF)

© 2021 by the authors. Articles in this book are Open Access and distributed under the Creative Commons Attribution (CC BY) license, which allows users to download, copy and build upon published articles, as long as the author and publisher are properly credited, which ensures maximum dissemination and a wider impact of our publications.

The book as a whole is distributed by MDPI under the terms and conditions of the Creative Commons license CC BY-NC-ND.

Contents

About the Editor vii

Alan Jovic
Intelligent Biosignal Analysis Methods
Reprinted from: *Sensors* **2021**, *21*, 4743, doi:10.3390/s21144743 1

Tianqi Zhu, Wei Luo and Feng Yu
Multi-Branch Convolutional Neural Network for Automatic Sleep Stage Classification with Embedded Stage Refinement and Residual Attention Channel Fusion
Reprinted from: *Sensors* **2020**, *20*, 6592, doi:10.3390/s20226592 7

Pei-Chun Su, Elsayed Z. Soliman and Hau-Tieng Wu
Robust T-End Detection via T-End Signal Quality Index and Optimal Shrinkage
Reprinted from: *Sensors* **2020**, *20*, 7052, doi:10.3390/s20247052 23

Heekyung Yang, Jongdae Han and Kyungha Min
EEG-Based Estimation on the Reduction of Negative Emotions for Illustrated Surgical Images
Reprinted from: *Sensors* **2020**, *20*, 7103, doi:10.3390/s20247103 41

Alessandro Tonacci, Lucia Billeci, Irene Di Mambro, Roberto Marangoni, Chiara Sanmartin and Francesca Venturi
Wearable Sensors for Assessing the Role of Olfactory Training on the Autonomic Response to Olfactory Stimulation
Reprinted from: *Sensors* **2021**, *21*, 770, doi:10.3390/s21030770 61

Jia-Zheng Jian, Tzong-Rong Ger, Han-Hua Lai, Chi-Ming Ku, Chiung-An Chen, Patricia Angela R. Abu and Shih-Lun Chen
Detection of Myocardial Infarction Using ECG and Multi-Scale Feature Concatenate
Reprinted from: *Sensors* **2021**, *21*, 1906, doi:10.3390/s21051906 75

Hui Huang, Jianhai Zhang, Li Zhu, Jiajia Tang, Guang Lin, Wanzeng Kong, Xu Lei and Lei Zhu
EEG-Based Sleep Staging Analysis with Functional Connectivity
Reprinted from: *Sensors* **2021**, *21*, 1988, doi:10.3390/s21061988 93

Andrea Giorgi, Vincenzo Ronca, Alessia Vozzi, Nicolina Sciaraffa, Antonello di Florio, Luca Tamborra, Ilaria Simonetti, Pietro Aricò, Gianluca Di Flumeri, Dario Rossi and Gianluca Borghini
Wearable Technologies for Mental Workload, Stress, and Emotional State Assessment during Working-Like Tasks: A Comparison with Laboratory Technologies
Reprinted from: *Sensors* **2021**, *21*, 2332, doi:10.3390/s21072332 109

Kei Suzuki, Tipporn Laohakangvalvit, Ryota Matsubara and Midori Sugaya
Constructing an Emotion Estimation Model Based on EEG/HRV Indexes Using Feature Extraction and Feature Selection Algorithms
Reprinted from: *Sensors* **2021**, *21*, 2910, doi:10.3390/s21092910 131

Alexander Kamrud, Brett Borghetti and Christine Schubert Kabban
The Effects of Individual Differences, Non-Stationarity, and the Importance of Data Partitioning Decisions for Training and Testing of EEG Cross-Participant Models
Reprinted from: *Sensors* **2021**, *21*, 3225, doi:10.3390/s21093225 153

Igor Stancin, Mario Cifrek and Alan Jovic
A Review of EEG Signal Features and Their Application in Driver Drowsiness Detection Systems
Reprinted from: *Sensors* **2021**, *21*, 3786, doi:10.3390/s21113786 . . . . **183**

Haijing Sun, Anna Wang, Wenhui Wang and Chen Liu
An Improved Deep Residual Network Prediction Model for the Early Diagnosis of Alzheimer's Disease
Reprinted from: *Sensors* **2021**, *21*, 4182, doi:10.3390/s21124182 . . . . **213**

Goran Šeketa, Lovro Pavlaković, Dominik Džaja, Igor Lacković and Ratko Magjarević
Event-Centered Data Segmentation in Accelerometer-Based Fall Detection Algorithms
Reprinted from: *Sensors* **2021**, *21*, 4335, doi:10.3390/s21134335 . . . . **229**

About the Editor

Alan Jović

Alan Jović received Dipl. Ing. and Ph.D. degrees in computing from the Faculty of Electrical Engineering and Computing, University of Zagreb, in 2006 and 2012, respectively, where he is currently an Associate Professor. He has mostly worked on the applications of artificial intelligence methods in biomedicine. His research interests include data mining, knowledge representation, biomedical engineering and software engineering. He has published more than 60 papers in scientific journals and international conference proceedings. He is a managing editor for CIT. Journal of Computing and Information Technology. He has reviewed more than 100 papers for international journals in the areas of artificial intelligence, computer science and biomedical engineering. He has led several research and industrial projects. He has received several awards for his work, including the Vera Johanides young scientist award from Croatian Academy of Engineering. He is a member of IEEE and EMBS.

Editorial

Intelligent Biosignal Analysis Methods

Alan Jovic

Faculty of Electrical Engineering and Computing, University of Zagreb, Unska 3, 10000 Zagreb, Croatia; alan.jovic@fer.hr

Citation: Jovic, A. Intelligent Biosignal Analysis Methods. *Sensors* **2021**, *21*, 4743. https://doi.org/10.3390/s21144743

Received: 2 July 2021
Accepted: 7 July 2021
Published: 12 July 2021

Publisher's Note: MDPI stays neutral with regard to jurisdictional claims in published maps and institutional affiliations.

Copyright: © 2021 by the author. Licensee MDPI, Basel, Switzerland. This article is an open access article distributed under the terms and conditions of the Creative Commons Attribution (CC BY) license (https://creativecommons.org/licenses/by/4.0/).

This Editorial presents the accepted manuscripts for the special issue "Intelligent Biosignal Analysis Methods" of the Sensors MDPI journal.

The special issue consists of 12 accepted manuscripts (11 regular papers and 1 review paper) that present advances in research and development of intelligent biosignal analysis methods. These methods are involved in a variety of significant biomedical applications, ranging from clinical decision support systems and portable personal devices used for screening and monitoring patients to modeling organism states and disorders. The focus of this special issue is on different types of methods used for intelligent analysis, and therefore, the accepted manuscripts mostly use different types of machine learning and deep learning algorithms for classification tasks on different types of biosignals. Both the regular contributions and the review paper reach valuable conclusions and discuss avenues for future work in this exciting field. In continuation of this Editorial, the motivation, methods, results, and conclusions of the accepted papers are presented.

The first paper [1], titled "Multi-Branch Convolutional Neural Network for Automatic Sleep Stage Classification with Embedded Stage Refinement and Residual Attention Channel Fusion", was authored by T. Zhu, W. Luo, and F. Yu, from Zhejiang University, China.

The paper addresses a machine learning method developed for automatic sleep stage classification, which is an important and currently unsolved problem. An efficient and accurate solution could allow clinicians to efficiently assess a person's sleep quality and help diagnose a possible sleep disorder. The sleep stage refinement process was integrated into a neural network model to enable true end-to-end processing. Since detection can be made more efficient by incorporating multichannel signals, the authors used Sleep-EDF Expanded Database (Sleep-EDFx) and the University College Dublin Sleep Apnea Database (UCDDB), both of which include electroencephalogram (EEG), electrooculogram (EOG), and chin electromyogram (EMG). A multibranch convolutional neural network (CNN) was combined with a proposed residual attention method, and achieved a classification accuracy of 85.7% and 79.4% on the Sleep-EDFx and UCDDB databases, respectively, for the awake state and four sleep stages (N1, N2, N3, and REM). The proposed residual attention method had a more robust channel-information fusion ability than the respective average and concatenation methods.

The second paper [2], titled "Robust T-End Detection via T-End Signal Quality Index and Optimal Shrinkage", was authored by P.-C. Su, E.Z. Soliman, and H.-T. Wu, from Duke University and Wake Forest School of Medicine, USA, and from the National Center for Theoretical Sciences, Taiwan.

The authors address the problem of accurately detecting the end of the T-wave for providing automatic annotations in the electrocardiogram (ECG). This problem is difficult to solve due to the presence of noise in ECG signals. The authors propose an algorithm based on the signal quality index (SQI) for the T-wave end (tSQI) and the optimal shrinkage (OS). For segments with low tSQI, the OS is applied to enhance the signal-to-noise ratio. They evaluate their method on a set of 11 short-term ECG recordings from the freely available QT database and on four long-term ECG recordings. They find that tSQI captures signal quality well, and that the proposed OS denoising helps stabilize existing T-end detection algorithms under noisy situations. The methods could be well-suited for clinical applications and large ECG databases; however, the current study is limited by the small size of the annotated datasets available for consideration.

The paper [3], titled "EEG-Based Estimation on the Reduction of Negative Emotions for Illustrated Surgical Images", was authored by H. Yang, J. Han, and K. Min, from Sangmyung University, Korea.

The paper describes an approach to emotion recognition from EEG biosignals that aims to demonstrate that illustrated surgical images reduce negative emotional reactions compared to that of photographic surgical images. Because surgical images are important in communicating procedures to patients and nonspecialists, it is important to evaluate whether illustrated images that are similarly informative produce the same emotional response. To demonstrate the difference in emotional response, the authors recorded the emotional responses of 40 subjects to 10 pairs of images (surgical images and their illustrated counterparts). They combined their responses with a deep learning network to obtain accurate predictions of emotions. The results show that the estimated valence of illustrated surgical images is significantly higher than the valence of photographic surgical images and vice-versa for arousal, suggesting that illustrated images are better suited for communication with patients and nonspecialists.

The paper [4], titled "Wearable Sensors for Assessing the Role of Olfactory Training on the Autonomic Response to Olfactory Stimulation", was authored by A. Tonacci, L. Billeci, I. Di Mambro, R. Marangoni, C. Sanmartin, and F. Venturi, from the following institutions in Italy: National Research Council of Italy (IFC-CNR), University of Pisa, and NexFood Srl.

The authors focus on the key psychophysiological drivers of olfactory-related pleasantness, as the current literature demonstrated the relationship between odor familiarity and odor valence but has not clarified the consequential relationship between the two domains. They use analysis of ECG and galvanic skin response at the beginning and end of the olfactory training for 25 subjects enrolled in the study. The authors observed different autonomic system responses, with a higher parasympathetically-mediated response at the end of the training period. They conclude that increased familiarity with the suggested stimuli could lead to a higher tendency towards relaxation, which could be important for applications in personalized treatments based on odors and foods.

The paper [5], titled "Detection of Myocardial Infarction Using ECG and Multi-Scale Feature Concatenate", was authored by J.-Z. Jian, T.-R. Ger, H.-H. Lai, C.-M. Ku, C.-A. Chen, P.A.R. Abu, and S.-L. Chen, from Chung Yuan Christian University and Ming Chi University of Technology, Taiwan, and from Ateneo de Manila University, Philippines.

The authors investigate different convolutional neural networks (CNN) architectures that can be used for automatic detection of myocardial infarction (MI). Based on data from 200 patients from open-access PTB ECG database, the authors determined that the best network structure can be obtained via tuning both the number of filters in the convolutional layers and the number of input signal scales in the CNN. A multi-lead features-concatenate narrow network (N-Net) achieved 95.76% accuracy on the MI detection task, while multi-scale features-concatenate network (MSN-Net) achieved 61.82% accuracy on the MI locating task, which is a much more difficult task than MI detection. Both results outperfomed the state-of-the-art. The authors note that the constructed models are small in size, making them suitable for incorporation into wearable devices for offline monitoring.

The paper [6], titled "EEG-Based Sleep Staging Analysis with Functional Connectivity", was authored by H. Huang, J. Zhang, L. Zhu, J. Tang, G. Lin, W. Kong, X. Lei, and L. Zhu, from the following institutions in China: Hangzhou Dianzi University, Southwest University, and the Ministry of Education.

Similar to [1], this paper also deals with automatic sleep staging. The authors propose to use indices of functional connectivity from multiple EEG signal channels to classify sleep stages. The main idea of the paper is that brain functional connectivity during a sleep stage process is characterized by different frequency bands and that the interaction between brain regions may be specific to a particular sleep stage. They applied phase-locked value (PLV) to characterize phase synchronization between pairs of signals from different brain regions.

The authors demonstrate the effectiveness of using PLV for sleep stage discrimination, which is due to PLV increasing in the lower frequency band (delta and alpha bands) during different stages of nonrapid eye movement (NREM) sleep. They achieved a classification accuracy of feature-level fusion from six frequency bands for NREM, N2, and N3 stages of 96.91% and 96.14% for intrasubject and intersubject evaluations, respectively.

The paper [7], titled "Wearable Technologies for Mental Workload, Stress, and Emotional State Assessment during Working-Like Tasks: A Comparison with Laboratory Technologies", was authored by A. Giorgi, V. Ronca, A. Vozzi, N. Sciaraffa, A. di Florio, L. Tamborra, I. Simonetti, P. Aricò, G. Di Flumeri, D. Rossi, and G. Borghini, from several institutions in Italy: BrainSigns, Sapienza University of Rome, Ernst & Young, IRCCS Fondazione Santa Lucia, and LUISS University.

The authors contend that consumer wearables are characterized by their ease of use and their comfortability, and therefore, may be an ideal substitute for laboratory technologies in the real-time assessment of human performance in ecological settings. The study evaluated the reliability and capability of two consumer wearable devices, Empatica E4 and Muse 2, to assess stress, mental workload, and emotional state evaluation, while 17 participants performed 3 work-like tasks. The results were compared to that of laboratory devices. The study showed that the parameters computed by the consumer wearable devices and the laboratory sensors were positively and significantly correlated. In addition, wearable devices were shown to be able to discriminate stress levels, but not mental workload or emotional state.

The paper [8], titled "Constructing an Emotion Estimation Model Based on EEG/HRV Indexes Using Feature Extraction and Feature Selection Algorithms", was authored by K. Suzuki, T. Laohakangvalvit, R. Matsubara, and M. Sugaya, from Shibaura Institute of Technology, Japan.

This study investigated the use of inexpensive and simple EEG and photoplethysmography (PPG) sensors to classify emotions using EEG and heart rate variability (HRV) signal features. The authors extracted the features and then used feature selection methods to improve the accuracy of the model. Multiple feature combinations of EEG and/or HRV indices selected using feature selection criteria were used to construct emotion estimation models based on a deep neural network. The model was evaluated using the stratified k-fold cross-validation method on a dataset consisting of 25 young and healthy subjects. The results suggest that it is possible to construct an emotion classification model using only a small number of features from physiological indices. Using the proposed methodology, an accuracy of approximately 98% was achieved for classification into 4 emotion classes.

The paper [9], titled "The Effects of Individual Differences, Non-Stationarity, and the Importance of Data Partitioning Decisions for Training and Testing of EEG Cross-Participant Models", was authored by A. Kamrud, B. Borghetti, and C. Schubert Kabban, from the Air Force Institute of Technology, USA.

The study points out the problems associated with dataset construction and partitioning for EEG studies. Due to the nonstationarity of the EEG signal as well as individual differences, EEG-based deep learning models may either not generalize well or, if improperly learned, achieve overly optimistic accuracy. Therefore, it is important that the evaluation procedure strictly follows the evaluation guidelines, as explained in this paper. The data must be partitioned into training, validation, and testing sets so that cross-participant models avoid overestimating model accuracy. The authors build the models for five publicly available datasets and demonstrate how model accuracy is significantly reduced when proper guidelines for cross-participant EEG model are followed. They show that if the guidelines are not followed, the error rates of the cross-participant models can be underestimated by between 35% and 3900%. The authors believe that misrepresentations of model performance in related EEG studies impede scientific progress toward truly more accurate models.

The review paper [10], titled "A Review of EEG Signal Features and Their Application in Driver Drowsiness Detection Systems", was authored by I. Stancin, M. Cifrek, and A. Jovic, from the University of Zagreb, Croatia.

The work has several contributions. First, it provides a comprehensive overview, systematization, and brief description of the existing features of the EEG signal, including: time-domain, frequency-domain, time-frequency domain, nonlinear, entropies, undirected and directed spatiotemporal, and complex network features. Second, it provides a comprehensive review of drowsiness detection systems reported in the relevant scientific literature. Third, it provides a comprehensive overview of the existing similar reviews, as several related yet different reviews were published in the literature on this topic. Finally, it discusses various ways to improve the state-of-the-art of drowsiness detection systems. Some of the important conclusions reached regarding drowsiness detection systems are: (1) systems should consider raw data, features from all seven categories, and deep learning models; (2) systems should base ground truth labels on the unified, standardized definition and description of drowsiness or be confirmed by multiple independent sources to reduce subjectivity bias; (3) systems should be evaluated on a large number of participants, such as 100 or more, because electrophysiological signals have high interindividual differences.

The paper [11], titled, "An Improved Deep Residual Network Prediction Model for the Early Diagnosis of Alzheimer's Disease", was authored by H. Sun, A. Wang, W. Wang, and C. Liu, from the Northeastern University and the Shenyang University, China.

This paper deals with the early diagnosis of Alzheimer's disease (AD) from magnetic resonance imaging (MRI) of subjects. The authors use a deep residual network model (ResNet) based on spatial transformer networks and the nonlocal attention mechanism for diagnosing AD. The proposed approach can solve the problems of local information loss and extract the long-distance correlation in MRI feature space, both of which are problematic for conventional convolutional neural networks. The method was evaluated with the Alzheimer's disease neuroimaging experimental dataset and proved superior to other methods, including the original ResNet model. It achieved 97.1% accuracy, 95.5% macro precision, 95.3% macro recall, and 95.4% macro F1 score. The authors conclude that the proposed method is of great importance for early diagnosis of AD.

Finally, the paper [12], titled "Event-Centered Data Segmentation in Accelerometer-Based Fall Detection Algorithms", was authored by G. Šeketa, L. Pavlaković, D. Džaja, I. Lacković, and R. Magjarević, from the University of Zagreb, Croatia.

This study addresses the problem of improving algorithms for automatic fall detection. It investigates how different configurations of windows for data segmentation affect the detection accuracy of a fall detection system. The study showed that the best configuration consists of three sequential windows (preimpact: 3.5 or 3.75 s, impact: 0.5 or 1.0 s, and postimpact: 3.5 or 3.75 s). The method was evaluated on three publicly available datasets on falls and activities of daily living using a support vector machine classifier. The achieved F-scores for the public datasets were: 99.7% for ErciyesUni, 96.1% for FallAllD, and 98.4% for the SisFall dataset. The authors conclude that data segmentation is an important component of automatic fall detection systems as it affects the overall detection accuracy. The results of the study clearly suggest that using three windows for data segmentation results in better fall detection performance than using one or two windows.

Acknowledgments: The guest editor would like to thank all the authors, reviewers, and members of MDPI's editorial team whose work led to the publication of this special issue.

Conflicts of Interest: The author declares no conflict of interest.

References

1. Zhu, T.; Luo, W.; Yu, F. Multi-Branch Convolutional Neural Network for Automatic Sleep Stage Classification with Embedded Stage Refinement and Residual Attention Channel Fusion. *Sensors* **2020**, *20*, 6592. [CrossRef] [PubMed]
2. Su, P.-C.; Soliman, E.Z.; Wu, H.-T. Robust T-End Detection via T-End Signal Quality Index and Optimal Shrinkage. *Sensors* **2020**, *20*, 7052. [CrossRef] [PubMed]

3. Yang, H.; Han, J.; Min, K. EEG-Based Estimation on the Reduction of Negative Emotions for Illustrated Surgical Images. *Sensors* **2020**, *20*, 7103. [CrossRef]
4. Tonacci, A.; Billeci, L.; Di Mambro, I.; Marangoni, R.; Sanmartin, C.; Venturi, F. Wearable Sensors for Assessing the Role of Olfactory Training on the Autonomic Response to Olfactory Stimulation. *Sensors* **2021**, *21*, 770. [CrossRef] [PubMed]
5. Jian, J.-Z.; Ger, T.-R.; Lai, H.-H.; Ku, C.-M.; Chen, C.-A.; Abu, P.A.R.; Chen, S.-L. Detection of Myocardial Infarction Using ECG and Multi-Scale Feature Concatenate. *Sensors* **2021**, *21*, 1906. [CrossRef] [PubMed]
6. Huang, H.; Zhang, J.; Zhu, L.; Tang, J.; Lin, G.; Kong, W.; Lei, X.; Zhu, L. EEG-Based Sleep Staging Analysis with Functional Connectivity. *Sensors* **2021**, *21*, 1988. [CrossRef] [PubMed]
7. Giorgi, A.; Ronca, V.; Vozzi, A.; Sciaraffa, N.; Di Florio, A.; Tamborra, L.; Simonetti, I.; Aricò, P.; Di Flumeri, G.; Rossi, D.; et al. Wearable Technologies for Mental Workload, Stress, and Emotional State Assessment during Working-Like Tasks: A Comparison with Laboratory Technologies. *Sensors* **2021**, *21*, 2332. [CrossRef] [PubMed]
8. Suzuki, K.; Laohakangvalvit, T.; Matsubara, R.; Sugaya, M. Constructing an Emotion Estimation Model Based on EEG/HRV Indexes Using Feature Extraction and Feature Selection Algorithms. *Sensors* **2021**, *21*, 2910. [CrossRef] [PubMed]
9. Kamrud, A.; Borghetti, B.; Schubert Kabban, C. The Effects of Individual Differences, Non-Stationarity, and the Importance of Data Partitioning Decisions for Training and Testing of EEG Cross-Participant Models. *Sensors* **2021**, *21*, 3225. [CrossRef] [PubMed]
10. Stancin, I.; Cifrek, M.; Jovic, A. A Review of EEG Signal Features and Their Application in Driver Drowsiness Detection Systems. *Sensors* **2021**, *21*, 3786. [CrossRef] [PubMed]
11. Sun, H.; Wang, A.; Wang, W.; Liu, C. An Improved Deep Residual Network Prediction Model for the Early Diagnosis of Alzheimer's Disease. *Sensors* **2021**, *21*, 4182. [CrossRef] [PubMed]
12. Šeketa, G.; Pavlaković, L.; Džaja, D.; Lacković, I.; Magjarević, R. Event-Centered Data Segmentation in Accelerometer-Based Fall Detection Algorithms. *Sensors* **2021**, *21*, 4335. [CrossRef] [PubMed]

Article

Multi-Branch Convolutional Neural Network for Automatic Sleep Stage Classification with Embedded Stage Refinement and Residual Attention Channel Fusion

Tianqi Zhu, Wei Luo and Feng Yu *

College of Biomedical Engineering and Instrument Science, Zhejiang University, Hangzhou 310027, China; terryzhu@zju.edu.cn (T.Z.); willi4m@zju.edu.cn (W.L.)
* Correspondence: osfengyu@zju.edu.cn

Received: 11 October 2020; Accepted: 17 November 2020; Published: 18 November 2020

Abstract: Automatic sleep stage classification of multi-channel sleep signals can help clinicians efficiently evaluate an individual's sleep quality and assist in diagnosing a possible sleep disorder. To obtain accurate sleep classification results, the processing flow of results from signal preprocessing and machine-learning-based classification is typically employed. These classification results are refined based on sleep transition rules. Neural networks—i.e., machine learning algorithms—are powerful at solving classification problems. Some methods apply them to the first two processes above; however, the refinement process continues to be based on traditional methods. In this study, the sleep stage refinement process was incorporated into the neural network model to form real end-to-end processing. In addition, for multi-channel signals, the multi-branch convolutional neural network was combined with a proposed residual attention method. This approach further improved the model classification accuracy. The proposed method was evaluated on the Sleep-EDF Expanded Database (Sleep-EDFx) and University College Dublin Sleep Apnea Database (UCDDB). It achieved respective accuracy rates of 85.7% and 79.4%. The results also showed that sleep stage refinement based on a neural network is more effective than the traditional refinement method. Moreover, the proposed residual attention method was determined to have a more robust channel–information fusion ability than the respective average and concatenation methods.

Keywords: sleep stage scoring; neural network-based refinement; residual attention

1. Introduction

Sleep is an essential component of daily human activity. Obtaining adequate sleep is necessary for individuals to perform tasks when they are awake. Long-term lack of sleep can cause mental fatigue and impairment of decision-making and learning abilities. It can also cause migraines, Parkinson's syndrome, and other diseases [1,2]. To effectively evaluate the human sleep state, researchers have established a scientific sleep evaluation and diagnosis system, such as the American Academy of Sleep Medicine Manual (AASM) [3]. In this guide, the sleep-related physiological signals collected by sensors are divided into wake, rapid eye movement, and nonrapid eye movement stages according to the signal characteristics. The nonrapid eye movement stage is further divided into N1, N2, and N3 stages according to the sleep depth. For example, the signal characteristics of the rapid eye movement (REM) stage (Figure 1b) are broadly described as low-amplitude mixed-frequency electroencephalography (EEG) activity, with minimal muscle activity and typical rapid eye movement. These activities are reflected in the signals collected by the corresponding sensors. According to the description of the characteristics of each stage in the AASM guide, an experienced medical technician must read each 30-s sleep epoch, one at a time, and determine the sleep stage to form a hypnogram, as shown in Figure 1a (only one cycle). This process is time-intensive and relies heavily on human resources. To alleviate this constraint, automated sleep staging based on modern signal processing technology can be used. This approach can significantly improve the efficiency of sleep disorder diagnosis.

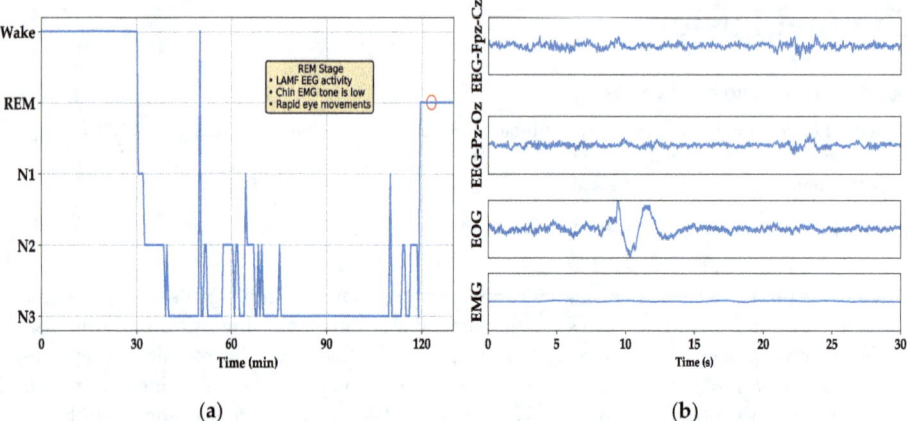

Figure 1. (a) Hypnogram of one sleep cycle. (b) Multi-channel physiological signal for the rapid eye movement (REM) stage corresponding to the red cycle in (a).

The automatic sleep stage classification process (Figure 2) can be divided into three steps—feature extraction, classification, and refinement—based on the transition rules of the stages. The first step is feature extraction. Before automatic feature extraction methods based on neural networks were developed, the features used for sleep staging were manually designed by researchers. Because brain activity changes in each sleep stage, the spectral energy density of the EEG signal in different frequency bands can effectively classify the signal. Other features used in sleep stage classification include spectral entropy [4], signal kurtosis [5], Hurst and fractal exponents [6,7], and others. With the development of deep learning methods in recent years [8–10], automatic feature extraction based on deep learning has become widely used in the biomedical field [11–14]. For example, Acharya et al. [15] used convolutional neural networks (CNNs) to classify Alzheimer's disease lesions. Li et al. [16] used CNNs to classify EEG signals for motor image classification and achieved good results. For sleep staging classification, Supratak et al. [17] used a CNN to extract signal features and recurrent neural networks (RNNs) [18] to extract temporal features. Their technique achieved good performance on the Sleep-EDF dataset.

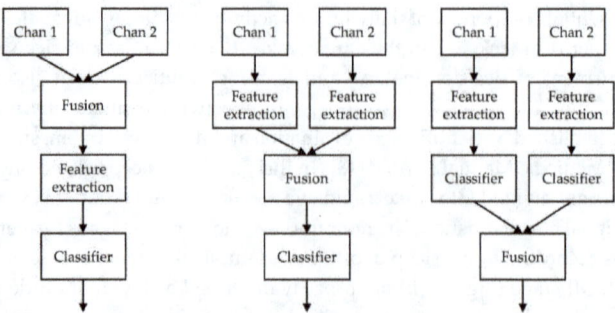

Figure 2. Diagrams of different channel fusion methods, which from left to right are data fusion, feature fusion, and decision fusion, respectively.

After the feature extraction step is completed, a classifier is selected in the second step to classify the features. Shi et al. [19] used the K-nearest neighbor (KNN) method, an unsupervised classifier based on joint sparse representation features. Other supervised methods for sleep staging include the support vector machine (SVM) [20], random forest [21], and neural network classifiers based on fully connected networks. Feature extraction by a CNN or RNN combined with a fully connected network classifier makes sleep staging classification an end-to-end process.

The last step is sleep stage refinement. As a cyclical process, the transition between adjacent sleep stages is not random, as shown in Figure 1a. Therefore, applying transition rules for refining the preliminary results can effectively improve the classification accuracy [22–24]. Because sleep continuity is one of the most important sleep transition rules, Liang et al. applied the rule to a smoothing method [22] to correct their preliminary results, such as by modifying (Wake, N1, Wake) to (Wake, Wake, Wake). Jiang et al. [23] employed a strategy based on the hidden Markov model (HMM) to refine the classification results and improve the classification performance. However, because the training process of end-to-end deep neural networks relies on the gradient backward propagation method, we cannot use these nondifferentiable traditional methods to build end-to-end models.

To score sleep stages, a single-channel signal or multi-channel signals are used. The selected type depends on the given application scenario. For example, owing to the limitation of collection equipment in wearable devices and household devices, it is more feasible to use single-channel signals in these scenarios. In clinical auxiliary diagnosis, methods based on multi-channel signals can obtain more reliable classification results [24–28]. Channel fusion is a crucial part of these methods. As shown in Figure 2, these methods can be divided into different fusion types—data-level, feature-level, and decision-level—according to the channel fusion stage. The fusion step that precedes feature extraction is called data fusion. As an example of data fusion, Phan et al. [28] proposed the conversion of EEG, electrooculography (EOG), and electromyography (EMG) signals into the frequency domain through a short-time Fourier transform. Then, a three-channel frequency image is applied as the input of the neural network model.

Feature fusion methods often use a multi-branch feature extractor to separately extract features from different channels and then join the features [26] or superimpose them. They are then input into the classifier. Decision fusion involves the same feature extraction method as feature fusion; however, the channel fusion is placed after the classifier. These methods use voting or maximum posterior probability (MAP) [24] to determine the final category after each channel is independently classified. The channel fusion method often requires different choices according to the given task.

To achieve complete end-to-end processing and more effective use of multi-channel signal data, we propose a multi-branch convolutional neural network model with embedded stage refinement and a residual attention channel fusion method. The main contributions of the proposed approach are the following:

- Data from the previous sleep epoch stage are encoded through a neural network and embedded in the final classification process to correct the current stage. The proposed model thereby realizes end-to-end processing of feature extraction, classification, and transition refinement based on a deep neural network.
- The model uses multiple neural network branches (Figure 3) to extract the features of different channels. The model accounts for the importance of the channels in decision making. It thus employs a channel fusion method based on a self-attention mechanism [29] to dynamically adjust the decision weights of multiple channels.
- The model performance was evaluated on two public datasets. The model achieved better results than other state-of-the-art methods. At the same time, through these two datasets, we explained the performance differences of the model in stages.

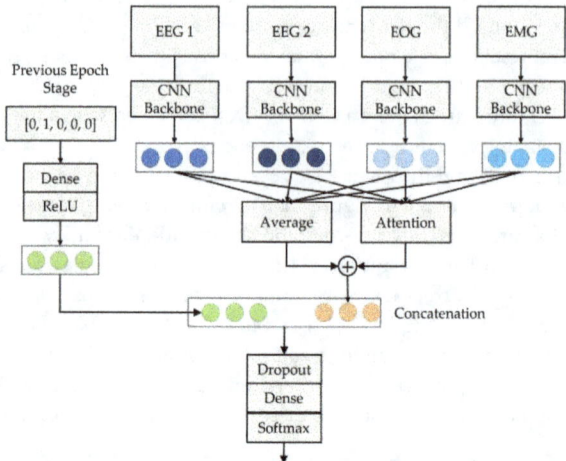

Figure 3. Schematic diagram of the proposed multi-branch convolution neural network combined with embedded stage refinement and residual attention-based channel fusion.

2. Materials and Methods

2.1. Datasets

In this study, we employed two public datasets to evaluate the performance of the model: the Sleep-EDF Database Expanded (Sleep-EDFx) [30] and the University College Dublin Sleep Apnea Database (UCDDB) [31]. Both datasets are publicly available on PhysioNet [31] and contain multimodal and multi-channel data, including EEG, EOG, and chin EMG. The latest version of the Sleep-EDFx dataset contains two subsets—sleep cassette (SC) and sleep telemetry (ST)—which include a total of 104 individuals and 197 complete nights of polysomnographic sleep recordings. The data in the SC subset were collected from healthy individuals; the data in the ST subset were obtained from subjects who experience mild difficulty falling asleep.

To facilitate a comparison of the proposed approach with existing methods, we employed the records of 39 nights of 20 individuals in the age range of 25 to 34 in the SC subset (the second night of subject 13 was missing). We adopted the same method in [17], which retained only portions of wake epochs. The Sleep-EDFx dataset contains two EEG channels, Fpz-Cz and Pz-Oz; one EOG channel; and one chin EMG channel. The sampling rate of the first three channels was 100 Hz, and the sampling rate of the EMG channel was 1 Hz. To maintain processing consistency, we upsampled the rate to 100 Hz. The UCDDB dataset contains complete night data of 25 individuals with sleep-disorder breathing collected at St Vincent's University Hospital. The dataset includes two EEG channels, C3-A2 and C4-A1; two left and right EOG channels; and one chin EMG channel. The sampling rate of both EEG and EOG was 128 Hz, and the sampling rate of the EMG channel was 64 Hz. We upsampled the EMG channel to 128 Hz for the same reason as in Sleep-EDFx.

Here, we define as the "transition epoch" the epoch that occurs between the preceding epoch and the subsequent epoch. If the given epoch is not a transitional one, it is called a "nontransition epoch." Table 1 shows the stage distribution of the two datasets and the distributions of the transition and nontransition epochs in each stage. It is observed in the table that the transition epoch ratio of stage N1 is significantly higher in both datasets than in the other stages. Furthermore, the UCDDB dataset has a higher transition epoch proportion than the Sleep-EDFx dataset.

Table 1. Details on the datasets used in this study.

Stage	Sleep-EDFx			UCDDB		
	Transition (%)	Nontransition	Total	Transition (%)	Nontransition	Total
Wake	844 (10.2)	7402	8246	1239 (26.3)	3468	4707
N1	1554 (55.4)	1250	2804	1349 (39.6)	2054	3403
N2	2873 (16.1)	14,926	17,799	1154 (16.5)	5831	6985
N3	1237 (21.7)	4466	5703	293 (11.0)	2370	2663
REM	761 (9.9)	6956	7717	258 (8.6)	2758	3016
Total	7268 (17.2)	35,001	42,269	4293 (20.7)	16,481	20,774

Manual labeling of the two datasets was performed according to the R&K guideline [32], which defines six stages of sleep: Wake, N1, N2, N3, N4, and REM. Before their application as input to the model, the datasets were preprocessed in two simple steps. The first step was to merge N3 and N4 into a single stage, N3—also called the slow-wave stage—according to the AASM guidelines. The second step was to perform z-score normalization for each respective channel of each subject. That is, the mean and variance of each channel were respectively calculated and each channel was normalized.

2.2. Model Architecture

The overall architecture of the proposed model consists of four parts, as shown in Figure 3: a feature extraction module based on the convolutional neural network; a channel fusion module based on residual attention; an encoding module, which is used to embed the previous epoch stage into the model; and a classification module based on the fully connected layer.

In the feature extraction part of the proposed model, different branches of the CNN are used to extract the channel features of each channel signal. This means that the CNN does not share parameters between channels. The feature extraction module is composed of five convolutional blocks and a global average pooling layer. Each convolution block employs a convolution layer [10] to extract shift-invariant intermediate features. Each block also uses a batch normalization layer [33] to normalize the features to avoid model overfitting and to accelerate model convergence. Finally, the normalized features are input to the rectified linear unit layer (ReLU) [34] for nonlinear activation. The specific hyperparameters of the backbone are listed in Table 2.

Table 2. Hyperparameters of convolution neural network backbone.

Layer Name	Kernel Size	Stride	Padding	Output Size	
				Sleep-EDFx	UCDDB
Input				[3000 × 1]	[3840 × 1]
conv_block_1	[1 × 5]	3	VALID	[999 × 64]	[1279 × 64]
conv_block_2	[1 × 5]	3	VALID	[332 × 64]	[425 × 64]
conv_block_3	[1 × 3]	2	VALID	[165 × 128]	[212 × 128]
conv_block_4	[1 × 3]	1	VALID	[163 × 128]	[210 × 128]
conv_block_5	[1 × 3]	1	VALID	[161 × 256]	[208 × 256]
global average pooling				[1 × 256]	

We input the channel features obtained through the convolution backbone into the average module and the attention module. The outputs of these two modules are added to obtain the fused channel features. The full composition of these two modules is called the residual attention module. In this module, we mark the channel feature as v_i. The feature vector obtained by concatenating all channels is V. The channel weight α_i can be calculated by the following formula, where W_i^s, W_i^v, W, and b are learnable parameters:

$$V = \text{Concat}([v_1, v_2, \cdots, v_C]) \tag{1}$$

$$s_i = W_i^s * \text{ReLU}\big(W_i^v v_i + WV + b\big) \tag{2}$$

$$\alpha_i = \frac{\exp(s_i)}{\sum_{i=1}^{C} \exp(s_i)} \tag{3}$$

The weight of the channel may be saturated, which means that the model only focuses on one channel and completely ignores the other channels. To avoid the lack of information caused by this situation, we incorporate a threshold to the weight of each channel by adding the mean value of the multi-channel features to the output of the attention module. Therefore, the final fusion feature is

$$V_{\text{fusion}} = v_{\text{avg}} + \sum_{i=1}^{C} \alpha_i v_i \tag{4}$$

Owing to the continuity of sleep and the hidden transition rules between adjacent sleep epochs, the current epoch stage can be corrected by using the stage information of the previous epoch. We use the truth value of the previous epoch during training. In addition, the probability vector of the model's output at the previous epoch during inference is employed. To maintain consistency of the training and inference, we use one-hot encoding as input during training. Then, the model employs a single-layer fully connected layer to re-encode the stage into a vector of length 256 and concatenates it with the fused channel features. The connected vector passes through the classifier composed of the dropout layer [10], the fully connected layer, and the softmax layer.

The fully connected layer is shown in equation (5). It is evident that the concatenation between the re-encoded stage vector (v_c) and the fused signal feature (v_{fusion}) is equivalent to having an additive refinement for the probability vector (P_{fusion}) corresponding to the fused feature vector. The dropout layer zeroes the neurons according to a certain probability to achieve regularization and avoid model overfitting. The softmax layer normalizes the stage probability vector for the loss calculation.

$$P = Wh^T = [W_c, W_f][v_c, v_{\text{fusion}}]^T = W_c v_c + W_f v_{\text{fusion}} = P_c + P_{\text{fusion}} \tag{5}$$

2.3. Experiment Details

To evaluate the performance of the model on the entire dataset, we used the leave-one-subject-out method for testing. The experiment used one subject as the test set; the remaining subjects composed the training and validation sets. We repeated the experiment many times and then merged the results of each experiment on the test set to obtain the final result. For the Sleep-EDFx dataset, we set up 20 experiments, with each training set consisting of 18 subjects, and one individual composed the validation set. The remaining subjects composed the test set. The UCDDB dataset was used for a 25-fold experiment with 23 individuals as the training set and one subject as the validation set. We used cross-entropy as the loss function (Equation (6)), which y_i is the one-hot label and $\hat{y}_i$ is predicted probability vector, and the Adam [35] optimizer to update the model parameters during training. The model and training parameters are summarized in Table 3.

$$L = -\sum_{i \in \Omega} y_i \log(\hat{y}_i) \tag{6}$$

Owing to the small size of the training set, and to improve the generalization performance of the model on the test set during the inference process, we used an ensemble method. That method is based on multiple training epochs and infers the test set. The first step in the ensemble method is to use the model's performance on the validation set as a reference to obtain the top 10% intermediate models during the training process, which included seven models in our experiment. Then, we used each intermediate model as an independent model to separately infer the test set. Finally, we used the maximum likelihood method to ensemble multiple results on the same test set and obtain the final results.

Table 3. Hyperparameters of the proposed neural network.

Model		Training	
Encoding size in embedded refinement	256	Batch size	64
Number of channels	4	Number of training epochs	70
Weights size in attention module	256	Loss function	Cross-entropy
Batch normalization (momentum and epsilon)	0.99, 0.001	Optimizer	Adam
Dropout rate	0.5	Learning rate	0.0001
		Clip value of the gradient	0.1

In this study, we employed accuracy, macro-average F1-score (MF1), and Cohen's kappa coefficient to evaluate the overall performance of the model. Because MF1 and kappa provide different categories of the same importance, these two metrics could more reliably assess the actual performance of the model on the dataset with an imbalanced category distribution. In addition, MF1 was used as a verification indicator for selecting the training epoch during ensemble inference. Moreover, we calculated the precision, recall, and F1-score of each stage to evaluate the performance of the model in stages.

3. Results

3.1. Model Performance on Public Datasets

As evident in Table 4, the overall performance of the model on the two datasets has some gaps. The overall accuracy, MF1, and kappa of the Sleep-EDFx dataset are 85.8, 81.2, and 0.80, respectively, while the corresponding metrics of UCDDB are 79.4, 78.8, and 0.73, respectively. The performance of the proposed model is lower on UCDDB than on Sleep-EDFx. Specifically, the performance of stage N3 is comparable on the two datasets, the result of stage N2 is better than that of Sleep-EDFx on UCDDB. The performance in the other stages on UCDDB is significantly lower than on Sleep-EDFx.

Table 4. Overall performance of the proposed model.

	W	N1	N2	N3	REM
Sleep-EDFx	Accuracy: 85.8 Macro-Average F1-Score: 81.2 Cohen's Kappa: 0.80				
Precision	93.4	54.0	87.8	86.6	84.5
Recall	91.2	55.0	87.9	84.3	87.4
F1-score	92.3	54.5	87.8	85.4	85.9
UCDDB	Accuracy: 79.4 Macro-Average F1-Score: 78.8 Cohen's Kappa: 0.73				
Precision	81.3	64.8	79.5	87.0	83.7
Recall	82.5	56.1	83.9	84.4	85.9
F1-score	81.9	60.1	81.7	85.7	84.8

The common point of the model performance on the two datasets is that stage N1 has the lowest accuracy, and the model performance has a clear gap in the other stages. The classification confusion matrix of the two datasets is shown in Figure 4. Their misclassification rules are the same. That is, the main misclassifications of Wake and REM are N1 and N2. N1 is more likely to be misclassified into stages other than N3. N2 has an even distribution of misclassifications, while N3 is almost only misclassified as N2.

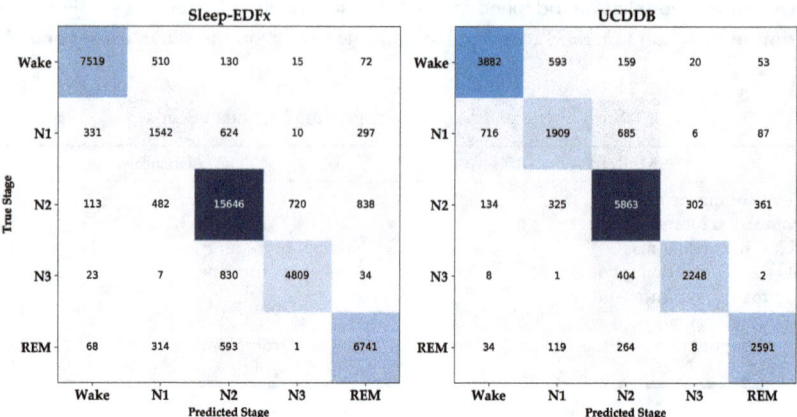

Figure 4. Classification confusion matrix of Sleep-EDFx and UCDDB.

Table 5 shows the performance comparison between the proposed model and existing models on the two datasets. The inclusion of a large number of wake stages will significantly improve the model performance. Moreover, subject-independent or nonindependent testing methods will also influence the model performance [17,25]. Therefore, we chose methods that use the same dataset. Furthermore, we employed a subject-independent testing method in the comparison of all models except that of [19], which only tested the nontransition epoch in the UCDDB dataset. It is observed in the table that our method is superior to the other methods in terms of accuracy, MF1, and kappa. Shi et al. [19] tested their model only on the nontransition window. It achieved an accuracy of 81%, while the accuracy of our model on the same data is 85.1%, and MF1 is 83.4%. The performance of our model is still better than that of Shi et al.

Table 5. Performance of different methods on the Sleep-EDFx and UCDDB datasets.

| Reference | Methods | | | Channels | Overall Performances | | |
	Feature	Classifier	Refinement		Acc	MF1	Kappa
Sleep-EDFx							
Supratak et al. [17]	CNN & RNN	FC	-	1	82.0	76.9	0.76
Tsinalis et al. [36]	Handcraft	AE	-	1	78.9	73.7	-
Yu et al. [37]	ACNN	FC	-	1	82.8	77.8	-
Phan et al. [20]	ARNN	SVM	-	1	82.5	72.0	0.76
Mousavi et al. [38]	CNN & ARNN	FC	-	1	84.3	79.7	0.79
Zhang et al. [24]	MB-CNN	FC	Expert Rules	4	83.6	78.1	0.77
Proposed	MB-CNN	FC	FC	4	85.8	81.2	0.80
UCDDB							
Shi et al. [19]	Handcraft	RF	-	2	81.1	-	-
Martin et al. [39]	Handcraft	DBN	HMM	3	72.2	70.5	0.64
Yuan et al. [40]	MB-CNN	FC	-	4	74.2	68.2	-
Cen et al. [41]	CNN	FC	HMM	4	69.7	-	-
Proposed	MB-CNN	FC	FC	4	79.4	78.8	0.73

ACNN: attentional CNN, ARNN: attentional RNN, AE: auto encoder, DBN: deep brief nets.

In addition, Zhang et al. [24] and Yuan et al. [40] used a multi-branch (MB) CNN-based multi-channel feature extraction method and a fully connected network-based classification method on the Sleep-EDFx and UCDDB datasets, respectively. Zhang et al.'s method uses decision-level channel fusion and expert rule-based refinement. Yuan's method employs a multi-channel fusion method based on global information. Our method uses neural-network-based stage correction. Our channel fusion method based on residual attention is better than those methods.

3.2. Model Component Analysis

3.2.1. Influence of Neural Network-Based Embedded Stage Refinement

To explore the effect of neural-network-based stage refinement on the model performance, we constructed a set of comparative experiments. The neural-network-based refinement module in the model was removed as the baseline model. The smoothing method based on expert rules [22] and the method based on the hidden Markov model (HMM) [23] were used to correct the stages. The rule-based refinement method set the matching rules and refinement rules. All sequences that met the matching rules were corrected according to the corresponding refinement rules. The specific rules are listed in Table 6.

Table 6. Refinement rules [22] (X represents any stage).

Rule No.	Matching Rules	Refinement Rules
1	Any REM epoch before the first appearance of N2	N1
2	Wake, REM, N2	Wake, N1, N2
3	N1, REM, N2	N1. N1, N2
4	N2, X, N2	N2, N2, N2
5	REM, X, REM	REM, REM, REM

Refinement based on the hidden Markov model is divided into two steps. The first step was to use the ground truth stages of the validation set as the hidden state. The inference value of our model on the validation set was used as the observation value. Then, the state transition probability and emission probability of the HMM were obtained through a frequency-counting method. The second step was to maintain the HMM parameters as unchanged, and take the model's inference result on the test set as the observation value, and obtain the hidden states of the HMM through the Viterbi [42] algorithm as the corrected results of the test set.

The comparison results are shown in Figure 5. The smoothing refinement and the HMM-based refinement improve the overall MF1 performance of the Sleep-EDFx, while the MF1 of the UCDDB dataset is slightly increased by 1.3% and 1.2%, respectively. It is apparent that these two methods improve the nontransition epoch performance by sacrificing the transition epoch performance. Moreover, the HMM-based correction method causes more degradation of the transition epochs performance, while engendering greater nontransition epoch improvement. In comparison, the refinement process based on the neural network improves the performance without causing the performance degradation of the transition epochs.

Figure 6 shows a hypnogram of subject 3 on the first night in the Sleep-EDFx dataset. From top to bottom is manual labeling by experts, the classification results based on the baseline model, and the results of the baseline neural network combined with embedded refinement. As shown in the figure, compared with the baseline model, the revised hypnogram is smoother and retains many critical transition processes that occur during sleep.

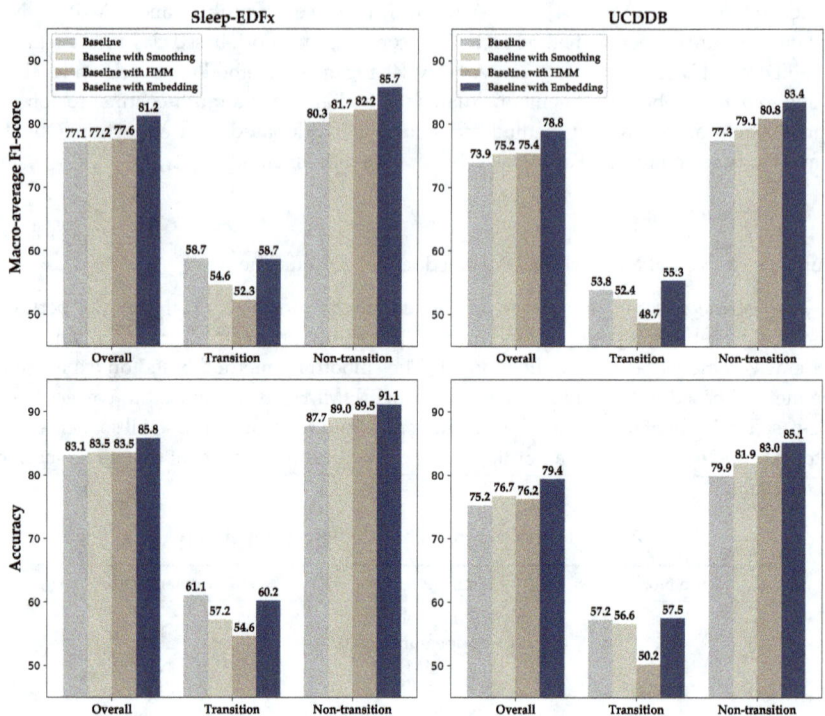

Figure 5. Performance comparison of different refinement methods on overall, transitional, and nontransitional epochs.

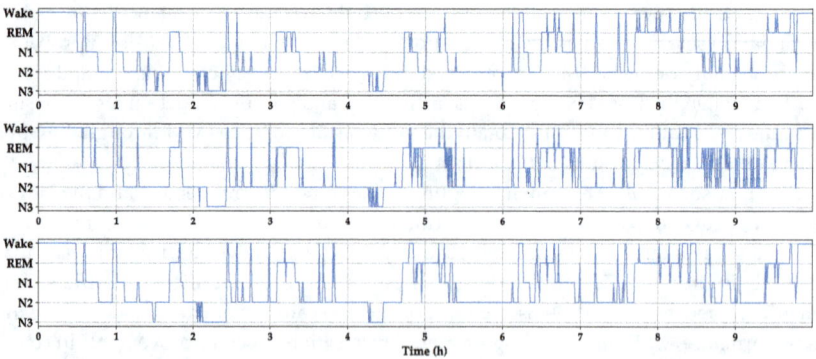

Figure 6. Hypnogram of subject 4 on the first night in the Sleep-EDFx. The graphs from top to bottom are derived from a human expert, baseline model, and baseline model with embedded stage refinement.

3.2.2. Efficacy of Multi-Channel and Residual Attention

In Figure 7, we show the performance gain obtained by multiple channels compared to a single channel. In the Sleep-EDFx dataset, the signals increase from one channel to four channels—Fpz-Cz, EOG, EMG, and Pz- Oz. The corresponding channels in the UCDDB dataset are C4-A1, EOG, EMG, and C3-A2. In the UCDDB dataset, each additional channel improves the overall performance, whereas on the Sleep-EDFx dataset, the performance decreases slightly after adding the EMG signal. This may have been due to the low sampling rate of the original EMG signal.

Meanwhile, stage N1 and stage REM achieve greater performance improvement on the two datasets, which shows that the recognition process of N1 and REM staging is more dependent on multi-channel signal characteristics.

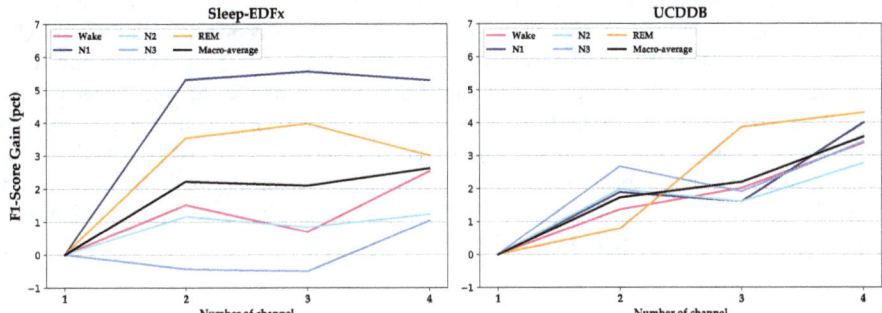

Figure 7. Performance gain for each stage by adding channels on Sleep-EDFx and UCDDB. The gain is computed by using the F1-score of each channel setting to subtract the F1-score of one channel.

Figure 8 shows the performance comparison of different channel fusion methods. In data fusion, the residual attention module is removed, and we use the same CNN backbone in which the four channels are concatenated with shape (3000, 4) as the model input. The decision fusion method trains an independent model for each channel. Then, the inference results of each model are fused by voting or the method of maximum posterior probability, as shown in Figure 2.

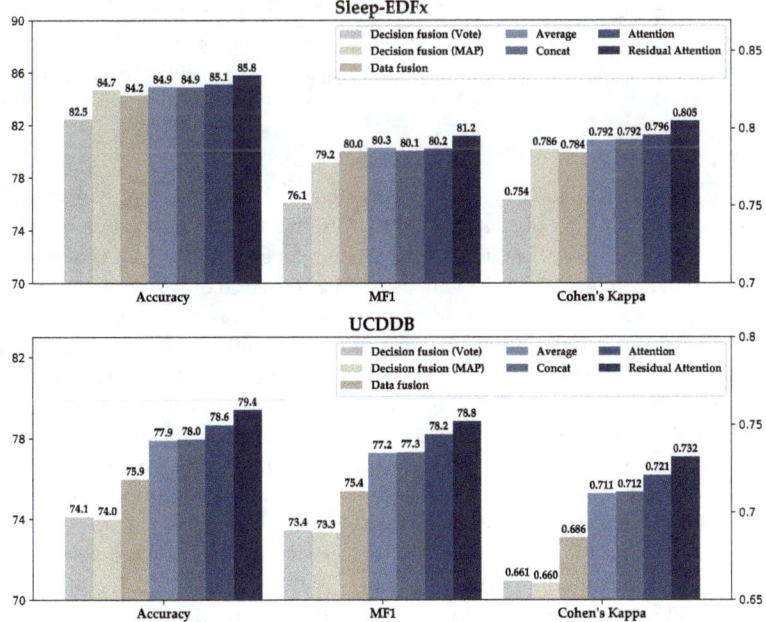

Figure 8. Performance comparison of different channel fusion methods.

In addition, we experimented with feature fusion methods based on the average, concatenation, and attention. It is observed from the results in Figure 8 that the performance of the method based on data fusion and decision fusion is lower than that of the method based on feature fusion. The performance of the model obtained by directly fusing the multi-channel features through average and concatenation is similar. After removing the average part of the proposed residual attention module, the model performance is slightly improved on the Sleep-EDFx dataset and it shows an accuracy increase of approximately 0.6% on the UCDDB dataset. The further application of the complete residual attention increases the classification accuracy of the model on the Sleep-EDFx dataset and UCDDB dataset by approximately 1% and 1.5%, respectively, and on MF1 by 1% and 1.5%, respectively.

In Figure 9, we show the attention module's weight response to different stages when the model uses the residual attention method. This stage sequence was obtained from the Sleep-EDFx dataset after subject 1 fell asleep on the first night at approximately 3.7 h to 4.5 h. It is observed on the heat map that the model mainly focuses on the Cz-Oz channel and the Fpz-Cz channel for the wake stage. For N1 and N3, the model confers greater weight to the Fpz-Cz channels. When identifying N2 and REM, the model mainly relies on EOG and EMG channels.

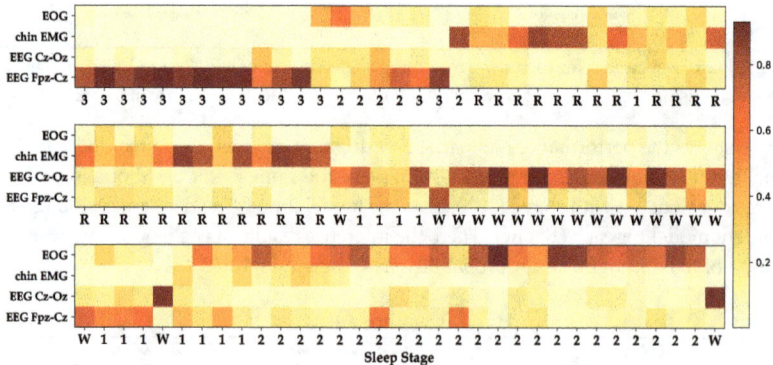

Figure 9. Attention weights for each channel in stage sequence, which W, 1, 2, 3, R refer to Wake, N1, N2, N3, and REM.

4. Discussion

On the basis of previous studies [17,24,36], we embedded the refinement stage into the neural network model and used the residual attention-based multi-channel signal fusion method to make the performance of our proposed model achieve the human expert level [43]. However, it should be noted that, similar to those of other methods, the performance of the proposed model for the different stages was inconsistent, and the accuracy of stage N1 was much lower than those of the other stages. In most previous studies, this was attributed to the underfitting caused by using fewer samples. However, in the UCDDB dataset, N1 had more samples than N3 and REM; however, its performance was far worse than in the other two stages. This shows that underfitting was only part of the cause rather than the main reason. From Table 1 and Figure 5, it is apparent that the actual cause of the poor performance of stage N1 was that the proportion of transition epochs in N1 was much higher than those in other stages. At the same time, the performance of the model on the transition epoch was much lower than that of the nontransition epoch.

For example, on the Sleep-EDFx dataset, the proportion of the transition epoch in stage N1 is 55.4%, and the highest proportion in the other stages is 21.7% of stage N3. The MF1 of the model in the transition and nontransition epochs is 58.7% and 85.7%, respectively. Such a vast distribution and performance difference ultimately leads to the stage N1 performance being far lower than in the other stages. In addition, the UCDDB dataset is composed of individuals who have difficulty falling asleep. The proportion of the transition epoch is greater than that of the Sleep-EDFx dataset. Therefore, the performance of the model on UCDDB is lower than that on Sleep-EDFx.

Multi-channel data provides richer information than single-channel data. Nevertheless, owing to unreasonable channel fusion methods on occasion, more signal channels will not significantly improve the model [27]. It is also evident in Figure 8 that only using the self-attention module can only slightly improve the model. Figure 9 shows that the model can correctly learn the attention mode corresponding to the AASM guidelines. However, it is easier to have attention saturation on a specific channel. In other words, it completely ignores the information of other channels, which may affect the model performance. To solve this problem, we added the average module, which sets a threshold for the weight of each channel. The performance of the model was further improved by this method.

Based on the above experimental results and discussion, we found that the proposed approach still has some shortcomings. In future work, we will strive to address these limitations and improve our method. First, the refinement process of the model can significantly improve the performance of the nontransition epoch, but it cannot improve the performance of the transfer epoch, which also leads to a lower accuracy of stage N1. Therefore, we intend to develop models for the transition epoch, such as by enabling the model to identify the transition and nontransition epochs and by using different refinement modules to implement different correction strategies. Second, inter-individual differences also limit the generalization ability of the model across individuals. We will strive to use adversarial-learning-based methods to eliminate the differences between individuals and improve the model robustness.

5. Conclusions

In this paper, we proposed a multi-branch neural network model for automatic sleep stage classification. The model integrates feature extraction, feature classification, and stage refinement into a neural network model to form an end-to-end processing method. The model thereby significantly improves the performance of the nontransition epoch without lowering the accuracy of the transition epoch. In addition, the channel fusion method based on residual attention can further improve the performance of the model based on a naive fusion method (average, concatenation). On the Sleep-EDFx dataset composed of healthy individuals and the UCDDB dataset composed of patients with sleep-disorder breathing, the proposed model achieved better performance than existing models.

Author Contributions: Conceptualization, T.Z. and F.Y.; data curation, T.Z.; formal analysis, T.Z. and W.L.; investigation, T.Z.; methodology, T.Z. and W.L.; project administration, F.Y.; software, T.Z.; supervision, F.Y.; validation, T.Z. and W.L.; visualization, T.Z.; writing—original draft, T.Z.; writing—review & editing, T.Z., W.L. and F.Y. All authors have read and agreed to the published version of the manuscript.

Funding: This research received no external funding.

Conflicts of Interest: The authors declare no conflict of interest. The funder had no role in the design of the study; in the collection, analyses, or interpretation of data; in the writing of the manuscript; or in the decision to publish the results.

References

1. Zhong, G.; Naismith, S.L.; Rogers, N.L.; Lewis, S.J.G. Sleep–wake disturbances in common neurodegenerative diseases: A closer look at selected aspects of the neural circuitry. *J. Neurol. Sci.* **2011**, *307*, 9–14. [CrossRef] [PubMed]
2. Buysse, D.J. Sleep Health: Can We Define It? Does It Matter? *Sleep* **2014**, *37*, 9–17. [CrossRef] [PubMed]
3. Iber, C.; Ancoli-Israel, S.; Chesson, A.L.; Quan, S.F. *The AASM Manual for the Scoring of Sleep and Associated Events: Rules, Terminology and Technical Specification*; American Academy of Sleep Medicine: Westchester, NY, USA, 2007.
4. Noviyanto, A.; Isa, S.; Wasito, I.; Arymurthy, A.M.; Barat, J. Selecting Features of Single Lead ECG Signal for Automatic Sleep Stages Classification using Correlation-based Feature Subset Selection. *IJCSI Int. J. Comput. Sci. Issues* **2011**, *8*.

5. Gasser, T.; Bächer, P.; Möcks, J. Transformations towards the normal distribution of broad band spectral parameters of the EEG. *Electroencephalogr. Clin. Neurophysiol.* **1982**, *53*, 119–124. [CrossRef]
6. Pereda, E.; Gamundi, A.; Rial, R.; González, J. Nonlinear behaviour of human EEG: Fractal exponent versus correlation dimension in awake and sleep stages. *Neurosci. Lett.* **1998**, *250*, 91–94. [CrossRef]
7. Acharya, U.R.; Chua, E.C.; Faust, O.; Lim, T.C.; Lim, L.F. Automated detection of sleep apnea from electrocardiogram signals using nonlinear parameters. *Physiol. Meas.* **2011**, *32*, 287–303. [CrossRef]
8. LeCun, Y.; Bengio, Y.; Hinton, G. Deep learning. *Nature* **2015**, *521*, 436–444. [CrossRef]
9. Yoshua, B.; Xavier, G.; Antoine, B. Deep Sparse Rectifier Neural Networks. In *Proceedings of the Fourteenth International Conference on Artificial Intelligence and Statistics*; PMLR: Fort Lauderdale, FL, USA, 2011; Volume 15, pp. 315–323.
10. Krizhevsky, A.; Sutskever, I.; Hinton, G.E. ImageNet Classification with Deep Convolutional Neural Networks. In *Advances in Neural Information Processing Systems 25*; Pereira, F., Burges, C.J.C., Bottou, L., Weinberger, K.Q., Eds.; Curran Associates, Inc.: Red Hook, NY, USA, 2012; pp. 1097–1105.
11. Esmaelpoor, J.; Moradi, M.H.; Kadkhodamohammadi, A. A multistage deep neural network model for blood pressure estimation using photoplethysmogram signals. *Comput. Biol. Med.* **2020**, *120*, 103719. [CrossRef]
12. Kiranyaz, S.; Ince, T.; Gabbouj, M. Real-Time Patient-Specific ECG Classification by 1-D Convolutional Neural Networks. *IEEE Trans. Biomed. Eng.* **2016**, *63*, 664–675. [CrossRef]
13. Zaimi, A.; Wabartha, M.; Herman, V.; Antonsanti, P.L.; Perone, C.S.; Cohen-Adad, J. AxonDeepSeg: Automatic axon and myelin segmentation from microscopy data using convolutional neural networks. *Sci. Rep.* **2018**, *8*, 3816. [CrossRef]
14. Li, P.; Wang, Y.; He, J.; Wang, L.; Tian, Y.; Zhou, T.S.; Li, T.; Li, J.S. High-Performance Personalized Heartbeat Classification Model for Long-Term ECG Signal. *IEEE Trans. Biomed. Eng.* **2017**, *64*, 78–86. [CrossRef] [PubMed]
15. Acharya, U.R.; Oh, S.L.; Hagiwara, Y.; Tan, J.H.; Adeli, H. Deep convolutional neural network for the automated detection and diagnosis of seizure using EEG signals. *Comput. Biol. Med.* **2018**, *100*, 270–278. [CrossRef]
16. Li, Y.; Zhang, X.R.; Zhang, B.; Lei, M.Y.; Cui, W.G.; Guo, Y.Z. A Channel-Projection Mixed-Scale Convolutional Neural Network for Motor Imagery EEG Decoding. *IEEE Trans. Neural Syst. Rehabil. Eng.* **2019**, *27*, 1170–1180. [CrossRef] [PubMed]
17. Supratak, A.; Dong, H.; Wu, C.; Guo, Y. DeepSleepNet: A Model for Automatic Sleep Stage Scoring Based on Raw Single-Channel EEG. *IEEE Trans. Neural Syst. Rehabil. Eng.* **2017**, *25*, 1998–2008. [CrossRef] [PubMed]
18. Hochreiter, S.; Schmidhuber, J. Long Short-Term Memory. *Neural Comput.* **1997**, *9*, 1735–1780. [CrossRef]
19. Shi, J.; Liu, X.; Li, Y.; Zhang, Q.; Li, Y.; Ying, S. Multi-channel EEG-based sleep stage classification with joint collaborative representation and multiple kernel learning. *J. Neurosci. Methods* **2015**, *254*, 94–101. [CrossRef]
20. Phan, H.; Andreotti, F.; Cooray, N.; Chen, O.Y.; Vos, M. Automatic Sleep Stage Classification Using Single-Channel EEG: Learning Sequential Features with Attention-Based Recurrent Neural Networks. *Conf. Proc. IEEE Eng. Med. Biol. Soc.* **2018**, *2018*, 1452–1455. [CrossRef]
21. Memar, P.; Faradji, F. A Novel Multi-Class EEG-Based Sleep Stage Classification System. *IEEE Trans. Neural Syst. Rehabil. Eng.* **2018**, *26*, 84–95. [CrossRef]
22. Liang, S.-F.; Kuo, C.-E.; Hu, Y.-H.; Cheng, Y.-S. A rule-based automatic sleep staging method. *J. Neurosci. Methods* **2012**, *205*, 169–176. [CrossRef]
23. Jiang, D.; Lu, Y.-N.; Ma, Y.; Wang, Y. Robust sleep stage classification with single-channel EEG signals using multimodal decomposition and HMM-based refinement. *Expert Syst. Appl.* **2019**, *121*, 188–203. [CrossRef]
24. Zhang, X.; Xu, M.; Li, Y.; Su, M.; Xu, Z.; Wang, C.; Kang, D.; Li, H.; Mu, X.; Ding, X.; et al. Automated multi-model deep neural network for sleep stage scoring with unfiltered clinical data. *Sleep Breath* **2020**. [CrossRef]
25. Phan, H.; Andreotti, F.; Cooray, N.; Chen, O.Y.; De Vos, M. Joint Classification and Prediction CNN Framework for Automatic Sleep Stage Classification. *IEEE Trans. Biomed. Eng.* **2019**, *66*, 1285–1296. [CrossRef] [PubMed]
26. Chambon, S.; Galtier, M.N.; Arnal, P.J.; Wainrib, G.; Gramfort, A. A Deep Learning Architecture for Temporal Sleep Stage Classification Using Multivariate and Multimodal Time Series. *IEEE Trans. Neural Syst. Rehabil. Eng.* **2018**, *26*, 758–769. [CrossRef] [PubMed]

27. Andreotti, F.; Phan, H.; Cooray, N.; Lo, C.; Hu, M.T.M.; De Vos, M. Multichannel Sleep Stage Classification and Transfer Learning using Convolutional Neural Networks. *Conf. Proc. IEEE Eng. Med. Biol. Soc.* **2018**, *2018*, 171–174. [CrossRef]
28. Phan, H.; Andreotti, F.; Cooray, N.; Chen, O.Y.; De Vos, M. SeqSleepNet: End-to-End Hierarchical Recurrent Neural Network for Sequence-to-Sequence Automatic Sleep Staging. *IEEE Trans. Neural Syst. Rehabil. Eng.* **2019**, *27*, 400–410. [CrossRef]
29. Vaswani, A.; Shazeer, N.; Parmar, N.; Uszkoreit, J.; Jones, L.; Gomez, A.N.; Kaiser, Ł.; Polosukhin, I. Attention is All you Need. In *Advances in Neural Information Processing Systems 30*; Guyon, I., Luxburg, U.V., Bengio, S., Wallach, H., Fergus, R., Vishwanathan, S., Garnett, R., Eds.; Curran Associates, Inc.: Red Hook, NY, USA, 2017; pp. 5998–6008.
30. Kemp, B.; Zwinderman, A.H.; Tuk, B.; Kamphuisen, H.A.C.; Oberye, J.J.L. Analysis of a sleep-dependent neuronal feedback loop: The slow-wave microcontinuity of the EEG. *IEEE Trans. Biomed. Eng.* **2000**, *47*, 1185–1194. [CrossRef]
31. Goldberger, A.L.; Amaral, L.A.N.; Glass, L.; Hausdorff, J.M.; Ivanov, P.C.; Mark, R.G.; Mietus, J.E.; Moody, G.B.; Peng, C.-K.; Stanley, H.E. PhysioBank, PhysioToolkit, and PhysioNet: Components of a New Research Resource for Complex Physiologic Signals. *Circulation* **2000**, *101*. [CrossRef] [PubMed]
32. Wolpert, E.A. A Manual of Standardized Terminology, Techniques and Scoring System for Sleep Stages of Human Subjects. *Arch. Gen. Psychiatry* **1969**, *20*, 246. [CrossRef]
33. Ioffe, S.; Szegedy, C. Batch Normalization: Accelerating Deep Network Training by Reducing Internal Covariate Shift. *arXiv* **2015**, arXiv:1502.03167.
34. Vinod, N.; Geoffrey, E.H. Rectified Linear Units Improve Restricted Boltzmann Machines. In Proceedings of the ICML, Haifa, Israel, 21–24 June 2010; pp. 807–814.
35. Kingma, D.P.; Ba, J. Adam: A Method for Stochastic Optimization. *arXiv* **2017**, arXiv:1412.6980.
36. Tsinalis, O.; Matthews, P.M.; Guo, Y. Automatic Sleep Stage Scoring Using Time-Frequency Analysis and Stacked Sparse Autoencoders. *Ann. Biomed. Eng.* **2016**, *44*, 1587–1597. [CrossRef] [PubMed]
37. Zhu, T.; Luo, W.; Yu, F. Convolution-and Attention-Based Neural Network for Automated Sleep Stage Classification. *Int. J. Environ. Res. Public Health* **2020**, *17*, 4152. [CrossRef] [PubMed]
38. Mousavi, S.; Afghah, F.; Acharya, U.R. SleepEEGNet: Automated sleep stage scoring with sequence to sequence deep learning approach. *PLoS ONE* **2019**, *14*, e0216456. [CrossRef] [PubMed]
39. Längkvist, M.; Karlsson, L.; Loutfi, A. Sleep Stage Classification Using Unsupervised Feature Learning. *Adv. Artif. Neural Syst.* **2012**, *2012*, 1–9. [CrossRef]
40. Yuan, Y.; Jia, K.; Ma, F.; Xun, G.; Wang, Y.; Su, L.; Zhang, A. A hybrid self-attention deep learning framework for multivariate sleep stage classification. *BMC Bioinform* **2019**, *20*. [CrossRef]
41. Cen, L.; Yu, Z.L.; Tang, Y.; Shi, W.; Kluge, T.; Ser, W. Deep Learning Method for Sleep Stage Classification. *Neural Inf. Process.* **2017**, 796–802. [CrossRef]
42. Viterbi, A.J. Error Bounds for Convolutional Codes and an Asymptotically Optimum Decoding Algorithm. *IEEE Trans. Inf. Theory* **1967**, *13*, 260–269. [CrossRef]
43. Danker-Hopfe, H.; Anderer, P.; Zeitlhofer, J.; Boeck, M.; Dorn, H.; Gruber, G.; Heller, E.; Loretz, E.; Moser, D.; Parapatics, S.; et al. Interrater reliability for sleep scoring according to the Rechtschaffen & Kales and the new AASM standard. *J. Sleep Res.* **2009**, *18*, 74–84. [CrossRef]

Publisher's Note: MDPI stays neutral with regard to jurisdictional claims in published maps and institutional affiliations.

© 2020 by the authors. Licensee MDPI, Basel, Switzerland. This article is an open access article distributed under the terms and conditions of the Creative Commons Attribution (CC BY) license (http://creativecommons.org/licenses/by/4.0/).

Article

Robust T-End Detection via T-End Signal Quality Index and Optimal Shrinkage

Pei-Chun Su [1], Elsayed Z. Soliman [2,3] and Hau-Tieng Wu [1,4,5,*]

1 Department of Mathematics, Duke University, Durham, NC 27708, USA; peichun.su@duke.edu
2 Department of Epidemiology and Prevention, Epidemiological Cardiology Research Center (EPICARE), Wake Forest School of Medicine, Winston-Salem, NC 27101, USA; esoliman@wakehealth.edu
3 Section on Cardiovascular Medicine, Department of Internal Medicine, Wake Forest School of Medicine, Winston-Salem, NC 27101, USA
4 Department of Statistical Science, Duke University, Durham, NC 27708, USA
5 Mathematics Division, National Center for Theoretical Sciences, Taipei 106, Taiwan
* Correspondence: hauwu@math.duke.edu; Tel.: +1-919-660-2861

Received: 20 October 2020; Accepted: 28 November 2020; Published: 9 December 2020

Abstract: An automatic accurate T-wave end (T-end) annotation for the electrocardiogram (ECG) has several important clinical applications. While there have been several algorithms proposed, their performance is usually deteriorated when the signal is noisy. Therefore, we need new techniques to support the noise robustness in T-end detection. We propose a new algorithm based on the signal quality index (SQI) for T-end, coined as tSQI, and the optimal shrinkage (OS). For segments with low tSQI, the OS is applied to enhance the signal-to-noise ratio (SNR). We validated the proposed method using eleven short-term ECG recordings from QT database available at Physionet, as well as four 14-day ECG recordings which were visually annotated at a central ECG core laboratory. We evaluated the correlation between the real-world signal quality for T-end and tSQI, and the robustness of proposed algorithm to various additive noises of different types and SNR's. The performance of proposed algorithm on arrhythmic signals was also illustrated on MITDB arrhythmic database. The labeled signal quality is well captured by tSQI, and the proposed OS denoising help stabilize existing T-end detection algorithms under noisy situations by making the mean of detection errors decrease. Even when applied to ECGs with arrhythmia, the proposed algorithm still performed well if proper metric is applied. We proposed a new T-end annotation algorithm. The efficiency and accuracy of our algorithm makes it a good fit for clinical applications and large ECG databases. This study is limited by the small size of annotated datasets.

Keywords: T-end annotation; signal quality index; tSQI; optimal shrinkage

1. Introduction

The electrocardiogram (ECG) is a ubiquitous diagnostic tool for cardiovascular diseases. One important clinical application is information about the QT interval, a measure of ventricular repolarization. A prolonged heart rate corrected QT is associated with ventricular arrhythmia and sudden death [1], and also used to study adverse drug reactions [2].

The accuracy of QT measurement directly depends on the ability to accurately determine the Q onset and T offset. Compared with the Q onset, determination of the T-end is challenging. Nevertheless, various techniques have been proposed for automatic T-end detection. This includes threshold on the first derivative [3,4], threshold on an area connected by points around the T-wave [5–7], wavelet transform [8,9], mathematical model [10], support vector machine [11], artificial neural network (ANN) [12–14], hidden Markov model (HMM) [15,16], partially collapsed Gibbs sample and Bayesian [17], "wings" function [18], derivative curve [19], adaptive technique [20], TU complex analyses [21], correlation analysis [22], and k-nearest neighbor [23]. While those algorithms are widely applied, they are only validated on databases without severe noise contamination. It is thus unclear how robust they are to the inevitable noise and artifacts. The emerging wide use of long-term ECG recording that extends for days calls for robust automatic T-end annotation algorithms that handle marked prolonged noise such as myogenic noise, electrode contact noise, motion artifacts, and powerline interference [24,25].

In this report we propose a novel denoising tool to stabilize existing T-end annotation algorithms. The niche of the algorithm is twofold. First, we defined a signal quality index (SQI) that is suitable for the T-end annotation. This SQI describes the signal quality from a different perspective compared with other SQI aiming for R peak detection. Second, we applied a recently developed denoise technique called optimal shrinkage (OS) [26]. In our previous publication [27], we have demonstrated that a better and more adaptive template for each cardiac cycle is obtained through OS, which helps recover ECG morphology from noisy signals. However, we observed a morphology distortion after the application of OS on clean signals, where "clean" means the noise is dominated by the beat to beat variation. The noise level is thus overestimated and results in the distorted templates of cardiac cycle. Therefore, in this work, we incorporated the SQI thresholding step, such that the OS is only applied to signals with low signal quality. This part will be further addressed in the discussion section. Moreover, for those arrhythmic beats, we demonstrated that our algorithm still recovers their morphology when the proper metric between different cardiac cycles is selected.

2. Materials and Methods

2.1. Three Existing T-End Detection Algorithms

To keep things self-contained, we summarize three commonly applied T-end detection algorithms here. The algorithms are referred to by the last name of the first author, including Zhang [5], Carlos [6], and Martinez [8]. All these three algorithms require the locations of the QRS complex and T-wave before estimating T-end points. Both Zhang's and Carlos's algorithms are based on the idea that inside the designed searching window related to the detected R peaks, the maximum value of an area function is reached over the T-end point. Martinez's algorithm uses dyadic wavelet transform to find the peaks and limit points of QRS cycles, P waves, and T waves. The T-end points are defined as the local maximum or minimum in the wavelet transform with dilation factor 2^4 or 2^5. These algorithms have been evaluated on the PhysioNet QT database [28] with low T-end detection errors. The performance of Martinez's algorithm has also been validated on the dataset 3 of the CSE multilead measurement database (CSEDB) [29]. The MATLAB package of Zhang's algorithm can be downloaded at http://www.irisa.fr/sosso/zhang/biomedical/ and Martinez's algorithm can be downloaded at https://github.com/marianux/ecg-kit. We coded Carlos's algorithm according to the original paper's description. For T-wave locations, Zhang's and Martinez's algorithms have their built-in algorithms, so we simply adopted them. The T-wave locations estimated by Martinez were applied in Carlos. The other parameters of each algorithm were tuned in the same settings described in the original papers.

2.2. Signal Quality Index (SQI) for T-End Detection

Signal quality index (SQI) has been a critical quantity in the analysis of biomedical time series. It could be considered as an index summarizing the relationship between noise, artifact, and the signal of interest. In the ideal situation, if both the clean signal and the noise are clearly defined, the concept of signal-to-noise ratio (SNR) is a common approach to define SQI. However, usually it is challenging to get the clean signal and the noise or artifact from the given noisy signal, particularly when there is only one channel. Therefore, we need a different approach to determine the SQI.

There have been various ideas in the past decades to define SQI for different biomedical signals [30–33]. The bSQI proposed by Li et al. [32] is a typical example. They applied two different R peak detection algorithms to the given ECG signal and obtained two sets of estimated R peak locations. If an ECG signal has a high signal quality, the estimated R-peak locations should be the same, or at least similar. This similarity is quantified as the SQI. This idea is simple but brilliant, and it can help us understand the quality of a given ECG signal. However, it only tells us the quality of the given ECG signal in the sense of R peak detection but not from all aspects. Specifically, it may not tell us how good the P wave is, or how clean the T wave is. See Figure 1 for an example. In this example we have a noisy ECG recording. Although R-peak locations estimated by two different R-peak detection algorithms, the Elgendi's [34] and jqrs [30] algorithms, are similar, visually the T waves are not of high quality. Quantitatively, the T-end's estimated by Zhang's and Martinez's algorithms are quite different. In summary, the bSQI only describes the signal quality from the aspect of R peak locations, and it cannot well manifest the signal quality for T-wave, and hence the T-end location.

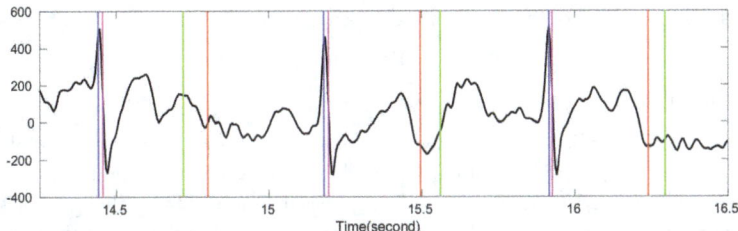

Figure 1. The comparison of bSQI and tSQI. The black line is the ECG signal from the Ultra-Long-Term ECG recordings Database with intermediate quality. The intersection of x-axis and blue (magenta) vertical lines are the time stamps of R peak locations estimated by Elgendi's algorithm [34] (jqrs [30]). The intersection of x-axis and red (green) vertical lines are the time stamps of T-end locations estimated by Zhang's algorithm (Martinez's algorithm). The magenta vertical lines are shifted right by 10 milliseconds to avoid the overlap with blue lines. The value of bSQI is 0.99, and the value of tSQI is 0.66, which are calculated by matching points from two different algorithms as the same point if the time difference between them is smaller than 50 ms.

Motivated by this observation, we propose a new SQI for the automatic T-end detection here. Similar to the idea behind the bSQI, we take two sequences of T-end locations detected by two T-end detection algorithms, and then determine the SQI in the following way. For each ECG segment, we assume that the R peak detection algorithm performs well and use the detected R peaks to estimate T-end points by two chosen algorithms. Denote $A \in \mathbb{N}$ to be the number of detected R peaks and hence estimated T-end points. Given a grace period $\gamma > 0$, we consider that two chosen algorithms match if the time difference between the two estimated T-ends is smaller than γ. Assuming we have $B \in \mathbb{N}$ of T-end points that match, we denote a value tSQI $\in [0, 1]$ as

$$\text{tSQI} := \frac{B}{2A - B},$$

which is the desired SQI for the T-end detection. When tSQI = 1, it means that the two sequences of estimated T-end locations are perfectly matched, and hence the T-end quality is high; a lower tSQI stands for less matched estimations, and hence a lower T-end quality. In this work, we chose Zhang's and Martinez's algorithms to determine the tSQI in the following sections.

2.3. Proposed Algorithm

We detail the propose automatic T-end annotation algorithm, step by step, here.

2.3.1. Step 0: Preprocessing

Given an ECG recording, we resample it at the sampling rate 250 Hz. To remove the baseline wandering, a Butterworth lowpass filter of order 4 with the cut-off frequency l_{off} Hz is applied. Since the source of data is unknown, we apply two notch filters with the notches centered at 50 and 60 Hz to reduce the powerline interference. The recording after the preprocessing is denoted as $z \in \mathbb{R}^N$, where $N \in \mathbb{N}$ is the number of samples.

2.3.2. Step 1: Estimate QRS Complex

There have been several works [30,34,35] discussing how to detect the location of QRS complexes. Since the T-end detection is our focus, here we simply use QRS locations estimated by Elgendi's algorithm before applying any T-end detection algorithm. We denote the collected timestamps of estimated R-peak locations as

$$\mathbf{R} = \{R(i)\}_{i=1}^n \qquad (1)$$

where $R(i)$ is the timestamp of the i-th detected R peak and $n \in \mathbb{N}$ is the total number of estimated R peaks.

2.3.3. Step 2: Evaluate tSQI

For the i-th cardiac cycle, we evaluate its tSQI on a signal segment $[z(R(i) - 1250), \ldots, z(R(i) + 1250)]^\top$ with a grace period γ. Given a threshold number $q \in [0, 1]$, if the tSQI $\geq q$, the final estimated T-end of each cardiac cycle is determined by applying the desired T-end detection algorithm. Otherwise, the following steps are applied, and the final estimation would be made in Step 4.

2.3.4. Step 3: Denoise Low Quality Cardiac Cycles by Optimal Shrinkage

- *Construct ECG templates.* On the i-th cardiac cycle determined by the i-th R peak, we find a window large enough, so that the whole P-QRS-T waveform is covered. For instance, denote $w \in \mathbb{N}$ to be the rounding number of the 95% quantile of R to R intervals in $\mathbf{R}$, and denote the corresponding ECG segment over the cardiac cycle as

$$s_i := [z(R(i) - L_w), \ldots, z(R(i) + R_w)]^\top \in \mathbb{R}^p \qquad (2)$$

where $L_w \in \mathbb{N}$, $R_w \in \mathbb{N}$, and $p := L_w + R_w + 1$. A library for the ECG template is built and denoted as

$$\mathcal{L} := \{s_i\}_{i=1}^n \qquad (3)$$

- *Remove nuisance variables by optimal shrinkage.* Define a metric $d(s_a, s_b)$ between the a-th and b-th template. For instance, we can use R-R interval difference in respect to the cycles or l_2 norm $\|s_a - s_b\|_{l2}$ as the metric. For the i-th cardiac cycle s_i, from the library $\mathcal{L}$ we selecte $\xi \in \mathbb{N}$ neighbors that have the smallest difference. We then construct a data matrix S of size $p \times (\xi + 1)$ consisting of the i-th cardiac cycle in the first column and all other neighbors in the remaining ξ columns. We assume that the S can be decomposed into two parts, $S = X + N$, where X is the clean data matrix containing QRS cycles and N is the matrix modeling noise. We also assume each entry of N has independent and identical noisy component with zero mean and the same variance and finite fourth moment, and X has a low rank. Under these assumptions, there is an elegant solution based on the random matrix theory proposed by Gavish and Donoho [26] to recover X from S, which is named as optimal shrinkage (OS). We apply OS on the data matrix S in the following manner:

Suppose $\frac{p}{\ell} \leq 1$ (if not, we simply take the transpose of S and apply the same approaches on $S^\top$ as the following). Denote the SVD of the data matrix S as

$$S = \sum_{i=1}^{r} \lambda_i u_i v_i', \qquad (4)$$

where r is the matrix rank, u_i and v_i' are the i-th left and right singular vector corresponding to the singular value λ_i, and $\lambda_1 \geq \lambda_2 \geq \ldots \geq \lambda_p$. We normalize S with the noise level estimated by

$$\sigma := \sqrt{\frac{1}{n \cdot p} \sum_{i=1}^{n} \sum_{k=1}^{p} (s_i(k) - \bar{s}(k))^2}, \qquad (5)$$

and

$$\bar{s}(k) = \text{median } \{s_1(k), \ldots, s_n(k)\}, \qquad (6)$$

where $k = 1, \ldots, p$. Then, the denoised data matrix is estimated from S by OS and denoted as

$$\widetilde{S}^{\eta^*} = \sigma \sum_{i=1}^{r} \eta^*\left(\frac{\lambda_i}{\sigma}\right) u_i v_i', \qquad (7)$$

where $\eta^* : [0, \infty) \to [0, \infty)$ is the optimal shrinker. In this work, we let η^* be the optimal shrinker that minimize the asymptotic loss with respect to the operator norm, such that

$$\eta^*(\lambda) = \frac{1}{\sqrt{2}} \sqrt{\lambda^2 - \beta - 1 + \sqrt{(\lambda^2 - \beta - 1)^2 - 4\beta}}, \qquad (8)$$

when $\lambda \geq 1 + \sqrt{\beta}$ and $\eta^*(\lambda) = 0$ otherwise. The first column of $\widetilde{S}^{\eta^*}$ is the estimated QRS complex of s_i, denoted as $\widetilde{s}_i$. Applying OS on every cardiac cycle in $\mathcal{L}$, we acquire a denoised library and denote it as

$$\widetilde{\mathcal{L}} := \{\widetilde{s}_i\}_{i=1}^n. \qquad (9)$$

2.3.5. Step 4: Evaluate T-End Locations

As mentioned earlier, T-end detection algorithms of Zhang, Carlos, and Martinez are chosen for T offset delineation. Chosen T-end detection algorithm is applied in the library $\widetilde{\mathcal{L}}$, and locations of T-end are estimated for each denoised cardiac cycles. Based on the R-peak locations **R** estimated in Equation (2), estimated T-end locations on the signal z are the final output of the proposed algorithm.

2.4. QT Database

The first database we considered is a common benchmark database, the PhysioNet QT database [28]. It includes ECG signals chosen from the MIT-BIH database [36] and the European ST-T database [37]. The database contains 105 subjects. Each subject has fifteen-minutes recordings of 2-channel ECG signals sampled at the 250 Hz, which include a broad variety of QRS and ST morphology. A subset of cardiac cycles in the database have been manually annotated with waveform boundaries, and only a small portion of signals was annotated for T-end. The manual annotations were made by two cardiologists using an interactive graphic display to view both signals simultaneously. The first cardiologist (Cardio 1) made annotations on all 105 subjects, and the second cardiologist (Cardio 2) made annotations on only 11 subjects. Following the same approach in Zhang's work [5], we separated the QT database into three sets for analysis according to which cardiologists made the annotations. The first set (Set 1) contains all 105 subjects, in which we considered the 3542 annotations made by Cardio 1 as the true T-end points. The second set (Set 2) is from the 11 subjects annotated by both

Cardio 1 and Cardio 2, in which we considered the 487 T-end points annotated by Cardio 1 as the ground truth. The third set (Set 3) also includes the same 11 subjects as Set 2, but the ground truth is the 402 annotations made by Cardio 2.

To evaluate our proposed algorithm under various noisy environment, we considered two additive noise models, the random Gaussian noise and the ARMA(1,1) noise [38], and contaminated the QT database by these noises. Assume the original signal is $z \in \mathbb{R}^N$, where $N \in \mathbb{N}$ is the number of samples. The Gaussian noise was generated by N random points following the Gaussian distribution with mean 0 and variance 1. The ARMA (1,1) noise was generated by the ARMA (1,1) process:

$$X_t - \phi X_{t-1} = c + Z_t + \theta Z_{t-1},$$

where $t = 1, \ldots, N$ is the sampling point, X_t is the ARMA (1,1) process sampled at point t, Z_t is a random variable following Student t-4 distribution sampled at point t, and c, ϕ and θ are selected constant. We set $c = 0.5$, $\phi = 0.5$ and $\theta = -0.5$ for following evaluation. The desired ARMA (1,1) noise at point t with variance 1 was then acquired by

$$X_t / SD\left(\{X_t\}_{t=1}^N\right),$$

where $SD(\{X_t\}_{t=1}^N)$ is the standard deviation of the sequence $\{X_t\}_{t=1}^N$. Define a constant S

$$S := \sqrt{P_z}/10^{SNR/20},$$

where SNR is the desired signal to noise ratio and P_z is the power of original signal. We then multiplied both Gaussian and ARMA (1,1) noise by S and added them to z to create the noisy signal with desired SNR. We evaluated SNR of 10 dB and 5 dB in the following evaluation.

2.5. 14-Day ECG Recordings Database

Our database of single-lead, ultra-long-term ECG recordings comprised of four recordings; each recording is approximately two weeks (14 days) in length. The data was recorded using the ZIO® Patch cardiac monitor (iRhythm Technologies, Inc., San Francisco, CA, USA) at a sampling rate of 200 Hz. The underlying information of the subjects was unknown to us. Across the four 14-day recordings, we randomly selected 51, 11, 24, 80, and 32 segments of 10 s for manual review and annotation at the Epidemiological Cardiology Research Center (EPICARE Center, Wake Forest School of Medicine, Winston Salem, NC, USA). The ECG core laboratory was provided with the automated T annotation generated by our algorithm, and the results were reviewed by the ECG core readers for accuracy and editing. The quality of each ECG segment was also documented as part of the annotation process. In total, 173 segments were labeled good, 16 segments were labeled intermediate, and 9 segments were labeled bad.

2.6. Evaluation

We evaluated our proposed T-end annotation algorithm, which is an enhancement of Zhang, Carlos, or Martinez, on the above-mentioned databases. For each ECG recording, we cropped a segment for analysis, which started from 1 min before the first T-end annotations and ended at 1 min after the last T-end annotation. The R-R interval difference between cardiac cycles was applied as the metric $d(s_a, s_b)$. Since our focus was automatically annotating T-end, the R peaks were assumed to be known. The T-end detection error is the time difference between the automatically detected T-end points and the provided annotations. In the QT database, since each subject has two recordings, the estimated T-end points were chosen from the best result that minimized the detection error among the two computed T-end positions. This approach is the same as that used by Zhang and Carlos. The justification of this approach is that the cardiologists made their annotations by evaluating both

ECG records. For the Ultra-Long-Term ECG recordings database, since there is only one channel for each recording, we simply calculated the estimated T-end locations and provided annotations.

In our previous work, the effects of noise robustness and morphology recovery by optimal shrinkage and other template estimation algorithms had been compared for the purpose of extracting fetal ECG from the trans-abdominal maternal ECG [27] over the Physionet CinC Challenge 2013 database [39]. These methods included independent component analysis (ICA), principal component analysis (PCA), least mean square (LMS), recursive least square (RLS), echo state neural network (ESN), and extended Kalman filter (EKF). To further demonstrate the strength of optimal shrinkage, in this work we compared with another ECG denoising method named wavelet shrinkage [40,41]. The idea is similar to the optimal shrinkage, where the empirical wavelet coefficients are shrunk, and the signals are recovered by the inverse wavelet transform. The main difference is that in OS, the basis is adaptive to the data, while in the wavelet shrinkage, the basis is predetermined. We compared these two algorithms on the QT database with the additive Gaussian or ARMA (1,1) noise. The wavelet shrinkage is applied after *Step 0: preprocessing*, where wavelet shrinkage is applied on the denoised signal $z \in \mathbb{R}^N$ following the setup detailed [42]. Then, *Step 1* and *Step 4* are applied for R peaks and T offset delineation.

To evaluate the performance of each algorithm, the mean (ME) for the absolute values of detection errors of each recording were calculated. Then, the median and MAD and 2.5–97.5% quantile interval of ME over all recordings were computed and reported. To evaluate if the proposed OS approach improved the existing algorithm, we applied the Wilcoxon signed rank test with the statistical significance level set to 0.05.

3. Results

The parameters of proposed algorithm were set as follows. We set the grace period $\gamma = 50$ ms for the tSQI evaluation. Moreover, we set the cutoff frequency for low pass filter as $l_{off} = 0.5$ Hz, window length $L_w = R_w = \lceil \frac{1}{2} \rceil$, where $\lceil x \rceil$ is the smallest integer larger than x, and number of neighbors $\xi = 19$. The evaluation was performed on MATLAB 2019b, Microsoft 10 system, Intel i7-6700HQ CPU@2.60GHz 4 cores, and 16GB RAM. The code can be downloaded at: https://github.com/MagineZ/Tend-Project.

3.1. tSQI and Quality in the 14-Day ECG Database

The comparison of the signal quality provided in the 14-day ECG database and the proposed tSQI in the ultra-long ECG recording database is reported in Table 1. We observe that the ECG signals labeled as good (or bad) quality have higher (or lower) tSQI's. If we view label good as 1, label intermediate as 3, and label bad as 5, the correlation coefficient between the tSQI and labeled quality is −0.71.

Table 1. The relationship between the tSQI and quality.

Labeled Quality	Good	Average	Bad
tSQT	0.98 ± 0.06	0.84 ± 0.12	0.68 ± 0.08

Note: If we view label good as 1, label intermediate as 3, and label bad as 5, the correlation coefficient between the tSQ and labeled quality is −0.71.

3.2. Noise Suppression

We examined if the proposed OS denoising could help stabilize existing T-end detection algorithms under various noise types and noise levels. The results for different SNR levels are reported in Table 2 for the Gaussian noise and ARMA (1,1) noise respectively. It is clear that the proposed OS algorithm helps improve the traditional algorithms and outperforms wavelet shrinkage. Wilcoxon signed rank test over the 20 rounds' rejects the null hypothesis with statistical significance. To appreciate how the OS recovers the ECG signal, some examples are shown in Figures 2 and 3. We see that the deviations of estimated T-end from the annotation is obvious on the signals without OS applied, and the OS helps recover the ECG morphology and thus reduces the automatic annotation errors. This suggests the potential of the proposed denoise algorithm to help stabilize existing algorithms.

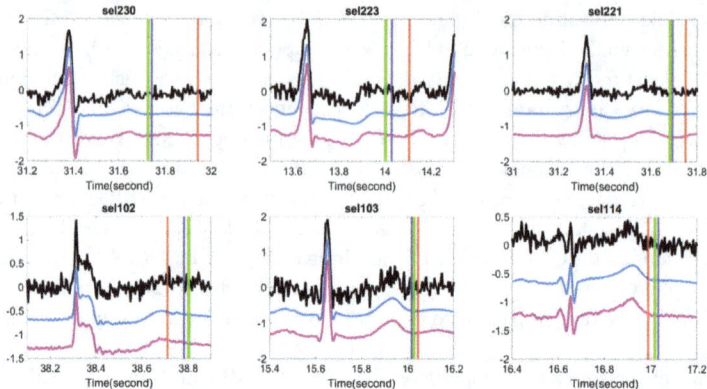

Figure 2. Comparison of different T-end detection algorithms with or without optimal shrinkage when the signal is contaminated by the additive Gaussian noise. In each subplot, the black line is the ECG signal from the first channel of a subject in the QT database with additive noise, the light blue line is the denoised ECG signal by the optimal shrinkage, and the magenta line is the original ECG signal without adding any noise. The red (green) vertical lines indicate the estimated T-end by the chosen detection algorithm on noisy signals without (with) OS applied. The deep blue vertical line indicates the annotated T-end by Cardio 1. The plots in the first (second) row are the results when the SNR is 10 dB (5 dB). The chosen T-end algorithm in the first, second and third column is Zhang's, Carlos's, and Martinez's algorithms respectively. The case index of each plot is in the title.

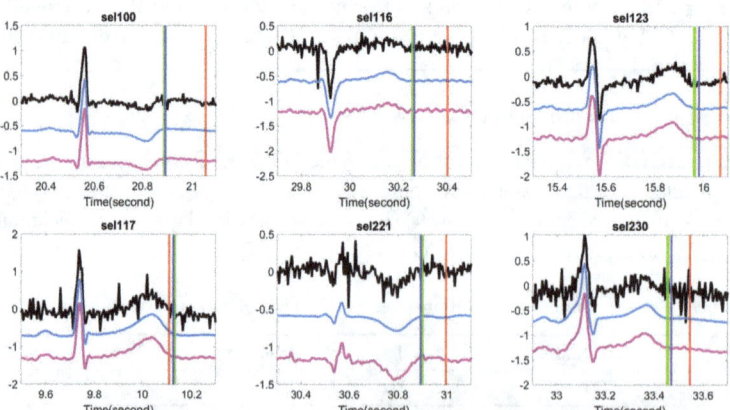

Figure 3. Comparison of different T-end detection algorithms with or without optimal shrinkage when the signal is contaminated by the additive ARMA (1,1) noise. In each subplot, the black line is the ECG signal from the first channel of a subject in the QT database with additive noise, the light blue line is the denoised ECG signal by the optimal shrinkage, and the magenta line is the original ECG signal without adding any noise. The red (green) vertical lines indicate the estimated T-end by the chosen detection algorithm on noisy signals without (with) OS applied. The deep blue vertical line indicates the annotated T-end by Cardio 1. The plots in the first (second) row are the results when the SNR is 10 dB (5 dB). The chosen T-end algorithm in the first, second and third column is Zhang's, Carlos's, and Martinez's algorithms respectively. The case index of each plot is in the title.

Table 2. Evaluation of algorithms on the QT database under contamination of Gaussian/ARMA (1,1) noise.

	SNR		Zhang					
			Gaussian			ARMA (1,1)		
			$q = 0$	WS	$q = 0.9$ (OS)	$q = 0$	WS	$q = 0.9$ (OS)
Set 1	10 dB		22.32 ± 0.26 [21.47, 22.99]	20.15 ± 0.24 [19.58, 20.75]	17.43 ± 0.19 ** [16.97, 17.76]	22.39 ± 0.22 [21.47, 22.60]	20.15 ± 0.22 [19.64, 20.74]	17.53 ± 0.17 ** [17.16, 18.01]
	5 dB		29.22 ± 0.51 [28.12, 30.]	23.84 ± 0.33 [22.82, 24.25]	18.35 ± 0.44 ** [17.62, 19.30]	28.55 ± 0.38 [27.97, 29.57]	24.13 ± 0.35 ** [23.62, 25.02]	18.57 ± 0.49 ** [17.71, 19.65]
Set 2	10 dB		17.91 ± 0.67 [15.95, 20.04]	16.81 ± 0.51 [15.65, 17.85]	15.35 ± 0.47 ** [14.07, 16.16]	17.95 ± 0.75 [15.68, 19.24]	16.65 ± 0.56 ** [15.87, 18.78]	15.20 ± 0.46 ** [14.41, 16.92]
	5 dB		23.96 ± 0.61 [22.85, 25.55]	19.68 ± 0.62 [18.49, 21.16]	16.08 ± 0.43 ** [15.04, 17.18]	23.23 ± 1.01 [21.48, 26.42]	19.76 ± 0.88 [18.21, 21.78]	15.66 ± 0.70 ** [15.09, 18.89]
Set 3	10 dB		21.85 ± 1.63 [20.06, 27.38]	19.81 ± 1.22 [18.55, 23.38]	20.33 ± 0.50 * [18.74, 21.09]	22.36 ± 1.06 [19.97, 24.42]	20.22 ± 0.60 * [17.87, 22.54]	20.07 ± 0.57 * [18.79, 21.91]
	5 dB		26.85 ± 1.16 [24.99, 30.09]	21.40 ± 1.69 [19.13, 27.01]	21.43 ± 0.62 ** [19.52, 23.02]	26.87 ± 1.33 [23.33, 31.10]	22.77 ± 1.30 [19.36, 25.74]	20.82 ± 0.67 ** [19.96, 24.22]

			Carlos					
			Gaussian			ARMA (1,1)		
			$q = 0$	WS	$q = 0.9$ (OS)	$q = 0$	WS	$q = 0.9$ (OS)
Set 1	10 dB		25.12 ± 0.34 [24.41, 25.93]	24.70 ± 0.34 [24.07, 25.42]	22.78 ± 0.33 ** [22.18, 23.58]	25.82 ± 0.28 [25.13, 26.51]	25.36 ± 0.26 [25.03, 26.00]	22.98 ± 0.28 ** [22.35, 23.86]
	5 dB		32.27 ± 0.41 [31.28, 32.86]	29.12 ± 0.30 [28.31, 29.63]	23.19 ± 0.45 ** [21.96, 24.44]	32.53 ± 0.57 [30.83, 34.14]	29.75 ± 0.45 [28.69, 31.01]	23.39 ± 0.27 ** [22.53, 23.90]
Set 2	10 dB		21.20 ± 0.71 [19.01, 22.22]	20.10 ± 0.56 [17.56, 20.61]	19.49 ± 0.79 ** [16.81, 21.47]	22.01 ± 0.93 [19.18, 23.53]	20.59 ± 0.67 [19.09, 22.97]	19.56 ± 0.63 * [18.67, 21.45]
	5 dB		25.62 ± 0.75 [23.45, 26.81]	23.14 ± 0.75 [20.43, 24.67]	19.99 ± 1.10 ** [16.41, 22.16]	26.61 ± 1.10 [24.91, 29.69]	25.46 ± 0.70 [23.20, 26.88]	20.29 ± 0.87 ** [18.32, 22.28]
Set 3	10 dB		19.96 ± 0.98 [17.89, 24.02]	17.15 ± 1.28 [14.37, 19.65]	14.67 ± 0.54 ** [13.22, 15.99]	20.33 ± 1.14 [18.04, 22.90]	18.32 ± 1.25 [15.35, 20.59]	14.62 ± 0.78 ** [13.76, 17.12]
	5 dB		26.12 ± 1.24 [23.56, 31.77]	21.15 ± 1.30 [18.50, 24.36]	16.03 ± 0.83 ** [14.07, 17.69]	27.21 ± 1.74 [23.51, 31.32]	23.72 ± 1.06 [20.58, 26.85]	15.67 ± 0.92 ** [13.51, 18.45]

			Martinez					
			Gaussian			ARMA (1,1)		
			$q = 0$	WS	$q = 0.9$ (OS)	$q = 0$	WS	$q = 0.9$ (OS)
Set 1	10 dB		26.64 ± 0.29 [26.16, 27.29]	25.74 ± 0.26 [25.01, 26.25]	22.86 ± 0.25 ** [22.22, 23.54]	26.35 ± 0.22 [25.77, 26.80]	25.47 ± 0.25 [24.75, 25.85]	22.91 ± 0.26 ** [22.13, 23.15]
	5 dB		33.87 ± 0.29 [33.04, 34.38]	30.38 ± 0.30 [29.40, 31.35]	23.39 ± 0.34 ** [22.43, 24.41]	33.51 ± 0.24 [32.42, 33.84]	30.17 ± 0.30 [29.40, 30.90]	23.43 ± 0.48 ** [22.85, 24.86]
Set 2	10 dB		19.49 ± 0.73 [17.88, 21.35]	17.41 ± 0.68 [15.83, 18.84]	17.12 ± 0.79 ** [14.91, 18.69]	19.24 ± 0.69 [17.38, 20.61]	17.30 ± 0.43 [16.18, 18.14]	17.02 ± 0.55 ** [15.91, 18.76]
	5 dB		25.67 ± 0.83 [23.19, 27.49]	21.33 ± 0.84 [17.89, 22.92]	17.52 ± 0.72 ** [16.29, 19.33]	25.38 ± 0.79 [23.75, 27.94]	21.03 ± 0.96 [18.78, 23.25]	16.93 ± 0.74 ** [14.87, 18.45]
Set 3	10 dB		20.20 ± 0.97 [18.30, 23.09]	17.38 ± 0.88 [15.71, 21.57]	16.87 ± 0.79 ** [15.40, 18.52]	20.12 ± 1.03 [18.27, 21.79]	18.12 ± 1.18 [15.36, 21.93]	17.55 ± 0.81 * [14.58, 18.80]
	5 dB		27.12 ± 1.39 [23.92, 30.58]	22.30 ± 1.61 [17.96, 27.41]	18.77 ± 0.77 ** [16.51, 20.09]	26.62 ± 1.62 [24.09, 32.05]	23.02 ± 1.71 [19.46, 27.78]	18.57 ± 0.79 ** [16.69, 19.58]

Note: Column one stands for which set is used for error computation. Column 2 is the signal to noise ratio. Column 3–5 (Gaussian noise) and 4–6 (ARMA(1,1) noise) are the results of T-wave end detection error using algorithms of Zhang, Carlos, and Martinez respectively, where q stands for the tSQI threshold for deciding when to apply the optimal shrinkage, WS stands for wavelet shrinkage, and OS stands for optimal shrinkage. The results are shown by taking median ± MAD of ME over 20 rounds' random noise addition. The unit is millisecond. The 2.5% and 97.5% quantile interval of ME are also listed beneath median ± MAD. * (**) stands for p-value < 0.05 (0.01).

3.3. Evaluation in the QT and 14-Day ECG Databases

We applied the proposed tSQI and OS denoising to the QT and 14-day ECG recording databases. We considered tSQI thresholds $q = 0.9$ when applying the proposed algorithm; that is, the OS was applied to those cardiac cycles with the tSQI less than 0.9. Note that $q = 0$ means we do not apply the OS. The results are shown in Tables 3 and 4. First, note that in Zhang's and Carlos's algorithms, the ME and SD were defined without taking the absolute value. The error is thus underestimated since the detection error of the estimated T-end has positive or negative values. Therefore, smaller MEs were reported by Zhang and Carlos in comparison with our results when $q = 0$, even if we applied their announced codes on the same database. We see that, overall, the MAD and 97.5% quantile are improved, while there is no statistical significance. To have a better feeling about how the algorithm performs, the scatterplots of T-end detection errors of the QT database are shown in Figure 4.

Table 3. Evaluation of algorithms on the QT database.

	# of Beats	Zhang		Carlos		Martinez	
		Before OS	After OS	Before OS	After OS	Before OS	After OS
Set 1	1417	12.00 ± 20.83 [0, 128.00]	12.00 ± 18.96 [0, 116.00]	12.00 ± 35.82 [0, 212.30]	12.00 ± 32.84 [0, 224.00]	12.00 ± 40.59 [0, 304.60]	12.00 ± 37.88 [0, 332.00]
Set 2	169	12.00 ± 9.43 [0, 44.80]	16.00 ± 9.17 [0, 44.00]	12.00 ± 20.41 [0, 108.00]	12.00 ± 19.94 [0, 101.60]	12.00 ± 20.33 [0, 92.00]	12.00 ± 18.47 [0, 84.80]
Set 3	132	16.00 ± 27.49 [0, 100.00]	12.00 ± 27.37 [0, 100.80]	8.00 ± 14.22 [0, 72.00]	8.00 ± 13.35 [0, 49.6]	16.00 ± 22.60 [0, 79.20]	12.00 ± 21.87 [0, 81.60]

Note: Column one indicates which set is analyzed. Column 2 is the number of heart beats. Column 3, 4, and 5 are the results of T-wave end detection error using algorithms of Zhang, Carlos, and Martinez respectively. The median ± mean absolute deviation (MAD) of detection errors are evaluated. The unit is millisecond. Note that since the sampling rate is 250 Hz, the median error is the multiple of 4 ms.

Table 4. Evaluation of algorithms on the Ultra-Long-Term ECG recordings database.

Labeled Quality	# of Beats	Zhang		Carlos		Martinez	
		Before OS	After OS	Before OS	After OS	Before OS	After OS
Good	538	0.00 ± 17.05 [0, 125.00]	5.00 ± 13.55 [0, 115.25]	5.00 ± 13.65 [0, 105.00]	5.00 ± 12.95 [0, 95.50]	10.00 ± 14.09 [0, 120.25]	10.00 ± 13.68 [0, 115.50]
Averaged	148	0.00 ± 33.99 [0, 168.00]	10.00 ± 29.94 [0, 159.00]	10.00 ± 33.88 [0, 145.00]	15.00 ± 38.23 [0, 200.00]	10.00 ± 33.73 [0, 157.00]	15.00 ± 34.10 [0.00, 169.00]
Bad	127	0.00 ± 45.04 [0, 208.25]	30.00 ± 47.90 [0, 208.25]	25.00 ± 50.46 [0, 236.63]	35.00 ± 50.38 [0, 230.00]	35.00 ± 54.88 [0, 216.63]	50.00 ± 50.07 [0, 225.00]

Note: Column one indicates which set is analyzed. Column 2 is the number of heart beats. Column 3, 4, and 5 are the results of T-wave end detection error using algorithms of Zhang, Carlos, and Martinez respectively. The median ± mean absolute deviation (MAD) of detection errors are evaluated. The unit is millisecond. Note that since the sampling rate is 200 Hz, the median error is the multiple of 5 ms.

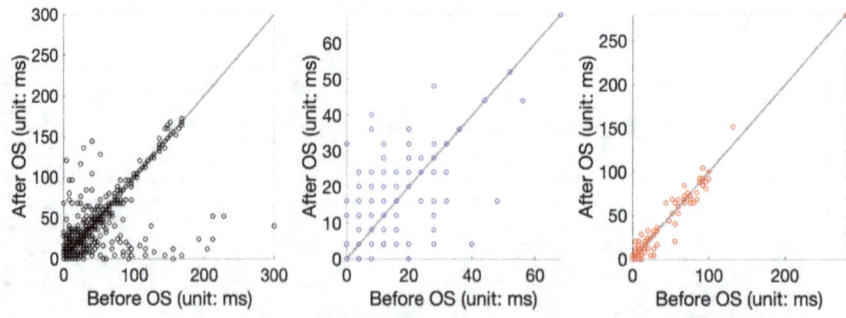

Figure 4. Scatterplot of T-end prediction error before and after applying the OS. From left to right are the scatterplot of applying Zhang's algorithm to the set 1, set 2, and set 3 of the QT database.

4. Discussion

In this report, we showed that the labeled quality in the 14-day ECG database provided by the ECG core lab is well captured by the proposed tSQI. We also showed how the noise deteriorates the signal quality and thus induces high detection errors in both databases when the commonly applied T-end detection algorithms are applied. The proposed OS denoise was able to recover the ECG morphology when the signal was contaminated by noise, and hence stabilized the T-end detection algorithm. In the arrhythmic cases, the T-wave morphologies could be visually better recovered by selecting proper metric between cardiac cycles.

The spike model underlying the proposed algorithm deserves discussion. As shown in Figure 5, there is T-wave distortion after the OS, and hence the T-end location shifts. In other words, when the ECG signal is clean, a morphology distortion after the OS is applied. This observation suggests that the cardiac cycles cannot be fully captured by the spike model used in Gavish's and Donoho's work [26] for the OS, and hence the morphology is distorted when the noise is dominated by the beat to beat variation. Recall that the PQRST morphology is not fixed from cycle to cycle, and the variation is caused by various physiological dynamics such as the respiratory and heart rate [2]. See Figure 6 for an example, where 20 cycles of clean PQRST waves from the same subject were superimposed. It is also clear that the PQRST variation from cycle to cycle is small compared with the dominant PQRST pattern. Therefore, the data matrix for a set of clean cardiac cycles can be modeled by $E = \sum_{i=1}^{p} \mu_i e_i a_i' \in \mathbb{R}^{p \times n}$, where $\mu_1 \gg \mu_2 \geq \mu_3 \geq \cdots$, $e_1 \in \mathbb{R}^p$ is the dominant PQRST pattern, $a_1 \in \mathbb{R}^n$ describes the magnitude the dominant PQRST pattern of each cycle, $e_2 \ldots e_p \in \mathbb{R}^p$ describe the variation of the PQRST pattern, and $a_2 \ldots a_p \in \mathbb{R}^n$ describe the magnitude of each variation of the PQRST pattern. Clearly, E can be well approximated by a spike model $\widetilde{E} = \mu_1 e_1 a_1' \in \mathbb{R}^{p \times n}$. While this seems to be a nice approximation, it does generate trouble when we apply the OS. Specifically, when the signal is clean, Equation (5) for noise level estimation will consider the physiological variation $\sum_{i=2}^{p} \mu_i e_i a_i'$ between each PQRST cycle as a source of noise. Thus, the noise level of the clean signal is overestimated. As a result, the OS might eliminate $\sum_{i=2}^{p} \mu_i e_i a_i'$ in order to recover the "clean matrix" $\mu_1 e_1 a_1'$, which leads to a distortion of morphology. The critical observation is that the variation of T wave morphology from cycle to cycle is quantified by the variation term $\sum_{i=2}^{p} \mu_i e_i a_i'$. However, due to the nonlinear relationship among T waves from cycle to cycle, it is not clear how to directly use the T wave information in $\sum_{i=2}^{p} \mu_i e_i a_i'$. When the signal is heavily contaminated by noise, $\overline{E} = \sum_{i=1}^{p} \mu_i e_i a_i' + \xi$, where ξ is the noise matrix, the small variation term $\mu_2 e_2 a_2', \ldots, \mu_p e_p a_p'$ will be dominated by the noise, particularly those with small singular values. Hence, there is benefit from applying the OS because it will balance between recovering the morphology and reducing the noise. This explains why we only apply OS to those cycles with low tSQI. We mention that in general, the dynamics of T wave morphology can be modeled by a low dimension manifold, which is referred to by the wave-shape manifold [43]. An exploration of this model to further improve the denoising performance, or even noise estimation shown in Equation (5), is out of the scope of this paper.

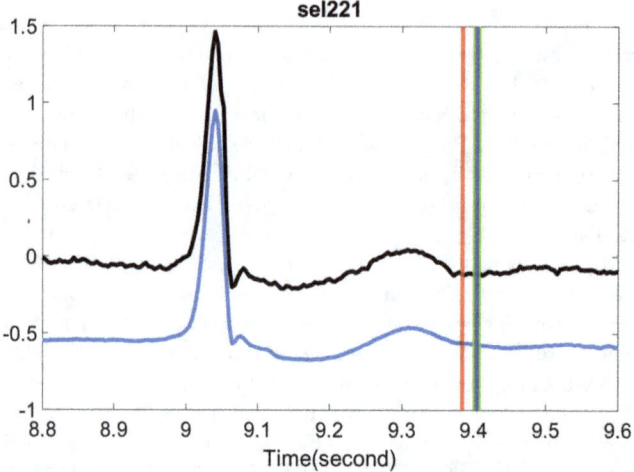

Figure 5. Comparison of the estimated T-end with or without optimal shrinkage on P-QRS-T cycles with high signal quality in the QT database. The black line is the preprocessed ECG signals from the first channel of one subject, and the light blue line is the same signals with the optimal shrinkage applied, where the whole signal is shifted down by 0.5 to enhance visualization. The red vertical line indicates the T-end point estimated by the chosen algorithm on the original signal. The green vertical line indicates the T-end point by the chosen algorithm on the denoised signal. The deep blue vertical line indicates the time point of T-end annotations provided by Cardio 1. Zhang's algorithm is applied for the T-end detection. The case index is in the title.

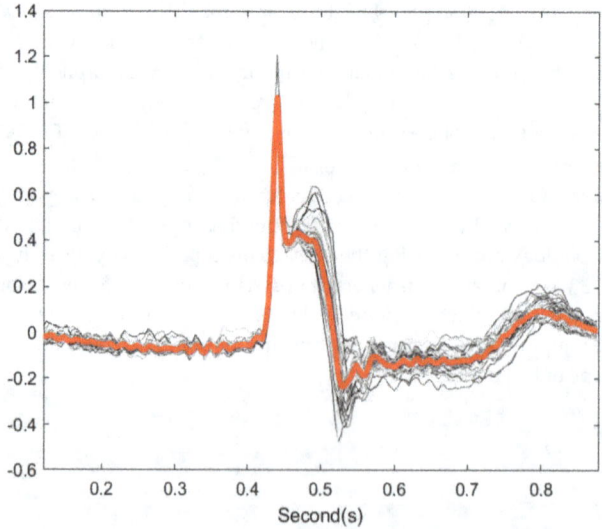

Figure 6. Illustration of cardiac cycles variation. The gray lines are 20 cardiac cycles from subject id sel30 in QT database. The red line is the median over the 20 cycles.

In the QT and ultra-long-term ECG recordings databases, while there was improvement of the T-end algorithm after applying OS with a properly chosen tSQI threshold, this improvement did not reach statistical significance. See Table 3. There are two possible explanations. First, the motion or other artifacts are inevitable. Usually, artifacts have structures that are unknown to us, unless we have other ECG channels to confirm. Due to these artifacts, visual manual annotation of T-end might be challenging. Consider the following scenario. Suppose the visual manual annotation of T-end was deviated by the existence of noise or artifacts. On the other hand, the denoising tool recovered the T wave, and hence the automatic T-end annotation algorithm provided the correct T-end annotation. In this case, the "correctly detected T-end" will be viewed as a bad annotation compared with visual manual annotation of T wave. To visualize this effect, we show some results in Figure 7. When the signal quality is labeled as average in the ultra-long-term ECG recording database, it is challenging even for experts to annotate the T-end due to noise and artifacts.

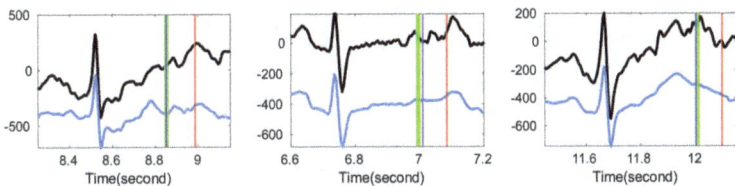

Figure 7. Comparison of the estimated T-end points with or without optimal shrinkage over Ultra-Long-Term ECG recordings Database with intermediate quality. In each subplot, the black line is the original ECG signal, and the blue line is the denoised ECG signal estimated by the optimal shrinkage. The red (green) vertical lines indicate the estimated T-end by the chosen detection algorithm on noisy signals without (with) OS applied. The deep blue vertical line indicates the annotated T-end provided by EPICARE Center. The chosen T-end algorithm in the first, second and third column is Zhang's, Carlos's, and Martinez's algorithm respectively.

Second, the OS performance might be masked by the experts' annotation process. This can be observed clearly in the ultra-long-term ECG recording database. Due to the labor-intensive annotation process, the data analysis team provided the automatic annotated labels by applying Zhang's algorithm, and the experts only provided a corrected T-end when they disagreed with the automatic label. This "semi-automatic" process might bias the experts' T-end annotation. We can see this potential bias in Table 4. Before applying the OS, the Zhang's algorithm outperforms other algorithms with or without OS. Therefore, we may conclude that it is possible that the non-statistical significance comes partially from the label uncertainty issue. Combining these facts and its performance when marked noise of different kinds exists, we may argue that the proposed stabilization algorithm by combining tSQI and OS is potential for automatic T-end annotation purpose in practice. We may also discuss a relevant but different topic. The labeling procedure for the ultra-long-term ECG recording database in this study can be viewed as an artificial intelligence aided approach to speed up the standard annotation procedure. By and large, the common labeling procedure is composed of two steps. First, one group of experts provide an initial manual annotation of ECG waveform. Then, another group of experts doubly confirm the provided annotation and edit extreme values as a quality control. In this study, we replace the first step by the existing best automatic annotation system and control the overall quality by a human expert intervention. How to improve this semi-automatic labeling procedure to avoid the above-mentioned issues is of its own interest, and it will be explored in our future work.

Another topic deserves a discussion is arrhythmic ECGs. It is well-known that occasional arrhythmias, like premature ventricular contraction (PVC), can cause sudden T wave changes in normal rhythms. Although we cannot find a publicly available arrhythmia database with T-end annotation, we provide some preliminary visual evaluation of the OS algorithm on the ECG signals with arrhythmia. We consider the Physionet MITDB [44] that contains 48 half hour excerpts of two-channel ambulatory ECG recordings. Each recording has 2 channels with the sampling frequency 360 Hz and the 11-bit resolution over a 10-mV range. The R peak annotations are provided. To see the performance of our proposed algorithm on arrhythmic ECGs, we applied OS on MITDB with Zhang's method for T-end annotation. Both the R-R interval difference and the l_2-norm of difference between cardiac cycles were applied as the metric $d(s_a, s_b)$. See Figure 8 for a typical result. We see that the distortion of T-wave morphology is obvious when the RRI metric is applied. The distortion is less when the l_2 norm is used as the metric to compare two cardiac cycles. For example, for the cycles around 1719.2 s and 1723 s, the T wave is distorted when the RRI metric is applied, and these distortions disappear when the l_2 norm is considered and the ECG signal is better recovered. While we do not have experts' label for T end, visually when the l_2 norm is applied, the detected T ends are closer to those detected from the original ECG signal, while the detected T-ends might not be correct. This preliminary result is encouraging, but an extensive study is needed to evaluate its performance. While developing a more accurate T-end detection algorithm is not the focus of this paper, we mention that developing such an algorithm that is suitable for arrhythmic ECG is another critical topic for exploration.

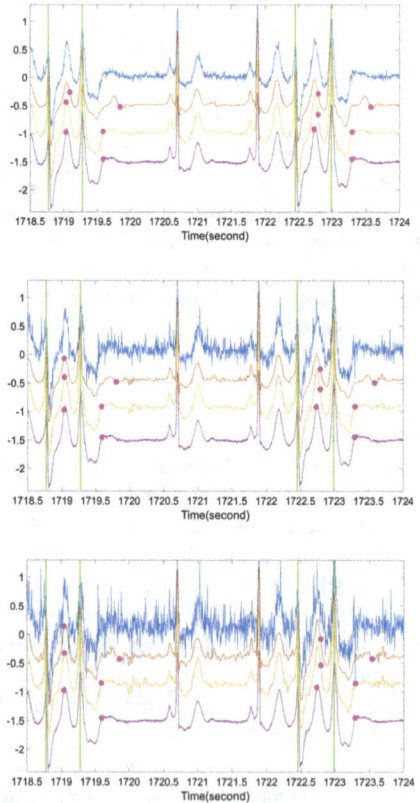

Figure 8. A preliminary comparison of ECG morphologies with different metrics for arrhythmic ECG. For each subplot, the blue line is the ECG contaminated by ARMA (1,1) noise, the orange line is the ECG after OS with RRI as the metric, the yellow line is the ECG after OS with l_2 norm as the metric, the purple line is the original ECG, green vertical lines are the locations of R peaks in each PVC occurrence, and the magenta spots are the corresponding estimations of T-end locations by Zhang's algorithm. The signal is from the first channel of case 106 in MITDB. From top to bottom subplot, the noise level is 20 dB, 10 dB, and 5 dB respectively.

There are several limitations in this study. First, the labeled database is small. Because manual T-end labeling for ultra-long ECG recording to validate the algorithm is a labor intense process, even with the help of the initial labels, the sample size was small. Second, we need to develop a new denoising algorithm that can handle structured artifacts. The main challenge is how to model artifacts when there is no extra information. A basis pursuit approach might be suitable, and we will report our theoretical research result in our future work. Third, in this article we focus on the tSQI and ECG denoising. To further improve the T-end annotation accuracy, we may need to further improve existing T-end annotation algorithms, probably by incorporating some machine learning algorithms.

In conclusion, our proposed T-end annotation algorithm has the efficiency and accuracy that make it a good fit for clinical applications and large ECG databases.

Author Contributions: Conceptualization, P.-C.S., E.Z.S. and H.-T.W.; Methodology, P.-C.S. and H.-T.W.; Software, P.-C.S.; Validation, E.Z.S. and H.-T.W.; Formal Analysis, P.-C.S. and H.-T.W.; Investigation, E.Z.S. and H.-T.W.; Resources, E.Z.S. and H.-T.W.; Data Curation, P.-C.S. and E.Z.S.; Writing—Original Draft Preparation, P.-C.S.; Writing—Review & Editing, E.Z.S. and H.-T.W.; Visualization, P.-C.S.; Supervision, E.Z.S. and H.-T.W.; Project Administration, E.Z.S. and H.-T.W.; Funding Acquisition, H.-T.W. All authors have read and agreed to the published version of the manuscript.

Funding: This work is partially supported by Ministry of Science and Technology 109-2119-M-002-014-, NCTS Taiwan.

Conflicts of Interest: The authors declare no conflict of interest.

References

1. Glassman, A.H.; Bigger, J.T., Jr. Antipsychotic drugs: Prolonged QTc interval, torsade de pointes, and sudden death. *Am. J. Psychiatry* **2001**, *158*, 1774–1782. [CrossRef] [PubMed]
2. Malik, M. Problems of heart rate correction in assessment of drug-induced QT interval prolongation. *J. Cardiovasc. Electrophysiol.* **2001**, *12*, 411–420. [CrossRef] [PubMed]
3. Laguna, P.; Thakor, N.V.; Caminal, P.; Jane, R.; Yoon, H.-R.; de Luna, A.B.; Marti, V.; Guindo, J. New algorithm for QT interval analysis in 24-h Holter ECG: Performance and applications. *Med Biol. Eng. Comput.* **1990**, *28*, 67–73. [CrossRef] [PubMed]
4. Laguna, P.; Jané, R.; Caminal, P. Automatic detection of wave boundaries in multilead ECG signals: Validation with the CSE database. *Comput. Biomed. Res.* **1994**, *27*, 45–60. [CrossRef] [PubMed]
5. Zhang, Q.; Manriquez, A.I.; Médigue, C.; Papelier, Y.; Sorine, M. An algorithm for robust and efficient location of T-wave ends in electrocardiograms. *IEEE Trans. Biomed. Eng.* **2006**, *53*, 2544–2552. [CrossRef]
6. Vázquez-Seisdedos, C.R.; Neto, J.E.; Reyes, E.J.M.; Klautau, A.; de Oliveira, R.C.L. New approach for T-wave end detection on electrocardiogram: Performance in noisy conditions. *Biomed. Eng. Online* **2011**, *10*, 77. [CrossRef]
7. Shang, H.; Wei, S.; Liu, F.; Wei, D.; Chen, L.; Liu, C. An Improved Sliding Window Area Method for T Wave Detection. *Comput. Math. Methods Med.* **2019**, *2019*. [CrossRef]
8. Martínez, J.P.; Almeida, R.; Olmos, S.; Rocha, A.P.; Laguna, P. A wavelet-based ECG delineator: Evaluation on standard databases. *IEEE Trans. Biomed. Eng.* **2004**, *51*, 570–581. [CrossRef]
9. Ghaffari, A.; Homaeinezhad, M.; Akraminia, M.; Atarod, M.; Daevaeiha, M. A robust wavelet-based multi-lead electrocardiogram delineation algorithm. *Med. Eng. Phys.* **2009**, *31*, 1219–1227. [CrossRef]
10. Madeiro, J.P.; Nicolson, W.B.; Cortez, P.C.; Marques, J.A.; Vázquez-Seisdedos, C.R.; Elangovan, N.; Ng, G.A.; Schlindwein, F.S. New approach for T-wave peak detection and T-wave end location in 12-lead paced ECG signals based on a mathematical model. *Med. Eng. Phys.* **2013**, *35*, 1105–1115. [CrossRef]
11. Mehta, S.; Lingayat, N.; Sanghvi, S. Detection and delineation of P and T waves in 12-lead electrocardiograms. *Expert Syst.* **2009**, *26*, 125–143. [CrossRef]
12. Vijaya, G.; Kumar, V.; Verma, H. Artificial neural network based wave complex detection in electrocardiograms. *Int. J. Syst. Sci.* **1997**, *28*, 125–132. [CrossRef]
13. Leon, A.A.S.; Molina, D.M.; Seisdedos, C.R.V.; Goovaerts, G.; Vandeput, S.; Van Huffel, S. Neural network approach for T-wave end detection: A comparison of architectures. In Proceedings of the 2015 Computing in Cardiology Conference (CinC), Nice, France, 6–9 September 2015; pp. 589–592.
14. Suárez-León, A.A.; Varon, C.; Willems, R.; Van Huffel, S.; Vázquez-Seisdedos, C.R. T-wave end detection using neural networks and Support Vector Machines. *Comput. Biol. Med.* **2018**, *96*, 116–127. [CrossRef] [PubMed]
15. Coast, D.A.; Stern, R.M.; Cano, G.G.; Briller, S.A. An approach to cardiac arrhythmia analysis using hidden Markov models. *IEEE Trans. Biomed. Eng.* **1990**, *37*, 826–836. [CrossRef] [PubMed]
16. Akhbari, M.; Shamsollahi, M.B.; Sayadi, O.; Armoundas, A.A.; Jutten, C. ECG segmentation and fiducial point extraction using multi hidden Markov model. *Comput. Biol. Med.* **2016**, *79*, 21–29. [CrossRef] [PubMed]

17. Lin, C.; Mailhes, C.; Tourneret, J.-Y. P- and T-wave delineation in ECG signals using a Bayesian approach and a partially collapsed Gibbs sampler. *IEEE Trans. Biomed. Eng.* **2010**, *57*, 2840–2849.
18. Zarrini, M.; Sadr, A. A real-time algorithm to detect inverted and symmetrical T-wave. In Proceedings of the 2009 Second International Conference on Computer and Electrical Engineering, Dubai, United Arab Emirates, 28–30 December 2009; pp. 318–322.
19. Singh, Y.N.; Gupta, P. An Efficient and Robust Technique of T Wave Delineation in Electrocardiogram. In Proceedings of the International Conference on Bio-inspired Systems and Signal Processing, Porto, Portugal, 14–17 January 2009; pp. 146–154.
20. Bayasi, N.; Tekeste, T.; Saleh, H.; Khandoker, A.; Mohammad, B.; Ismail, M. Adaptive technique for P and T wave delineation in electrocardiogram signals. In Proceedings of the 2014 36th Annual International Conference of the IEEE Engineering in Medicine and Biology Society, Chicago, IL, USA, 26–30 August 2014; pp. 90–93.
21. Vila, J.A.; Gang, Y.; Presedo, J.M.R.; Fernández-Delgado, M.; Barro, S.; Malik, M. A new approach for TU complex characterization. *IEEE Trans. Biomed. Eng.* **2000**, *47*, 764–772. [CrossRef]
22. Homaeinezhad, M.R.; ErfanianMoshiri-Nejad, M.; Naseri, H. A correlation analysis-based detection and delineation of ECG characteristic events using template waveforms extracted by ensemble averaging of clustered heart cycles. *Comput. Biol. Med.* **2014**, *44*, 66–75. [CrossRef]
23. Saini, I.; Singh, D.; Khosla, A. K-nearest neighbour-based algorithm for P-and T-waves detection and delineation. *J. Med. Eng. Technol.* **2014**, *38*, 115–124. [CrossRef]
24. Limaye, H.; Deshmukh, V. ECG noise sources and various noise removal techniques: A survey. *Int. J. Appl. Innov. Eng. Manag.* **2016**, *5*, 86–92.
25. Barrett, P.M.; Komatireddy, R.; Haaser, S.; Topol, S.; Sheard, J.; Encinas, J.; Fought, A.J.; Topol, E.J. Comparison of 24-hours Holter monitoring with 14-day novel adhesive patch electrocardiographic monitoring. *Am. J. Med.* **2014**, *127*, 95.e11–95.e17. [CrossRef] [PubMed]
26. Gavish, M.; Donoho, D.L. Optimal shrinkage of singular values. *IEEE Trans. Inf. Theory* **2017**, *63*, 2137–2152. [CrossRef]
27. Su, P.-C.; Miller, S.; Idriss, S.; Barker, P.; Wu, H.-T. Recovery of the fetal electrocardiogram for morphological analysis from two trans-abdominal channels via optimal shrinkage. *Physiol. Meas.* **2019**, *40*, 115005. [CrossRef] [PubMed]
28. Laguna, P.; Mark, R.G.; Goldberg, A.; Moody, G.B. A database for evaluation of algorithms for measurement of QT and other waveform intervals in the ECG. In Proceedings of the Computers in Cardiology 1997, Lund, Sweden, 7–10 September 1997; pp. 673–676.
29. Willems, J.L.; Arnaud, P.; Van Bemmel, J.H.; Bourdillon, P.J.; Degani, R.; Denis, B.; Graham, I.; Harms, F.M.; Macfarlane, P.W.; Mazzocca, G. A reference data base for multilead electrocardiographic computer measurement programs. *J. Am. Coll. Cardiol.* **1987**, *10*, 1313–1321. [CrossRef]
30. Johnson, A.E.; Behar, J.; Andreotti, F.; Clifford, G.D.; Oster, J. Multimodal heart beat detection using signal quality indices. *Physiol. Meas.* **2015**, *36*, 1665. [CrossRef]
31. Clifford, G.; Behar, J.; Li, Q.; Rezek, I. Signal quality indices and data fusion for determining clinical acceptability of electrocardiograms. *Physiol. Meas.* **2012**, *33*, 1419. [CrossRef]
32. Li, Q.; Mark, R.G.; Clifford, G.D. Robust heart rate estimation from multiple asynchronous noisy sources using signal quality indices and a Kalman filter. *Physiol. Meas.* **2007**, *29*, 15. [CrossRef]
33. Redmond, S.J.; Xie, Y.; Chang, D.; Basilakis, J.; Lovell, N.H. Electrocardiogram signal quality measures for unsupervised telehealth environments. *Physiol. Meas.* **2012**, *33*, 1517. [CrossRef]
34. Elgendi, M. Fast QRS detection with an optimized knowledge-based method: Evaluation on 11 standard ECG databases. *PLoS ONE* **2013**, *8*, e73557. [CrossRef]
35. Lindecrantz, K.; Lilja, H. New software QRS detector algorithm suitable for real time applications with low signal-to-noise ratios. *J. Biomed. Eng.* **1988**, *10*, 280–284. [CrossRef]
36. Moody, G.B.; Mark, R.G. The MIT-BIH arrhythmia database on CD-ROM and software for use with it. In Proceedings of the 1990 Computers in Cardiology, Chicago, IL, USA, 23–26 September 1990; pp. 185–188.
37. Taddei, A.; Biagini, A.; Distante, G.; Emdin, M.; Mazzei, M.; Pisani, P.; Roggero, N.; Varanini, M.; Mark, R.; Moody, G. The European ST-T database: Development, distribution and use. In Proceedings of the 1990 Computers in Cardiology, Chicago, IL, USA, 23–26 September 1990; pp. 177–180.

38. Brockwell, P.J.; Davis, R.A. *Introduction to Time Series and Forecasting*; Springer: Berlin/Heidelberg, Germany, 2016.
39. Silva, I.; Behar, J.; Sameni, R.; Zhu, T.; Oster, J.; Clifford, G.D.; Moody, G.B. Noninvasive fetal ECG: The PhysioNet/computing in cardiology challenge 2013. In Proceedings of the Computing in Cardiology 2013, Zaragoza, Spain, 22–25 September 2013; pp. 149–152.
40. Donoho, D.L.; Johnstone, J.M. Ideal spatial adaptation by wavelet shrinkage. *Biometrika* **1994**, *81*, 425–455. [CrossRef]
41. Donoho, D.L.; Johnstone, I.M.; Kerkyacharian, G.; Picard, D. Wavelet shrinkage: Asymptopia? *J. R. Stat. Soc. Ser. B (Methodol.)* **1995**, *57*, 301–337. [CrossRef]
42. Popescu, M.; Cristea, P.; Bezerianos, A. High resolution ECG filtering using adaptive Bayesian wavelet shrinkage. In Proceedings of the Computers in Cardiology 1998 (Cat. No. 98CH36292), Cleveland, OH, USA, 13–16 September 1998; Volume 25, pp. 401–404.
43. Lin, Y.-T.; Malik, J.; Wu, H.-T. Wave-shape oscillatory model for biomedical time series with applications. *arXiv* **2019**, arXiv:1907.00502.
44. Saeed, M.; Villarroel, M.; Reisner, A.T.; Clifford, G.; Lehman, L.-W.; Moody, G.; Heldt, T.; Kyaw, T.H.; Moody, B.; Mark, R.G. Multiparameter Intelligent Monitoring in Intensive Care II (MIMIC-II): A public-access Intensive Care Unit Database. *Crit. Med.* **2011**, *39*, 952. [CrossRef]

Publisher's Note: MDPI stays neutral with regard to jurisdictional claims in published maps and institutional affiliations.

© 2020 by the authors. Licensee MDPI, Basel, Switzerland. This article is an open access article distributed under the terms and conditions of the Creative Commons Attribution (CC BY) license (http://creativecommons.org/licenses/by/4.0/).

Article

EEG-Based Estimation on the Reduction of Negative Emotions for Illustrated Surgical Images

Heekyung Yang [1], Jongdae Han [2,*,†] and Kyungha Min [2,*,†]

1. Division of Software Convergence, Sangmyung University, Seoul 03016, Korea; yanghk@smu.ac.kr
2. Department of Computer Science, Sangmyung University, Seoul 03016, Korea
* Correspondence: elvenwhite@smu.ac.kr (J.H.); minkh@smu.ac.kr (K.M.); Tel.: +82-2-2287-7170 (J.H.); +82-2-2287-5377 (K.M.)
† These authors contributed equally to this work.

Received: 3 November 2020; Accepted: 9 December 2020; Published: 11 December 2020

Abstract: Electroencephalogram (EEG) biosignals are widely used to measure human emotional reactions. The recent progress of deep learning-based classification models has improved the accuracy of emotion recognition in EEG signals. We apply a deep learning-based emotion recognition model from EEG biosignals to prove that illustrated surgical images reduce the negative emotional reactions that the photographic surgical images generate. The strong negative emotional reactions caused by surgical images, which show the internal structure of the human body (including blood, flesh, muscle, fatty tissue, and bone) act as an obstacle in explaining the images to patients or communicating with the images with non-professional people. We claim that the negative emotional reactions generated by illustrated surgical images are less severe than those caused by raw surgical images. To demonstrate the difference in emotional reaction, we produce several illustrated surgical images from photographs and measure the emotional reactions they engender using EEG biosignals; a deep learning-based emotion recognition model is applied to extract emotional reactions. Through this experiment, we show that the negative emotional reactions associated with photographic surgical images are much higher than those caused by illustrated versions of identical images. We further execute a self-assessed user survey to prove that the emotions recognized from EEG signals effectively represent user-annotated emotions.

Keywords: emotion; EEG; DEAP; CNN; surgery image; disgust

---

1. Introduction

From the early days of brain science, many researchers have studied negative human emotions that come from surgical images showing blood, injection, and injury (BII). Usually, the negative emotion caused by surgical images is classified as fear and disgust. Even though emotional responses can be different according to the subject's experience, knowledge, and personality, the emotional responses are located in close distances when mapped on widely used Russell's emotional coordinate [1].

Ordinary people rarely have the chance to view surgical images. However, there are certain situations in which people should carefully inspect surgical images. For example, when we or our family members face surgical operation, surgeons explain the process of the operation by showing surgical images. Even though we feel very negative emotions in response to the images, we still have to study them very carefully to understand the procedure. In cases such as this, the negative emotional response to surgical images can prevent people from understanding necessary surgical procedures.

Some studies have tried to reduce impact of the image by simplifying the color of the images through image abstraction schemes [2,3]. They employed existing image abstraction techniques on surgical images to produce illustrated expressions in order to reduce the negative affective responses.

Even though many of the existing image abstraction techniques fail to present the details of the surgical images, some surgeons participating in these studies recommend the illustrated surgical images for explaining the images to ordinary people or training students [4,5].

Even though several image abstraction algorithms such as [4,5] have demonstrated effectiveness for abstracting surgical images, it is difficult to retain the diverse and fine details of human organic structures which is especially important for educational purposes while reducing negative emotional response. It would take a lot of cost and effort to develop an algorithm that satisfies the above requirements. Before undertaking such an effort, we need objective evidence that the illustrated surgical images can reduce the severity of negative emotional reactions to photographic surgical images. Unfortunately, the works of Besancon et al.'s [2,3] lack such an evidence, as they did not include quantitative study such as EEG-based emotion measurement on the emotional reactions comparing abstracted surgical images from original images.

We argue that objective and quantitative strategies including biosignal-based methods are needed to confirm the hypothesis that illustrated surgical images can reduce negative emotional reactions. The cost of developing an automatic algorithm that produces illustrative representations of surgical images with preserving sufficient details would be surprisingly expensive; before deciding whether to develop such an algorithm, we need concrete evidence that supports our hypothesis. Among the various kinds of biosignals, the electroencephalogram (EEG) is very widely used to measure emotional responses. Recently, many deep learning-based methods employing EEG have been presented [6–18].

We employ an EEG-based emotion recognition framework in order to present a quantitative measure of the difference in emotional reactions to illustrated surgical images and photographic surgical images. To this end, we employ professional scientific illustrators to produce illustrations of surgical images, and execute a user study with a deep learning-based emotion recognition model with EEG biosignals. Our study seeks to provide a confidence that the negative emotional reactions caused by surgical images can be reduced through abstraction via illustration.

We employ two groups of participants who view photographic surgical images and illustrated surgical images, respectively. Their emotional responses are measured through an EEG capturing device and processed with a deep learning-based emotion recognition model. To show the effectiveness of the model, we additionally execute a nine-metric user survey for the participants, then compare those results with those of the model. From the results of this experiment, we suggest that the illustrated surgical images successfully reduce the negative emotional responses caused by their photographic counterparts.

2. Related Work

2.1. Emotional Reactions to Surgical Images

Many researchers have studied human emotional reactions on BII (blood, injection, and injury) scenes including body mutilation [19], surgical procedures [20,21], blood drawing [22], open-heart surgery [23], and surgical amputation [24]. Other studies presented human reactions to repelling scenes including homicide scenes [25], spiders [21], vomit [23], and dirty toilets [26]. To estimate human reactions to these scenes, most studies employed either estimation of physical reactions or subjective methods. For estimating physical reactions, they examined heart rate [19,23], facial expression [27], electromyography [23,28], skin conductance [28], neural activation by fMRI [26], eye tracking [29], and visuomotor processing [30]. The subjective methods include user survey [20,21], rate of refusal to watch [23], and experienced vasovagal symptoms [22]. Even though these schemes are used to estimate human reactions to repelling scenes including surgery images, Cisler et al. found that there is no universal scheme to consistently estimate human reactions [31].

Surgical images incur various human reactions including anxiety, fear, disgust, and vicarious pain [31,32]. Among them, fear and disgust are suggested to be the most prominent. Cisler et al. and Olatunji et al. reported disgust as the most representative emotion [31,33]. Their reason is that fear is an emotion of avoiding danger, which is not induced by watching images of bodily injury or surgery. Chapman and Anderson classified blood-injury disgust as a subtype of physical disgust [34]. Olatunji et al. further divided blood-injury disgust into contamination disgust and animal-reminder disgust, where animal-reminder disgust is defined as the reminder of one's mortality and inherent animal nature [23].

2.2. CNN-Based Emotion Recognition from EEG

From the great success of AlexNet [35] and VGGNet [36] in image classification, deep convolutional neural networks are employed in various EEG analytic tasks.

Tang et al. [6] proposed an early deep CNN-based classification model for single-trial EEG. Their model, which is composed of five layers, is applied to classify motor imagery of left and right hand movement. The model recorded F1 scores of 87.76% 86.64% for classification of motor imagery. While the performance of the model does not show significant improvement over conventional hand-crafted feature-based models, this study has shown the promise of CNN for EEG recognition.

Schirrmeister et al. [7] presented a deep CNN to analyze EEG biosignals. Their model is composed of four blocks, each of which executes convolution and max pooling operations. The first block is distinguished from the others, as it executes spatial filtering between the convolution and max pooling operations. The result of fourth block is linearly classified to four soft max units including left hand, right hand, feet, and rest. They also visualized the features of their CNN to analyze the relationships between the features and EEG signals.

Li et al. [17] presented a hybrid model of convolutional neural network and recurrent neural network to recognize emotions from a multi-channel EEG dataset. As a preprocessing of their data, they employ wavelet and scalogram transform to encapsulate multi-channel neuro-signals into grid-like frames. Their model extracts task-related features and mines correlation between channels, incorporating contextual information. They demonstrate their accuracy by estimating valence and arousal.

Salama et al. [8] presented a 3-dimentional CNN approach for recognizing emotions from multi-channel EEG signals. Their model is constructed using two convolutional layers and two max pooling layers, followed by a fully connected layer. The 3D representation of EEG data is fed into a data augmentation phase, which improves the performance of their 3D CNN model. The simple structure of their model leaves many aspects to be improved. They achieved 87.44% accuracy for valence and 88.49% for arousal.

Moon et al. [9] applied CNN models for EEG-based emotion recognition. They tested three CNN models: CNN-2, CNN-5, and CNN-10, which are distinguished by the number of convolutional layers. The CNN-2 model has one convolutional layer followed by one max pooling layer; CNN-10 has five convolutional layers followed by five max pooling layers. Among the three models, CNN-5, which has three convolutional layers and two max pooling layers, shows the best accuracy for PSD, PCC, and PLV features.

Chiarelli et al. [10] presented a hybrid framework to construct a brain-computer interface using EEG and infrared spectroscopy (fNIRS). They employed DNN, which recorded unprecedented classification outcomes, for their framework. They performed a guided left and right hand motor task on 15 participants. The left-to-right classification accuracy of the DNN was estimated and compared to a stand-alone EEG and fNIRS. The results of their multi-modal recording and DNN classifier significant improvement over the state-of-the-art techniques.

Lawhern et al. [11] presented an EEGNet, a DNN-based approach for constructing brain-computer interface using EEG biosignals. Their EEGNet has three blocks of layers: Conv2D, DepthwiseConv2D, and SeparableConv2D. In this network, they introduce depthwise convolution and separable convolution to process the EEG signals effectively. They tested their method on three datasets: P300 Event-related Potential, Feedback Error-related Negativity, and Movement-related Corticial Potential. The results demonstrate EEGNet's improved performance over reference algorithms.

Croce et al. [12] applied a CNN model to a large dataset of independent component (IC)s extracted from multi-channel EEG and magnetoencephalographic (MEG) signals. Their aim was to classify brain IC and artifactual IC from the biosignals. The EEG, MEG, and combined EEG + MEG signals were processed through a CNN model to compare its accuracy of classification with state-of-the-art models; their classification accuracies reached 92.4% for EEG, 95.4% for MEG and 95.0% for EEG + MEG.

Yang et al. [13] proposed a CNN-based approach to recognize valence and arousal from unstationary EEG signals. Their model has a multi-column structure of independent modules, each of which was designed using DenseNet [37]. The independent decisions from the modules were merged using a voting strategy to make a final decision. Their model was trained and optimized using DEAP dataset, and applied to distinguish the emotional responses between photographs and artwork images [38] and to verify the influence of contrast on valence [39].

2.3. RNN-Based Emotion Recognition from EEG

The spatio-temporal aspect of EEG biosignals invites the use of a recurrent neural network (RNN), which is known as an effective model for processing time-serial data, to analyze EEG signals.

Khosrowabadi et al. [14] presented a biologically inspired feedforward neural network (ERNN), which has six layers, to recognize human emotions from EEG biosignals. The ERNN model employs a serial-in/parallel-out shift register to simulate the short term memory of emotion. This model with a radial basis function shows very competitive accuracy compared with other feature extraction methods.

Alhagry et al. [16] presented an RNN-based emotion recognition model from EEG biosignals. Their model has two long short term memory (LSTM) layers, one dropout layer and one fully connected layer. Since the EEG biosignal captured from subjects watching a movie clip has a time-serial property, the RNN structure demonstrates competitive accuracy in emotion recognition. Their model showed 85.65% accuracy for arousal and 85.45% for valence.

Soleymani et al. [15] employed an LSTM RNN with conditional random fields to trace the emotions captured from EEG biosignals of subjects watching video. They also captured facial expressions of the subjects. The combination of EEG biosignals and facial expressions was able to provide adequate information for emotion recognition.

Xing et al. [18] presented a framework consisting of a linear EEG mixing model and an LSTM RNN model. For EEG mixing, they employed stack auto encoder (SAE), which is similar to the standard auto encoder; the difference lies in the processing of source signals, which are separated by brain region. The EEG source signals processed by SAE are fed into the LSTM RNN model, which then extracts features from them. This model achieved 81.10% accuracy for valence and 74.38% for arousal.

3. Overview of Our Framework

Our assumption is that the negative emotions caused by photographic surgical images would hinder non-professional people in understanding necessary information conveyed by the images. Since these people are not trained with surgical images, the negative emotions such as fear and disgust arise at their first glance of the images. To reduce negative emotion and to increase the understanding of the information conveyed by surgical images, anatomy textbooks tend to use illustrations, rather than photographs. From this point, we build our assumption that illustrated surgical images evoke less negative emotion from ordinary people than photographic surgical images.

To prove our assumption, we chose 10 photographic surgical images and produced their illustrated versions by hiring professional scientific illustrators. The photographic surgical images and their illustrated counterparts are presented in Figures 1–3. Before producing the illustrations, the illustrators were instructed to preserve as much fine details as possible. The target images were collected from various sources and are released under 'fair use' purpose.

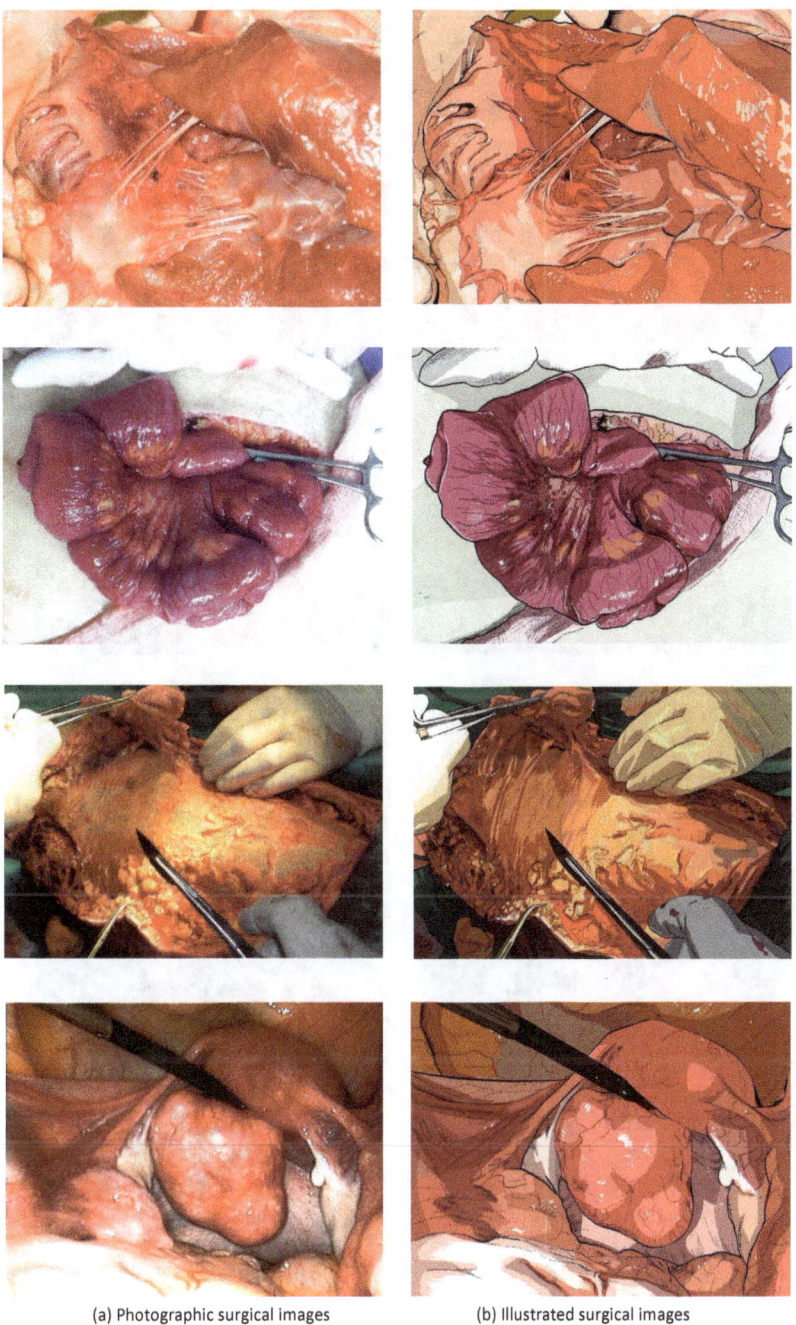

(a) Photographic surgical images   (b) Illustrated surgical images

Figure 1. The first comparison of photographic surgical images and illustrated surgical images.

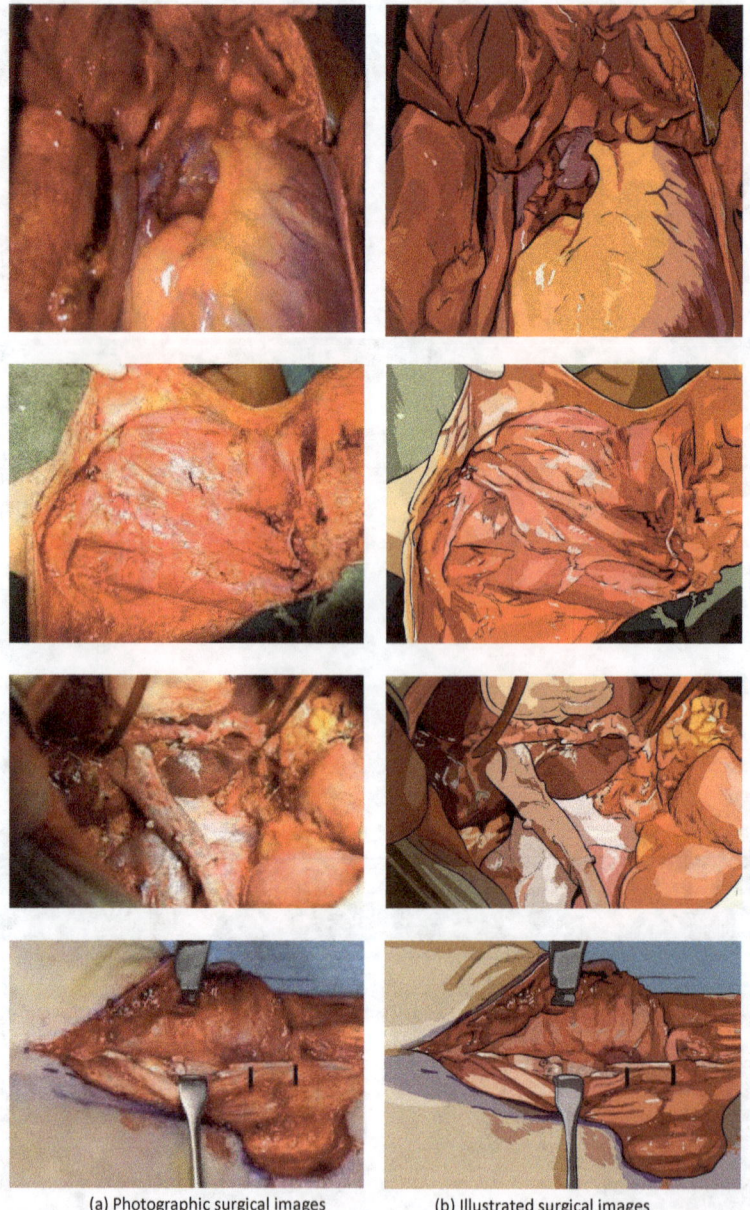

(a) Photographic surgical images (b) Illustrated surgical images

Figure 2. The second comparison of photographic surgical images and illustrated surgical images.

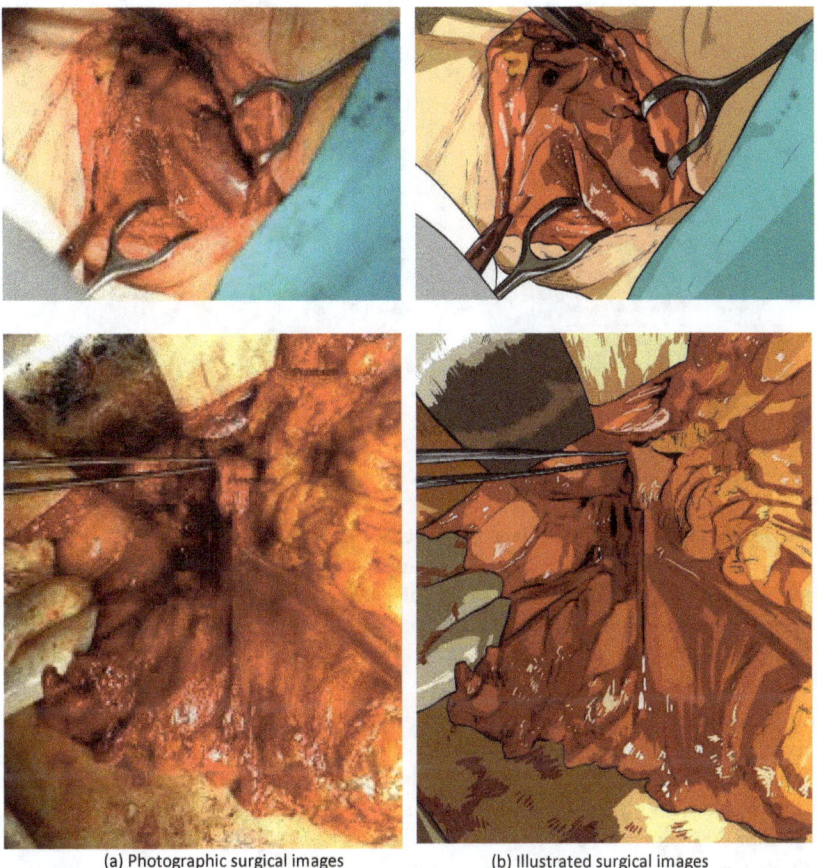

(a) Photographic surgical images   (b) Illustrated surgical images

Figure 3. The third comparison of photographic surgical images and illustrated surgical images.

From the ten pairs of photographic and illustrated surgical images, we hired 40 participants to record their emotional reactions to both photographic surgical images and illustrated images. To record their emotional reactions, we employed two different processes. One was the usage of EEG biosignals; the EEG signals captured from participants were processed through a deep multi-channel emotion recognition model [13] and quantized into valence and arousal scores. The other process was a self-assessed user survey. The participants were given a 9-metric survey to record their valence and arousal.

The 40 participants were randomly partitioned into two groups. The first group underwent the above processes for photographic surgical images, while the second worked with illustrated images. The results of these two groups are analyzed and discussed; the outline of this study is illustrated in Figure 4.

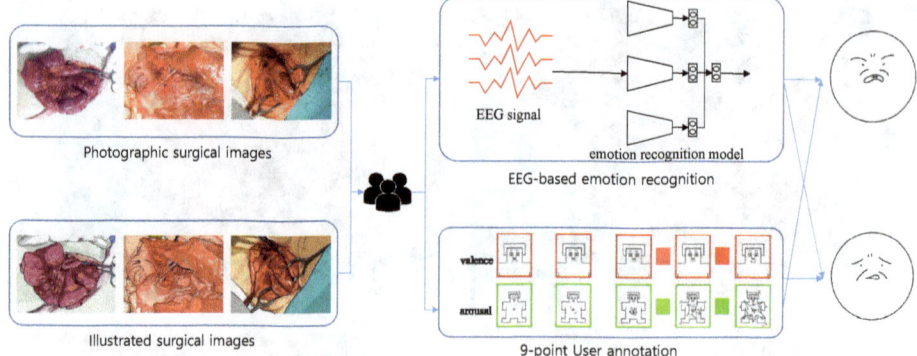

Figure 4. Overview of our framework.

4. Deep Emotion Recognition Model

4.1. Structure of the Model

In this section, we describe our deep emotion recognition model, which was presented in our previous study [13]. Our model is based on a multi-column structure: five independent modules process the EEG signal and make estimations of valence and arousal. Results from these modules are ensembled into concerted valence and arousal scores, effectively recognizing emotional responses.

4.2. Dataset Preparation

For the training of our model, we employ the DEAP dataset [40], one of the most widely used EEG datasets. The DEAP dataset consists of preprocessed EEG signals and their corresponding labels which describe emotional states. As instructed by the original authors [40], and similar to our previous study [38], we downsample the EEG signal in DEAP to 128 Hz and process it with a 4.0–45.0 Hz band pass filter. Therefore, we extract 128×60 samples from a trial for 40 channels of the dataset. Among the 40 channels, we exclude 8 for normalization and employ 32 channels for the input of our model. For each input channel, we prepare 32 consecutive samples for an input for each module of our model, effectively creating 32×32-sized input data. Figure 5 (a) illustrates the sampling process of EEG data, (b) shows the structure of a recognition module, and (c) shows the overall multi-column structure of the model.

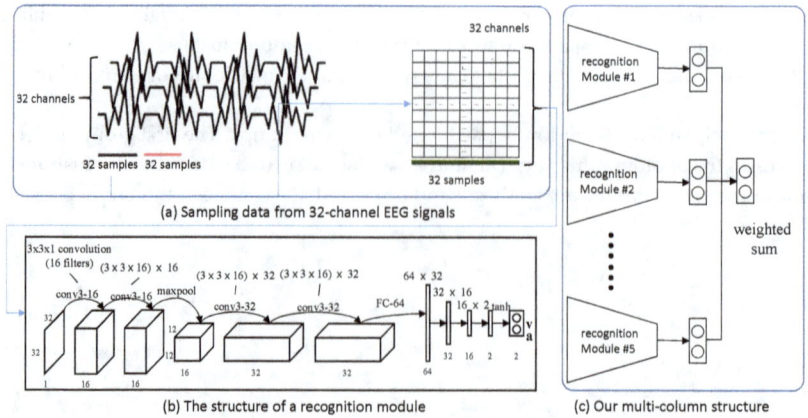

Figure 5. Structure and dataflow of our model, which is constructed according to [13].

4.3. Model Training

The DEAP dataset is constructed using the EEG signals captured from 32 participants. We segment the dataset into three groups: training, validation and test. Out of the 32, EEG signals from 22 participants are used for training, validation and the remaining 5 for test. Each participant executed 40 experiments. Therefore, the numbers of the EEG signal data for training, validation, and test are 880, 200, and 200, respectively.

5. Implementation and Experiment

5.1. Implementation

We implemented our emotion recognition model with Pytorch library on a machine with an Intel Core i7 CPU, 64 GB main memory, and nVidia GTX 2080TI GPU. We employed LiveAmp32 with LiveCap [41], which supports 32 channels following a standard 10/20 system [42].

5.2. Preparation of Surgical Images

While preparing our dataset of surgical images, we surveyed various open emotional image datasets including IAPS [43], GAPED [44], NAPS [45], CAPD [46], SMID [47], ISEE [48] and COMPASS [49]. Some of the datasets are specialized for scary images (SFIP) [50], disgusting images (DIRTI) [51], natural disaster images (NDPS) [52], and adult images (BAPS-adult) [53]. However, there was no existing dataset dedicated to surgical images; therefore, we collected several "fair-use" images from various sources for our experiment.

5.3. Preparing of User Annotation

For user annotation of emotional responses, we presented participants with a nine-point metric separated into valence and arousal. They were asked to mark the metric for the photographic and illustrated surgical images they saw. The leftmost point means very negative reaction, which matches to -1 in EEG-based estimation, and the rightmost point means very positive reaction, which matches to 1. The mid-point signifies a neutral reaction, which matches to 0. The nine-point metric form for user annotation is presented in Figure 6.

5.4. Experiment

For the experiment, we hired 40 participants and separated them into two groups: $group1$ watched photographic surgical images and $group2$ watched the illustrated versions. The characteristics of the two groups are suggested in Table 1. In the case of a participant watching both photographic and illustrated surgical images in a short timeframe, the emotional response from the images they watched first can affect that from the images that they watched later. This was our motivation for employing disjoint groups. We address the issue that personal differences between participants may affect their emotional responses by increasing the number of participants. Before participants watched the images, we explained what they were about to see and allowed withdrawal from the experiment. The participants were asked to watch a 100 s movie clip, wich each image lasting 10 s. In the first round of our experiment, we extracted EEG biosignals from the participants for objective responses. We performed the second round by asking the participants to mark their valence and arousal on a 9-point metric for subjective responses. To avoid the diminishment of emotional reactions in the second round, the participants were instructed to remember their emotions during the first round and mark those. The results of both rounds of the experiment on each group are illustrated in Table 2 and Figure 7. We further visualize the comparison of personal responses for EEG-based and user-annotated emotion in Figures 8 and 9.

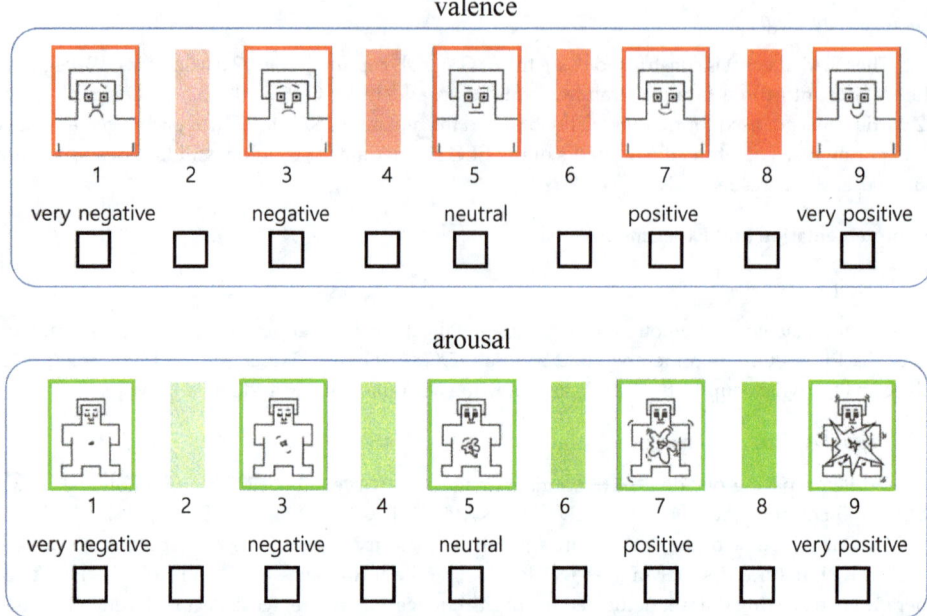

Figure 6. Nine-point metric for user annotation.

Table 1. Gender and age distribution of the participants.

	Total	Gender		Age		
		Female	Male	20 s	30 s	>40
group1	20	10	10	13	6	1
group2	20	10	10	12	8	0

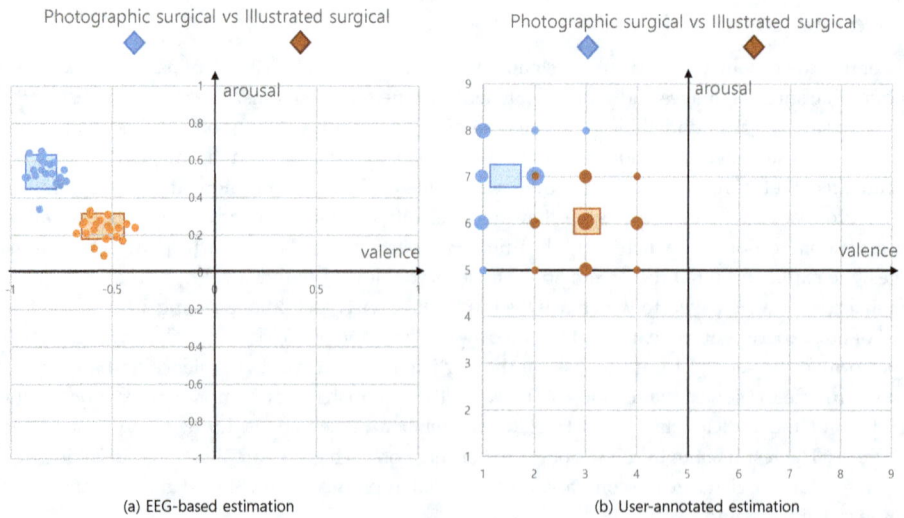

Figure 7. Results plotted in Russell's emotion circumplex model.

Table 2. Results of our experiment valence and arousal values in EEG-estimated matrix are rearranged to (−1∼1) scale.

EEG-Estimated						User-Annotated					
Photographic Surgical			Illustrated Surgical			Photographic Surgical			Illustrated Surgical		
Part. No.	Val.	Arou.	Part. No.	Val.	Arou.	Part. No.	Val.	Arou.	Part. No.	Val.	Arou.
01	−0.86	0.34	21	−0.68	0.21	01	2	6	21	2	3
02	−0.91	0.64	22	−0.39	0.24	02	1	9	22	4	5
03	−0.76	0.47	23	−0.54	0.09	03	2	7	23	1	4
04	−0.85	0.55	24	−0.48	0.19	04	3	7	24	4	5
05	−0.73	0.49	25	−0.45	0.17	05	3	7	25	4	4
06	−0.93	0.51	26	−0.53	0.18	06	1	7	26	3	5
07	−0.81	0.58	27	−0.59	0.13	07	2	7	27	2	5
08	−0.84	0.63	28	−0.52	0.25	08	1	8	28	3	6
09	−0.85	0.65	29	−0.63	0.21	09	1	8	29	2	5
10	−0.86	0.61	30	−0.61	0.311	10	1	9	30	3	6
11	−0.84	0.59	31	−0.43	0.26	11	3	8	31	3	6
12	−0.88	0.52	32	−0.47	0.24	12	1	7	32	5	6
13	−0.92	0.51	33	−0.51	0.23	13	1	7	33	3	5
14	−0.78	0.48	34	−0.56	0.28	14	2	5	34	3	5
15	−0.83	0.53	35	−0.64	0.27	15	1	7	35	3	6
16	−0.89	0.55	36	−0.65	0.26	16	1	7	36	1	7
17	−0.79	0.59	37	−0.59	0.23	17	1	7	37	3	5
18	−0.80	0.53	38	−0.58	0.26	18	2	7	38	3	6
19	−0.76	0.51	39	−0.52	0.31	19	4	6	39	2	6
20	−0.74	0.55	40	−0.61	0.33	20	2	7	40	3	6

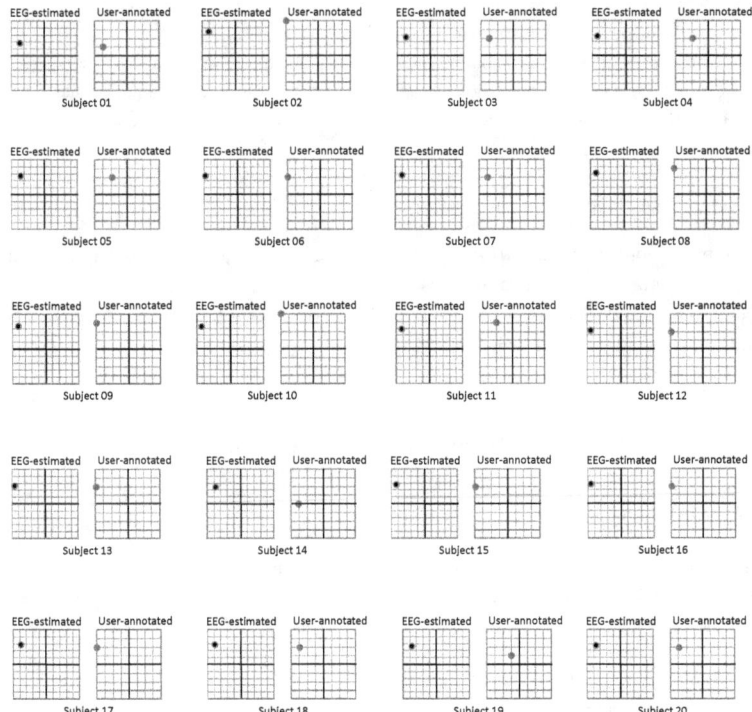

Figure 8. Results from photographic surgical images. Subjects 01∼20 participated in the experiment for photographic surgical images. The left box, which corresponds to EEG-based recognition has a range of $(-1, 1) \times (-1, 1)$, while the right box corresponding to user-annotated emotion has a range of $(1, 9) \times (1, 9)$. The x-axis of each box represents valence and the y-axis represents arousal.

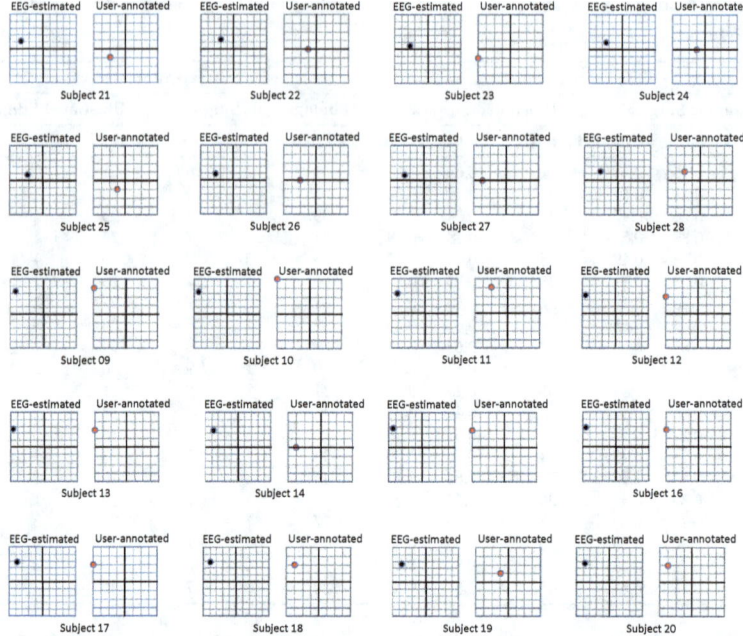

Figure 9. Results from illustrated surgical images. Subjects 21~40 participated in the experiment for illustrated surgical images. The left box, which corresponds to EEG-based recognition has a range of $(-1,1) \times (-1,1)$, while the right box corresponding to user-annotated emotion has a range of $(1,9) \times (1,9)$. The x-axis of each box represents valence and the y-axis represents arousal.

6. Analysis

We have two research questions regarding our experiment.

- RQ1 Are emotional responses from illustrated surgical images discernably less negative than those from photographic surgical images?
- RQ2 Is our emotional recognition model reliable? In other words, is there sufficient evidence that the emotions recognized by our model resemble self-assessed ones?

6.1. Analysis 1: t-Test

We have set up our null hypothesis for RQ1 as follows:

- H_0 There is no notable difference between emotional responses from photographic surgical images and illustrated images.

To answer RQ1, a *t*-test is executed between *group*1 who watch photographic surgical images and *group*2 who watch illustrated surgical images. The *p* values of this *t*-test are presented in Table 3. According to the very small *p* values in Table 3, we can reject H_0 in favor of the alternative hypothesis.

Table 3. *p* values for *t*-test between photographic and illustrated surgical images.

	EEG-Estimated		User-Annotated	
	Photographic Surgical (*group*1)	Illustrated Surgical (*group*2)	Photographic Surgical (*group*1)	Illustrated Surgical (*group*2)
valence	2.27×10^{-15}		7.6×10^{-4}	
arousal	2.07×10^{-17}		2.2×10^{-7}	

Another *t*-test regarding the emotions estimated by EEG and the emotions annotated by users, leads us to answer RQ2. RQ2's null hypothesis is:

- H_1 There is no notable difference between EEG-based assessment and user-annotated approach.

The *p* values for this second *t*-test are presented in Table 4. For *group*1, who watched photographic surgical images, the valence and arousal estimated from EEG biosignals and annotated by users are very closely related; the strong negative emotion recognized from photographic surgical images is consistent regardless of the recognition scheme. However, for *group*2, who watched illustrated surgical images, the valence is closely related, while the arousal is not. Therefore, we cannot reject H_1 except in case of arousal. We assume that pictures of organs, blood, and flesh effect similar negative emotions in viewers, even though they are reduced by the illustrated representation. Therefore, the different approaches for estimating emotions show consistently similar valence scores; for arousal, however, ordinary people have only rarely seen surgical images even, even in their illustrated form. Users who have watched illustrated surgical images in the first round of the emotion recognition experiment through EEG biosignals may pay less attention in the second stage experiment using user annotation. Therefore, the arousal values for illustrated surgical images in user annotation can be lower than those in EEG-based estimation.

Table 4. *p* values for *t*-test between EEG-estimated and user-annotated valence and arousal.

	Photographic Surgical (*group*1)		Illustrated Surgical (*group*2)	
	EEG-Estimated	User-Annotated	EEG-Estimated	User-Annotated
valence	0.72134		0.844513	
arousal	0.942176		0.007345	

6.2. Analysis 2: Effect Size

We estimate the effect size by calculating Cohen's *d* values for the pairs of the emotions. The formula for Cohen's *d* (*X*, *Y*) is suggested as follows:

$$d(X, Y) = \frac{Exp(X) - Exp(Y)}{SD_{pooled}},$$

where $Exp(X)$ and $Exp(Y)$ are the mean values of the distributions *X* and *Y*, respectively, and SD_{pooled} is the pooled standard deviation of *X* and *Y*.

We estimate Cohen's *d* to measure the difference between the emotional reactions of photographic and illustrated surgical images in the following four combinations in Table 5:

(i) the valence estimated by EEG between photographic and illustrated surgical images,
(ii) the arousal estimated by EEG between photographic and illustrated surgical images,
(iii) the valence estimated by user-annotation between photographic and illustrated surgical images,
(iv) the arousal estimated by user-annotation between photographic and illustrated surgical images.

The Cohen's *d* values for these four matches are greater than 0.8, which denotes that the effect size is very large.

Table 5. Cohen's *d* values to measure the difference in emotional reaction between photographic and illustrated surgical images.

	EEG-Estimated		User-Annotated	
	Photographic Surgical (*group*1)	Illustrated Surgical (*group*2)	Photographic Surgical (*group*1)	Illustrated Surgical (*group*2)
valence		(i) 1.78		(ii) 1.01
arousal		(iii) 1.82		(iv) 1.37

We also estimate Cohen's d to measure the difference between the emotions estimated by EEG and the emotions estimated by user-annotation in the following four combinations in Table 6:

(i) the valence for photographic surgical images estimated by EEG biosignal and user annotation,
(ii) the arousal for photographic surgical images estimated by EEG biosignal and user annotation,
(iii) the valence for illustrated surgical images estimated by EEG biosignal and user annotation,
(iv) the arousal for illustrated surgical images estimated by EEG biosignal and user annotation.

The Cohen's d values for cases (i)~(iii) are less than 0.23, which denotes that the effect size is small, and the d value for case (iv) implies there is relatively larger effect size. The reason case (iv) has a medium effect size can be described as similar to the reason results from the case (iv) in the prior t-test are more weakly related.

Table 6. Cohen's d values to measure the difference of the emotional reaction estimation methods: EEG-biosignal and user-annotation.

	Photographic Surgical (group1)		Illustrated Surgical (group2)	
	EEG-Estimated	User-Annotated	EEG-Estimated	User-Annotated
valence	(i) 0.12		(ii) 0.06	
arousal	(iii) 0.23		(iv) 0.64	

7. Discussion

7.1. Discussion 1: Comparison of Performances

In the relevant literatures, many models, including conventional machine learning techniques or deep learning techniques, have been employed to estimate valence and arousal from EEG signal. According to [13], models using machine learning-based approaches such as SVM or decision tree show 71.66% average accuracy for valence and 69.37% for arousal, while the models using deep learning schemes such as CNN or RNN show 81.4% for valence and 80.5% for arousal. Clearly, emotion recognition schemes based on deep learning techniques outperform those based on conventional machine learning techniques. The accuracy of our model is compared to that of several important existing studies that estimate emotion through valence and arousal, as shown in Table 7.

Table 7. Comparison to existing models that recognizes valence and arousal using DEAP dataset.

Existing Models	Classifier	Accuracy (%)	
		Valence	Arousal
Khosrowabadi et al. 2014 [14]	RNN	71.43	70.83
Alhagry et al. 2017 [16]	LSTM RNN	85.00	85.00
Li et al. 2017 [17]	CRNN	72.06	74.12
Salama et al. 2018 [8]	3D CNN	87.44	88.49
Xing et al. 2019 [18]	LSTM	81.10	74.38
Ours	multi-column	90.01	90.65

7.2. Discussion 2: Increase of Valence

Our experiment reveals that the valence estimated from illustrated surgical images is significantly higher than the valence from photographic surgical images. We assume that the unpleasant feelings from photographic blood and flesh are decreased by substituting the color of photographic blood and flesh with a similar color that has higher saturation or intensity. Classic artistic media, such as pencil or watercolor brush, produce similar effects. It is also notable to invoke the conclusion of the work of Yang et al's work [38] that the artwork images induce higher valence than photographs. Since the illustrated surgical image can be regarded as a kind of artwork, the increased valence for the illustrated surgical image reinforces the conclusion of [38].

The change in valence in our study, however, is greater than that in [38]. We assume that emotional reactions to surgical images generally more negative: fearsome or disgusting. Therefore, the increase of valence between the surgical image and its illustrated version is greater than the increase of valence between a photograph and an artwork image when the image itself is neutral.

7.3. Discussion 3: Decrease of Arousal

Our result shows a decrease in arousal for the illustrated surgical images compared to the photographic surgical images. Since photographic surgical images are distinguished from other images, their engendered arousal is very great. The reason for the photographic surgical images showing higher arousal is reasoned to be that seeing flesh and blood usually occurs only in very frightening or alerting situations. The decrease in arousal for the illustrated images can be explained by the fact that the realistic colors of flesh and blood are converted to less threatening colors frequently seen in animations or cartoons. The simple and friendly color of the illustrated flesh and blood reduces the sense of actual alert or frightening, which results in the decrease of arousal.

7.4. Discussion 4: Evaluation from a Surgeon

We have asked a surgeon to evaluate the illustrated surgical images. The surgeon marked some regions of the photographic and illustrated surgical images and suggested the following opinions:

(1) Color transform of the illustrated images is reasonable. Replacing vivid colors such as red and violet by less vivid colors can help reducing negative reactions from the people who do not have an experience in the surgical images
(2) In the illustrated versions, the reflections on the surface of organs are illustrated as a narrow spot with higher brightness (the yellow circles in Figure 10). Since the spots on organs can be from some disease or from the reflection, the reflections should be illustrated in different style.
(3) The blood vessels, which play important role in many diagnosis cases, are not illustrated in a consistent way. In some figures, they are preserved in a very salient way (the blue circles in Figure 10), and in others, they are omitted (the green circles in Figure 10). Presenting details such as blood vessels should be expressed in a consistent way.

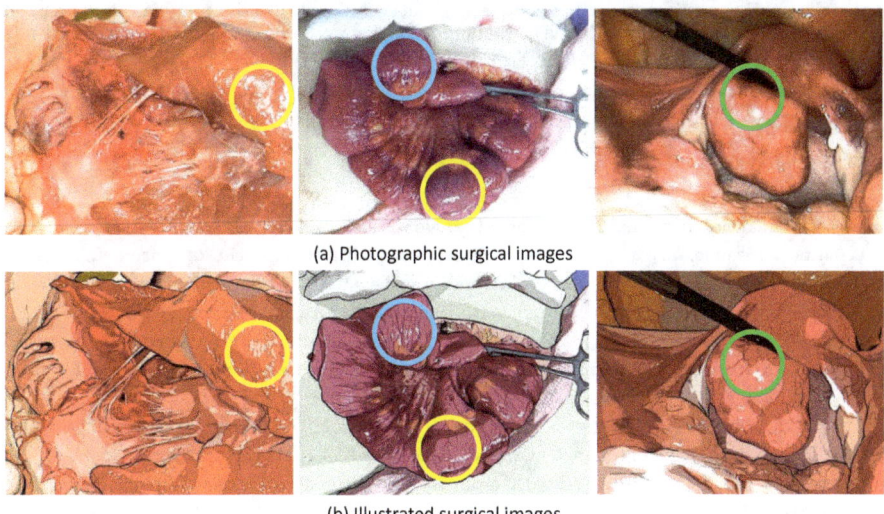

Figure 10. The marks drawn by a surgeon for the evaluation of the illustrated images.

As a conclusion, the surgeon suggested a positive answer for using the illustrated images to reduce negative emotional reactions from ordinary people. However, he suggested several points to improve for educational or professional purposes.

7.5. Discussion 5: Limitations

The limitation of this study is that we have not taken into account the opinions of experts, such as surgeons or pathologists in producing the illustrative surgical images. Surgeons may provide productive insights in the illustration of surgical images, for example, which fine details are important and must be kept. They may also be able to suggest proper colors to replace the original colors of flesh and blood.

This limitation of this study can be addressed in two points. Similar studies [2,3] hired a small group of surgeons to confirm that the illustrated surgical images could be used for communication and education. In another point, we collected a series of opinions from a surgeon for the illustrative surgical images in Section 7.4. The opinions can be employed to give a guidance for developing an automatic algorithm that produces illustrative surgical images.

8. Conclusions and Future Work

In this paper, we produced illustrated surgical images to prove their ability to reduce the negative emotional responses engendered by photographic surgical images. We executed emotion recognition processes on 40 participants to compare their emotional responses to photographic and illustrated surgical images. The emotional responses were estimated in a bi-modal approach: a deep learning-based emotion recognition model from EEG biosignals was combined with a 9-point metric user annotation. From the results, we conclude that illustrated surgical images indeed capable of reducing the negative emotions of participants.

In our future research, we will study relevant methods to create appropriate illustrated images. We will consult with experts including surgeons and pathologists to enrich the illustration schemes on surgical images. We will also examine the illustrated surgical images from experts to improve the quality of the illustrations. These approaches will help developing an automatic algorithm for generating illustrated surgical images that satisfy both ordinary people and experts.

Author Contributions: Conceptualization, H.Y., J.H. and K.M.; methodology, H.Y.; software, J.H.; validation, J.H.; formal analysis, J.H.; investigation, K.M.; resources, J.H.; data curation, J.H.; writing–original draft preparation, H.Y.; writing–review and editing, K.M.; visualization, K.M.; supervision, K.M.; project administration, K.M. All authors have read and agreed to the published version of the manuscript.

Funding: This research received no external funding.

Conflicts of Interest: The authors declare no conflict of interest.

References

1. Russell, J. Evidence for a three-factor theory of emotions. *J. Res. Personal.* **1977**, *11*, 273–294. [CrossRef]
2. Besancon, L.; Semmo, A.; Biau, D.; Frachet, B.; Pineau, V.; Sariali, E.H.; Taouachi, R.; Isenberg, T.; Dragicevic, P. Reducing affective responses to surgical images and videos through color manipulation and stylization. In Proceedings of the Expressive, Vancouver, BC, Canada, 17–19 August 2018; pp. 11:1–11:13.
3. Besancon, L.; Semmo, A.; Biau, D.; Frachet, B.; Pineau, V.; Sariali, E.H.; Soubeyrand, M.; Taouachi, R.; Isenberg, T.; Dragicevic, P. Reducing affective responses to surgical images and videos through stylization. *Comput. Graph. Forum* **2020**, *39*, 462–483. [CrossRef]
4. Kyprianidis, J.; Dollner, J. Image abstraction by structure adaptive filtering. In Proceedings of the EG UK—Theory and Practice of Computer Graphics, Manchester, UK, 9–11 June 2008; pp. 51–58.
5. Kyprianidis, J.; Kang, H. Image and video abstraction by coherence-enhancing filtering. *Comput. Graph. Forum* **2011**, *30*, 593–602. [CrossRef]
6. Tang, Z.; Li, C.; Sun, S. Single-trial EEG classification of motor imagery using deep convolutional neural networks. *Optik* **2017**, *130*, 11–18. [CrossRef]

7. Schirrmeister, R.T.; Springenberg, J.T.; Fiederer, L.D.J.; Glasstetter, M.; Eggensperger, K.; Tangermann, M.; Hutter, F.; Burgard, W.; Ball, T. Deep learning with convolutional neural networks for EEG decoding and visualization. *Hum. Brain Map.* **2017**, *38*, 5391–5420. [CrossRef]
8. Salama, E.S.; El-Khoribi, R.A.; Shoman, M.E.; Shalaby, M.A.E. EEG-based emotion recognition using 3D convolutional neural networks. *Int. J. Adv. Comput. Sci. Appl.* **2018**, *9*, 329–337. [CrossRef]
9. Moon, S.-E.; Jang, S.; Lee, J.-S. Convolutional neural network approach for EEG-based emotion recognition using brain connectivity and its spatial information. In Proceedings of the IEEE International Conference on Acoustics, Speech and Signal Processing, Calgary, AB, Canada, 15–20 April 2018; pp. 2556–2560.
10. Chiarelli, A.M.; Croce, P.; Merla, A.; Zappasodi, F. Deep learning for hybrid EEG-fNIRS brain-computer interface: Application to motor imagery classification. *J. Neural. Eng.* **2018**, *15*, 036028. [CrossRef]
11. Lawhern, V.J.; Solon, A.J.; Waytowich, N.R.; Gordon, S.M.; Hung, C.P.; Lance, B.J. EEGNet: A compact convolutional neural network for EEG-based brain–computer interfaces. *J. Neural. Eng.* **2018**, *15*, 056013. [CrossRef]
12. Croce, P.; Zappasodi, F.; Marzetti, L.; Merla, A.; Pizzella, V.; Chiarelli, A.M. Deep Convolutional Neural Networks for Feature-Less Automatic Classification of Independent Components in Multi-Channel Electrophysiological Brain Recordings. *IEEE Trans. Biom. Eng.* **2019**, *66*, 2372–2380. [CrossRef]
13. Yang, H.; Han, J.; Min, K. A Multi-Column CNN Model for Emotion Recognition from EEG Signals. *Sensors* **2019**, *19*, 4736. [CrossRef]
14. Khosrowabadi, R.; Chai, Q.; Kai, K.A.; Wahab, A. ERNN: A biologically inspired feedforward neural network to discriminate emotion from EEG signal. *IEEE Trans. Neural Netw. Learn. Syst.* **2014**, *25*, 609–620. [CrossRef] [PubMed]
15. Soleymani, M.; Asghari-Esfeden, S.; Fu, Y.; Pantic, M. Analysis of EEG signals and facial expressions for continuous emotion detection. *IEEE Trans. Affect. Comput.* **2016**, *7*, 17–28. [CrossRef]
16. Alhagry, S.; Fahmy, A.A.; El-Khoribi, R.A. Emotion recognition based on EEG using LSTM recurrent neural network. *Int. J. Adv. Comput. Sci. Appl.* **2017**, *8*, 355–358. [CrossRef]
17. Li, X.; Song, D.; Zhang, P.; Yu, G.; Hou, Y.; Hu, B. Emotion recognition from multi-channel EEG data through convolutional recurrent neural network. In Proceedings of the IEEE International Conference on Bioinformatics and Biomedicine, Kansas City, MO, USA, 13–16 November 2017; pp. 352–359.
18. Xing, X.; Li, Z.; Xu, T.; Shu, L.; Hu, B.; Xu, X. SAE + LSTM: A New framework for emotion recognition from multi-channel EEG. *Front. Nuerorobot.* **2019**, *13*, 37. [CrossRef]
19. Klorman, R.; Weissberg, R.; Wiesenfeld, A. Individual differences in fear and autonomic reactions to affective stimulation. *Psychophysiology* **1977**, *14*, 45–51. [CrossRef]
20. Sawchuk, C.; Lohr, J.; Westendorf, D.; Meunier, S.; Tolin, D. Emotional responding to fearful and disgusting stimuli in specific phobics. *Behav. Res. Ther.* **2002**, *40*, 1031–1046. [CrossRef]
21. Tolin, D.; Lohr, J.; Sawchuk, C.; Lee, T. Disgust and disgust sensitivity in blood-injection-injury and spider phobia. *Behav. Res. Ther.* **1997**, *35*, 949–953. [CrossRef]
22. Gilchrist, P.; Ditto, B. The effects of blood-draw and injection stimuli on the vasovagal response. *Psychophysiology* **2012**, *49*, 815–820. [CrossRef]
23. Olatunji, B.; Haidt, J.; McKay, D.; David, B. Core, animal reminder, and contamination disgust: Three kinds of disgust with distinct personality, behavioral, physiological, and clinical correlates. *J. Res. Personal.* **2008**, *42*, 1243–1259. [CrossRef]
24. Rohrmann, S.; Hopp, H. Cardiovascular indicators of disgust. *Int. J. Psychophysiol.* **2008**, *68*, 201–208. [CrossRef]
25. Hare, R.; Wood, K.; Britain, S.; Shadman, J. Autonomic responses to affective visual stimulation. *Psychophysiology* **1970**, *7*, 408–417. [CrossRef] [PubMed]
26. Schienle, A.; Stark, R.; Walter, B.; Blecker, C.; Ott, U.; Kirsch, P.; Sammer, G.; Vaitl, D. The insula is not specifically involved in disgust processing: An fMRI study. *Neuroreport* **2002**, *13*, 2023–2026. [CrossRef] [PubMed]
27. Lumley, M.; Melamed, B. Blood phobics and nonphobics: Psychological differences and affect during exposure. *Behav. Res. Ther.* **1992**, *30*, 425–434. [CrossRef]
28. Lang, P.; Greenwald, M.; Bradley, M.; Hamm, A. Looking at pictures: Affective, facial, visceral, and behavioral reactions. *Psychophysiology* **1993**, *30*, 261–273. [CrossRef]

29. Armstrong, T.; Hemminger, A.; Olatunji, B. Attentional bias in injection phobia: Overt components, time course, and relation to behavior. *Behav. Res. Ther.* **2013**, *51*, 266–273. [CrossRef]
30. Haberkamp, A.; Schmidt, T. Enhanced visuomotor processing of phobic images in blood-injury-injection fear. *J. Anxiety Disord.* **2014**, *28*, 291–300. [CrossRef]
31. Cisler, J.; Olatunji, B.; Lohr, J. Disgust, fear, and the anxiety disorders: A critical review. *Clin. Psychol. Rev.* **2009**, *29*, 34–46. [CrossRef]
32. Benuzzi, F.; Lui, F.; Duzzi, D.; Nichelli, P.; Porro, C. Does it look painful or disgusting? Ask your parietal and cingulate cortex. *J. Neurosci.* **2008**, *28*, 923–931. [CrossRef]
33. Olatunji, B.; Cisler, J.; McKay, D.; Phillips, M. Is disgust associated with psychopathology? Emerging research in the anxiety disorders. *Psychiatry Res.* **2010**, *175*, 1–10. [CrossRef]
34. Chapman, H.; Anderson, A. Understanding disgust. *Ann. N. Y. Acad. Sci.* **2012**, *1251*, 62–76. [CrossRef]
35. Krizhevsky, A.; Sutskever, I.; Hinton, G.E. Imagenet classification with deep convolutional neural networks. In Proceedings of the Advances in Neural Information Processing Systems, Lake Tahoe, NV, USA, 3–6 December 2012; pp. 1097–1105.
36. Simonyan, K.; Andrew, Z. Very deep convolutional networks for large-scale image recognition. *arXiv* **2014**, arXiv:1409.1556.
37. Huang, G.; Liu, Z.; Van Der Maaten, L.; Weinberger, K.Q. Densely connected convolutional networks. In Proceedings of the IEEE Conference on Computer Vision and Pattern Recognition (CVPR), Honolulu, HI, USA, 21–26 July 2017; pp. 4700–4708.
38. Yang, H.; Han, J.; Min, K. Distinguishing emotional responses to photographs and artwork using a deep learning-based approach. *Sensors* **2019**, *19*, 5533. [CrossRef]
39. Yang, H.; Han, J.; Min, K. Emotion variation from controlling contrast of visual contents through EEG-Based deep emotion recognition. *Sensors* **2020**, *20*, 4543. [CrossRef]
40. Koelstra, S.; Muhl, C.; Soleymani, M.; Lee, J.; Yazdani, A.; Ebrahimi, T.; Pun, T.; Nijholt, A.; Patras, I. DEAP: A Database for Emotion Analysis; Using Physiological Signals. *IEEE Trans. Affect. Comput.* **2012**, *3*, 18–31. [CrossRef]
41. BCI+: LiveAmp. Compact Wireless Amplifier for Mobile EEG Applications. BCI+ Solutions by Brain Products. Available online: bci.plus/liveamp/ (accessed on 12 December 2019).
42. Klem, G.H.; Lüders, H.O.; Jasper, H.H.; Elger, C. The ten-twenty electrode system of the International Federation. The International Federation of Clinical Neurophysiology. *Electroencephalogr. Clin. Neurophysiol. Suppl.* **1999**, *52*, 3–6.
43. Lang, P.; Bradley, M.; Cuthbert, B. *International Affective Picture System (IAPS): Technical Manual and Affective Ratings*; Technical Report A-8; University of Florida: Belle Glade, FL, USA, 2008.
44. Dan-Glauser, E.; Scherer, K. The Geneva affective picture database (GAPED): A new 730-picture database focusing on valence and normative significance. *Behav. Res. Methods* **2011**, *43*, 468. [CrossRef] [PubMed]
45. Marchewka, A.; Zurawski, L.; Jenorog, K.; Grabowska, A. The Nencki Affective Picture System (NAPS): Introduction to a novel, standardized, wide-range, high-quality, realistic picture database. *Behav. Res. Methods* **2014**, *46*, 596–610. [CrossRef] [PubMed]
46. Moyal, N.; Henik, A.; Anholt, G. Categorized Affective Pictures Database (CAP-D). *J. Cogn.* **2018**, *1*, 41. [CrossRef]
47. Crone, D.; Bode, S.; Murawski, C.; Laham, S. The Socio-Moral Image Database (SMID): A novel stimulus set for the study of social, moral and affective processes. *PLoS ONE* **2018**, *13*, e0190954. [CrossRef]
48. Kim, H.; Lu, X.; Costa, M.; Kandemir, B.; Adams Jr., R.; Li, J.; Wang, J.; Newman, M. Development and validation of Image Stimuli for Emotion Elicitation (ISEE): A novel affective pictorial system with test-retest repeatability. *Psychiatry Res.* **2018**, *261*, 414–420. [CrossRef]
49. Weierich, M.; Kleshchova, O.; Reider, J.; Reilly, D. The Complex Affective Scene Set (COMPASS): Solving the Social Content Problem in Affective Visual Stimulus Sets. *Collabra Psychol.* **2019**, *5*, 53. [CrossRef]
50. Michalowski, J.; Drozdziel, D.; Matuszewski, J.; Koziejowski, W.; Jednorog, K.; Marchewka, A. The Set of Fear Inducing Pictures (SFIP): Development and validation in fearful and nonfearful individuals. *Behav. Res. Methods* **2017**, *49*, 1407–1419. [CrossRef] [PubMed]
51. Haberkamp, A.; Glombiewski, J.; Schmidt, F.; Barke, A. The DIsgust-RelaTed-Images (DIRTI) database: Validation of a novel standardized set of disgust pictures. *Behav. Res. Ther.* **2017**, *89*, 86–94. [CrossRef] [PubMed]

52. Merlhiot, G.; Mermillod, M.; Le Pennec, J.; Mondillon, L. Introduction and validation of the Natural Disasters Picture System (NDPS). *PLoS ONE* **2018**, *13*, e0201942. [CrossRef]
53. Szymanska, M.; Comte, A.; Tio, G.; Vidal, C.; Monnin, J.; Smith, C.; Nezelof, S.; Vulliez-Coady, L. The Besançon affective picture set-adult (BAPS-Adult): Development and validation. *Psychiatry Res.* **2019**, *271*, 31–38. [CrossRef]

Publisher's Note: MDPI stays neutral with regard to jurisdictional claims in published maps and institutional affiliations.

© 2020 by the authors. Licensee MDPI, Basel, Switzerland. This article is an open access article distributed under the terms and conditions of the Creative Commons Attribution (CC BY) license (http://creativecommons.org/licenses/by/4.0/).

Article

Wearable Sensors for Assessing the Role of Olfactory Training on the Autonomic Response to Olfactory Stimulation

Alessandro Tonacci [1], Lucia Billeci [1,*], Irene Di Mambro [2], Roberto Marangoni [3,4], Chiara Sanmartin [5] and Francesca Venturi [5,6]

1. Institute of Clinical Physiology, National Research Council of Italy (IFC-CNR), 56124 Pisa, Italy; atonacci@ifc.cnr.it
2. School of Engineering, University of Pisa, 56122 Pisa, Italy; i.dimambro@studenti.unipi.it
3. Department of Biology, University of Pisa, 56127 Pisa, Italy; roberto.marangoni@unipi.it
4. Institute of Biophysics, National Resarsch Council of Italy (IBF-CNR), Via Moruzzi 1, 56124 Pisa, Italy
5. Department of Agriculture, Food and Environment, University of Pisa, 56124 Pisa, Italy; chiara.sanmartin@unipi.it (C.S.); francesca.venturi@unipi.it (F.V.)
6. NexFood Srl, 57121 Livorno, Italy
* Correspondence: lucia.billeci@ifc.cnr.it

Citation: Tonacci, A.; Billeci, L.; Di Mambro, I.; Marangoni, R.; Sanmartin, C.; Venturi, F. Wearable Sensors for Assessing the Role of Olfactory Training on the Autonomic Response to Olfactory Stimulation. *Sensors* **2021**, *21*, 770. https://doi.org/10.3390/s21030770

Academic Editor: Alan Jović
Received: 31 December 2020
Accepted: 21 January 2021
Published: 24 January 2021

Publisher's Note: MDPI stays neutral with regard to jurisdictional claims in published maps and institutional affiliations.

Copyright: © 2021 by the authors. Licensee MDPI, Basel, Switzerland. This article is an open access article distributed under the terms and conditions of the Creative Commons Attribution (CC BY) license (https://creativecommons.org/licenses/by/4.0/).

Abstract: Wearable sensors are nowadays largely employed to assess physiological signals derived from the human body without representing a burden in terms of obtrusiveness. One of the most intriguing fields of application for such systems include the assessment of physiological responses to sensory stimuli. In this specific regard, it is not yet known which are the main psychophysiological drivers of olfactory-related pleasantness, as the current literature has demonstrated the relationship between odor familiarity and odor valence, but has not clarified the consequentiality between the two domains. Here, we enrolled a group of university students to whom olfactory training lasting 3 months was administered. Thanks to the analysis of electrocardiogram (ECG) and galvanic skin response (GSR) signals at the beginning and at the end of the training period, we observed different autonomic responses, with higher parasympathetically-mediated response at the end of the period with respect to the first evaluation. This possibly suggests that an increased familiarity to the proposed stimuli would lead to a higher tendency towards relaxation. Such results could suggest potential applications to other domains, including personalized treatments based on odors and foods in neuropsychiatric and eating disorders.

Keywords: autonomic nervous system; electrocardiogram; galvanic skin response; olfactory training; psychophysics; smell; wearable sensors; wine sensory analysis

1. Introduction

As recently reviewed by Kryklywy and co-workers [1], from an evolutionary point of view, representations of valence-labeled sensation in emotion-processing regions are not an ancillary feature developed to inform centralized affect representation. Rather, they reflect the ancestral role of these structures; they are relics of a time when the experiences of sensory information and emotional-motivational states were one and the same.

While the whole mechanism still seems far from being fully understood, interactions between cortical and thalamic regions appear to play a key role in cognitive functions, with several lines of research now suggesting that a fundamental aspect of thalamic functioning is that it fuses perceptual, emotional and cognitive information into one single meaningful experience [2].

More than any other sensory modality, olfaction is like emotion in attributing positive (appetitive) or negative (aversive) valence to the environment, and the close anatomic relations between the systems deployed for olfaction and for emotion [3] account for the important links found between these two functions [4–7].

In this context, in the clinical field the sense of smell is mainly related to neurodegenerative processes, where olfactory impairments are reported, somewhat linked to the disease progression [8].

Notably, abnormal olfactory processing is also seen in other neurodevelopmental [9] and neuropsychiatric disorders, including those where an impaired attitude towards feeding represents one of the hallmarks of the condition [10].

Among them, anorexia (AN) and bulimia nervosa (BN) experience, especially in more severe cases, a peculiar olfactory processing, made up of distorted sensitivity and reactivity to sensory stimulation, possibly related to the food aversion typical of those individuals [10–12].

Recently, a significant literature has been focused on the positive effects of olfactory training [13]. Indeed, the unprecedented worldwide pandemic represented by COVID-19 has put anosmia and dysgeusia at the forefront of clinical investigation, the loss of smell and taste being some of the most prevalent side effects of the infection, often occurring also in asymptomatic or pauci-symptomatic subjects, possibly representing a biomarker of infection occurrence and, somewhat, severity [14,15]. In this specific domain, Liu et al. [16] demonstrated the capability of the sense of smell to regenerate, in turn contributing to an overall improvement of the quality of life in individuals already challenged by the diverse physically-, psychologically- and socially-disrupting consequences of the COVID-19 infection [17–19].

Until now, olfactory training was seen to be effective in individuals where a significant related sensory impairment is present; however, it was never analyzed in terms of enhancement of the sensory function in individuals where the olfactory pathway is already optimal, nor in relation to psycho-physiological changes eventually occurring in the human body following the modification of odor familiarity and/or valence, two dimensions of the olfactory stimulus often neglected but worth investigation.

Previous studies conducted on healthy subjects have hypothesized the existence of a significant correlation between odor familiarity and pleasantness, intended as the positive attitude experienced by an individual towards an odorous compound [20–22]. However, those works have not clarified exhaustively and objectively the consequentiality between those two domains of the olfactory processing. This represents a significant gap in the current literature, since knowing how those two domains interact to each other can be critical to thinking about possible therapeutic strategies based on sensory, particularly olfactory, stimulation, addressed to several disorders where an abnormal attitude towards feeding represents one of the main clinical features.

To objectively and quantitatively assess the physiological response to olfactory stimulation, several strategies have been adopted throughout the years, with a number of either invasive or unobtrusive techniques applied, each displaying significant drawbacks in terms of applicability, acceptability and informativity [23–25]. A reasonable solution, merging acceptability, low cost and reliability and providing useful information about the physiological reactions to odorous stimuli is represented by the assessment of biomedical signals triggered by the activity of the autonomic nervous system (ANS), including electrocardiogram (ECG) and galvanic skin response (GSR), already studied in relationship with the olfactory assessment [26,27]. Such signals can be acquired in a completely non-invasive manner using wearable sensors, as demonstrated in several literature works published to date (e.g., [26,27]).

Therefore, the aim of the present article is to investigate the relationship between odor familiarity and pleasantness, the latter studied not using basic questionnaires, possibly associated with conscious responses and subsequent biases, but evaluating the activation of the ANS in a cohort of healthy individuals. This first approach is mandatory to understand, net of any possible clinical condition, the relationship between the two odor-related domains paving the way, in case of significant correlations, for more tailored investigations on specific clinical disorders.

2. Materials and Methods

2.1. Selection and Training of Panelists

For this study, 25 students (9 females and 16 males; ranging from 21 to 29 years old) enrolled in the bachelor degree in "Oenology and Viticulture" of the University of Pisa (Italy) were initially recruited based on their motivation and willingness.

Selection and training of panelists was performed according to the University of Pisa, Department of Agriculture, Food and Environment (DAFE) internal procedure, which is based on a normalized technical procedure reported in literature with some modifications [21]. The trained panelists are then included in the official panel of the DAFE. They have to repeat and pass re-qualification tests once a year, considering their efficacy as tasting judge, in terms of their own repeatability, discrimination ability and compliance. Re-qualification tests, in addition to providing information about panelists' suitability, help to keep the panelists alert, avoiding relaxation and undervaluation of training.

A multi-step training period was therefore arranged in order to select a group of students characterized by the necessary motivation during the whole activity (attendance at more than 75% of training sessions) together with the minimum sensory skills required for wine tasting and description (including visual, aroma and taste attributes).

The training of the 25 students was arranged as follows over a period of three months:

(i) Step 1 (15 h): Theoretical introduction to the principles of human physiology of sight, smell and taste.
(ii) Step 2 (20 h): Arrangement of preliminary training tests, mainly based on the utilization of model standard solutions, to collect information about the tasting capacity of each panelist (i.e., sensory acuity (detection thresholds); odor and flavor memory; term use and recall; scoring consistency).
(iii) Step 3 (30 h): As discrimination is probably based as much on odor memory (that accumulates with experience) as on sensory acuity, ten wine tasting sessions were carried out in the morning, in a well-ventilated quiet room and in a relaxed atmosphere. During each of the ten tasting sessions, the panelists evaluated three different commercial wines (globally thirty different wines were assessed including white, rosé and red wines). The assessors used a sensorial sheet, specifically developed for this purpose, consisting of a non-structured, parametric, descriptive wine scoring chart [28]. Before starting the sensory evaluations, panelists were provided with the synthetic definitions of each descriptors proposed in the sensorial sheet. Furthermore, the panelists were also asked to freely describe the specific olfactory expression of each tasted wine to familiarize themselves with the main descriptors generally utilized for wine's sensory analysis [29].

The overall experimental design, including the sensory assessment, is displayed in Figure 1.

2.2. Model Solutions Used for the Olfactory Stimulation

To reproduce, as much as possible, the main olfactory sensations that are mostly utilized for the description of wine's olfactory behavior, some model solutions were prepared in an affordable and easily reproducible way by utilizing raw material widely available at the supermarket (i.e., commercial fruit juices; fresh fruits and vegetables; distilled flower water). Furthermore, as threshold values are significantly influenced by the solvent (i.e., water vs. ethanol) model solutions were prepared in a neutral white wine base.

As during tasting experience both synergistic and suppressive influences among different wine's aromatic compounds must be always taken into account, our approach allowed us to create a more real tasting experience than what could have been obtained by utilizing model solutions produced starting from chemical pure standards diluted in artificial model wine.

In Table 1, the odorous solutions used for the olfactory stimulation are reported.

cleaning the nasal cavity from the previous odor [30] as well to let the GSR signal return to the baseline condition. The subjects were asked to report the identifier for each of the odor presented on a paper sheet.

2.4. ANS Assessment

The assessment of the ANS activity was performed studying physiological signals acquired by wearable sensors.

Notably, two signals of interest to this extent included (i) the ECG, one of the most important biomedical signals as it relies on the electrical activity of the heart, and (ii) the GSR, related to the electrical activity of the skin caused by the activation of the sweat glands.

Both those signals are normally correlated with the activation of the ANS, thus representing a useful, non-invasive means to assess its functioning, as demonstrated in [26,27].

2.4.1. ECG Acquisition and Processing

The acquisition of the ECG signal was performed using a commercial wearable, Bluetooth-equipped sensor, named Shimmer ECG (Shimmer Sensing, Dublin, Republic of Ireland), attached to a commercial fitness-like chest strap (Polar Electro Oy, Kempele, Finland). In order to comply with the international guidelines for the estimation of the Heart Rate (HR) and its variability (heart rate variability (HRV)) [31], the ECG signal was acquired at 500 Hz, not requiring particular controls about the battery duration given the structured experimental setting.

The ECG signal was analyzed using a dedicated routine implemented in MATLAB (The MathWorks, Inc., Natick, MA, USA) [32] and optimized for the present work.

ECG signals were pre-processed for artifact removal, QRS complexes were detected and then the RR series were reconstructed and corrected (for an example, see Figure 2). The correction was applied to remove correction of non-sinusoidal beats in order to obtain an RR series that only contains variations due to the sinus node and thus reflects the activity of the ANS [32]. From the corrected RR series, a number of significant features were extracted, notably:

- Time-domain features:
  - Heart rate (HR): number of heart beats per unit of time. Measured in beats per minute (bpm), it is usually associated with the sympathetic branch of the ANS [33];
  - Standard deviation of the normal R–R intervals (SDNN): measured in ms, it is an estimate of the HRV influenced by both the sympathetic and para-sympathetic branches of the ANS [33];
  - Root mean square of the successive differences (RMSSD): measured in ms, it represents the root mean square of the differences between neighboring R–R intervals. It is an estimate of the parasympathetic activity of the ANS [33];
  - Number of normal R–R intervals differing for more than 50 ms (NN50): it estimates the number (or the percentage) of the normal R–R intervals differing for more than 50 ms from each other. Under resting state short-term recordings, it refers to the parasympathetic activity of the ANS [33];
  - Variance of the R–R intervals (VAR): it refers to the variability of the R–R intervals;
  - SD1: standard deviation of the projection of the Poincaré plot on the perpendicular line to the identity. It estimates the short-term HRV;
  - SD2: standard deviation of the projection of the Poincaré plot on the parallel line to the identity. It estimates the long-term HRV;
  - Cardiac sympathetic index (CSI): obtained by the Poincaré plot and calculated as SD2/SD1, it is employed as a reliable indicator of the sympathetic activity of the ANS [34];
  - Cardiac vagal index (CVI): obtained by the Poincaré plot and calculated as $\log_{10}(SD1 \times SD2)$, it is employed as a reliable indicator of the parasympathetic activity of the ANS [34].

- Frequency–domain features:
  - Low frequency (LF): power spectral density of the ECG signal at low frequencies (0.04–0.15 Hz), it is employed as an estimator of the sympathetic activity of the ANS [33];
  - High frequency (HF): power spectral density of the ECG signal at high frequencies (0.15–0.4 Hz), it is employed as an estimator of the sympathetic and parasympathetic activity of the ANS [33];
  - Low-to-high frequency components ratio (LF/HF): it indicates the overall balance between low and high frequency components of the ECG signal. A ratio exceeding 1 suggests a sympathetic dominance, whereas for values below 1, the parasympathetic nervous system appears to be prevalently activated [33]. It should be stated that the reliability of the LF/HF ratio in quantifying the overall sympathetic/parasympathetic balance is often questioned by several works in the scientific literature, as it is judged less accurately and is more affected by artifacts than what occur with time-domain features [35].

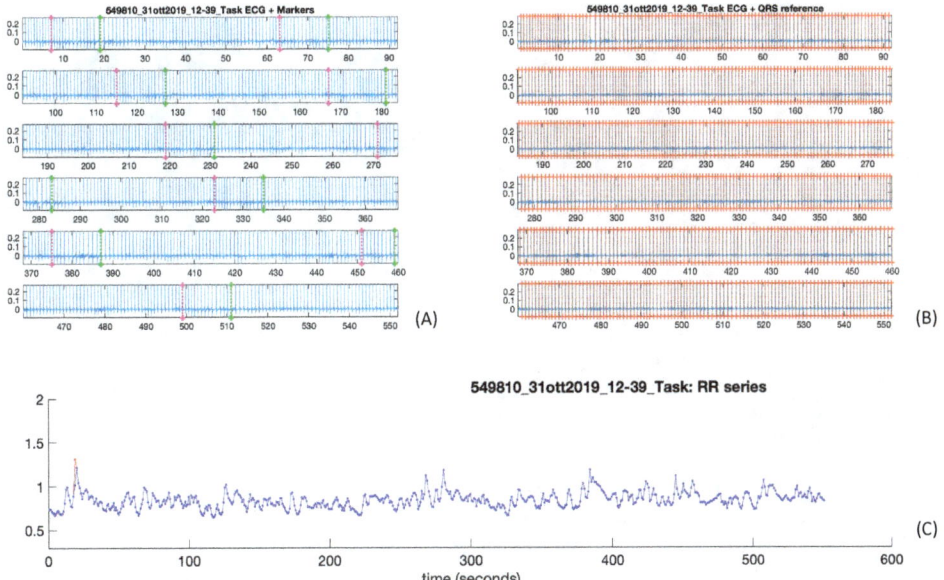

Figure 2. ECG signal processing for a sample data: (**A**) original ECG signal with the markers indicating the start (purple) and the end (green) of each odor stimulation; (**B**) the same signal after the application of the QRS complexes detector (QRS markers indicated in red); (**C**) the RR series obtained from the ECG signal before (red) and after (blue) correction.

2.4.2. GSR Acquisition and Processing

The acquisition of the GSR signal was conducted with a commercial wearable sensor, Shimmer3GSR (Shimmer Sensing, Dublin, Republic of Ireland), communicating via Bluetooth to the manufacturer user interface. Here, the sampling frequency was kept at 51.2 Hz, which was one of the higher with respect to the available choices allowed by the sensor firmware and in compliance with previously published protocols [36]. The GSR sensor captured the corresponding signal, being attached to two adjacent fingers of the subject's non-dominant hand at the phalanx level with the support of two comfortable soft rings in turn worn by the individual studied.

Concerning the processing, the GSR signal was analyzed using Ledalab, a MATLAB-based tool devoted to the processing of this specific biomedical signal [37]. The GSR signal was filtered at first with a first order Butterworth low-pass filter at 5 Hz to remove high frequency noise, and then continuous decomposition analysis was applied for the extraction of both tonic and phasic activities (see Figure 3 for an example). As such, the following features were extracted:

- Global GSR signal: composed of the sum of the tonic and phasic components of the signal;
- Tonic GSR component: mainly refers to slow changes of the electrical skin signal, dominant at rest and during relaxing activities not including specific stimuli;
- Phasic GSR component: extracted to study the response to the sensory (olfactory) stimulation, as it refers to quick responses to specific stimuli. It is often termed skin conductance response (SCR).

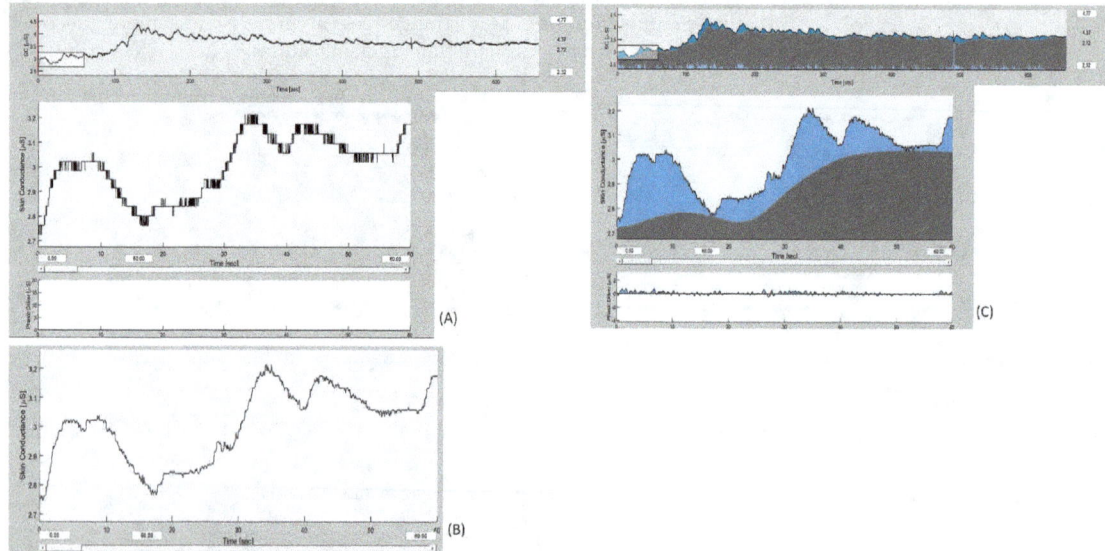

Figure 3. Galvanic skin response (GSR) signal processing: (**A**) the Ledalab interface displaying the raw signal (upper plot) and a 60-s portion of it (medium plot); (**B**) the same 60-s portion after the application of the first order Butterworth low-pass filter at 5 Hz; (**C**) the signal filtered (upper plot), the 60-s portion (medium plot) and the phasic component extraction after applying a continuous decomposition analysis (lower plot).

2.5. Statistical Analysis

Data normality was assessed using the Shapiro–Wilk test for each of the parameters studied [38]. In case of parameters displaying a normal distribution, Student's t-test was applied to compare couples (e.g., scores at baseline vs. task, or at T0 vs. T1), whereas with data deviating from normality, the Wilcoxon signed-rank test was applied.

For all the analyses conducted, statistical significance was set at $p < 0.05$.

3. Results

3.1. ECG Signal

In the ECG signal, the features extracted and described above were analyzed in terms of the comparison between T0 and T1 of the baseline, as well as within each testing session (e.g., at T0 and at T1) in terms of the comparison between baseline and task. Due to the nature of the HRV, it is quite infrequent (and useless) to calculate HRV features within short time windows like the ones dealing with the odorous stimulation (e.g., 10 s); therefore at both T0 and T1, the task phase was further divided into task ON and task OFF, being, respectively, the portion of the task phase where the odorous stimulation took place and the inter-stimulus portion of the task phase.

The results obtained are displayed in Table 3.

Table 3. Main results concerning the ECG features throughout the protocol phases (B: baseline, T OFF: task inter-stimulus, T ON: task with olfactory stimulation; *: $p < 0.05$; **: $p < 0.01$; n.s.: not significant).

Feature	B T0	B T1	T ON T0	T ON T1	T OFF T0	T OFF T1	B T0 vs. B T1	B T0 vs. T ON T0	B T1 vs. T ON T1	T ON T0 vs. T OFF T0	T ON T1 vs. T OFF T1
HR (bpm)	71.9 ± 10.6	67.7 ± 9.4	78.8 ± 12.1	75.1 ± 9.0	78.3 ± 9.6	74.0 ± 7.1	n.s.	0.005 **	<0.001 **	n.s.	n.s.
RMSSD (ms)	0.063 ± 0.031	0.071 ± 0.031	0.083 ± 0.055	0.067 ± 0.031	0.063 ± 0.045	0.050 ± 0.015	n.s.	n.s.	n.s.	n.s.	0.018*
NN50	18.9 ± 12.8	47.8 ± 34.4	4.4 ± 2.1	4.5 ± 1.8	12.1 ± 7.1	9.1 ± 4.4	0.036 *	0.002 **	0.002 **	<0.001 **	<0.001 **
SD1	0.044 ± 0.022	0.050 ± 0.022	0.058 ± 0.039	0.047 ± 0.022	0.044 ± 0.032	0.035 ± 0.011	n.s.	n.s.	n.s.	n.s.	0.018 *
CSI	2.238 ± 0.770	2.100 ± 0.546	2.224 ± 0.939	2.346 ± 0.512	2.825 ± 0.919	2.783 ± 0.451	n.s.	n.s.	n.s.	0.020*	0.036 *
CVI	−2.490 ± 0.362	−2.361 ± 0.309	−1.510 ± 0.521	−2.418 ± 0.351	−2.474 ± 0.444	−2.545 ± 0.260	n.s.	n.s.	n.s.	n.s.	0.007 **
LF (ms^2)^2/Hz	0.264 ± 0.167	0.233 ± 0.048	0.119 ± 0.031	0.098 ± 0.021	0.240 ± 0.049	0.237 ± 0.046	n.s.	0.004 **	<0.001 **	0.017 *	<0.001 **
HF (ms^2)^2/Hz	0.255 ± 0.450	0.802 ± 0.569	0.255 ± 0.156	0.288 ± 0.195	0.329 ± 0.318	0.351 ± 0.216	n.s.	0.010*	0.001 **	n.s.	n.s.
LF/HF	2.364 ± 3.620	0.535 ± 0.458	1.227 ± 1.479	0.098 ± 0.021	1.969 ± 1.769	1.177 ± 0.687	n.s.	n.s.	n.s.	0.013*	0.016 *

3.2. GSR Signal

As for the GSR signal, comparisons between baseline at T0 and at T1, as well between baseline at T0 and task at T0 (and baseline at T1 and task at T1) were conducted evaluating differences arising in terms of global and tonic GSR. The responses to single odorants at T0 with respect to T1 were compared by means of the phasic component of the GSR. This analysis, slightly different with respect to those carried out with the ECG signal, was possible thanks to the fact that the GSR analysis, particularly concerning the tonic phase evaluation, can be performed also on very short time windows like the ones represented by the 10 s of olfactory stimulation foreseen in the present protocol.

The results obtained are displayed in Table 4.

Table 4. Main results concerning the GSR signal analysis (B: baseline, T: task; *: $p < 0.05$; **: $p < 0.01$; n.s.: not significant).

Feature	B T0	B T1	T T0	T T1	B T0 vs. B T1	B T0 vs. T T0	B T1 vs. T T1
GSR global (μS)	2.13 ± 2.33	3.75 ± 4.90	3.09 ± 3.16	4.73 ± 6.88	n.s.	0.015 *	n.s.
GSR tonic (μS)	1.93 ± 2.14	3.56 ± 4.64	2.84 ± 2.73	4.53 ± 6.58	n.s.	0.009 **	n.s.

On the other hand, no significant differences between the GSR phasic signals were seen for any of the odorants administered at T1 with respect to T0.

4. Discussion and Conclusions

The analysis of such results should be performed taking into account the physiological meanings of both ECG and GSR signals and their ability to map the activity of the ANS.

Notably, the various features extracted from the ECG signal can reliably detect changes occurring at both the sympathetic and parasympathetic branches of the ANS (see [33] for a review), whereas the GSR signal is capable of monitoring the sympathetic arousal [39], albeit often reported to be less sensitive to subtle modifications of the ANS activity with respect to the ECG-related features [40–42].

In fact, more specifically, it is well known that different components of the ANS activated by emotional reactions can be detected by both signals. Concerning the ECG, the heart rhythm and its variability are modulated by the activity of both sympathetic and parasympathetic nerves, whereas the GSR only reflects the activation of the sympathetic branch of the ANS, probably representing the elective method for assessing the emotional arousal [43]. Several works have demonstrated the higher performance of the ECG signal with respect to the GSR in representing a useful indicator of emotions (see [44]) for some related description), but the use of both signals is basically justified by their informative value.

As such, it is reasonable that slight, sometimes pleasant sensory stimulations, as represented by olfactory stimuli, could drive quite subtle changes in the ANS activity, therefore requiring a comprehensive analysis of both ECG and GSR signals to be appreciated, at least in individuals with preserved sensory ability.

Overall, the results obtained in the present work suggest that the engagement in an emotionally-demanding task like sniffing an odorant might drive the ANS towards a higher sympathetic activation and somewhat vagal withdrawal in cognitively- and sensory-intact individuals. Indeed, both the ECG and GSR features are consistent about this point, especially during the first session (T0), conducted prior to the olfactory training. Such a result appears consistent with previous literature works, proving once more this existing, albeit subtle association [26,45].

Interestingly, ECG features were also able to retrieve some differences between the "sub-phases" of the task, displaying higher vagal activation while sniffing and higher sympathetic activity during inter-stimulus phases, where individuals are engaged in a more cognitively demanding task, again consistently with the literature [26].

The effect noticed comparing results at the two testing sessions also suggests a slightly different behavior at T1 with respect to T0. In fact, the higher vagal withdrawal highlighted by RMSSD at T1 during inter-stimuli with respect to the olfactory stimulation sub-phase, and the absence of any sympathetically-driven arousal detectable by the tonic GSR signal suggest that the more odors become familiar to the panelists (as occurring after the training period, at T1, in our protocol), the more they show a tendency to provoke higher vagal responses in the individuals evaluated.

Such results lead to the consideration about a clear link between familiarity and pleasantness [46], the latter being studied through the "implicit" assessment of the ANS [47].

Generally, sensory channels, at least concerning unpleasant triggers, display an adaptation for repeated stimulations, with lower autonomic reactivity as much as the stimulus becomes familiar. However, this was demonstrated only limited to unpleasant stimuli and excluding the olfactory channel [48], this domain remaining yet poorly explored in the literature.

The results obtained in the present article go beyond such retrievals and makes sense also from an evolutionary perspective. Indeed, the main survival role of the olfactory system is to identify potential environmental hazards and to adopt the optimal approach to the surrounding universe [49], including that with respect to feeding, activating an approach/avoidance behavior, which is critical to ensure the individual's survival [50,51]. As such, odors are highly capable of eliciting affective responses and emotions, thanks to the direct connections between primary olfactory areas and the areas of the limbic systems, without a thalamic relay [52], making olfaction a particularly useful, non-invasive mean to somewhat access some specific information processed by specific areas of the brain.

Proving, using an implicit methodology and thus relying on the study of the autonomic changes brought by odors, that olfactory training, beyond enhancing familiarity, also leads to different autonomic reactivity, particularly on domains concerned with odor pleasantness, can be of critical importance from a clinical perspective. Indeed, although this work has demonstrated the association only on healthy individuals, and in particularly university students, which are probably interested and more favorable to the present approach, it could form the basis for future investigations on clinically relevant cohorts.

Administering a similar protocol, for example, to subjects characterized by disturbed sensoriality, in turn leading to abnormal behavior towards feeding, such as extreme food aversion, binge eating or overfeeding, would help in understanding eventual autonomic abnormalities in such specific cohorts and eventually in hypothesizing a treatment based on repeated olfactory stimuli tailored on the specific disease phenotype and, in some instances, on an individual-basis. If proven to be beneficial, this would represent an undoubted advancement in the current clinical practice that the development of Information and Communication Technology would enable.

Author Contributions: Conceptualization, A.T., L.B., C.S. and F.V.; Data curation, A.T., L.B. and F.V.; Formal analysis, A.T. and I.D.M.; Investigation, A.T., L.B., I.D.M., R.M., C.S. and F.V.; Methodology, A.T., L.B., R.M., C.S. and F.V.; Project administration, A.T., L.B. and F.V.; Resources, F.V.; Software, A.T.; Supervision, A.T., L.B. and F.V.; Validation, A.T., I.D.M., C.S. and F.V.; Visualization, I.D.M.; Writing—original draft, A.T., L.B. and F.V.; Writing—review and editing, A.T., L.B., I.D.M., R.M., C.S. and F.V. All authors have read and agreed to the published version of the manuscript.

Funding: This research received no external funding.

Institutional Review Board Statement: The study was conducted according to the guidelines of the Declaration of Helsinki, and approved by the Ethical Clearance Committee of CNR (protocol code 0087922/2019, of 6 December 2019).

Informed Consent Statement: Informed consent was obtained from all subjects involved in the study.

Data Availability Statement: The data presented in this study are available on request from the corresponding author. The data are not publicly available due to ethical reasons.

Conflicts of Interest: The authors declare no conflict of interest.

References

1. Kryklywy, J.H.; Ehlers, M.R.; Anderson, A.K.; Todd, R.M. From Architecture to Evolution: Multisensory Evidence of Decentralized Emotion. *Trends Cogn. Sci.* **2020**, *24*, 916–929. [CrossRef] [PubMed]
2. Wolff, M.; Morceau, S.; Folkard, R.; Martin-Cortecero, J.; Groh, A. A thalamic bridge from sensory perception to cognition. *Neurosci. Biobehav. Rev.* **2021**, *120*, 222–235. [CrossRef] [PubMed]
3. Soudry, Y.; Lemogne, C.; Malinvaud, D.; Consoli, S.-M.; Bonfils, P. Olfactory system and emotion: Common substrates. *Eur. Ann. Otorhinolaryngol. Head Neck Dis.* **2011**, *128*, 18–23. [CrossRef] [PubMed]
4. De Luca, R.; Botelho, D. The unconscious perception of smells as a driver of consumer responses: A framework integrating the emotion-cognition approach to scent marketing. *AMS Rev.* **2019**, 1–17. [CrossRef]
5. Álvarez-Pato, V.M.; Sánchez, C.N.; Domínguez-Soberanes, J.; Méndoza-Pérez, D.E.; Velázquez, R. A Multisensor Data Fusion Approach for Predicting Consumer Acceptance of Food Products. *Foods* **2020**, *9*, 774. [CrossRef]
6. Morquecho-Campos, P.; De Graaf, K.; Boesveldt, S. Smelling our appetite? The influence of food odors on congruent appetite, food preferences and intake. *Food Qual. Prefer.* **2020**, *85*, 103959. [CrossRef]
7. Baccarani, A.; Brand, G.; Dacremont, C.; Valentin, D.; Brochard, R. The influence of stimulus concentration and odor intensity on relaxing and stimulating perceived properties of odors. *Food Qual. Prefer.* **2021**, *87*, 104030. [CrossRef]
8. Hawkes, C.H. Olfaction in neurodegenerative disorder. *Mov. Disord.* **2003**, *18*, 364–372. [CrossRef]
9. Tonacci, A.; Billeci, L.; Tartarisco, G.; Ruta, L.; Muratori, F.; Pioggia, G.; Gangemi, S. Olfaction in autism spectrum disorders: A systematic review. *Child Neuropsychol.* **2015**, *23*, 1–25. [CrossRef]
10. Tonacci, A.; Calderoni, S.; Billeci, L.; Maestro, S.; Fantozzi, P.; Ciuccoli, F.; Morales, M.A.; Narzisi, A.; Muratori, F. Autistic traits impact on olfactory processing in adolescent girls with Anorexia Nervosa restricting type. *Psychiatry Res.* **2019**, *274*, 20–26. [CrossRef]

11. Bentz, M.; Guldberg, J.; Vangkilde, S.; Pedersen, T.; Plessen, K.J.; Jepsen, J.R.M. Heightened Olfactory Sensitivity in Young Females with Recent-Onset Anorexia Nervosa and Recovered Individuals. *PLoS ONE* **2017**, *12*, e0169183. [CrossRef] [PubMed]
12. Islam, M.A.; Fagundo, A.B.; Arcelus, J.; Agüera, Z.; Jiménez-Murcia, S.; Fernandezreal, J.M.; Tinahones, F.J.; De La Torre, R.; Botella, C.; Frühbeck, G.; et al. Olfaction in eating disorders and abnormal eating behavior: A systematic review. *Front. Psychol.* **2015**, *6*, 1431. [CrossRef] [PubMed]
13. Kattar, N.; Do, T.M.; Unis, G.D.; Migneron, M.R.; Thomas, A.J.; McCoul, E.D. Olfactory Training for Postviral Olfactory Dysfunction: Systematic Review and Meta-analysis. *Otolaryngol. Neck Surg.* **2020**. [CrossRef] [PubMed]
14. Aghagoli, G.; Marin, B.G.; Katchur, N.J.; Chaves-Sell, F.; Asaad, W.F.; Murphy, S.A. Neurological Involvement in COVID-19 and Potential Mechanisms: A Review. *Neurocritical Care* **2020**, 1–10. [CrossRef] [PubMed]
15. Kang, Y.J.; Cho, J.H.; Lee, M.H.; Kim, Y.J.; Park, C.-S. The diagnostic value of detecting sudden smell loss among asymptomatic COVID-19 patients in early stage: The possible early sign of COVID-19. *Auris Nasus Larynx* **2020**, *47*, 565–573. [CrossRef] [PubMed]
16. Liu, D.T.; Sabha, M.; Damm, M.; Philpott, C.M.; Oleszkiewicz, A.; Hähner, A.; Hummel, T. Parosmia is Associated with Relevant Olfactory Recovery After Olfactory Training. *Laryngoscope* **2020**. [CrossRef] [PubMed]
17. Ellul, M.A.; Benjamin, L.; Singh, B.; Lant, S.; Michael, B.D.; Easton, A.; Kneen, R.; Defres, S.; Sejvar, J.; Solomon, T. Neurological associations of COVID-19. *Lancet Neurol.* **2020**, *19*, 767–783. [CrossRef]
18. Leschak, C.J.; Eisenberger, N.I. The role of social relationships in the link between olfactory dysfunction and mortality. *PLoS ONE* **2018**, *13*, e0196708. [CrossRef]
19. Saltzman, L.Y.; Hansel, T.C.; Bordnick, P.S. Loneliness, isolation, and social support factors in post-COVID-19 mental health. *Psychol. Trauma: Theory Res. Pr. Policy* **2020**, *12*, S55–S57. [CrossRef]
20. Delplanque, S.; Grandjean, D.; Chrea, C.; Aymard, L.; Cayeux, I.; Le Calvé, B.; Velazco, M.I.; Scherer, K.R.; Sander, D. Emotional Processing of Odors: Evidence for a Nonlinear Relation between Pleasantness and Familiarity Evaluations. *Chem. Senses* **2008**, *33*, 469–479. [CrossRef]
21. Knaapila, A.; Laaksonen, O.; Virtanen, M.; Yang, B.; Lagström, H.; Sandell, M. Pleasantness, familiarity, and identification of spice odors are interrelated and enhanced by consumption of herbs and food neophilia. *Appetite* **2017**, *109*, 190–200. [CrossRef] [PubMed]
22. Luisier, A.-C.; Petitpierre, G.; Bérod, A.C.; Garcia-Burgos, D.; Bensafi, M. Effects of familiarization on odor hedonic responses and food choices in children with autism spectrum disorders. *Autism* **2018**, *23*, 1460–1471. [CrossRef] [PubMed]
23. Huart, C.; Legrain, V.; Hummel, T.; Rombaux, P.; Mouraux, A. Time-Frequency Analysis of Chemosensory Event-Related Potentials to Characterize the Cortical Representation of Odors in Humans. *PLoS ONE* **2012**, *7*, e33221. [CrossRef] [PubMed]
24. Sato, M.; Kodama, N.; Sasaki, T.; Ohta, M. Olfactory evoked potentials: Experimental and clinical studies. *J. Neurosurg.* **1996**, *85*, 1122–1126. [CrossRef] [PubMed]
25. Wang, J.; Rupprecht, S.; Sun, X.; Freiberg, D.; Crowell, C.; Cartisano, E.; Vasavada, M.; Yang, Q.X. A Free-breathing fMRI Method to Study Human Olfactory Function. *J. Vis. Exp.* **2017**, *125*, e54898. [CrossRef]
26. Tonacci, A.; Billeci, L.; Burrai, E.; Sansone, F.; Conte, R. Comparative Evaluation of the Autonomic Response to Cognitive and Sensory Stimulations through Wearable Sensors. *Sensors* **2019**, *19*, 4661. [CrossRef]
27. Tonacci, A.; Di Monte, J.; Meucci, M.B.; Sansone, F.; Pala, A.P.; Billeci, L.; Conte, R. Wearable Sensors to Characterize the Autonomic Nervous System Correlates of Food-Like Odors Perception: A Pilot Study. *Electronics* **2019**, *8*, 1481. [CrossRef]
28. Venturi, F.; Andrich, G.; Sanmartin, C.; Taglieri, I.; Scalabrelli, G.; Ferroni, G.; Zinnai, A. Glass and wine: A good example of the deep relationship between drinkware and beverage. *J. Wine Res.* **2016**, *27*, 153–171. [CrossRef]
29. Venturi, F.; Sanmartin, C.; Taglieri, I.; Xiaoguo, Y.; Quartacci, M.F.; Sgherri, C.; Andrich, G.; Zinnai, A. A kinetic approach to describe the time evolution of red wine as a function of packaging conditions adopted: Influence of closure and storage position. *Food Packag. Shelf Life* **2017**, *13*, 44–48. [CrossRef]
30. Lötsch, J.; Lange, C.; Hummel, T. A Simple and Reliable Method for Clinical Assessment of Odor Thresholds. *Chem. Senses* **2004**, *29*, 311–317. [CrossRef]
31. Malik, M.; Bigger, J.T.; Camm, A.J.; Kleiger, R.E.; Malliani, A.; Moss, A.J.; Schwartz, P.J. Heart rate variability: Standards of measurement, physiological interpretation, and clinical use. *Eur. Heart J.* **1996**, *17*, 354–381. [CrossRef]
32. Billeci, L.; Marino, D.; Insana, L.; Vatti, G.; Varanini, M. Patient-specific seizure prediction based on heart rate variability and recurrence quantification analysis. *PLoS ONE* **2018**, *13*, e0204339. [CrossRef] [PubMed]
33. Shaffer, F.; Ginsberg, J.P. An Overview of Heart Rate Variability Metrics and Norms. *Front. Public Health* **2017**, *5*, 258. [CrossRef] [PubMed]
34. Dodo, N.; Hashimoto, R. Autonomic Nervous System Activity During a Speech Task. *Front. Neurosci.* **2019**, *13*, 406. [CrossRef] [PubMed]
35. Herzig, D.; Eser, P.; Omlin, X.; Riener, R.; Wilhelm, M.; Achermann, P. Reproducibility of Heart Rate Variability Is Parameter and Sleep Stage Dependent. *Front. Physiol.* **2018**, *8*, 1100. [CrossRef]
36. Tonacci, A.; Billeci, L.; Sansone, F.; Masci, A.; Pala, A.P.; Domenici, C.; Conte, R. An Innovative, Unobtrusive Approach to Investigate Smartphone Interaction in Nonaddicted Subjects Based on Wearable Sensors: A Pilot Study. *Medical* **2019**, *55*, 37. [CrossRef]

37. Benedek, M.; Kaernbach, C. A continuous measure of phasic electrodermal activity. *J. Neurosci. Methods* **2010**, *190*, 80–91. [CrossRef]
38. Shapiro, S.S.; Wilk, M.B. An analysis of variance test for normality (complete samples). *Biometrika* **1965**, *52*, 591–611. [CrossRef]
39. Mackersie, C.L.; Calderon-Moultrie, N. Autonomic Nervous System Reactivity During Speech Repetition Tasks. *Ear Hear.* **2016**, *37*, 118S–125S. [CrossRef]
40. Thompson, K.J.; Adams, H.E. Psychophysiological characteristics of headache patients. *Pain* **1984**, *18*, 41–52. [CrossRef]
41. Gass, J.J.; Glaros, A.G. Autonomic Dysregulation in Headache Patients. *Appl. Psychophysiol. Biofeedback* **2013**, *38*, 257–263. [CrossRef] [PubMed]
42. Andersson, L.; Claeson, A.-S.; Dantoft, T.M.; Skovbjerg, S.; Lind, N.; Nordin, S. Chemosensory perception, symptoms and autonomic responses during chemical exposure in multiple chemical sensitivity. *Int. Arch. Occup. Environ. Health* **2015**, *89*, 79–88. [CrossRef] [PubMed]
43. Bach, D.R. Sympathetic nerve activity can be estimated from skin conductance responses—A comment on Henderson et al. (2012). *NeuroImage* **2014**, *84*, 122–123. [CrossRef] [PubMed]
44. Goshvarpour, A.; Abbasi, A. An accurate emotion recognition system using ECG and GSR signals and matching pursuit method. *Biomed. J.* **2017**, *40*, 355–368. [CrossRef] [PubMed]
45. Tonacci, A.; Sansone, F.; Pala, A.P.; Centrone, A.; Napoli, F.; Domenici, C.; Conte, R. Effect of feeding on neurovegetative response to olfactory stimuli. In Proceedings of the 2017 E-Health and Bioengineering Conference (EHB), IEEE, Sinaia, Romania, 22–24 June 2017.
46. Joussain, P.; Rouby, C.; Bensafi, M. A pleasant familiar odor influences perceived stress and peripheral nervous system activity during normal aging. *Front. Psychol.* **2014**, *5*, 113. [CrossRef] [PubMed]
47. He, W.; De Wijk, R.A.; De Graaf, C.; Boesveldt, S. Implicit and Explicit Measurements of Affective Responses to Food Odors. *Chem. Senses* **2016**, *41*, 661–668. [CrossRef] [PubMed]
48. Croy, I.; Laqua, K.; Suess, F.; Joraschky, P.; Ziemssen, T.; Hummel, T. The sensory channel of presentation alters subjective ratings and autonomic responses toward disgusting stimuli—Blood pressure, heart rate and skin conductance in response to visual, auditory, haptic and olfactory presented disgusting stimuli. *Front. Hum. Neurosci.* **2013**, *7*, 510. [CrossRef]
49. Stevenson, R.J. An Initial Evaluation of the Functions of Human Olfaction. *Chem. Senses* **2010**, *35*, 3–20. [CrossRef]
50. Khan, R.M.; Luk, C.-H.; Flinker, A.; Aggarwal, A.; Lapid, H.; Haddad, R.; Sobel, N. Predicting Odor Pleasantness from Odorant Structure: Pleasantness as a Reflection of the Physical World. *J. Neurosci.* **2007**, *27*, 10015–10023. [CrossRef]
51. Yeshurun, Y.; Sobel, N. An Odor is Not Worth a Thousand Words: From Multidimensional Odors to Unidimensional Odor Objects. *Annu. Rev. Psychol.* **2010**, *61*, 219–241. [CrossRef]
52. Lundström, J.N.; Boesveldt, S.; Albrecht, J. Central Processing of the Chemical Senses: An Overview. *ACS Chem. Neurosci.* **2010**, *2*, 5–16. [CrossRef] [PubMed]

Article

Detection of Myocardial Infarction Using ECG and Multi-Scale Feature Concatenate

Jia-Zheng Jian [1], Tzong-Rong Ger [1,*,†], Han-Hua Lai [1], Chi-Ming Ku [1], Chiung-An Chen [2,*], Patricia Angela R. Abu [3] and Shih-Lun Chen [4]

1. Department of Biomedical Engineering, Chung Yuan Christian University, Taoyuan City 320314, Taiwan; g10875014@cycu.edu.tw (J.-Z.J.); g10975008@cycu.edu.tw (H.-H.L.); g10575014@cycu.edu.tw (C.-M.K.)
2. Department of Electrical Engineering, Ming Chi University of Technology, New Taipei City 243303, Taiwan
3. Department of Information Systems and Computer Science, Ateneo de Manila University, Quezon City 1108, Philippines; pabu@ateneo.edu
4. Department of Electronic Engineering, Chung Yuan Christian University, Taoyuan City 320314, Taiwan; chrischen@cycu.edu.tw
* Correspondence: sunbow@cycu.edu.tw (T.-R.G.); joannechen@mail.mcut.edu.tw (C.-A.C.); Tel.: +886-3-265-4536 (T.-R.G.); +886-2-2908-9899 (C.-A.C.)
† Equal contribution to the first author.

Abstract: Diverse computer-aided diagnosis systems based on convolutional neural networks were applied to automate the detection of myocardial infarction (MI) found in electrocardiogram (ECG) for early diagnosis and prevention. However, issues, particularly overfitting and underfitting, were not being taken into account. In other words, it is unclear whether the network structure is too simple or complex. Toward this end, the proposed models were developed by starting with the simplest structure: a multi-lead features-concatenate narrow network (N-Net) in which only two convolutional layers were included in each lead branch. Additionally, multi-scale features-concatenate networks (MSN-Net) were also implemented where larger features were being extracted through pooling the signals. The best structure was obtained via tuning both the number of filters in the convolutional layers and the number of inputting signal scales. As a result, the N-Net reached a 95.76% accuracy in the MI detection task, whereas the MSN-Net reached an accuracy of 61.82% in the MI locating task. Both networks give a higher average accuracy and a significant difference of $p < 0.001$ evaluated by the U test compared with the state-of-the-art. The models are also smaller in size thus are suitable to fit in wearable devices for offline monitoring. In conclusion, testing throughout the simple and complex network structure is indispensable. However, the way of dealing with the class imbalance problem and the quality of the extracted features are yet to be discussed.

Keywords: accuracy; convolution neural network (CNN); classifiers; electrocardiography; k-fold validation; myocardial infarction; sensitivity

1. Introduction

Myocardial infarction (MI), defined in pathology as myocardial cell death due to prolonged ischemia, is a serious heart disease that can cause death and disability [1]. According to the American Heart Association, it is estimated that 750,000 Americans have a heart attack every year, with approximately 116,000 deaths [2]. Therefore, early diagnosis and detection are the utmost important task. Nowadays, several methods already exist to recognize MI, including electrocardiogram (ECG), biomarkers, imaging technique, or defined by pathology. Yet, the non-invasive ECG is the most economical and widely used one for the sake of immediate treatment strategies among them [3–7]. Performing ECG analysis manually may not merely be time-consuming but leads to inter-observer variability [8,9]. Consequently, a computer-aided diagnosis system may come in handy to solve these difficulties. Moreover, wearable devices are common technology in recent days and are rising in numbers. Wang et al. [10] provided a wearable ECG monitoring system with the benefits of low power and high data transmitted function. Wang used a micro control unit (MCU) to realize the adjustable radio frequency (RF) and power reduction that optimized the ECG system. Another novel technical design is the antenna for wireless devices. Chiang et al. [11] proposed a multiband and power efficiency antenna for a USB dongle application.

MI can be detected by the abnormalities waveform features of the ECG, including ST displacement, T wave inversion, silent Q wave, and so on [1,12]. Hence, it is effective to make use of machine learning algorithms to achieve an automated MI diagnosis [13–15]. In the past few years, deep learning (DL) methods, including convolutional neural networks (CNN), recurrent neural networks, restricted Boltzmann machines [16], autoencoder, and generative adversarial networks are proposed [17–20]. These network architectures or learning methods are used for ECG classification, denoising, reconstruction, annotation, data compression, data generation, and data synthesis purposes. Among all DL methods described above, CNN is the most commonly used method for MI detecting and locating [21]. Acharya et al. [22] proposed a CNN model for MI detection on noisy lead II ECG and reached an accuracy of 93.53%. Alghamdi et al. [23], on the other hand, treated the lead II ECG as a 2D image and employed the transfer learning method by utilizing a pre-trained visual geometry group network (VGG-Net) [24] as a feature extractor incorporating an additional trainable classifier where the yielded accuracy after model retraining was as high as 99.22%. However, the above methods only make use of single-lead ECG information. To this end, Baloglu et al. [25] implemented a simple approach where a single CNN model was trained using all lead signals, resulting in a model that is capable of detecting and locating MI regardless of the input lead. Another way is to regard 12-lead ECG as a 12-by-signal-length image and perform the convolution along the signal direction but not lead direction [26]. A limitation of this is that the features in each lead will be extracted by the same filters. To extract features in each lead independently, Lodhi et al. [27] trained a CNN model for each lead. The 12 models were then used for a voting mechanism to yield a unified prediction of MI appearance, yet such a high number of CNNs will not be practical for portable devices. To improve on this drawback, Reasat et al. [28] proposed a high-level architecture CNN model named shallow-CNN, where each lead was passed through an Inception module [29] to execute feature extraction. The features were then concatenated and performed classification. This way, each lead of features can be extracted independently while giving a single prediction. As those leads are more relevant to inferior MI (IMI), II, III and augmented vector foot (aVF) were utilized to output the prediction between healthy control (HC) and IMI. Liu et al. [30] came up with the same approach, but with a total of six diagnosis classes and using all 12-lead ECG compared to previously mentioned work. The classes include the anterolateral (ALMI), anterior (AMI), anteroseptal (ASMI), inferolateral (ILMI), IMI, and HC, and they called the proposed model MFB-CNN. Han et al. [31] also implemented a similar approach and experiment but with some structural improvements in their ML-ResNet, which includes the residual network (ResNet) to improve the gradient vanishing problem [32] and the batch normalization (BN) to reduce the internal covariant shift [33]. Last but not the least, Hao et al. [34] worked on a similar approach as well but using DenseNet [35], a novel network architecture. Although both ResNet [36] and DenseNet [37] are famous for their skip connection approach, the latter achieved better performance via feature concatenate, whereas the former adopted feature addition.

Among all aforementioned state-of-the-art methods, different issues appear in different studies. In [22–24], only single lead information was utilized, which is not sufficient if the multiple MI location predictions are applied. In [25,26], every lead was used together as an input into CNN while training, but the features should be extracted separately. In [27], 12 models were trained, one for each lead and the final prediction was considered using a voting mechanism. However, the fact is that the multi-lead features-concatenate technique used to accomplish extracting inter-lead ECG features independently can be utilized while getting a unified prediction [28–32,34]. While there are plenty of studies that achieve remarkable accuracy [22–26,34], none mentioned and considered intra-individual variability (AIV) nor inter-individual variability (RIV) in ECG [38]. AIV is defined as the variability between ECGs from the same individual or variability within one ECG, while RIV is the variability between ECGs from different individuals. Though not explicitly mentioned in [22–26,34], their experimental scheme can be referred to as a beat-to-beat AIV cross-validation (bAIV-CV) scheme. In [28–31], the RIV problem was taken into account through implementing RIV cross-validation (RIV-CV), which regards the data from the same individual as a whole to prevent ECGs from appearing in the different folds at the same time. bAIV-CV, on the other hand, simply randomly crop segments from an ECG to form different folds. Even though there may be bAIV contained in the ECG from various sources [38], most of the aforementioned studies have already shown that it is insignificant in the Physikalisch-Technische Bundesanstalt (PTB) database. Simonson et al. [39] showed that AIV is smaller than RIV in ECG. Another potential problem is the so-called class imbalance problem [40], which refers to the data in a class outnumbered the other class. Such scenarios may induce the models to classify samples as belonging to the majority class simply. It can be observed that, while validating MI detection performance, studies that were previously considered and mentioned earlier tend to allow the number of data in the class MI to be significantly larger than in HC. Finally, in [28–31], features in every lead were utilized independently, but the performance, especially in MI locating, has room for improvement. In machine learning, overfitting is a production of an analysis that corresponds to how close or how exact something is to a particular set of data and may, therefore, fail to fit the held-out data or predict future observations reliably. Overfitting is caused by exceeding some optimal network size, whereas overtraining refers to the excessive time for network training. Both may finally result in losing the predictive ability of the model [41]. Most of the aforementioned literature prevent overtraining by using an early stopping mechanism, which stops the training by monitoring the accuracy or loss. However, none of them take the overfitting problem into account in the process of designing and validating a model. To verify the occurrence of overfitting in the model development phase, one should start from the simplest architecture then gradually increase the complexity when observing the validated result [42]. A. Kumar et al. [43] used a novel fuzzy cross-entropy loss together with transfer learning to increase the accuracy of the model. The work from M. Piekarski et al. [44] mainly focused on the implementation of transfer learning by utilizing various pre-trained networks where the VGG16 outperformed among all models considered in the study. Toward this end, a network should be simple and adjustable where the sequence of double-convolution-follow-by-pooling structure observed in VGG13 [24], together with multiscale features concatenate structure, was inspired by [45,46]. A multi-lead features-concatenate and multiscale features-concatenate integrating structure were developed, which is much like a transposed version of the VGG13 structure. Signals will first be pooled then passed to the convolutional layers to extract features that exist in different scales. The number of inputting scales and the number of filters remain adjustable to find the best architecture and justify overfitting.

As technology advances, utilization of smaller computers together with faster internet speeds for smart devices makes the improvement in portable devices and the Internet of Things nowadays an advanced research area. These open a new and wide range of solutions in e-health, surveillance, and monitoring for medical purposes. However, portable devices are prone to having a lower level of computational capability as well as having a battery consumption problems. This research aims to demonstrate the solutions to address the research challenges in the development of MI detection models using the CNN algorithm to apply feature extraction, classification, and further detection for portable devices. Figure 1 is the schematic diagram of healthcare application related to the research, 12-lead ECG signals, or other physiological signal values captured by portable devices sent to a smart device. It can either choose offline monitoring or cloud computing if the internet is available. Physicians can investigate or diagnose and undertake further actions, such as calling ambulance control or ward management. In other words, the proposed models are kept in both smart devices and cloud servers. Once an abnormality on the ECG waveform is identified by the model, the ECG will be sent to the physician in the hospital for further investigation. A smaller yet more accurate model allows the whole system to be more sustainable and makes it possible to fit inside a smart device for offline monitoring. Since bAIV about the MI and HC is negligible in the PTB database and assessing the RIV-CV has more clinical significance, only RIV-CV will be implemented. Moreover, considering it may lead to model performance reduction, the class imbalance problem should be considered. The main contributions in this research are as follows: First, by carefully verify the occurrence of underfitting and overfitting, the proposed N-Net for MI detection task outperformed the previous works considered in this study. Second, the proposed MSN-Net outperformed both the N-Net and the previous works, which indicates that multiscale features can improve the performance of the model. Third, networks were trained with a different number of input signal scales and a different number of filters in the convolutional layer. The ones that achieved the best accuracy in MI detecting and MI locating were then compared with several state-of-the-art techniques. The comparison was conducted using several parameters, including the nonparametric Mann–Whitney U test, to determine the difference of performances between the previous works.

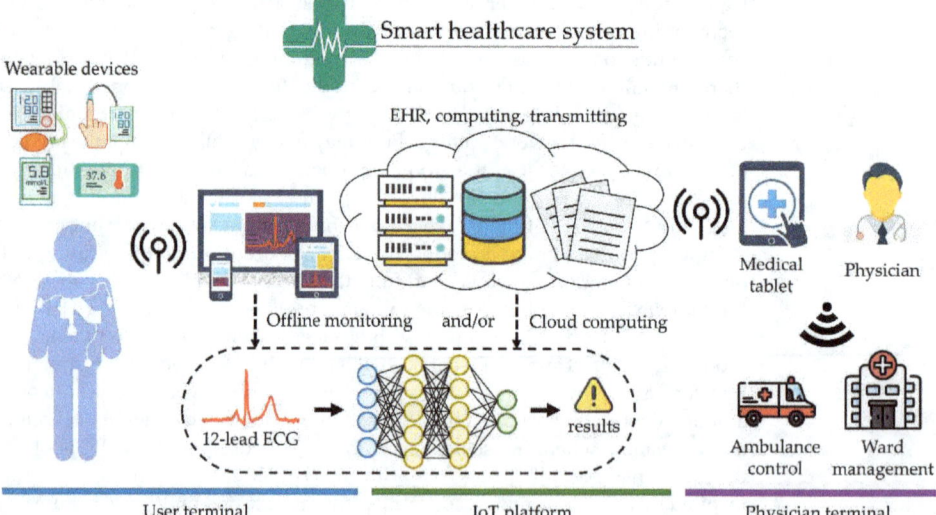

Figure 1. The schematic diagram of healthcare application with integration of Internet of Things (IoT) technology. 12-lead electrocardiogram (ECG) information can combine with other physiological signal values from different wearable devices, such as blood glucose, body temperature, and blood pressure, for algorithm models. Physicians can investigate or diagnosis and undertake further action, such as calling an ambulance or ward, through offline monitoring and/or cloud computing.

2. Materials and Methods

In this section, the experimental dataset and the signal preprocessing methods are first introduced, including signal denoising and data rearrangement. Next, the network architecture is presented and illustrated. Finally, verifying the performance of the models proposed in this research is discussed. Figure 2 demonstrates the block diagram of the research. The final objective is to build models that are capable of detecting and/or locating the occurrence of MI by analyzing the 12-lead ECG. First of all, the PTB 12-lead ECG databases were gathered, and signals were then denoised and segmented. When forming folders for 5-fold cross-validation, it was necessary to prevent patients' data from appearing in the different folders at the same time. Next, networks with a different number of inputting signal scales and a different number of filters in the convolutional layer were trained. The ones that achieved the best accuracy in MI detection and/or locating were then compared with several state-of-the-art networks. The comparison was conducted using several clinical indexes, including accuracy (ACC), sensitivity (SEN), specificity (SPE), and F1-score (F1), and area under curve (AUC), together with the nonparametric Mann–Whitney U test to determine whether the difference in performances between the previous works and the proposed networks are significant. The training was conducted on several computers with different hardware configurations. Yet, only the version of TensorFlow affected the network performance. In this study, the TensorFlow 2.0.0 GPU version was chosen.

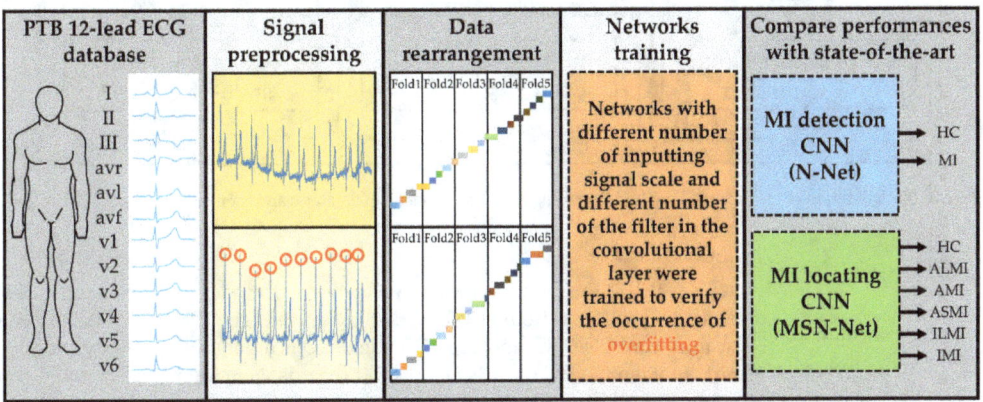

Figure 2. Block diagram of the research, including Physikalisch-Technische Bundesanstalt (PTB), 12-lead ECG database gathering, signal preprocessing, data rearrangement, study model networks training, and performance, compared with other studies. The final objective was to build models capable of detecting and/or locating the occurrence of MI by analyzing the 12-lead ECG.

Figure 3 is the block diagram of the method used in this research. During the signal preprocessing phase, the signal was down sampled to 100 Hz to reduce the computational cost of the subsequent steps. Next, segmentation using R-peak detection was conducted to shorten the length of the signals, thus simplifying the input layer of the neural network. Afterward, in the dataset rearrangement phase, under sampling was preferred to preliminary tackle the class imbalance issue since there was enough data for all classes. One of the main aims of the proposed research was to compare MI detection and locating performance of the model with previous works. With that, the MI locating dataset was created, and part of it was used to form the MI detection dataset. The k-fold CV was used to provide a measure of how accurately the model could predict across the whole dataset. To fulfill the inter-patient experimental scheme, it was necessary to prevent the patients' data from appearing in the different folds at the same time. Finally, in the model development phase, instead of testing the performance of one or more fixed network architecture, testing started from a simple network structure and gradually increased the complexity to find the maximum performance between underfitting and overfitting. The adjustable parameters included the number of inputting signal scales and the number of filters in the convolutional layers. The configuration that achieved the best ACC evaluated by k-fold CV was chosen and was compared with several state-of-the-art techniques by some clinical indexes, including ACC, SEN, SPE, F1, and AUC. The proposed networks showed promising results that achieved both higher average performance and significant differences evaluated by the U test.

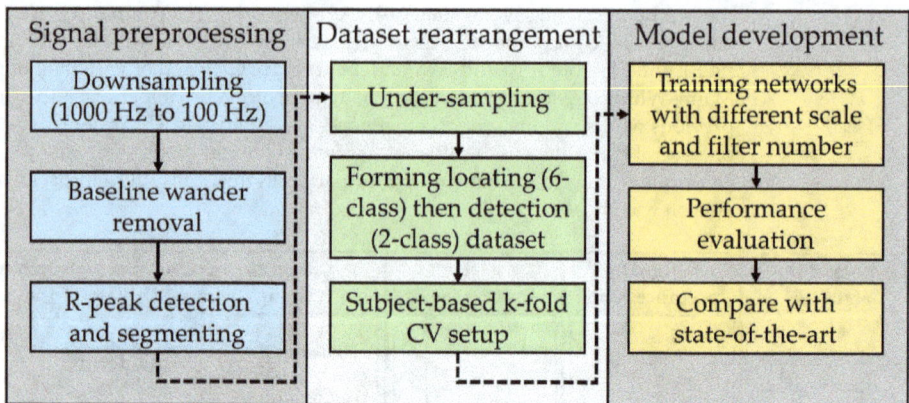

Figure 3. Block diagram of the proposed method, including signal preprocessing, dataset rearrangement, and model development.

2.1. ECG Dataset

To evaluate the performance of the proposed model, the open-access PTB ECG database [47] collected from PhysioNet [48] was used. The PTB ECG database comprises 52 healthy controls (HC) and 148 MI patients. Since patients may have more than one record, a total of 80 HC records and 368 MI records were found. Each record contains a standard 12-lead ECG together with 3 Frank lead ECGs under 1000 Hz sampling rate and 16-bit resolution ranging from −16,384 µV to 16,384 µV. Figure 4 shows the snapshot of the 12-lead HC and IMI ECG. According to the information provided by the header file in the database, MI records can be further divided by occurred MI locating. Five MI locations were utilized in this study, namely 43 ALMI, 47 AMI, 77 ASMI, 56 ILMI, 89 IMI.

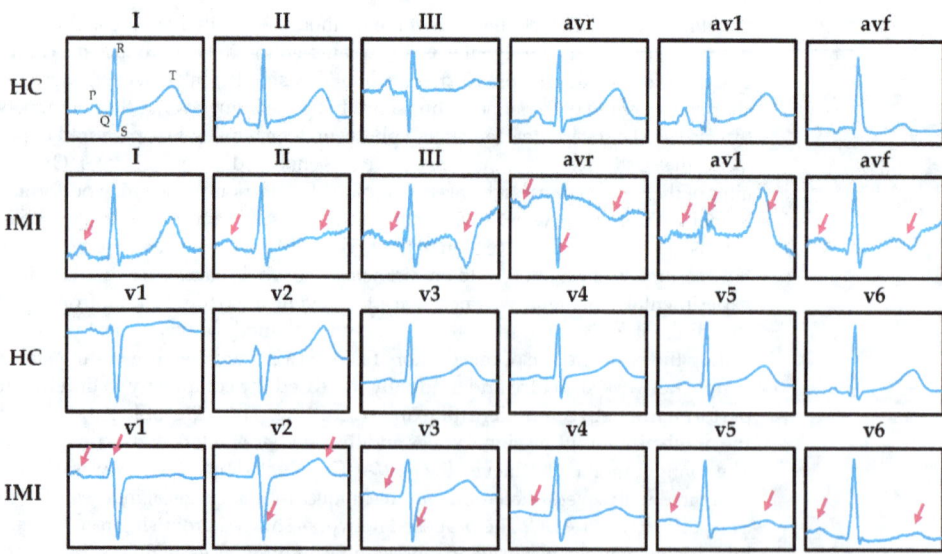

Figure 4. Samples of healthy control (HC) and inferior myocardial infarction (IMI) 12-lead ECG. IMI can be detected by the abnormalities waveform features of the ECG, as indicated by the arrows that include the ST displacement, T wave inversion, silent Q wave, and so on.

2.2. Signal Preprocessing

Since the ECG maximum frequency band is about 40 Hz [49], applying an anti-aliasing filter and down sampling to 100 Hz can eliminate high-frequency noise and reduce the computational cost on the later steps of the experiment while still taking the Nyquist theorem into consideration. A median filter with a 0.857-s window was then employed to find and remove baseline wander. The window size was calculated based on the objective of completely covering one cardiac cycle (PQRST waves) under a 70 beats per minute assumption. Denoised signals were then segmented into pieces using the R-peak detection algorithm proposed by Christov [50], while serving as a data augmentation method where every piece of data contained 50 points before the R-peak and 349 points after the R-peak. Lastly, to prevent the model from tending to predict classes that have more training data [40], the quantity of data in each class was required to be equal. This was achieved through random under sampling, a data level solution for imbalanced data [51]. Thirty (30) data pieces were chosen from every 40 chosen records in all 6 diagnostic classes, resulting in a total of 7200 data pieces in the MI locating dataset. Cross-validation (CV) was implemented after model training. A similar method to a CV is called leave-one-out, while the standard method is the leave-one-patient-out CV [52]. However, it was impractical to execute CV on a per subject basis since given a total of 96 chosen patients, 96-fold CV has to be performed. Thence, a subject-based k-fold CV was more suitable for the current investigation. A subject-based 5-fold CV was performed to evaluate the model performance, in which every fold contained multiple patient records. In the meantime, it was necessary to prevent a patient record from appearing in other folds. As for the MI detection dataset, 6 out of 30 were selected from each segmented data in all five MIs to fulfill class balancing. Table 1 summarizes the dataset after the rearrangement.

Table 1. Patient and data distribution after rearrangement.

Class	No. of Subjects	No. of Records	No. of Pieces (Detection)	No. of Pieces (Locating)
HC	25	40	1200	1200
ALMI	14	40	240	1200
AMI	14	40	240	1200
ASMI	13	40	240	1200
ILMI	16	40	240	1200
IMI	14	40	240	1200

2.3. Network Architecture

First of all, the network took 12-lead ECG at the input layer, as shown in Figure 5. Each lead was fed into a lead branch CNN to extract features independently. In the lead branch CNN, the input was passed through several parallel paths, as illustrated in Figure 6. In each parallel path, the input was sequentially passed through two convolutional layers marked in blue in Figure 6 for features extraction and a global average pooling (GAP) layer for overfitting prevention. To extract larger features, pooling the signal can let the features become smaller, which allows the filters with the same kernel size to extract it. This is in contrast to having a larger kernel size, which has a higher computational cost. Furthermore, instead of using common maximum pooling or average pooling, convolution with both kernel size (K) and stride (S) with the same value was introduced to accomplish the down sampling operation [53], which is considered a learnable pooling layer. Hence a specialized convolutional layer marked in purple in Figure 6 was used to pool the signal for larger features extraction. The extracted features were then concatenated and linked to a fully connected (FC) layer for classification. This FC layer was the only non-convolutional layer in the proposed model. It used the SoftMax activation function, which is the most commonly used activation function in the output layer of a model for classification tasks. To be more specific, 2 neurons for MI detection and 6 neurons for MI locating at the output FC layer were used. The parameter F represents the number of filters on a scale branch.

Since non-zero paddings were executed, the convolutional layers colored in blue in Figure 6 reduced the length of the passing signals by 2 since K was 3. All the convolutional layers used the rectified linear unit [54] as the activation function. Preventing overfitting is the utmost important task. Therefore, a dropout layer [55] was inserted with a rate of 0.5 right before FC. Finally, the number of filters and the number of scales were reserved as variables for tuning the best structure. Models using single-scale features were named narrow net (N-Net), while models using multi-scale features were named multi-scale narrow net (MSN-Net).

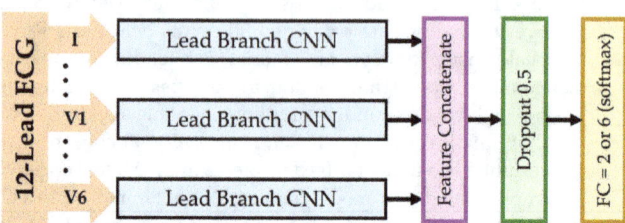

Figure 5. Multi-lead features-concatenate network. Twelve (12) lead branch convolutional neural networks (CNNs) were used to extract features in each lead independently and were then concatenated and classified.

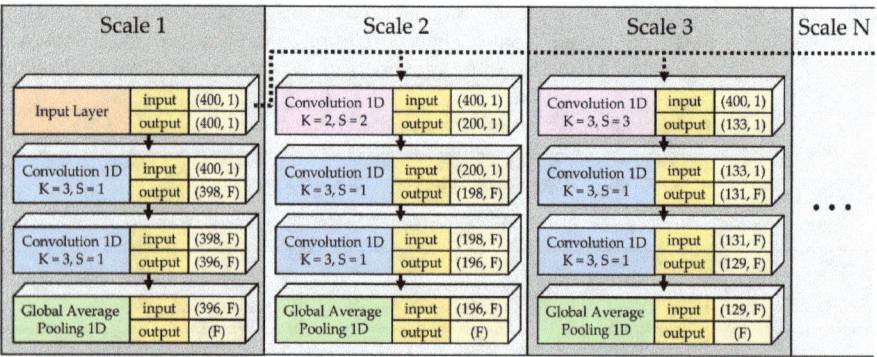

Figure 6. Multi-scale features-concatenate network in every lead branch. K represents kernel size, S represents strides. The N-Net only contained structures illustrated in scale 1, and MSN-Net that used two scales will contain the structure of both scale 1 and scale 2. MSN-Net that used three scales contained structures of scale 1, scale 2 and scale 3, and so on.

2.4. Model Training

The models described in Section 2.3 were trained with categorical cross-entropy loss, a common loss function for the multi-class classification task, and Adam optimizer [56] with a 0.001 learning rate. The model parameters updated after every 300 data were inputted. Training stops if it did not get any improvement for 20 continuous epochs or when a maximum of 200 epochs was reached. The accuracy and loss at each epoch were recorded. Additionally, how the number of filters and scales affect the model performance was explored. Performances of models with filter numbers from 1 to 10 and scale numbers from 1 to 5 were recorded. Since the robustness of MI locating models using single-scale features were too weak, the performances with filter number up to 15 were recorded. This resulted in a total of 50 different models for MI detection and 55 for MI locating. Since different starting conditions of model parameters led to different final accuracy, a total of 15 times subject-based 5-fold CV were executed for each model. In other words, one model would have 15 sets of CV results. The models were trained in a fixed order of data input to reduce the inter-model accuracy deviation. To compare the results with the current state-of-the-art models proposed by [24,26,27] were retrained since BN was removed and, more importantly, the dataset was different. All the networks were implemented using Keras [57], a neural network library.

2.5. Performance Metrics

Predictions given by subject-based 5-fold CV were gathered to form 15 sets of confusion matrixes for both detection and locating models proposed by [28,30,31] as well as this study. The performances of the models were then evaluated in terms of several clinical indexes, including accuracy (ACC), sensitivity (SEN), specificity (SPE), and F1-score (F1) with their corresponding equation for computation as shown in Equations (1)–(4), respectively. Only ACC was evaluated for MI locating models. All above criteria were calculated based on true positive (TP) rate, true negative (TN) rate, false positive (FP) rate, and false negative (FN) rate.

$$ACC\% = \frac{TP + TN}{TP + TN + FP + FN} \times 100 \qquad (1)$$

$$SEN\% = \frac{TP}{TP + FN} \times 100 \qquad (2)$$

$$SPE\% = \frac{TN}{TN + FP} \times 100 \qquad (3)$$

$$F1\% = \frac{2 \times TP}{2 \times TP + FP + FN} \times 100 \qquad (4)$$

In addition to the aforementioned indexes, the receiver operating characteristic (ROC) curve [58] and area under the ROC curve (AUC) of MI detection models were also calculated. As described in Section 2.4, the subject-based 5-fold CV 15 times was performed to evaluate the overall model performances. To verify whether a model had better performance than the other, aside from observing the box plot for comparing the distribution, statistical analysis was also included to determine whether there were significant differences between the performance of the models. Instead of using a t-test, the nonparametric Mann–Whitney U test [59], also known as the Wilcoxon rank–sum test, was utilized since it is more suitable for small population data. Finally, the AUC and U test were calculated using SPSS, a common statistical analysis tool.

3. Results

The data preprocessing and rearrangement were executed. The studies in [28,30,31] and the proposed networks in this study were implemented. Subject-based 5-fold and 10-fold CV was performed 15 times for each model in a 2-class detective dataset. Subject-based 5-fold was performed 15 times for each model in a 6-class detective dataset. Before picking the models that achieved the best average accuracy in MI detection or MI locating and compared them with the state-of-the-art, the training and validation accuracies, as well as the loss, were plotted to observe the training effectiveness. Afterward, the comparison was done by determining the significant difference in accuracy using the U test. The significant differences in SEN, SPE, F1, and AUC carried out by MI detection models were also calculated and compared.

3.1. Accuracy of N-Net and MSN-Net for MI Detection in 2-Class Dataset

Figure 7 shows the ACC trend of the proposed MI detection models with varying filter numbers and scale numbers. It can be observed that at low filter numbers, as the number of filters increased, the ACC increased significantly and gradually converges at about 95% for larger filter numbers. In addition, when using a low filter number, the ACC increased as the number of the inputted signal scale increased. But the increase was not as much as the filter number increase. By observing all the graphs, it can be seen that no matter how complex the network is, the ACC converged to about 95% with a small deviation. In using single-scale features, the best average ACC% of 95.76% was achieved with nine filters by 5-fold validation, and 94.30% was achieved with four filters by 10-fold validation. In using two-scale features, the best average ACC% of 95.60% was achieved with 10 filters by 5-fold validation, and 94.03% was achieved with six filters by 10-fold validation. In using three-scale features, the best average ACC% of 95.33% was achieved with six filters by 5-fold validation, and 96.29% was achieved with four filters by 10-fold validation. In using four-scale features, the best average ACC% of 95.27% was achieved with five filters by 5-fold validation, and 93.80% was achieved with five filters by 10-fold validation. In using five-scale features, the best average ACC% of 94.95% was achieved with nine filters by 5-fold validation, and 93.40% was achieved with seven filters by 10-fold validation. Models that were double confirmed by 5-fold or 10-fold validation demonstrated a similar trend of results. To reduce the number of computer calculations, subsequent verifications were conducted by 5-fold validation. To summarize, using the single-scale features together with nine filters yielded the best result among all models that are for the MI detection task. As the number of used scale features increased, the best average ACC gradually decreased. This may be caused by overfitting due to the excessive model strength, which is proven in Section 3.3.

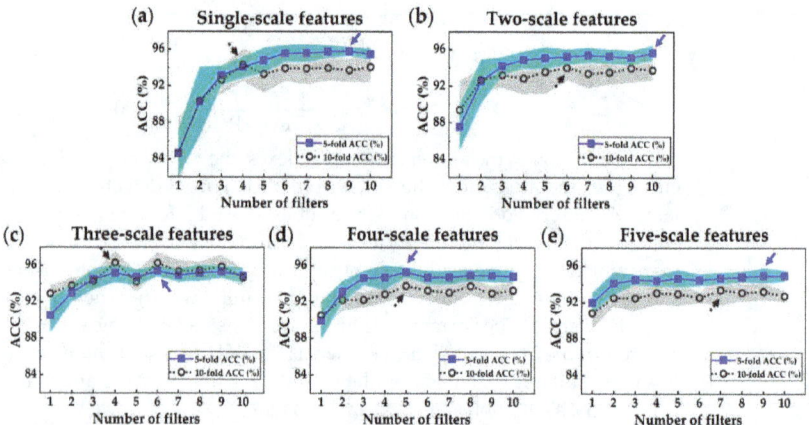

Figure 7. Accuracy trends of the proposed myocardial infarction (MI) detection models plotted in shaded error bar. Blue- and gray-shaded areas indicate the range of one standard deviation, and the best average accuracy under the same scale number is marked by an arrow: Accuracy of models using (**a**) single-scale features; (**b**) two-scale features; (**c**) three-scale features, (**d**) four-scale feature, and (**e**) five-scale features.

3.2. Accuracy of N-Net and MSN-Net for MI Locating in 6-Class Dataset

Figure 8 shows the ACC trend of the proposed MI locating models with different filter numbers and scale numbers. Similar to MI detection results, it can be observed that at low filter numbers, as the number of filters increased, the ACC increased significantly and gradually converge at about 60% when using larger filter numbers. Furthermore, when using a low filter number, the ACC increased as the number of the inputted signal scale increased. The increase was not as much as the increase in the filter number. By observing all the graphs in Figure 8, it can be seen that no matter how complex the network was, the ACC converged at about 60% with a slightly small deviation. Models that used single-scale features incorporating 15 filters achieved the best average ACC at about 60.49%. Two scales with 10 filters had an ACC of 61.19%, while three scales with 10 filters had an ACC of 61.52%. As for the four scales with nine filters, and five scales with 10 filters, an ACC of 61.82% and 60.87% were achieved, respectively. To summarize, using the four-scale features together with nine filters yielded the best result among all models for the MI locating task. As the number of used scale features increased, the best average ACC increased gradually. This indicates that multi-scale features can help the network in determining the location of MI, which was proved in Section 3.3.

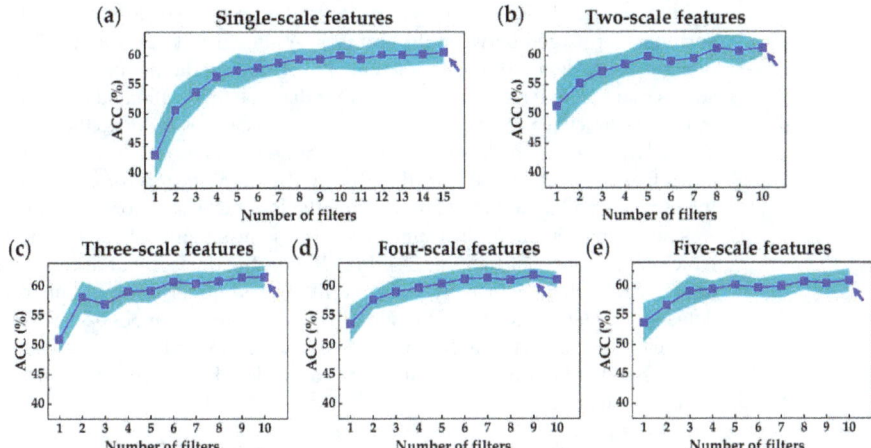

Figure 8. Accuracy trends of our proposed MI locating models plotted in shaded error bar. Blue- and gray-shaded areas indicate the range of one standard deviation and best average accuracy under the same scale number are marked by an arrow: Accuracy of models using (**a**) single-scale features, (**b**) two-scale features, (**c**) three-scale features, (**d**) four-scale features, and (**e**) five-scale features.

3.3. Verifying Training Effectiveness

To examine the occurrence of overfitting and overtraining, results were collected and analyzed. Figure 9 shows the box plot and significance of the accuracy of the proposed network. It can be observed in the left graph that using a model that was too robust for the current task will, on the contrary, lower the performance of the model from 95.76% to 94.95% ($p < 0.05$) due to overfitting.

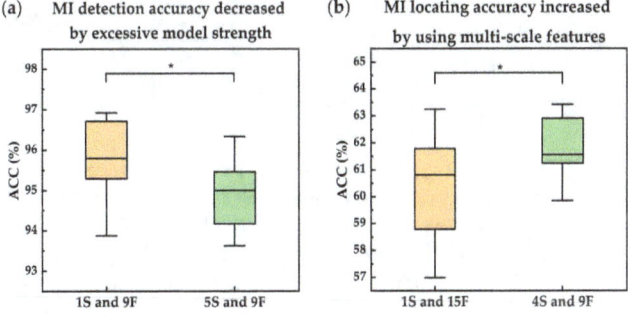

Figure 9. Box plot and significance of the accuracy of the proposed network where 1S indicates models using single-scale features, 9F indicates models using nine filters, and so on. (**a**) Evidence that supports accuracy decrease due to overfitting caused by excessive model strength. The average accuracy decreased from 95.76% to 94.95% ($p < 0.05$); (**b**) Evidence that supports using multi-scale features will increase MI locating accuracy. The average accuracy increased from 60.49% to 61.82% ($p < 0.05$).

Hence, the use N-Net instead of MSN-Net for MI detection tasks is preferred. On the other hand, using multi-scale features can increase the accuracy of the model from 60.49% to 61.82% ($p < 0.05$) during MI locating tasks. This can be observed in the graph on the right. It is, therefore, useful to use multi-scale features to enhance the performance of the model. In examining the occurrence of overtraining, one should normally be able to determine whether the validated loss was increased during training. However, in this case, both the training and validation curves had a similar trend. It can be found in Figure 10a that both trained and validated loss curves had a similar profile. The loss dropped exponentially and then converged between 0.1 and 0.15. A similar but opposite profile can be found in Figure 11b. Hence, the phenomenon of overtraining did not occur. A significant detail shows that the final trained loss was larger than the final validated loss, whereas the final trained accuracy was higher than validated accuracy. This is due to the fact that the model correctly predicted the label, but only with the confidence that was slightly above 50%. From Figure 10c, it can be seen that during the training stage of the MI locating model, the network had a harsh time optimizing the loss function. Moreover, the validated loss was not as low as that of the trained loss. The same situation can be found in Figure 10d, which points out that there was serious RIV in the dataset, but at least the model was not overtrained. Conclusively, both overfitting and underfitting did not occur in the MI detection model and MI locating model. This is because the models were simple or robust and selected the best one that lies between them. In addition, by examining both the training and validation curves, it can be concluded that overtraining and undertraining were not the case.

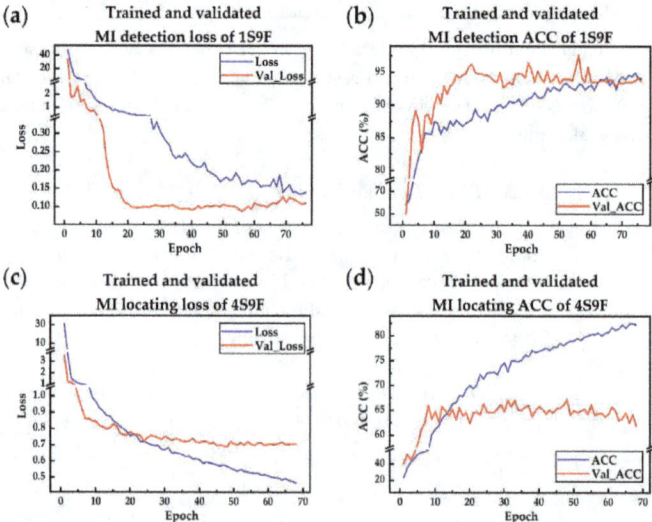

Figure 10. The performances of the proposed networks were recorded during each epoch where 1S indicates networks using single-scale features, 9F indicates networks using nine filters, and so on. (**a**) Trained and validated loss of MI detection model during each epoch; (**b**) Trained and validated the accuracy of MI detection model during each epoch; (**c**) Trained and validated loss of MI locating model during each epoch; (**d**) Trained and validated the accuracy of MI locating model during each epoch.

3.4. Comparing with State-of-the-Art

The MFB-CNN [26], ML-ResNet [31], and Shallow-CNN [28] were retrained under the validating scheme using the rearranged dataset. Fifteen (15) times subject-based 5-fold CV were executed on each model.

The ACC was recorded and used to generate the box plot and calculate the significant difference compared to the proposed model. Only MI detection performances were used to derive SEN, SPE, F1, and AUC, which is due to the fact that these parameters were internally designed to investigate the binary classification performance. By looking at the box plot in Figure 11a,b, it is clearly illustrated that the average accuracy was higher than the rest. By employing the U test, $p < 0.001$ was given in all previous works, which implies that the N-Net and MSN-Net outperformed in the MI detection task and MI locating task, respectively. As for clinical indexes shown in Figure 11c,f, the SEN was significantly higher than MFB-CNN ($p < 0.001$). It showed no difference compared to ML-ResNet and Shallow-CNN. The rest of the performances, including SPE, F1, and AUC, showed promising.

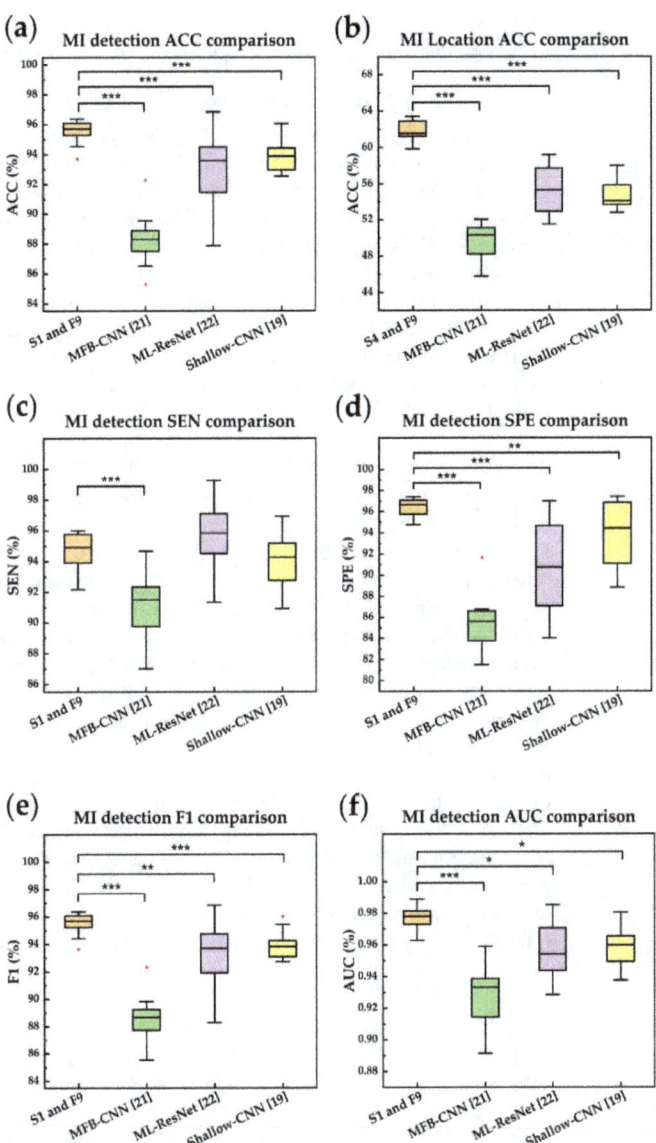

Figure 11. Comparison between the proposed model and literature where 1S indicates models using single-scale features, 9F indicates models using nine filters, and so on. Single star interprets $p < 0.05$, double star interprets $p < 0.01$, and triple star interprets $p < 0.001$. (**a**) MI detection accuracy comparison; (**b**) MI locating accuracy comparison; (**c**) MI detection sensitivity comparison; (**d**) MI detection specificity comparison; (**e**) MI detection F1-score comparison; and (**f**) MI detection area under the receiver operating characteristic curve comparison.

4. Discussion

N-Net for the MI detection task and an MSN-Net for MI locating task were developed. By carefully designing and validating the network robustness, the performance distribution of N-Net and MSN-Net under different parameters were recorded, and the best one was selected. The results showed that both MI detection and MI locating outperformed the current state-of-the-art. However, the results need to be justified. Furthermore, some detailed issues were not taken into consideration in this work. Additionally, to clarify some potential directions of on-going studies, all the above will be discussed in the following sections.

4.1. Verifying the Results of the Proposed N-Net and MSN-Net

In the developing phase of the model, by starting from the simplest network, incrementing the model complexity, and finding the best one among them, the issues of overfitting and underfitting were detected and thus, addressed. In other words, structures that were simpler with respect to the best one can refer to as underfitting and vice versa. Previous works straightforwardly start from a complex model, and as they are revalidated, excessive model strength exhibited a decrease in performances due to overfitting. As such, it is considered that overfitting has also occurred in the network design. Hence, the proposed networks exhibited better performance, and that the proposed networks were less overfitted compared to previous works. During the developing stage of the model, starting from the simplest model and proceeding with gradually increasing the model complexity should be considered.

4.2. Issues While Validating the Proposed Network Design

Though the structure of the proposed networks was carefully validated, some detailed issues need to be considered further. First of all, the validation scheme incremented the input signal scale and tested it on each network structure. To improve on this validation scheme, testing can be conducted independently on each kind of input scale. The best ones are then selected and incorporated into those structures and revalidate the new integrated network. Such an experimental scheme can validate which of the input scales contain more features that are more relevant to the task at that particular time, thus utilizing the multi-scale features more effectively. In addition, by comparing the proposed network structure, it can be seen that the design is quite similar to the Inception module [29] and the one that utilizes it on IMI detection [28]. Larger features were extracted by pooling the signals, whereas the latter extract larger features by expanding the kernel size. It remains a question as to which of the network structures would achieve better performance. Another interesting thing to consider is which network can complete one prediction faster. The Inception module [29] extracts larger features by using wider kernels which contain more parameters and will lengthen the time it takes in executing convolution. This directly affects the time required to complete a forward pass, which in turn directly affects the time it takes to give a prediction making it less suitable for real-time portable devices.

4.3. Limitations of the Proposed Experimental Scheme

One limitation of the proposed experimental scheme is that the class imbalance problem was addressed using under sampling, a data level method that is simple but makes it impossible to directly compare the results of the proposed model with the other existing works. This is due to the fact that a different dataset in this study was used. To overcome this drawback, a better data level approach can be utilized and can be found in [40] or consider using another category of approaches, called classifier level methods. These classifier level methods keep the dataset unchanged while adjusting the process of learning or training, as discussed in [50].

4.4. Potential for Future Study

This study can be extended by developing a computer-aided diagnosis system to lower the computational cost and achieve real-time functionality through a simple yet accurate model. In Section 4.2, examining which of the input scale will yield the best results can be explored. Further validation can be conducted to determine if the proposed design or the Inception modulus [29] is better at extracting multi-scale features. It is also significant to determine and compare the average time it takes for the network to complete a forward pass. Moreover, the geometric separability index [60] can be explored to examine the quality of features extracted by Inception modulus [29] and the proposed method and ultimately, implement the final model in portable devices.

5. Conclusions

In this research, data collection, preprocessing, and rearrangement were implemented for training the proposed N-Net and MSN-Net. To carefully verify the occurrence of underfitting and overfitting, two hyperparameters, the number of filters in the convolutional layer, and the number of inputting scales remained variable for tuning the best structure. Furthermore, 15 times patient-based 5-fold CV was run on each candidate model, and the best structures were obtained by comparing the average accuracy. As a result, the N-Net that used single-scale features together with nine filters (1S-9F) yielded a 95.76% average accuracy in MI detection, whereas the MSN-Net that used four-scale features together with nine filters yielded a 60.49% average accuracy in MI locating. By observing indexes including ACC, SEN, SPE, F1, and AUC, together with significant differences evaluated by the U test, both N-Net and MSN-Net outperformed the previous works considered in this study in MI detection and locating tasks, respectively, which indicates that previous works encountered the issue of overfitting. Furthermore, the MSN-Net outperformed the N-Net in MI locating tasks, which means that multi-scale features can improve the MI locating performance. More importantly, the proposed networks contained fewer parameters, which points out the potential and suitability in the applications of wearable devices. With all aforementioned promising results, several issues are yet to be explored, such as assessing the quality of the extracted features since it can provide a clearer idea of how to design the network. In future analysis, the testing model can be conducted independently on each kind of input scale. This contains more features relative to the particular time in each task, and then selecting these structures and incorporating them to revalidate the new integrated network to improve the validation. Another recommendation is to deploy the proposed models on portable devices to test their performance on a limited resource device further.

Author Contributions: Conceptualization, J.-Z.J., T.-R.G.; Data curation, J.-Z.J., H.-H.L.; Formal analysis, C.-M.K., T.-R.G., P.A.R.A., and S.-L.C.; Investigation, J.-Z.J., T.-R.G., and S.-L.C.; Methodology, J.-Z.J., T.-R.G., C.-A.C., and S.-L.C.; Project administration, T.-R.G. and S.-L.C.; Supervision, T.-R.G., P.A.R.A., C.-A.C., and S.-L.C.; Writing—original draft, J.-Z.J., T.-R.G.; P.A.R.A., C.-A.C., and S.-L.C.; Writing—review & editing, T.-R.G., P.A.R.A., C.-A.C., and S.-L.C. All authors have read and agreed to the published version of the manuscript.

Funding: This work was supported by the Ministry of Science and Technology (MOST), Taiwan, under grant numbers of MOST 108-2221-E-033-017-MY3, MOST-108-2628-E-033-001-MY3, MOST-108-2622-E-033-012-CC2, MOST-109-2622-E-131-001-CC3, MOST-109-2221-E-131-025, MOST 110-2823-8-033-002 Taoyuan Armed Forces General Hospital, Taiwan, under grant numbers of TYAFGH-D-110051. The National Chip Implementation Center, Taiwan.

Data Availability Statement: The PTB ECG database was downloaded from "https://physionet.org/content/ptbdb/1.0.0/, accessed on 9 March 2021", anyone can access the files, as long as they conform to the terms of the license at "https://physionet.org/content/ptbdb/view-license/1.0.0/, accessed on 9 March 2021".

Acknowledgments: The authors are grateful to the open-source neural network library provided by Keras and TensorFlow, so as the ECG database provided by PTB and PhysioNet.

Conflicts of Interest: The authors declare no conflict of interest.

References

1. Bax, J.J.; Baumgartner, H.; Ceconi, C. Third universal definition of myocardial infarction. *J. Am. Coll. Cardiol.* **2012**, *60*, 1581–1598.
2. Mozaffarian, D.; Benjamin, E.J. Executive summary: Heart disease and stroke statistics—2016 update: A report from the American Heart Association. *Circulation* **2016**, *133*, 447–454. [CrossRef] [PubMed]
3. Liu, B.; Liu, J. A novel electrocardiogram parameterization algorithm and its application in myocardial infarction detection. *Comput. Biol. Med.* **2015**, *61*, 178–184. [CrossRef] [PubMed]

4. Arif, M.; Malagore, I.A. Detection and localization of myocardial infarction using k-nearest neighbor classifier. *J. Med. Syst.* **2012**, *36*, 279–289. [CrossRef] [PubMed]
5. Wang, K.; Yang, G.; Huang, Y.; Yin, Y. Multi-scale differential feature for ECG biometrics with collective matrix factorization. *Pattern Recogn.* **2020**, *102*, 107211. [CrossRef]
6. Khan, M.A.; Kim, Y. Cardiac arrhythmia disease classification using LSTM deep learning approach. *CMC-Comput. Mater. Con.* **2021**, *67*, 427–443.
7. Zeng, W.; Yuan, J.; Yuan, C.; Wang, Q.; Liu, F.; Wang, Y. Classification of myocardial infarction based on hybrid feature extraction and artificial intelligence tools by adopting tunable-Q wavelet transform (TQWT), variational mode decomposition (VMD) and neural networks. *Artif. Intell. Med.* **2020**, *106*, 101848. [CrossRef] [PubMed]
8. Martis, R.J.; Acharya, U.R. Current methods in electrocardiogram characterization. *Comput. Biol. Med.* **2014**, *48*, 133–149. [CrossRef]
9. Chen, Z.; Brown, E.N. Characterizing nonlinear heartbeat dynamics within a point process framework. *IEEE Trans. Biomed. Eng.* **2010**, *57*, 1335–1347. [CrossRef]
10. Wang, L.-H.; Zhang, W.; Guan, M.-H.; Jiang, S.-Y.; Fan, M.-H.; Abu, P.A.R.; Chen, C.-A.; Chen, S.-L. A low-power high-data-transmission multi-lead ECG acquisition sensor system. *Sensors* **2019**, *19*, 4996. [CrossRef] [PubMed]
11. Chiang, W.-Y.; Ku, C.-H.; Chen, C.-A.; Wang, L.-Y.; Abu, P.A.R.; Rao, P.-Z.; Liu, C.-K.; Liao, C.-H.; Chen, S.-L. A power-efficient multiband planar USB dongle antenna for wireless sensor networks. *Sensors* **2019**, *19*, 2568. [CrossRef]
12. Dohare, A.K.; Kumar, V. Detection of myocardial infarction in 12 lead ECG using support vector machine. *Appl. Soft Comput.* **2018**, *64*, 138–147. [CrossRef]
13. Tripathy, R.K.; Dandapat, S. Detection of cardiac abnormalities from multilead ECG using multiscale phase alternation features. *J. Med. Syst.* **2016**, *40*, 143. [CrossRef] [PubMed]
14. Chang, P.-C.; Lin, J.-J.; Hsieh, J.-C.; Weng, J. Myocardial infarction classification with multi-lead ECG using hidden Markov models and Gaussian mixture models. *Appl. Soft Comput.* **2012**, *12*, 3165–3175. [CrossRef]
15. Sadhukhan, D.; Pal, S. Automated identification of myocardial infarction using harmonic phase distribution pattern of ECG data. *IEEE Trans. Instrum. Meas.* **2018**, *67*, 2303–2313. [CrossRef]
16. Xu, S.S.; Mak, M.W. Towards end-to-end ECG classification with raw signal extraction and deep neural networks. *IEEE J. Biomed. Health Inf.* **2018**, *23*, 1574–1584. [CrossRef]
17. Wang, Y.; Song, X.; Gong, G.; Li, N. A Multi-Scale Feature Extraction-Based Normalized Attention Neural Network for Image Denoising. *Electronics* **2021**, *10*, 319. [CrossRef]
18. Khan, M.A.; Kim, J. Toward Developing Efficient Conv-AE-Based Intrusion Detection System Using Heterogeneous Dataset. *Electronics* **2020**, *9*, 1771. [CrossRef]
19. Tor, H.T.; Ooi, C.P.; Lim-Ashworth, N.S.; Wei, J.K.E.; Jahmunah, V.; Oh, S.L.; Acharya, U.R.; Fung, S.S. Automated detection of conduct disorder and attention deficit hyperactivity disorder using decomposition and nonlinear techniques with EEG signals. *Comput. Meth. Prog. Bio.* **2021**, *200*, 105941. [CrossRef] [PubMed]
20. Ramesh, G.; Satyanarayana, D.; Sailaja, M. Composite feature vector based cardiac arrhythmia classification using convolutional neural networks. *J. Ambient. Intell. Human. Comput.* **2020**, 1–14. [CrossRef]
21. Hong, S.; Zhou, Y. Opportunities and challenges of deep learning methods for electrocardiogram data: A systematic review. *Comput. Biol. Med.* **2020**, *122*, 103801. [CrossRef] [PubMed]
22. Acharya, U.R.; Fujita, H. Application of deep convolutional neural network for automated detection of myocardial infarction using ECG signals. *Inf. Sci.* **2017**, *415*, 190–198. [CrossRef]
23. Detection of Myocardial Infarction Based on Novel Deep transfer Learning Methods for Urban Healthcare in Smart Cities. Available online: https://arxiv.org/abs/1906.09358 (accessed on 15 January 2021).
24. Very Deep Convolutional Networks for Large-Scale Image Recognition. Available online: https://arxiv.org/abs/1409.1556 (accessed on 15 January 2021).
25. Baloglu, U.B.; Talo, M. Classification of myocardial infarction with multi-lead ECG signals and deep CNN. *Pattern Recognit. Lett.* **2019**, *122*, 23–30. [CrossRef]
26. Liu, W.; Zhang, M. Real-time multilead convolutional neural network for myocardial infarction detection. *IEEE J. Biomed. Health Inf.* **2017**, *22*, 1431–1444. [CrossRef]
27. Lodhi, A.M.; Qureshi, A.N.; Sharif, U. A novel approach using voting from ECG leads to detect myocardial infarction. In Proceedings of the SAI Intelligent Systems Conference, Center for Healthcare Modeling & Informatics, Faculty of Information Technology, University of Central Punjab, Lahore, Pakistan, 8 November 2018.
28. Reasat, T.; Shahnaz, C. Detection of inferior myocardial infarction using shallow convolutional neural networks. In Proceedings of the 2017 IEEE Region 10 Humanitarian Technology Conference (R10-HTC), Dhaka, Bangladesh, Indonesia, 12 February 2018.
29. Szegedy, C.; Liu, W. Going deeper with convolutions. In Proceedings of the IEEE Conference on Computer Vision and Pattern Recognition, Boston, MA, USA, 7–12 June 2015.
30. Liu, W.; Huang, Q. Multiple-feature-branch convolutional neural network for myocardial infarction diagnosis using electrocardiogram. *Biomed. Signal Process* **2018**, *45*, 22–32. [CrossRef]
31. Han, C.; Shi, L. ML–ResNet: A novel network to detect and locate myocardial infarction using 12 leads ECG. *Comput. Methods Programs Biomed.* **2020**, *185*, 105138. [CrossRef] [PubMed]

32. He, K.; Zhang, X.; Ren, S. Deep residual learning for image recognition. In Proceedings of the IEEE Conference on Computer Vision and Pattern Recognition, Las Vegas, NV, USA, 27–30 June 2016.
33. Ioffe, S.; Szegedy, C. Batch normalization: Accelerating deep network training by reducing internal covariate shift. *IEEE ICMLA* **2015**, *37*, 448–456.
34. Hao, P.; Gao, X. Multi-branch fusion network for myocardial infarction screening from 12-lead ECG images. *Comput. Methods Programs Biomed.* **2020**, *184*, 105286. [CrossRef] [PubMed]
35. Huang, G.; Liu, Z.; Van Der Maaten, L. Densely connected convolutional networks. In Proceedings of the IEEE Conference on Computer Vision and Pattern Recognition, Honolulu, HI, USA, 21–26 July 2017.
36. Xi, Z.; Niu, Y.; Chen, J.; Kan, X.; Liu, H. Facial Expression Recognition of Industrial Internet of Things by Parallel Neural Networks Combining Texture Features. *IEEE Trans. Ind. Inf.* **2021**, *17*, 2784–2793.
37. Xie, J.; He, N.; Fang, L.; Ghamisi, P. Multiscale Densely-Connected Fusion Networks for Hyperspectral Images Classification. *IEEE Trans. Circ. Syst. Vid.* **2021**, *31*, 246–259. [CrossRef]
38. Schijvenaars, B.J.A.; van Herpen, G. Intraindividual variability in electrocardiograms. *J. Electrocardiol.* **2008**, *41*, 190–196. [CrossRef] [PubMed]
39. Simonson, E.; Brozek, J. Variability of the electrocardiogram in normal young men. *Am. Heart J.* **1949**, *38*, 407–422. [CrossRef]
40. Prati, R.C.; Batista, G.E. Data mining with imbalanced class distributions: Concepts and methods. In Proceedings of the Indian International Conference on Artificial Intelligence (IICAI), Tumkur, Karnataka, India, 16–18 December 2009.
41. Tetko, I.V.; Livingstone, D.J. Neural network studies. 1. Comparison of overfitting and overtraining. *J. Chem. Inf. Model.* **1995**, *35*, 826–833. [CrossRef]
42. Chicco, D. Ten quick tips for machine learning in computational biology. *BioData Min.* **2017**, *10*, 35. [CrossRef] [PubMed]
43. Kumar, A.; Vashishtha, G.; Gandhi, C.; Zhou, Y.; Glowacz, A.; Xiang, J. Novel Convolutional Neural Network (NCNN) for the Diagnosis of Bearing Defects in Rotary Machinery. *IEEE Trans. Instrum. Meas.* **2021**, *70*, 1–10. [CrossRef]
44. Piekarski, M.; Jaworek-Korjakowska, J.; Wawrzyniak, A.I.; Gorgon, M. Convolutional neural network architecture for beam instabilities identification in Synchrotron Radiation Systems as an anomaly detection problem. *Measurement* **2020**, *165*, 108116. [CrossRef]
45. Cui, Z.; Chen, W. Multi-scale convolutional neural networks for time series classification. *IEEE Access* **2016**, *8*, 109732–109746.
46. Jiang, G.; He, H. Multiscale convolutional neural networks for fault diagnosis of wind turbine gearbox. *IEEE Trans. Ind. Electron.* **2018**, *66*, 3196–3207. [CrossRef]
47. Bousseljot, R.; Kreiseler, D. Nutzung der EKG-Signaldatenbank CARDIODAT der PTB über das Internet. *Biomed. Tech.* **1995**, *40*, 317–318. [CrossRef]
48. Goldberger, A.L.; Amaral, L.A. PhysioBank, PhysioToolkit, and PhysioNet: Components of a new research resource for complex physiologic signals. *Circulation* **2000**, *101*, e215–e220. [CrossRef]
49. Thakor, N.V.; Webster, J.G. Estimation of QRS complex power spectra for design of a QRS filter. *IEEE Trans. Biomed. Eng.* **1984**, *BME-31*, 702–706. [CrossRef]
50. Christov, I.I. Real time electrocardiogram QRS detection using combined adaptive threshold. *Biomed. Eng. Online* **2004**, *3*, 28. [CrossRef]
51. Buda, M.; Maki, A. A systematic study of the class imbalance problem in convolutional neural networks. *Neural Netw.* **2018**, *106*, 249–259. [CrossRef] [PubMed]
52. Subject Cross Validation in Human Activity Recognition. Available online: https://arxiv.org/abs/1904.02666 (accessed on 15 January 2021).
53. Striving for Simplicity: The All Convolutional Net. Available online: https://arxiv.org/abs/1412.6806 (accessed on 15 January 2021).
54. Nair, V.; Hinton, G.E. Rectified linear units improve restricted boltzmann machines. In Proceedings of the International Conference on Machine Learning (ICML), Haifa, Israel, 21–24 June 2010.
55. Srivastava, N.; Hinton, G. Dropout: A simple way to prevent neural networks from overfitting. *J. Mach. Learn Res.* **2014**, *15*, 1929–1958.
56. A Method for Stochastic Optimization. Available online: https://arxiv.org/abs/1412.6980 (accessed on 15 January 2021).
57. Ketkar, N. Introduction to keras. In *Deep Learning with Python*, 2nd ed.; Springer: Mountain View, CA, USA, 2017; pp. 97–111.
58. Spackman, K.A. Signal detection theory: Valuable tools for evaluating inductive learning. In Proceedings of the Sixth International Workshop on Machine Learning, Ithaca, NY, USA, 26–27 June 1989.
59. Mann, H.B.; Whitney, D.R. On a test of whether one or two random variables is stochastically larger than the other. *Ann. Math. Stat.* **1947**, *18*, 50–60. [CrossRef]
60. Thornton, C. Separability is a learner's best friend. In Proceedings of the 4th Neural Computation and Psychology Workshop, London, UK, 9–11 April 1997.

Article

EEG-Based Sleep Staging Analysis with Functional Connectivity

Hui Huang [1,2], Jianhai Zhang [1,2], Li Zhu [1,2,*], Jiajia Tang [1,2], Guang Lin [1,2], Wanzeng Kong [2], Xu Lei [3,4] and Lei Zhu [5]

1. School of Computer Science and Technology, HangZhou Dianzi University, Hangzhou 310018, China; Hyoui7890@gmail.com (H.H.); jhzhang@hdu.edu.cn (J.Z.); hdutangjiajia@163.com (J.T.); lindandan@hdu.edu.cn (G.L.)
2. Key Laboratory of Brain Machine Collaborative Intelligence of Zhejiang Province, HangZhou Dianzi University, Hangzhou 310018, China; kongwanzeng@hdu.edu.cn
3. Sleep and NeuroImaging Center, Faculty of Psychology, Southwest University, Chongqing 400715, China; xlei@swu.edu.cn
4. Key Laboratory of Cognition and Personality, Ministry of Education, Chongqing 400715, China
5. School of Automation, HangZhou Dianzi University, Hangzhou 310018, China; zhulei@hdu.edu.cn
* Correspondence: zhuli@hdu.edu.cn

Citation: Huang, H.; Zhang, J.; Zhu, L.; Tang, J.; Lin, G.; Kong, W.; Lei, X.; Zhu, L. EEG-Based Sleep Staging Analysis with Functional Connectivity. *Sensors* **2021**, *21*, 1988. https://doi.org/10.3390/s21061988

Academic Editor: Yvonne Tran, Alan Jović

Received: 29 December 2020
Accepted: 8 March 2021
Published: 11 March 2021

Publisher's Note: MDPI stays neutral with regard to jurisdictional claims in published maps and institutional affiliations.

Copyright: © 2021 by the authors. Licensee MDPI, Basel, Switzerland. This article is an open access article distributed under the terms and conditions of the Creative Commons Attribution (CC BY) license (https://creativecommons.org/licenses/by/4.0/).

Abstract: Sleep staging is important in sleep research since it is the basis for sleep evaluation and disease diagnosis. Related works have acquired many desirable outcomes. However, most of current studies focus on time-domain or frequency-domain measures as classification features using single or very few channels, which only obtain the local features but ignore the global information exchanging between different brain regions. Meanwhile, brain functional connectivity is considered to be closely related to brain activity and can be used to study the interaction relationship between brain areas. To explore the electroencephalography (EEG)-based brain mechanisms of sleep stages through functional connectivity, especially from different frequency bands, we applied phase-locked value (PLV) to build the functional connectivity network and analyze the brain interaction during sleep stages for different frequency bands. Then, we performed the feature-level, decision-level and hybrid fusion methods to discuss the performance of different frequency bands for sleep stages. The results show that (1) PLV increases in the lower frequency band (delta and alpha bands) and vice versa during different stages of non-rapid eye movement (NREM); (2) alpha band shows a better discriminative ability for sleeping stages; (3) the classification accuracy of feature-level fusion (six frequency bands) reaches 96.91% and 96.14% for intra-subject and inter-subjects respectively, which outperforms decision-level and hybrid fusion methods.

Keywords: sleep staging; electroencephalography (EEG); brain functional connectivity; frequency band fusion; phase-locked value (PLV)

1. Introduction

With social pressure increasing in this high-speed development era, more and more people are faced with deep sleeping problems. The chronic lack of sleep or getting poor-quality sleep is a risk factor for cognitive disorders, mood disorders, and diseases such as high blood pressure, cardiovascular disease, diabetes, depression, and obesity [1,2]. Sleep staging is the basis of sleep quality evaluation, and plays an important role in the early diagnosis and intervention of sleep disorders. In 1968, R&K [3] identified sleep staging into awake, rapid eye movement (REM) and non-rapid eye movement (NREM) stages, and NREM is further subdivided into four stages: S1, S2, S3, and S4. Since S3 and S4 are similar in many aspects, American Academy of Sleep Medicine (AASM) [4] revised the R&K rules and used N1, N2, N3 to represent different sub-stages for NREM stage, combining both S3 and S4 into N3 stage.

In practice, clinical sleep staging is still based on visual inspection by sleep experts for decades according to the duration and proportion of special brain waves. Such waves during sleep include delta waves, alpha waves, sleep spindle waves and K-complex waves. Delta waves are slow waves, mainly appearing in N2 and N3 stages with different proportions. The frequency range of the alpha wave (8–13 Hz) and sleep spindle wave (12.5–15.5 Hz) is partially overlapping. Alpha waves generally appears in the REM stage. Both frequency band range and the occurring brain area of sleep spindle waves are different between N2 and N3 stage. The k-complex waves are the combination of apical waves and sleep spindle waves. The types and spatial distributions of these waves are different during sleep stages, see Table 1 for more details. Therefore, frequency bands should be considered in sleep staging analysis.

Table 1. Types and spatial distributions of brain waves during stages of sleep, '/' means no appearance.

	N1/S1	N2/S2	N3 S3	N3 S4	REM
delta waves	/	<20%	25~50% 0.75~3 Hz	>50%	/
alpha waves	<50%	/	/	/	mainly in Occipital lobe
sleep spindle waves	/	12.5~15.5 Hz, occur in central, bilateral frontal, parietal, forehead, temporal lobes	about 12 Hz gradually reduce, mainly in frontal lobe	6–10 Hz, gradually disappear, mainly in frontal lobe	/
K-complex waves	/	occur mainly in frontal lobe	evoked by external stimuli	evoked by strong stimuli	/

However, such manual sleep staging judgment by sleep experts easily brings problems of low efficiency, long time consuming, and subjective errors. Chapotot et al. [5] show that the average same judgment accuracy between two experts in labeling sleep-wake stage scores is only about 83%. Therefore, a more accurate and objective method for sleep staging is very required. Moreover, sleep is a complex and dynamic process, so that humans always hope to have a better understand of the brain mechanisms of sleep for human health. With the help of the signal recording technology, several sleep physiological signals acquisition methods are existed. For instance, polysomnography is a powerful tool for sleep signal acquisition including electroencephalography (EEG), electromyography (EMG), functional magnetic resonance imaging (fMRI), and electrooculography (EOG). Herein, EEG has advantages of low cost, high temporal resolution and easy operation which result in the wide application in sleep stages research [6,7]. Afterwards, sleep-related researchers take use of the recorded signals to conduct sleep staging research.

For computational sleep staging research, the main objective of this area is to find out discriminative features and good-performing classification strategies. Currently, EEG-based sleep staging research has brought out many desirable results such as most of the features are extracted from the single channel and end-to-end classifier models [8–14]. For instance, Ahmed et al. [15] designed a 34-layer deep residual neural network to classify the raw single-channel EEG sleep staging data and obtained the improved accuracy of 6.3%. This end-to-end classifier usually has a good classification performance, but it lacks the exploration of sleep mechanisms. On the other hand, Thiago et al. [16] proposed a feature extraction method based on wavelet domain, which increases the classification performance nearly 25% compared to the temporal and frequency domains; Zhang et al. [17] proposed a feature selection method based on metric learning to find out the optimal features. However, existing feature extraction methods (temporal, frequency and temporal-frequency domains) are difficult to explore the sleep staging information from a global level [18–20] since the calculation is performed on single-channel separately.

[21,22] also pointed out that the amount of information obtained through a single channel does not fully characterize the changes in brain activity during sleep.

Brain functional network is a relative new measurement to characterize the information exchanging between brain region through calculating the temporal correlation or coherence between brain areas. It is verified that each sleep stage is associated with a specific functional connectivity pattern in fMRI studies [23–25]. EEG-based brain functional connectivity has been employed in sleep research [26–28] to distinguish the sleep disease and health groups. We would use functional connectivity to explore the synchronization mechanisms between different brain regions and the classification accuracy for sleep staging.

In summary, in addition to pursuing the higher classification accuracy, we also want to, within different frequency bands, explore the information exchanging between brain areas for sleep staging. Specifically, this paper analyzed the sleep stage with single-band functional connectivity and then used the bi-serial correlation coefficient method to evaluate the frequency bands. Based on the evaluation results, features from frequency band are fused at the feature-level, decision-level and hybrid-level, respectively. Furthermore, we also investigated the mutual influence between frequency bands to identify the sleep stages. The remaining parts of this paper are organized as follows. Section 2 describes the materials and our method. Section 3 indicates all results. Section 4 and 5 provides the discussions and summarizes the future work, respectively.

2. Materials and Methods

2.1. Dataset Description

The data analyzed in this manuscript is from the public CAP Sleep Database [29,30]. The database was built to facilitate sleep research that includes 108 polysomnographic recordings provided by the Sleep Disorders Center of the Ospedale Maggiore of Parma, Italy. There are 16 healthy subjects without any neurological disorders and drug problems. The number of EEG channels varies from 3 to 12 and the data with the number of channels as more as possible are needed for functional brain connectivity calculation, therefore, we selected the subjects (namely n3, n5, n10, n11 respectively) who were recorded with 12 EEG channels, aging between 23 and 35 (mean 30.25) years old. According to the International 10–20 System, the placements of the bipolar electrodes were Fp2-F4, F4-C4, C4-P4, P4-O2, F8-T4, T4-T6, Fp1-F3, F3-C3, C3-P3, P3-O1, F7-T3, and T3-T5, shown in Figure 1. The sampling rate is set at 512 Hz. For each subject, the continuous recorded sleep EEG lasted about 9 h (from 10:30 p.m. to 7:30 a.m.).

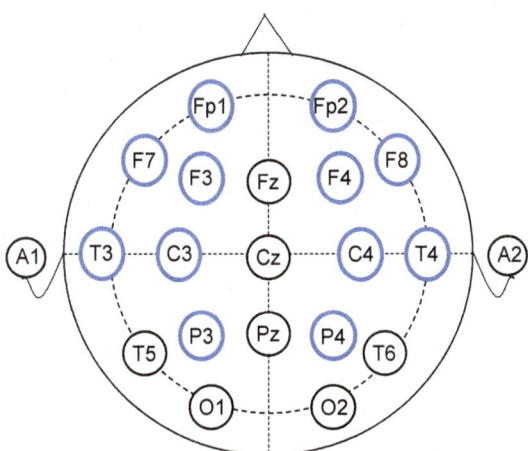

Figure 1. The layouts of EEG electrodes. The electrodes used in this study are labeled in blue circles.

The experts labeled sleep stages based on the standard rules by R&K every 30 s and sleep is a cyclical process, the duration of a cycle is about 90 to 110 min, humans generally experience 4 to 5 sleep cycles per night [3]. Since the N1 accounts for 5–10% or less of the total sleep duration (only lasts about 1–7 min) [31], we selected the other three sleep stages including the REM and N2, N3 during non-REM.

2.2. Framework of Our Method

In this study, we first perform data preprocessing, then calculated the brain functional connectivity for different frequency bands to compare the characteristics of brain mechanism during sleep stages. Moreover, bi-serial correlation coefficient was adopted to evaluate brain connectivity features across different frequency bands. Then, we used three fusion strategies for frequency band fusion to classify the sleep stages based on the findings in the frequency band evaluation results. The framework of our method was depicted in Figure 2.

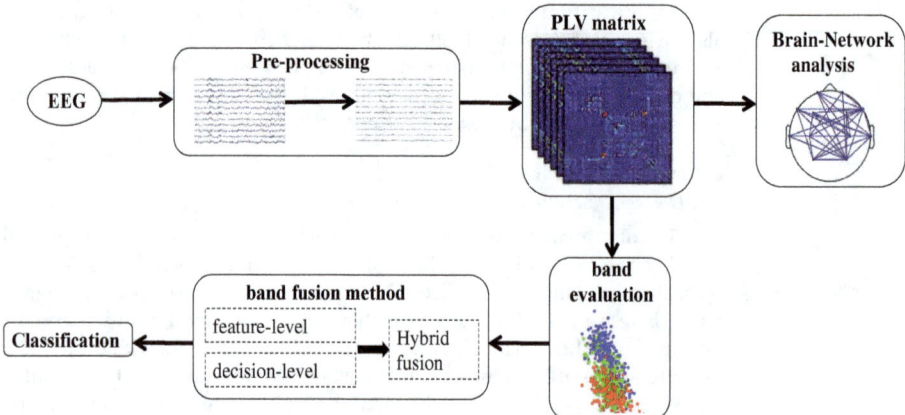

Figure 2. The flow diagram of the proposed method.

2.2.1. Data Preprocessing

It is difficult to draw clear boundaries between different sleep stages because the stage usually changes gradually and continuously. To confirm the sampling with the exact sleeping stage label, we delete the following three kinds of data that:

- belonging to the same stage, but duration is too short (such as only 2 to 3 min).
- the unusual waking duration (tens of seconds) and its before and after 30 s duration during a certain sleep stage.
- the beginning 30 s and the last 30 s of a certain sleep stage.

After that, we segmented the EEG into 30 s epochs as analyzed samples without overlapping. Note: for sleep staging, the adopted 30 s epoch is derived from the R&K and AASM rules [32], and related works also revealed that 30 s length of epoch is viable to characterize intrinsic brain activity [33,34]. The total number of samples with sleep staging labels REM, N2 and N3 is 801, 900, and 1001, respectively. Herein, the number of samples from subjects n3, n5, n10, n11 is 651, 639, 559 and 853, respectively.

For data preprocessing, we adopted common average reference (CAR) [35] to minimize the uncorrelated noise among channels, then we removed the artifacts with independent component analysis (ICA) [36] and Adjust plugin which is realized in EEGLAB [37] followed by the band-pass filtering with a passband from 0.5 to 40 Hz. Furthermore, we filtered the denoised EEG into six frequency bands: delta (0.5–4 Hz), theta (4–8 Hz), alpha (8–13 Hz), beta1 (13–22 Hz), beta2 (22–30 Hz), and gamma (30–40 Hz).

2.2.2. Phase-Locked Value

We estimated brain functional connectivity with phase-locked value (PLV). The PLV [38] was proposed to measure the phase synchronization between two signals which is only sensitive to phase but not to amplitude. Compared with other synchronization measures, PLV is simple to operate and can maintain the same information level as other more complex indicators [39]. Here, the PLV is used to analyze the phase synchronization between two channels of EEG in specific frequency, defined as follow:

$$PLV_n = \frac{1}{N} | \sum_{k=1}^{N} e^{i(\phi(t,k) - \psi(t,k))} | \tag{1}$$

where N represent the number of epochs, $\phi(t,k)$ and $\psi(t,k)$ indicates the phase values of channel ϕ and ψ for the epoch n at the time t. Specifically, we used HERMES toolbox [40] to obtain PLV matrices. In our case, 12 channels of EEG were used, which resulted in 12 × 12 symmetric matrix for each epoch. Each entry in matrix stood for synchronization of a pair of channels. This synchronization calculation was done for six frequency bands of each subject. The one-way ANOVA was used to assess differences between sleep stages or frequency bands of the PLV for REM, N2 and N3 stages. The observed returning values of ANOVA is p-value and lower p-value means more significant difference.

In addition, we also compared the brain network analysis between sleep stages with PLV matrices. We averaged the PLV matrix for each sleep stage and constructed the brain networks based on a threshold. The threshold is selected from the maximum value at which no isolated points appearing in the network.

2.2.3. Band Evaluation

We use bi-serial correlation coefficient as an indicator to measure the ability of features to classify classes. The bi-serial correlation coefficient, r^2, is a measurement to evaluate the performance of one feature in distinguishing various classes. For a two-classes classification scenario (class 1, 2), the bi-serial correlation coefficient is defined as:

$$r_X^2 = [\frac{\sqrt{N^+ \times N^-} \times [mean(X^+) - mean(X^-)]}{(N^+ \times N^-) \times std(X^+ \cup X^-)}]^2 \tag{2}$$

where X^+ and X^- represent all samples of class 1 and class 2, respectively. The N^+ and N^- indicate the number of two class samples [41]. The r^2 is ranging from 0 to 1 and its bigger value means more discriminate between the two classes. We calculated the bi-serial correlation coefficient between every two sleep stages (REM and N2, REM and N3, and N2 and N3) for PLV feature matrices. In total, we sorted the 3 × 66 × 6 (sleep stages × PLV × frequency bands) r^2 values to evaluate the features across different frequency bands. We also defined the discriminative ratio as setting a threshold t to represent the number of features, calculating the sum of the first sorted t r^2 between every two sleep stages and then obtaining the ratio of each frequency band. In our case, t is set to 36.

2.2.4. Classifier

We adopted support vector machine (SVM) with the Gaussian kernel function, which is implemented in the LIBSVM library [42]. The way to achieve multi-class classification is used the One-against-one strategy. We evaluated classification performance in terms of accuracy for single frequency band and the three level strategies fusion between frequency bands. The 75% samples were used for model training and the remaining 25% samples were used as testing data.

2.2.5. Frequency Band Fusion Strategy

Based on the evaluation of brain functional connectivity across different frequency bands, we used three band fusion strategies to integration of multiple information sources for classification. The multiple information sources refer to the brain functional connectivity features of different frequency bands and the three fusion strategies are feature-level fusion, decision-level fusion, and hybrid-level fusion. The graphical description of feature-level and decision-level fusion strategies are shown in Figure 3.

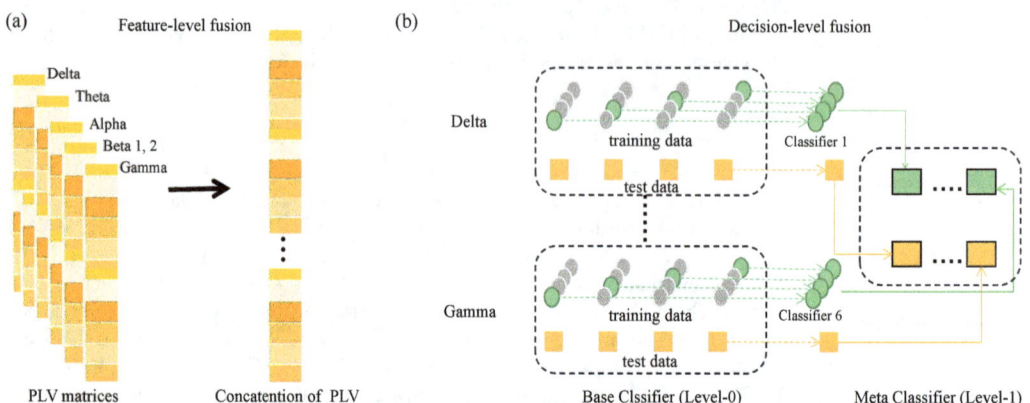

Figure 3. Schematic diagram of fusion strategy. (**a**) indicates the feature-level fusion and (**b**) is the decision-level fusion using stacking.

For feature-level fusion, we concatenated the PLV features of six frequency bands before feeding into classifier; For decision fusion using stacking [43], we constructed individual classifiers for PLV features of a single frequency band separately, namely base classifier and then a meta classifier learns to use the predictions of each base classifier to obtain a target decision result. For hybrid fusion, we combined feature-level and decision-level fusions, which includes two steps: first constructing individual classifiers for specific groups of selected two frequency bands based on the band evaluation result and then conducting ensemble classifier of these individual classifiers. Hereinafter, 'C', 'E' and 'E(C)' represent the classification result obtained by using the feature after feature-level fusion, decision-level fusion and hybrid fusion strategy, respectively.

3. Results

3.1. PLV Values between Six Frequency Bands for Different Sleep Stages

The comparisons on average PLV between six frequency bands for three sleep stages are in Figure 4. In some low frequency bands, delta and alpha bands, the PLV values are increased from N2 to N3 sleep stages while in high frequency bands, beta2 and gamma bands, the PLV values are decreased. Moreover, compared with N2 sleep stage, the PLV value for N3 is significantly bigger (with $p < 0.001$) in delta and alpha bands but smaller in beta 2 and gamma bands. Generally, the PLV values are significantly decreased as the frequency bands increase, from delta to gamma bands for REM, N2 and N3 sleep stages. Only the PLV value of alpha is significantly bigger than theta band, shown in Figure 5. Figure 6 displays the differences between sleep stages for brain network analysis from which the spatial distributions of PLV differences can be observed.

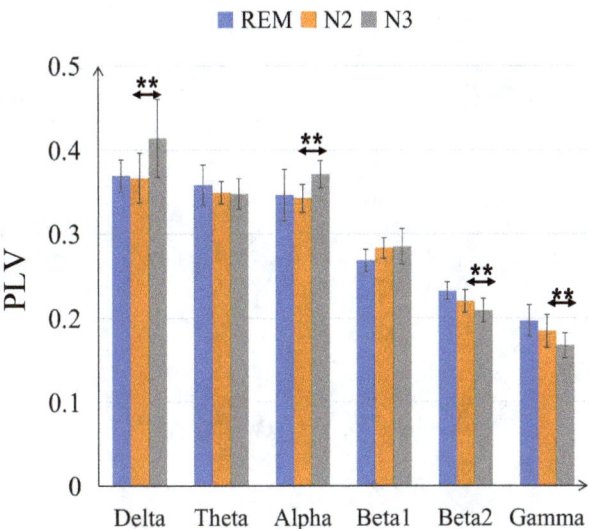

Figure 4. Comparisons of the average PLV values between six frequency bands for three sleep stages. The double-asterisk '**' indicates that there is a significant difference of $p < 0.001$ by ANOVA test.

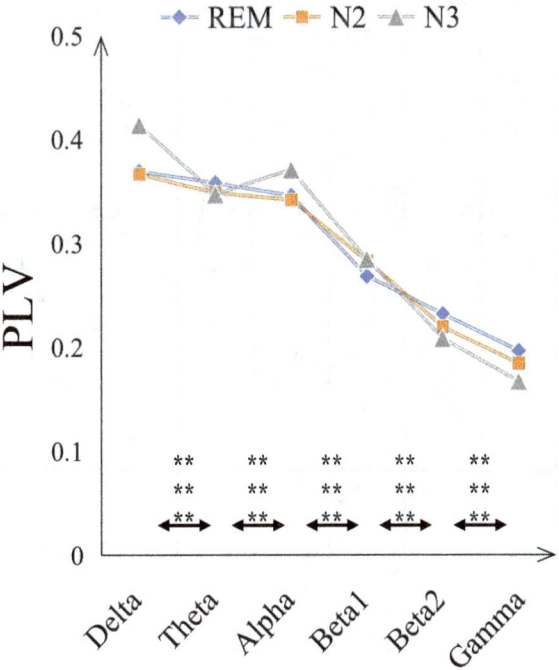

Figure 5. The averaged PLV value of three sleep stages in six frequency bands to observe the PLV distribution in different frequency bands. The double-asterisk '**' indicates that there is a significant difference of $p < 0.001$ by ANOVA test and three rows represent the significant difference result between two frequency bands for 'REM and N2', 'REM and N3' and 'REM and N2' respectively.

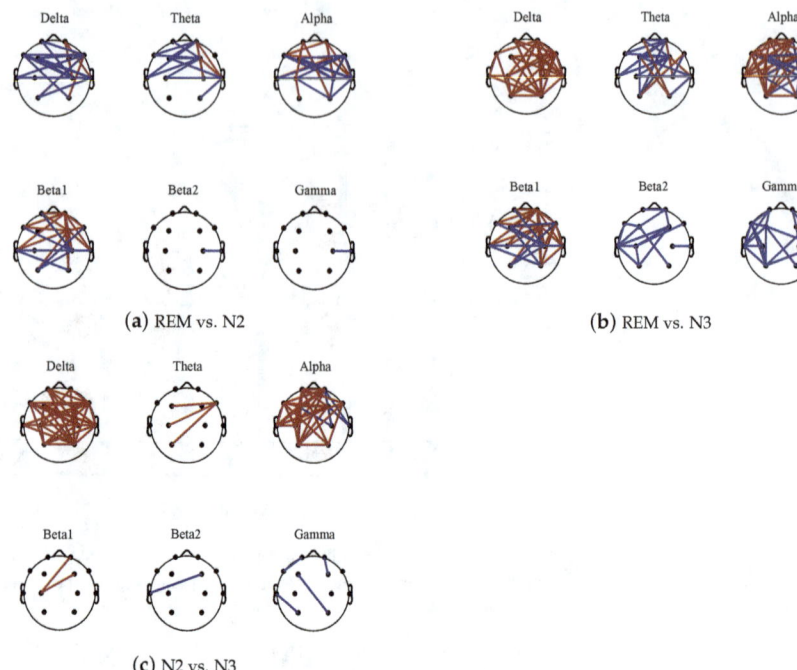

Figure 6. The brain network difference topoplot between REM and N2 (shown in (**a**)), REM and N3 (shown in (**b**)) and N2 and N3 (shown in (**c**)) for different frequency bands. The red line represents the increase area, and the blue line indicates the decrease area.

3.2. Evaluation of Different Frequency Bands

Figure 7 displays the percentage of corresponding frequency bands within the first 95 and 140 sorted r^2 values cases. Alpha band shows the largest percentage in both cases, accounting for 49.74% and 45.00% and followed by beta1, accounting for 30.79% and 27.14%, respectively. The smallest percentage is beta2 band with only 0.26% and 1.79%. The 2-D figure of PLV feature visualization for each frequency band is shown in Figure 8. The 'Feature 1' and 'Feature2' are the features with first two largest $\overline{r^2}$ and the $\overline{r^2}$ is averaged through the three r^2 obtained between each two classes. We can see that the PLV features extracted from alpha band shows a better discriminate ability. Figure 9 reveals the discriminative ratio of frequency bands for sleep staging. Alpha band also shows the higher ratio than other bands which is consistent with the Figure 7 as well as the following Table 2. The discriminative ratios are different for a certain frequency band (such as delta and beta1 bands) in distinguishing different paired sleep stages. For instance, the ratio is not high in distinguishing REM and N2, REM and N3 while it reaches 29.06% in distinguishing N2 and N3.

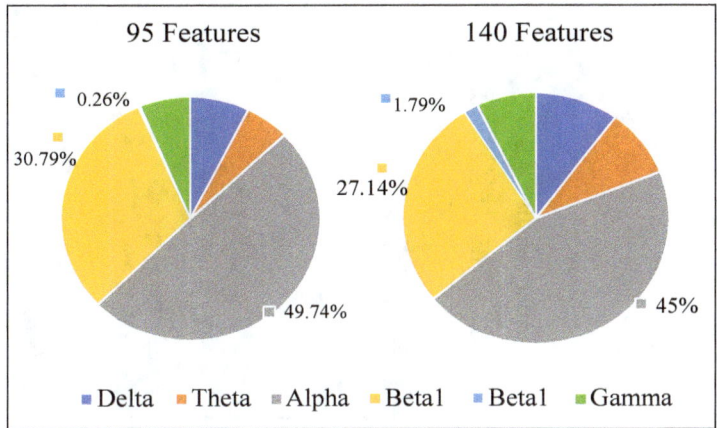

Figure 7. Percentage (%) of PLV features from different frequency bands in the features with first 95 and 140 sorted r^2 values

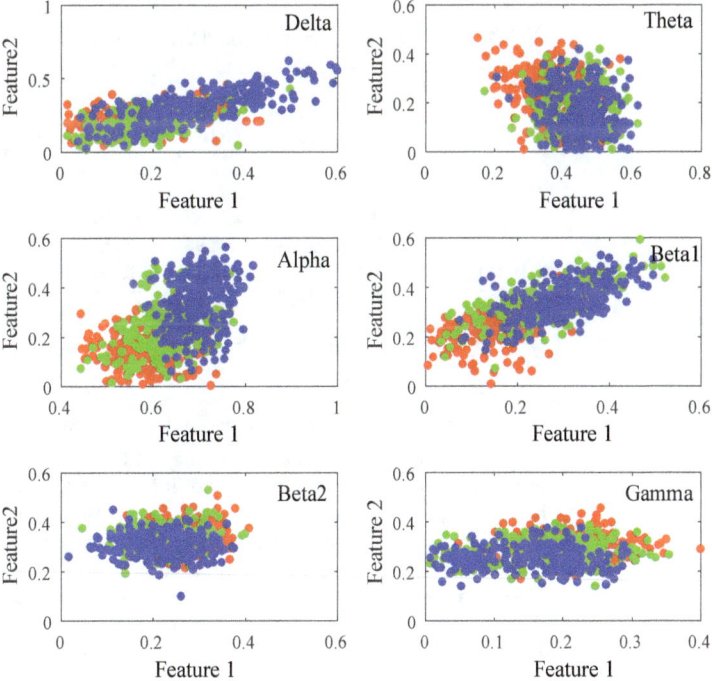

Figure 8. 2-D figure of PLV feature visualization for each frequency band. The Feature 1 and Feature 2 are the selected features with the first two largest $\overline{r^2}$ values, respectively. The dots represent different sleep stages (red:REM, green:N2, blue:N3).

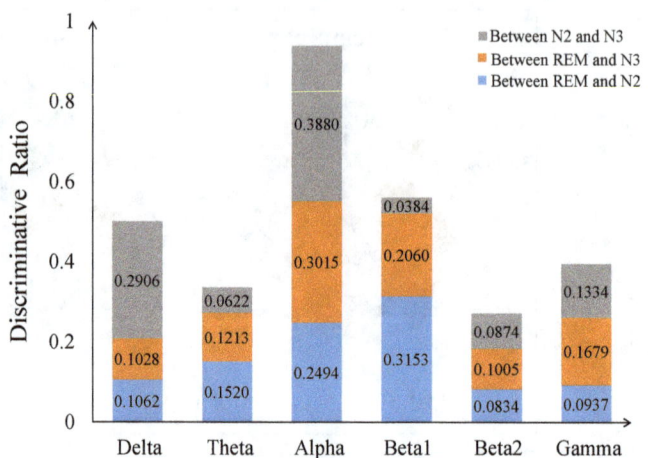

Figure 9. The discriminative ratio of per frequency band for distinguish two sleep stages (blue: REM and N2, orange: REM and N3, grey: N2 and N3).

Table 2. Classification accuracy (%) of PLV value with single-band. For inter-subject case, the true positive rate of each class is also given.

Band	n3	n5	n10	n11	Inter-Subjects			
					REM	N2	N3	ACC
delta	85.80	89.31	89.21	84.98	84.86	87.87	87.65	86.86
theta	82.10	85.53	74.82	82.16	86.24	81.87	87.24	84.86
alpha	88.27	86.79	94.96	88.73	93.58	88.70	90.53	90.86
beta1	76.54	74.74	92.81	82.63	91.74	76.57	81.07	82.86
beta2	85.80	79.25	87.05	78.87	81.19	80.75	86.01	82.71
gamma	82.72	75.47	76.98	85.92	85.78	79.50	85.19	83.43

3.3. Classification

3.3.1. Classification Performance of Single-Band Feature

The average classification accuracy of PLV with single-band for intra-subject and inter-subject are shown in Table 2. For intra-subject case, alpha band outperforms other bands except for subject n5 and the best classification accuracy reaches 94.96% followed by beta1 band 92.81% (from subject n10). For inter-subject case, alpha band also outperforms other bands. The best classification accuracy reaches 90.86% followed by delta 86.86%; There is a special result that the accuracy of beta1 reaches 92.81% from subject n10, while the accuracy is only 82.86% in inter-subject case. The true positive rates for N2 and N3 are 76.57% and 81.07%, respectively and they are smaller than other bands.

3.3.2. Classification Performance for Bands Fusion

Based on the results of different frequency bands evaluation (Section 3.2), we explored the three band fusion strategies for sleep staging. The two, three and four frequency bands are selected according to the r^2 values, respectively. Specifically, we combined 'delta and beta1', 'theta and gamma' and 'alpha and beta2' since the delta band is complementary to beta1, the beta2 matches the best discriminative alpha, and theta and gamma are combined to make the three splicing results all good. For three frequency bands fusion case, the alpha, beta1 and delta frequency bands are selected according to Figures 7 and 9 and further gamma frequency band is added to the four frequency bands fusion case. Finally, six frequency bands are used in feature-level, decision-level and hybrid-level fusions.

The classification performance of feature-level is better than decision-level and hybrid-level. Among the results of the fusion of six frequency bands, the best single subject is n3, with the accuracy rate of 96.91%, and the accuracy of inter-subjects is 96.14%. Note, compared with intra-subject and inter-subject cases, we can infer that there are not so big individual differences in sleep staging. The Table 3 shows detailed classification result.

Table 3. Classification accuracy (%) of PLV value with band fusion strategies. For inter-subject case, the true positive rate of each class is given.

		n3	n5	n10	n11	Inter-Subjects			
						REM	N2	N3	ACC
Two bands	C(delta+beta1)	87.65	93.08	91.37	91.08	92.20	88.70	88.48	89.71
	C(theta+gamma)	88.27	88.68	89.93	88.73	93.58	87.03	93.42	91.29
	C(alpha+beta2)	91.36	88.68	95.37	88.26	94.04	88.70	91.77	91.43
Three bands	C(alpha+beta1+delta)	94.41	93.08	92.81	94.37	93.12	92.05	95.06	93.43
	E(alpha+beta1+delta)	91.30	91.19	94.96	92.49	96.33	92.89	95.88	93.43
Four bands	C(alpha+beta1+delta+gamma)	96.89	94.34	92.81	94.37	94.95	94.14	95.47	94.86
	E(alpha+beta1+delta+gamma)	93.79	91.19	94.96	93.90	96.33	92.89	95.88	95.00
Six bands	Concatenation	**96.91**	95.60	94.24	96.71	96.33	94.98	97.12	**96.14**
	Ensemble	95.06	92.45	93.53	93.90	96.33	93.72	95.88	95.29
	E(C)	93.21	93.08	94.96	93.90	95.87	94.98	95.47	95.43

4. Discussion

4.1. The Dominant Role of Alpha Band in Sleep Staging

The assessment of sleep staging is based on specific EEG frequencies and on the recognition of corresponding sleep-related EEG patterns [44]. For instance, the amount of alpha decreases and an increase of EEG in alpha range can be found during REM sleep while the alpha frequency is 1 to 2 Hz lower compared with wakefulness during non-REM sleep [45,46]. More Other related works also revealed that alpha band shows important role in sleep staging. Dkhil et al. [47] proposed the importance of alpha band in the evaluation of drowsiness. Knaut et al. [48] finds the changes in alpha oscillations reflect different brain states associated with different levels of wakefulness and thalamic activity. Specifically, in our study, alpha band shows dominant role in sleep staging since the PLV values are decreased as the frequency band increased, but alpha band is higher than theta band (see Figure 5); in the frequency band evaluation section (Section 3.2), alpha band shows higher discriminative ratio revealed by bi-serial correlation and 2-D feature topoplot also shows alpha band has the less overlapping area than other bands; for classification results (see Section 3.3), alpha band outperforms other bands in both intra-subject (except for subject n5) and inter-subject cases.

4.2. Inconsistency between Frequency Band Evaluation and the Classification Accuracy of Beta1 Band

EEG beta activity represents a marker of cortical arousal [49]. The conventional power spectrum shows a significant increase of EEG in beta band of patients with primary insomnia during N2 stage [50] while a decrease of patients with idiopathic REM sleep behavior disorder during phasic REM [51] compared with sleep health people. In our study, we observed the inconsistency between frequency band evaluation and the classification accuracy of EEG functional connectivity pattern in beta1 frequency band. In frequency band evaluation, the number of selected features of beta1 band is only less than alpha band (see Figure 7) and discriminative ratios of beta1 between 'REM and N2' and 'REM and N3' are very high, but the classification accuracy is generally low. We can also observe that the discriminative ratios of beta1 between 'N2 and N3' is lowest in all bands (see Figure 9) and the true positive rate of the N2 and N3 stages is lower than other frequency bands (see Table 2). This may explain the inconsistency of the beta1 frequency band between band evaluation and classification accuracy. The special result from subject n10 shows achieved a high accuracy rate of 92.81% in beta1, while only 74.74–82.86% for other cases. Tracking the original data of subject n10, we found that there is no S3 stage which results in the deceasing decision error between N2 and N3.

4.3. Comparisons with Start-of-Arts Works

We compared our method with the start-of-arts in sleep staging classification research, shown in Table 4. Sors et al. [52] designed an end-to-end convolutional neural network(CNN) to classify the sleep stages using the raw signals and obtained the accuracy of 90.74%. Sharma et al. [53] used classical three time-domain features: log energy, signal fractal dimension, and signal sample entropy and multi-class SVM as the classifier and the ACC(N1 U N2, N3, REM) is 81.13%. Lajnef et al. [54] extracted 102 features covering the time-domain, frequency-domain and non-linear features. The accuracy of three classifications (REM, N2, N3) is 87.06% obtained by decision-tree-based multi-SVM; Michielli et al. [55] also combined feature extraction and deep learning and the ACC(REM U N1, N2, N3) is 90.6%. We also used their method on the CAP data set. Our method shows a better accuracy result compared with these related works. Hopefully, this method would be applied for automatic sleep staging and medical intervention of sleep disorders. For instance, in chronic insomnia, using transcranial direct current stimulation in N2 can increase the duration of N3 and sleep efficiency and the probability of transition from N2 to N3 [56] which requires more accurate separation of N2 and N3.

Table 4. Comparison of state-of-the-art studies.

Authors	Features	Database	Classifier	Results(%)			
				REM (+N1)	N2 (+N1)	N3	ACC
Sors et al. [52] 2018	raw signal samples	SSH-1	CNN	90.54	85.8	92.48	90.74
Sharma et al. [53] 2018	time-domain	Sleep-EDF	Multi-class SVM	71.81	82.57	84.48	81.13
		CAP	Multi-class SVM	84.40	84.10	85.60	84.71
Lajnef et al. [54] 2015	frequency-domain	DyCog Lab'PSD records	D-SVM	89.13	81.63	87.88	87.06
		CAP	Multi-class SVM	87.61	82.85	90.95	87.14
Michielli et al. [55] 2019	statistical features and spectral features	Sleep-EDF	LSTM-RNN	91.59	89.55	92.09	90.60
		CAP	Multi-class SVM	96.79	86.61	93.42	92.14
Proposed method	PLV	CAP	Multi-class SVM	96.33	94.98	97.12	**96.14**

5. Conclusions

In this paper, we proposed a method to classify sleep stages with brain functional connectivity. We analyzed the characteristics of brain network during different sleep stages and explored the influences of frequency bands for sleep staging classification. After applying a simple machine learning method (multi-class SVM) and a series of analysis, we obtained that:

1. For brain functional connectivity values, the average PLV increases in the delta and alpha band, while decreases in the high frequency beta2 and gamma band during non-REM periods;
2. Different frequency bands have different discriminative abilities for distinguishing between sleep stages. Herein, alpha band show the dominant role in sleeping stage. Beta1 band shows good performance for classifying 'REM and N2' and 'REM and N3' but higher classification error rate for 'N2 and N3'.
3. The classification performance of PLV is better than state-of-art studies. The best accuracy is 96.91% and 96.14% for intra-subject and inter-subject cases, respectively. We also replicated time-domain, frequency-domain and non-linear features on the data set used in our paper and results show the better performance of PLV.

In the future, we plan to develop on online brain computer interface for automatic sleep staging monitoring combined with this approach and graph convolution network.

Author Contributions: Conceptualization, L.Z. (Li Zhu); methodology, H. H., L.Z. (Li Zhu), J. Z.; programming, H. H., J.T, G. L.; writing, L.Z. (Li Zhu), H. H.; revising and writing-editing, L.Z. (Li Zhu), H.H., W. K., X. L., L.Z. (Lei Zhu); visualization, H.H., L.Z. (Lei Zhu); founding acquisition, L.Z. (Lei Zhu), W. K. All authors have read and agreed to the published version of the manuscript.

Funding: The work was supported by the National Natural Science Foundation of China (No.61633010) and Key Research and Development Project of Zhejiang Province (2020C04009, 2018C04012) and National Key Research & Development Project (2017YFE0116800), Fundamental Research Funds for the Provincial Universities of Zhejiang (GK209907299001-008), Joint Funds of the National Natural Science Foundation of China (U1609218) and was also supported by Laboratory of Brain Machine Collaborative Intelligence of Zhejiang Province (2020E10010).

Data Availability Statement: The data used in the manuscript is a public dataset, namely CAP Sleep Database, please see the link 'https://www.physionet.org/content/capslpdb/1.0.0/'. We conform to the terms of the specified license.

Acknowledgments: We would like to thank all the reviewers for their constructive comments.

Conflicts of Interest: The authors declare that there is no conflict of interest regarding the publication of this paper.

References

1. Altevogt, B.M.; Colten, H.R. Sleep Disorders and Sleep Deprivation: An Unmet Public Health Problem; *Washington: National Academies Press*, **2006**.
2. Younes, M. The Case for Using Digital EEG Analysis in Clinical Sleep Medicine. *Sleep Sci. Pract.* **2017**, 1, 1–15.
3. Rechtschaffen, A. A Manual of Standardized Terminology, Techniques and Scoring System for Sleep Stages of Human Subjects. *Public Health Service*, **1968**.
4. Iber, C.; Ancoli-Israel, S.; Chesson, A.L.; Quan, S.F. The AASM Manual for the Scoring of Sleep and Associated Events: Rules, Terminology and Technical Specifications; *American Academy of Sleep Medicine: Westchester, IL, USA*, **2007**; Volume 1.
5. Chapotot, F.; Becq, G. Automated Sleep-Wake Staging Combining Robust Feature Extraction, Artificial Neural Network Classification, and Flexible Decision Rules. *International Journal of Adaptive Control and Signal Processing*. **2010**, 24, 409–423.
6. Acharya, U.R.; Sree, S.V.; Swapna, G.; Martis, R.J.; Suri, J.S. Automated EEG Analysis of Epilepsy: A Review. *Knowledge-Based Systems* **2013**, 45, 147–165.
7. Aydın, S.; Tunga, M.A.; Yetkin, S. Mutual Information Analysis of Sleep EEG in Detecting Psycho-physiological Insomnia. *J. Med. Syst.* **2015**, 39, 43.
8. Liu, Y.; Yan, L.; Zeng, B.; Wang, W. Automatic Sleep Stage Scoring Using Hilbert-Huang Transform with BP Neural Network. In *2010 4th International Conference on Bioinformatics and Biomedical Engineering*, Chengdu, China, 18-20 June **2010**.

9. Gao, Q.; Zhou, J.; Ye, B.; Wu, X. Automatic Sleep Staging Method Based on Energy Features and Least Squares Support Vector Machine Classifier. *Journal of Biomedical Engineering* **2015**, *32*, 531–536.
10. Yuce, A.B.; Yaslan, Y. A Disagreement Based Co-active Learning Method for Sleep Stage Classification. In *Proceedings of the 2016 International Conference on Systems, Signals and Image Processing (IWSSIP)*, Bratislava, Slovak, 23–25 May **2016**.
11. Diykh, M.; Li, Y.; Wen, P. EEG Sleep Stages Classification Based on Time Domain Features and Structural Graph Similarity. *IEEE Trans. Neural Syst. Rehabil. Eng.* **2016**, *24*, 1159–1168.
12. Diykh, M.; Li, Y.; Wen, P.; Li, T. Complex Networks Approach for Depth of Anesthesia Assessment. *Measurement* **2018**, *119*, 178–189.
13. Phan, H.; Andreotti, F.; Cooray, N.; Chèn, Y.O.; De Vos, M. DNN Filter Bank Improves 1-max Pooling CNN for Single-channel EEG Automatic Sleep Stage Classification. In *Proceedings of the 2018 40th Annual International Conference of the IEEE Engineering in Medicine and Biology Society (EMBC)*, Honolulu, HI, USA, 17–21 July **2018**; pp. 453–456.
14. Zhou, J.; Tian, Y.; Wang, G.; Liu, J.; Hu, Y. Automatic Sleep Stage Classification with Single Channel EEG Signal Based on Two-layer Stacked Ensemble Model. *IEEE Access* **2020**, *8*, 57283–57297.
15. Humayun, A.I.; Sushmit, A.S.; Hasan, T.; Bhuiyan, M.I.H. End-to-end Sleep Staging with Raw Single Channel EEG using Deep Residual ConvNets. In *Proceedings of the 2019 IEEE EMBS International Conference on Biomedical & Health Informatics (BHI)*, Chicago, IL, USA, 19–22 May **2019**; pp. 1–5.
16. da Silveira, T.L.; Kozakevicius, A.J.; Rodrigues, C.R. Single-channel EEG Sleep Stage Classification Based on a Streamlined set of statistical features in wavelet domain. *Med. Biol. Eng. Comput.* **2017**, *55*, 343–352.
17. Zhang, T.; Jiang, Z.; Li, D.; Wei, X.; Guo, B.; Huang, W.; Xu, G. Sleep Staging Using Plausibility Score: A Novel Feature Selection Method Based on Metric Learning. *IEEE J. Biomed. Health Inform.* **2020**, *25*, 577–590.
18. Liang, S.F.; Kuo, C.E.; Hu, Y.H.; Cheng, Y.S. A Rule-based Automatic Sleep Staging Method. *J. Neuroence Methods* **2012**, *205*, 169–176.
19. Liu, X.; Shi, J.; Tu, Y.; Zhang, Z. Joint Collaborative Representation Based Sleep Stage Classification with Multi-channel EEG Signals. In *Proceedings of the 2015 37th Annual International Conference of the IEEE Engineering in Medicine and Biology Society (EMBC)*, Milan, Italy, 5–29 August **2015**.
20. Patrick, K.; Achim, S.; Judith, B.; Konstantin, T.; Claus, M.; Holger, S.; Maximilian, T. Analysis of Multichannel EEG Patterns During Human Sleep: A Novel Approach. *Front. Hum. Neurosci.* **2018**, *12*, 121.
21. Zhu, G.; Li, Y.; Wen, P.P. Analysis and Classification of Sleep Stages Based on Difference Visibility Graphs From a Single-Channel EEG Signal. *IEEE J. Biomed. Health Inform.* **2014**, *18*, 1813–1821.
22. Gopika, G.K.; Prabhu, S.S.; Sinha, N. Sleep EEG Analysis Utilizing Inter-channel Covariance Matrices. *Biocybern. Biomed. Eng.* **2020**, *40*, 527–545.
23. Stevner, A.B.A.; Vidaurre, D.; Cabral, J.; Rapuano, K.; Nielsen, S.F.V.; Tagliazucchi, E.; Laufs, H.; Vuust, P.; Deco, G.; Woolrich, M.W.A. Discovery of Key Whole-brain Transitions and Dynamics during Human Wakefulness and Non-REM Sleep. *Nat. Commun.* **2019**, *10*, 1035.
24. Tagliazucchi, E.; Wegner, F.V.; Morzelewski, A.; Brodbeck, V.; Laufs, H. Breakdown of Long-range Temporal Dependence in Default Mode and Attention Networks during Deep Sleep. *Proc. Natl. Acad. Sci. USA* **2013**, *110*, 15419–15424.
25. Enzo Tagliazucchi, H.L. Decoding Wakefulness Levels from Typical FMRI Resting-state Data Reveals Reliable Drifts between Wakefulness and Sleep. *Neuron* **2014**, *82*, 695–708.
26. Ralf.; Landwehr.; Andreas.; Volpert.; Ahmad.; Jowaed. A Recurrent Increase of Synchronization in the EEG Continues from Waking throughout NREM and REM Sleep. *ISRN Neurosci.* **2014**, *2014*, 756952.
27. Lv, J.; Liu, D.; Ma, J.; Wang, X.; Zhang, J. Graph Theoretical Analysis of BOLD Functional Connectivity during Human Sleep without EEG Monitoring. *PLoS ONE* **2015**, *10*, e0137297.
28. Marie-Ve, D.; Julie, C.; Jean-Marc, L.; Maxime, F.; Nadia, G.; Jacques, M.;Antonio, Z. EEG Functional Connectivity Prior to Sleepwalking: Evidence of Interplay Between Sleep and Wakefulness. *Sleep* **2017**, *40*.
29. Terzano, M.G.; Parrino, L.; Sherieri, A.; Chervin, R.; Chokroverty, S.; Guilleminault, C.; Hirshkowitz, M.; Mahowald, M.; Moldofsky, H.; Rosa, A.a. Atlas, Rules, and Recording Techniques for the Scoring of Cyclic Alternating Pattern (CAP) in human sleep. *Sleep Med.* **2002**, *2*, 537.
30. Ary L. Goldberger, Luis A. N. Amaral, L.G. PhysioBank, PhysioToolkit, and PhysioNet: Components of a New Research Resource for Complex Physiologic Signals. *Circulation* **2000**, *101*, 215–220.
31. Ohayon, M.M.; Carskadon, M.A.; Christian, G.; Vitiello, M.V. Meta-Analysis of Quantitative Sleep Parameters From Childhood to Old Age in Healthy Individuals: Developing Normative Sleep Values Across the Human Lifespan. *Sleep* **2004**, *27*, 1255–1273.
32. Berry, R.B.; Budhiraja, R.; Gottlieb, D.J.; Gozal, D.; Iber, C.; Kapur, V.K.; Marcus, C.L.; Mehra, R.; Parthasarathy, S.; Quan, S.F.A. Rules for Scoring Respiratory Events in Sleep: Update of the 2007 AASM Manual for the Scoring of Sleep and Associated Events. *J. Clin. Sleep Med.* **2012**, *8*, 597–619.
33. Brignol, A.; Al-Ani, T.; Drouot, X. EEG-based Automatic Sleep-wake Classification in Humans Using Short and Standard Epoch Lengths. In *Proceedings of the 2012 IEEE 12th International Conference on Bioinformatics & Bioengineering (BIBE)*, Larnaca, Cyprus, 11–13 November **2012**.

34. Wilson, R.S.; Mayhew, S.D.; Rollings, D.T.; Goldstone, A.; Przezdzik, I.; Arvanitis, T.N.; Bagshaw, A.P. Influence of Epoch Length on Measurement of Dynamic Functional Connectivity in Wakefulness and Behavioural Validation in Sleep. *Neuroimage* **2015**, *112*, 169–179.
35. Ludwig, K.A.; Miriani, R.M.; Langhals, N.B.; Joseph, M.D.; Anderson, D.J.; Kipke, D.R. Using a Common Average Reference to Improve Cortical Neuron Recordings from Microelectrode Arrays. *J. Neurophysiol.* **2009**, *101*, 1679–1689.
36. Lee, T.W. Independent Component Analysis. *Springer: Berlin, Germany*, **1998**; pp. 27–66.
37. Mognon, A.; Jovicich, J.; Bruzzone, L.; Buiatti, M. ADJUST: An Automatic EEG Artifact Detector Based on the Joint Use of Spatial and Temporal Features. *Psychophysiology* **2011**, *48*, 229–240.
38. Lachaux, J.P.; Rodriguez, E.; Martinerie, J.; Varela, F.J.J. Measuring Phase Synchrony in Brain Signals. *Hum. Brain Mapp.* **2015**, *8*, 194–208.
39. Quiroga, R.Q.; Kraskov, A.; Kreuz, T.; Grassberger, P. Performance of Different Synchronization Measures in Real Data: A Case Study on Electroencephalographic Signals. *Phys. Rev. E* **2002**, *65*, 041903.
40. Bruna, Ricardo, G.B.M.F. HERMES: Towards an Integrated Toolbox to Characterize Functional and Effective Brain Connectivity. *Neuroinformatics* **2013**, *11*, 405–434.
41. Blankertz, B.; Dornhege, G.; Krauledat, M.; Müller, K.R.; Curio, G. The Non-invasive Berlin Brain-Computer Interface: Fast acquisition of Effective Performance in Untrained Subjects. *NeuroImage* **2007**, *37*, 539–550.
42. Chang, C.C.; Lin, C.J. LIBSVM: A Library for Support Vector Machines. *ACM Trans. Intell. Syst. Technol.* **2011**.
43. Breiman, L. Stacked Regressions. *Mach. Learn.* **1996**, *24*, 49–64.
44. Rodenbeck, A.; Binder, R.; Geisler, P.; Danker-Hopfe, H.; Lund, R.; Raschke, F.; Weeß, H.G.; Schulz, H. A Review of Sleep EEG Patterns. Part I: A Compilation of Amended Rules for their Visual Recognition According to Rechtschaffen and Kales. *Somnologie* **2006**, *10*, 159–175.
45. Cantero, J.L.; Atienza, M.; Salas, R.M. Spectral Features of EEG Alpha Activity in Human REM Sleep: Two Variants with Different Functional Roles? *Sleep N. Y.* **2000**, *23*, 746–754.
46. Carskadon, M.A.; Rechtschaffen, A. Monitoring and Staging Human Sleep. *Princ. Pract. Sleep Med.* **2011**, *5*, 16–26.
47. Ben Dkhil, M.; Chawech, N.; Wali, A.; Alimi, A.M. Towards an Automatic Drowsiness Detection System by Evaluating the Alpha Band of EEG Signals. In *Proceedings of the IEEE International Symposium on Applied Machine Intelligence & Informatics*, Herl'any, 26–28 January **2017**; pp. 000371–000376.
48. Knaut, P.; von Wegner, F.; Morzelewski, A.; Laufs, H. EEG-correlated FMRI of Human Alpha (De-) synchronization. *Clin. Neurophysiol.* **2019**, *130*, 1375–1386.
49. Riemann, D.; Spiegelhalder, K.; Feige, B.; Voderholzer, U.; Berger, M.; Perlis, M.; Nissen, C. The Hyperarousa Model of Insomnia: A Review of the Concept and its Evidence. *Sleep Med. Rev.* **2010**, *14*, 19–31.
50. Spiegelhalder, K.; Regen, W.; Feige, B.; Holz, J.; Piosczyk, H.; Baglioni, C.; Riemann, D.; Nissen, C. Increased EEG Sigma and Beta Power during NREM Sleep in Primary Insomnia. *Biol. Psychol.* **2012**, *91*, 329–333.
51. Sunwoo, J.S.; Cha, K.S.; Byun, J.I.; Kim, T.J.; Jun, J.S.; Lim, J.A.; Lee, S.T.; Jung, K.H.; Park, K.I.; Chu, K.; et al. Abnormal Activation of Motor Cortical Network during Phasic REM Sleep in Idiopathic REM Sleep Behavior Disorder. *Sleep* **2019**, *42*, zsy227.
52. Sors, A.; Bonnet, S.; Mirek, S.; Vercueil, L.; Payen, J.F. A Convolutional Neural Network for Sleep Stage Scoring from Raw Single-channel EEG. *Biomed. Signal Process. Control.* **2018**, *42*, 107–114.
53. Sharma, M.; Goyal, D.; Pv, A.; Acharya, U.R. An Accurate Sleep Stages Classification System Using a New Class of Optimally Time-frequency Localized Three-band Wavelet Filter Bank. *Comput. Biol. Med.* **2018**, *98*, 58–75, doi:10.1016/j.compbiomed.2018.04.025.
54. Lajnef, T.; Chaibi, S.; Ruby, P.; Aguera, P.E.; Eichenlaub, J.B.; Samet, M.; Kachouri, A.; Jerbi, K. Learning Machines and Sleeping Brains: Automatic Sleep Stage Classification Using Decision-tree Multi-class Support Vector Machines. *J. Neurosci. Methods* **2015**, *250*, 94–105.
55. Michielli, N.; Acharya, U.R.; Molinari, F. Cascaded LSTM Recurrent Neural Network for Automated Sleep Stage Classification Using Single-channel EEG Signals. *Comput. Biol. Med.* **2019**, *106*, 71–81.
56. Saebipour, M.R.; Joghataei, M.T.; Yoonessi, A.; Sadeghniiat-Haghighi, K.; Khalighinejad, N.; Khademi, S. Slow Oscillating Transcranial Direct Current Stimulation during Sleep has A Sleep-stabilizing Effect in Chronic Insomnia: A Pilot Study. *J. Sleep Res.* **2015**, *24*, 518–525.

Article

Wearable Technologies for Mental Workload, Stress, and Emotional State Assessment during Working-Like Tasks: A Comparison with Laboratory Technologies

Andrea Giorgi [1,*], Vincenzo Ronca [1,2], Alessia Vozzi [1,2], Nicolina Sciaraffa [1,3], Antonello di Florio [1], Luca Tamborra [2,4], Ilaria Simonetti [2,4], Pietro Aricò [1,5,6], Gianluca Di Flumeri [1,5,6], Dario Rossi [1,6] and Gianluca Borghini [1,5,6]

1. BrainSigns, SRL, 00185 Rome, Italy; vincenzo.ronca@uniroma1.it (V.R.); alessia.vozzi@uniroma1.it (A.V.); nicolina.sciaraffa@uniroma1.it (N.S.); antonello.diflorio@brainsigns.com (A.d.F.); pietro.arico@uniroma1.it (P.A.); gianluca.diflumeri@uniroma1.it (G.D.F.); dario.rossi@brainsigns.com (D.R.); gianluca.borghini@uniroma1.it (G.B.)
2. Department of Anatomical, Histological, Forensic and Orthopaedic Sciences, Sapienza University, 00185 Rome, Italy; luca.tamborra@it.ey.com (L.T.); ilaria.simonetti@it.ey.com (I.S.)
3. Department of Molecular Medicine, Sapienza University of Rome, 00185 Rome, Italy
4. Ernst & Young, Department People Advisory Services, 00187 Rome, Italy
5. IRCCS Fondazione Santa Lucia, 00179 Rome, Italy
6. Department of Business and Management, LUISS University, 00197 Rome, Italy
* Correspondence: andrea.giorgi@brainsigns.com

Citation: Giorgi, A.; Ronca, V.; Vozzi, A.; Sciaraffa, N.; di Florio, A.; Tamborra, L.; Simonetti, I.; Aricò, P.; Di Flumeri, G.; Rossi, D.; et al. Wearable Technologies for Mental Workload, Stress, and Emotional State Assessment during Working-Like Tasks: A Comparison with Laboratory Technologies. *Sensors* **2021**, *21*, 2332. https://doi.org/10.3390/s21072332

Academic Editor: Alan Jović

Received: 24 February 2021
Accepted: 24 March 2021
Published: 26 March 2021

Publisher's Note: MDPI stays neutral with regard to jurisdictional claims in published maps and institutional affiliations.

Copyright: © 2021 by the authors. Licensee MDPI, Basel, Switzerland. This article is an open access article distributed under the terms and conditions of the Creative Commons Attribution (CC BY) license (https://creativecommons.org/licenses/by/4.0/).

Abstract: The capability of monitoring user's performance represents a crucial aspect to improve safety and efficiency of several human-related activities. Human errors are indeed among the major causes of work-related accidents. Assessing human factors (HFs) could prevent these accidents through specific neurophysiological signals' evaluation but laboratory sensors require highly-specialized operators and imply a certain grade of invasiveness which could negatively interfere with the worker's activity. On the contrary, consumer wearables are characterized by their ease of use and their comfortability, other than being cheaper compared to laboratory technologies. Therefore, wearable sensors could represent an ideal substitute for laboratory technologies for a real-time assessment of human performances in ecological settings. The present study aimed at assessing the reliability and capability of consumer wearable devices (i.e., Empatica E4 and Muse 2) in discriminating specific mental states compared to laboratory equipment. The electrooculographic (EOG), electrodermal activity (EDA) and photoplethysmographic (PPG) signals were acquired from a group of 17 volunteers who took part to the experimental protocol in which different working scenarios were simulated to induce different levels of mental workload, stress, and emotional state. The results demonstrated that the parameters computed by the consumer wearable and laboratory sensors were positively and significantly correlated and exhibited the same evidences in terms of mental states discrimination.

Keywords: wearable device; emotional state; mental workload; stress; heart rate; eye blinks rate; skin conductance level

1. Introduction

This paper aims to investigate the capability of two consumer wearable devices (i.e., Empatica 4 and Muse 2) in assessing different levels of mental and emotional states. The consumer devices were compared to laboratory ones (i.e., BeMicro and Shimmer) in order to validate their reliability in scientific research.

1.1. Monitoring Mental States

In recent years there was an increasing interest toward wearable monitoring devices to assess physiological and mental activity, both in research and industry [1,2].

These devices are particularly important to the world's increasingly aging population since this aspect constitutes a relevant risk factor for work-related accidents [3]. Both in research and industry domains the mental states' monitoring is becoming really important. Starting from few decades ago, there was a shift in the focus from operators' physical demands to their cognitive demands. This shift is particularly evident for some complex and safety-critical human activities such as air traffic control, and car and rail train driving [4–7]. In these contexts, it is evident that most of the fatal and non-fatal accidents occur because of Human Factors (HFs) concerns [8–11]. Among all the HFs, stress, mental overload, and lack of vigilance could cause tragic human errors in several working environments [12–14]. Giving the limitations imposed by subjective evaluation of mental states [15–17] and due to the fact that in some specific activities it is not possible to interrupt operators while working, researchers started to acquire biosignals to monitor and assess operators' mental states. Biomarkers such as skin conductance level (SCL), heart rate (HR), and eye blink rate (EBR) are investigated as correlates of users' mental states to develop a monitoring system to diminish and prevent fatal and non-fatal accidents [4,6,16,18–20]. For this reason, it is important to reduce at minimum the invasiveness of the monitoring equipment. Furthermore, the interest in consumer wearable devices was supported by the increasing advances in microelectronics which allowed to overcome the limitations imposed by the size of the electronic components and of the measuring sensor itself [21]. The size reduction, other than costs reduction and easiness to use, enhanced the application of such wearable devices to areas of research which were usually investigated using laboratory technologies, considered in scientific literature as the gold-standard [22–24]. Indeed, despite the improvements of the technology behind laboratory equipment such devices are often uncomfortable and obtrusive for the participants leading to a non-optimal condition to ecologically assess mental states [25].

1.2. Consumer Wearables in Scientific Research

Consumer wearable devices are ideal candidates to record operators' biosignals without negatively interfere with their activities and tasks. Given the emergence of an incredible amount of commercial and user-friendly wearable devices [23,24] and given the fact that they seem to better adapt to daily-life activities, their accuracy has to be investigated deeply. The reliability of wearable devices in measuring biomarkers such as HR and SCL was demonstrated. In fact, compared to gold-standard equipment, consumer wearable devices showed a similar accuracy in measuring different biomarkers such as HR, HRV and SCL in different conditions [26–28]. Ragot and colleagues successfully adopted the Empatica E4 wrist-band to measure physiological response in an emotion recognition task [29]. Based on these evidence wearable devices were also used to assess different mental states. Setz and colleagues [30] compared the reliability of a consumer wearable device (Empatica E4) in detecting drowsiness during a driving simulation task using HRV. The authors found that E4 wristband showed similar results compared to a medical-grade device and argued that the latter device could be substituted with the E4 in order to detect drowsiness. The possibility to discriminate between different levels of the same mental states was also explored. A study on simulated train traffic controlling [25] demonstrated that it is possible to differentiate between different level of mental workload (WL) using HRV acquired via wearable device. Compared to an FDA-approved medical device authors showed that a consumer wearable sensor (EmWave Pro, Boulder Creek, California, USA) had similar results in estimating changes in HRV, while the Empatica E3, a different consumer wearable device included in the same study, did not show the same reliability. The potentiality of consumer wearable devices in acquiring biosignals in an unobtrusive way brought to the development of devices to collect electroencephalographic (EEG) and electrooculographic (EOG) signals. Krigolson and colleagues [31] validated Muse 2 wearable device for ERP research demonstrating an adequate level of accuracy in measuring N200 and P300 components compared to standard 10-20 electrode configuration. Other researchers investigated the possibility to use Muse 2 to discriminate between different levels of enjoyment while playing videogames [32]. The authors reported no significant difference in cortical activity while subjective reports did but the absence of a gold standard reference did not allow to objectively assess the accuracy of the consumer wearable EEG device considered.

1.3. Aim of the Present Study

Summarizing, there are contrasting evidence in literature about the reliability of consumer wearable devices. The possibility of these devices to estimate different biosignals is well accepted [26–29,32]. Additionally, some authors successfully differentiated between several mental states using the neurometrics collected with consumer wearables devices [25,30] but in other cases a failure was reported [25,31]. This paper fits into this contest by comparing the Empatica E4 and Muse 2 with laboratory equipment. The reliability and capability of the two consumer wearable devices were investigated for stress, mental workload (WL), and emotional state (EmS) evaluation while participants were performing three working-like tasks, comparing them with laboratory equipment. To summarize, this paper aimed at responding to the following research questions (RQ):

- RQ1: Are the above-mentioned neurophysiological parameters (EBR, SCL and HR) gathered through consumer wearable devices comparable with those acquired with laboratory equipment?
- RQ2: Are consumer wearable devices reliable in discriminating different levels of the mental states considered (WL, Stress and EmS)?

2. Materials and Methods

2.1. Participants

Seventeen (17) participants were recruited from the Sapienza University of Rome (ten males and seven females, 31.1 ± 3.7 years old) with normal or corrected-to-normal vision. Due to artifacts and missing data caused by technical issues after signals processing twelve (12) participants were considered valid for the analysis. Informed consent was obtained from each participant after explanation of the study. The experiment was conducted following the principles outlined in the Declaration of Helsinki of 1975, as revised in 2000 and was approved by the Sapienza University of Rome Ethical Committee in Charge for the Department of Molecular Medicine (protocol number: 2507/2020, approved on 4 August 2020). To respect the privacy of participants, only aggregate results were reported.

2.2. Procedures

In order to test the reliability of consumer wearable devices in WL, stress, and EmS evaluation, an experimental protocol was designed including three tasks: N-back task, Doctor Game task, and Webcall task. These tasks were selected to respectively simulate an office-like environment, an assembly-line and a teleworking activity. N-back task was used to simulate an office related activity which usually do not demand a pronounced physical effort whilst keeping high the mental one. Doctor Game (i.e., "Operation") represents a fine motor skill task requiring participant to use a pair of tweezers to extract several items from their slots. This task was adopted because of its analogy with the assembly line activities. Finally, Webcall task was used to reproduce a teleworking case, in which people are often asked to communicate and coordinate with someone who is not physically present. The order of tasks completion was balanced and randomized among participants.

2.2.1. N-Back Task

The N-back task (NB) (Figure 1) is a robust psychological test to manipulate working memory load [33], one of the major components and a reasonable approximation of WL [34]. Participants are presented with a sequence of letters on a screen. The goal is to press a button when the letters appearing on the screen is the same that occurred in the series n steps before. The difficulty of the task can be manipulated increasing the value of n, thus forcing participants to retain more items in their mind. In this study, the task was composed of a baseline and three conditions: Low WL, high WL, and stress. Under all conditions, 21 uppercase letters were used, which were displayed for 500 ms and an inter-stimulus interval randomized between 500 to 3000 ms; 33% of the displayed letters were targets.

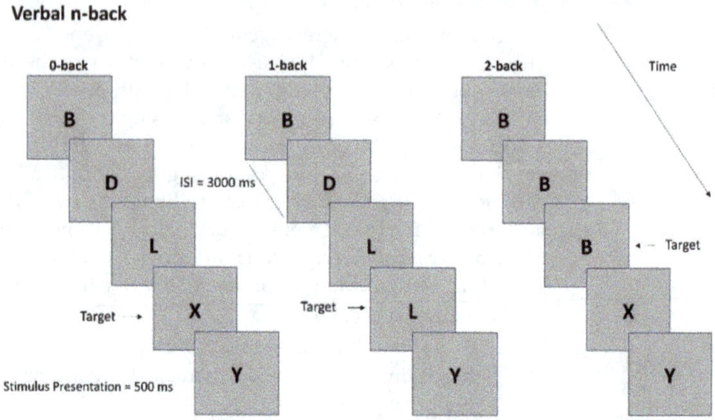

Verbal n-back

Figure 1. Example of N-back task under the 0-back, 1-back, and 2-back conditions.

- Baseline: Participants were instructed to watch the sequence of letters without giving any response.
- Low WL: 0-back. The task consisted in indicating when the stimulus on the screen matches a predetermined letter.
- High WL: 2-back. The task consisted in indicating when the stimulus occurred in the series 2 steps before. When investigating stress assessment, we referred to this condition as 'No Stress' condition (i.e., in the comparison 'No Stress vs. Stress') as it differed from the Stress one only in the presence of the stressors whilst the difficulty level was the same.
- Stress: The task was practically equivalent to the High WL one (indicating when the stimulus occurred in the series two steps before) but simultaneously high intensity noise was played (85 db) and the white-coat effect was used to stress the participant [35]. Four-minute relaxing music and video was played at the end of this phase for letting the participants recover from the stressful event before continuing with the remaining experimental conditions [36].

In all conditions, behavioral data like reaction time and number of errors were collected. The low WL and the high WL conditions were performed randomly while the baseline and the stress conditions were performed respectively at the beginning and at the end of the experimental task. Before the 0-back and the 2-back task, the participant performed a training session containing 21 stimuli, 33% of which were targets.

2.2.2. Doctor Game Task

This task is a fine motor skill task. We adopted the "Doctor Game" (DG) (i.e., "Operation") board game (Figure 2). Its goal consisted in removing small objects from the board without touching the metal edges. In this task a baseline, two difficulty levels and one stressful condition were performed as well.

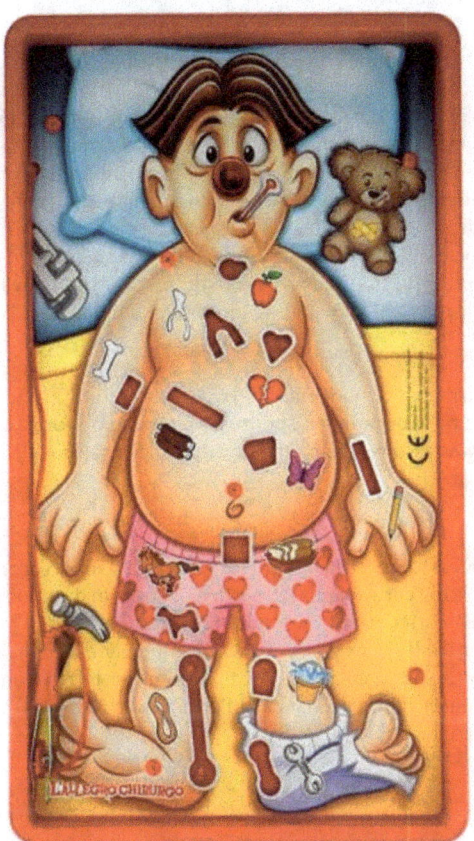

Figure 2. The Doctor Game task consisted in extracting as many objects as possible from the "patient" without touching the metal border. If an error occurred, the nose will emit a red light and the board will vibrate.

- Baseline: Participants were instructed to watch the board game without touching the board itself nor the objects.
- Low WL: Participants were asked to remove five predefined objects (the easiest ones). They had three minutes to complete the task.
- High WL: Participants were asked to remove all 12 objects. They had three minutes to complete the task. When investigating stress assessment, we referred to this condition as 'No Stress' condition (i.e., in the comparison 'No Stress vs. Stress') as it differed from the Stress one only in the presence of the stressors whilst the difficulty level was the same.
- Stress: Participants were asked to remove all 12 objects. They had one minute to complete the task. Additionally, high intensity noise was played (85 db) and the white-coat effect was used to stress the participant [35]. Then, a four-minute relaxing music and video was played at the end of this phase. This was done to let participants recover from the stressful event before continuing with the experiment.

In all conditions, behavioral data like number of objects removed and accomplishment time were collected. The Low WL and the High WL conditions were performed randomly while the baseline and the stress conditions were performed respectively at the beginning and at the end of the experimental task. Before the baseline the participant performed a training session by extracting a couple of objects from the board.

2.2.3. Webcall Task

This task consisted in an interactive Webcall to simulate a teleconference in smart-working condition. This task comprised a baseline, a positive, and a negative condition of two minutes each. The positive and negative conditions were achieved by asking the participant to respectively recall the happiest and the saddest memory of their past, while during the baseline condition the participant was asked to watch the teleconference platform interface without reacting. The positive condition was always performed at the beginning to avoid transients due to strong negative memories. One experimenter was sitting in another room interacting with the participant. The hypothesis was that asking the participant to talk about saddest/happiest memories will naturally induce these emotions and thereby enable them to feel and display the relevant expressions of emotions via multiple modalities, including physiological reactions [37,38].

2.3. Performance Assessment

Participants' performance was assessed for NB and DG tasks. Webcall task did not imply a right or wrong response therefore no performance was computed. Performance in NB was assessed using the Inverse Efficiency Score (IES) [34] computed as reported in Equation (1):

$$IES = \frac{RT}{1 - PE} \quad (1)$$

where RT is the participant's average (correct) reaction time within the condition considered, and PE is the participant's proportion of errors in the same condition. IES can be considered as the RT corrected for the amount of errors committed [34].

For the DG task we combined the number of errors, number of extracted objects, and the time spent to complete the task, in order to have an overall value representing the performance. Since no standard Performance Index (PI) are reported in the literature, we proposed the following one:

$$PI = \frac{\frac{OBJ}{OBJ_{max}} + \left(1 - \frac{ERR}{TIME}\right)}{2} \quad (2)$$

where OBJ is the number of extracted objects, OBJ_{max} is the total number of objects in the condition (5 in the low WL condition and 12 in the high WL and stress ones), ERR is the maximum number of errors a participant could make in the condition (one error per second, 180 in Low WL and High WL conditions and 60 in Stress one) and TIME is the time the participant spent to complete the task in the condition.

2.4. Subjective Reports

After each experimental condition, including the baseline, two questionnaires were administered to the participants:

- NASA Task-Load Index (NASA-TLX): It consists of six sub-scales representing independent groups of variables: mental, physical and temporal demands, frustration, effort and performance [39]. The participants were initially asked to rate on a scale from "low" to "high" (from 0 to 100) each of the six dimensions during the task. Afterwards, they had to choose the most important factor along pairwise comparisons. The NASA-TLX was selected for subjectively quantify the mental demand perceived by the participants with respect to the experimental condition of DG and NB tasks.
- GENEVA Emotion Wheel (GEW): It is a validated instrument to measure emotional reactions to several stimuli [40]. The participants were asked to indicate the emotion he/she experienced by choosing intensities for a single emotion or a blend of several emotions out of 20 distinct emotion families. Given the nature of the task, in this analysis we decided to use only the type of emotions selected by participants, without considering their intensities.

The reason why we selected these questionnaires is because they have been adopted in several studies. In particular, the NASA-TLX has been used for WL [41,42] subjective reports and GENEVA has been used for emotion categorization [40,43]. For the stress self-report, we utilized only the temporal demand and frustration parameters because they are the main components of the stressor used in this study.

2.5. EOG Recording and Analysis for Mental Workload Assessment

The vertical EOG pattern was estimated by acquiring simultaneously the EEG Fpz channel of the BeMicro (EB Neuro, Florence, Italy) and the EEG TP9 channel of the Muse 2 (Interaxon Inc, Toronto, OH, USA), with a sampling frequency of 256 Hz and 64 Hz respectively. Details are summarized in Table 1. The aim of the EOG analysis was to detect the eye blinks in order to estimate the eye blink rate (EBR) and finally correlate it with the WL variations) [7,44]. The same algorithm was adopted for the analysis of both datasets. Firstly, the EOG signal was band-pass filtered using a 5th-order Butterworth filter within the frequency range of 2–10 Hz, since in this range the main frequency contribute of eye blinks is contained [45,46].

Table 1. A summary of the devices and signals used in the presented work.

Signal	Laboratory Device	Consumer Wearable Device	Extracted Feature	Filter Frequency Range	Time Window
EOG	BeMicro	Muse 2	EBR	2–10 Hz	-
EDA	Shimmer	Empatica 4	SCL	1 Hz	60 s
PPG	-	Empatica 4	HR	1–4 Hz	60 s
ECG	BeMicro	-	HR	1–15 Hz	60 s

Secondly, the eyes open condition was used to identify a threshold for each participant that, when exceeded, identified a potential blink. The threshold was calculated as follows:

$$\text{Threshold} = \text{mean}(\text{EOG Eyes Open}) + 3 * \text{robustStdDev} \qquad (3)$$

where robustStdDev is the mean absolute deviation of the corresponding EOG channel.

Finally, every time the EOG signal exceeded the computed threshold, the Pearson correlation between a common blink template (the template was built averaging the blinks estimated from five random participants during the eyes open condition) and the EOG signal was computed within each experimental condition (i.e., pattern-matching phase). If this value was higher than 0.9, a potential blink would be classified as "real blink", similarly to what performed by the BLINKER algorithm [47].

The EBR estimated for each participant in each condition were calculated as the total number of blinks in every condition divided by the condition duration. EBR was evaluated under the different WL conditions to assess if it could differentiate user's mental workload. Previous studies demonstrated the capability of this parameter in estimating WL demand [16,44,48].

2.6. EDA Recording and Analysis for Stress Assessment

The EDA was recorded by both laboratory and consumer wearable devices. The sampling frequency of the Shimmer3 GSR+ unit (Shimmer Sensing, Dublin, Ireland) laboratory device was 64 Hz while the sampling frequency of the Empatica E4 was 4 Hz. Shimmer sensors were placed on the participant's no-dominant hand on the second and third fingers. In Empatica E4 the two electrodes are placed on the bottom part of the wrist. The EDA was firstly low-pass filtered with a cut-off frequency of 1 Hz and then processed by using the Ledalab suite [49], a specific open-source toolbox implemented within the MATLAB (MathWorks, Natik, Massachussets) environment for EDA processing (details in Table 1). The continuous decomposition analysis [50] was applied in order to estimate the tonic (SCL) and the phasic (SCR) components [51]. The SCL is the slow-changing component of the EDA signal, mostly related to the global arousal of the participant. On the contrary, the SCR is the fast-changing component of the EDA signal usually related to single stimuli reactions. The EDA components, as well as the other neurophysiological parameters, were estimated both using a 60 s time resolution and averaging within each experimental condition. Finally, only the SCL was analyzed accordingly with the objectives of the present study as demonstrated by Borghini et al. [7]. This parameter was chosen for stress estimation since previous studies demonstrated its relation with this mental state [7,52].

2.7. ECG Signal Recording and Analysis for Emotional State Assessment

Additonally, the HR estimation was performed using laboratory and consumer wearable technologies. ECG signal was collected using an electrode fixed on the participant's chest (laboratory device BeMicro) and referred to the potential recorded at both the earlobes with a sampling frequency of 256 Hz. At the same time, photoplethysmographic signal (PPG) was collected by means of Empatica E4 (Empatica, Milan, Italy). First, the ECG and PPG signal were filtered using a 5th-order Butterworth band-pass filter (1–1 Hz, and 1–4 Hz, respectively) in order to reject the continuous component and the high-frequency interferences, such as that related to the mains power source (details in Table 1). Another purpose of this filtering was to emphasize the QRS process of the ECG signal [53]. The following step consisted in computing the ECG (PPG) signal to the power of 3 to emphasize the heartbeat peaks, as they generally have the highest amplitude, and at the same time reduce spurious artifact peaks. Finally, the distance between consecutive peaks (i.e., each R peak corresponds to a heartbeat) was measured to estimate the HR values every 60 s. The Pan-Tompkins algorithm [54] was used for the HR estimation. A combination of HR and SCL measurements was adopted in order to estimate EmS [55,56]. In this regard, an Emotional Index (EI) was defined as:

$$EI = |SCL| * HR \qquad (4)$$

where SCL and HR were normalized by subtracting the corresponding baseline and dividing by the corresponding standard deviation. The resulting values were then averaged within the considered experimental condition. The combination of these two parameters was adopted because the sensitivity of this emotional index was already described in previous works [56].

2.8. Statistical Analysis

Statistical analyses were performed after normalizing each data condition with the corresponding task Baseline. For each participant, EBR, SCL, and HR data collected during baseline were subtracted from data collected during experimental conditions. The new EBR, SCL and HR values were named respectively EBR′, SCL′ and HR′. The Shapiro–Wilk test was used to assess the normality of the distribution related to each of the considered parameters. If normality was confirmed, Student's t-test would have been performed to pairwise compare the conditions (e.g., 'Low WL vs. High WL', or 'laboratory device vs. wearable device'). In case of non-normal distribution, the Wilcoxon signed-rank test was performed. In case of comparisons between three or more distributions, the analysis of variance (ANOVA) or its non-parametric equivalent (Friedman ANOVA) was performed. For all tests, statistical significance was set at $\alpha = 0.05$.

Pearson's repeated measure correlation (rmcorr) analysis [57] was then used to assess the reliability of the parameters estimated by the wearable device with respect to the laboratory one both at single- participant level and on the entire group. The rmcorr was performed on the average values of each parameter of wearable and laboratory devices gathered during the entire experimental session.

3. Results
3.1. Performance
3.1.1. N-back task

The Wilcoxon signed-rank test on the IES (Figure 3) revealed a significant difference between the low WL and high WL conditions ($p < 0.001$) and between the "no stress" (i.e., high WL) and stress conditions ($p < 0.001$). Furthermore, the three parameters involved in the IES computation (i.e., reaction times, wrong response, missed response) were analyzed to determine the one was most affecting the decreasing performance while executing the task. The Wilcoxon signed-rank test showed that both in high WL and Stress conditions (Figure 4) the number of missed responses increased significantly compared to the low WL condition ($p < 0.001$).

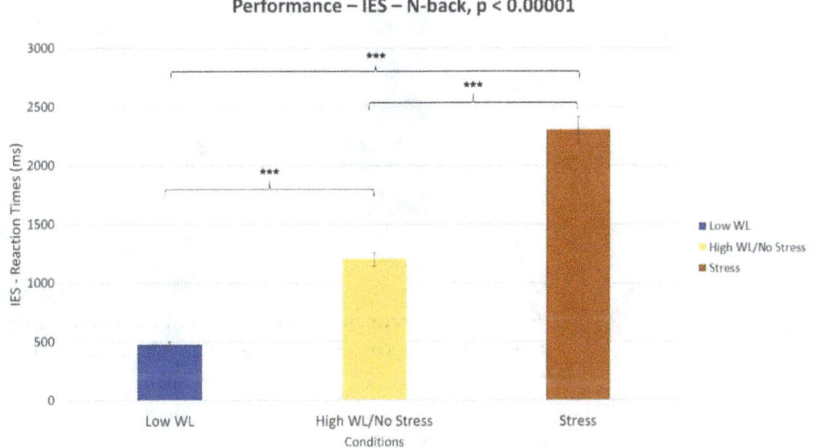

Figure 3. Difference in subjective performance during N-back task. Low vs. high Workload (WL) conditions ($p < 0.001$). No stress vs. stress conditions ($p < 0.001$).

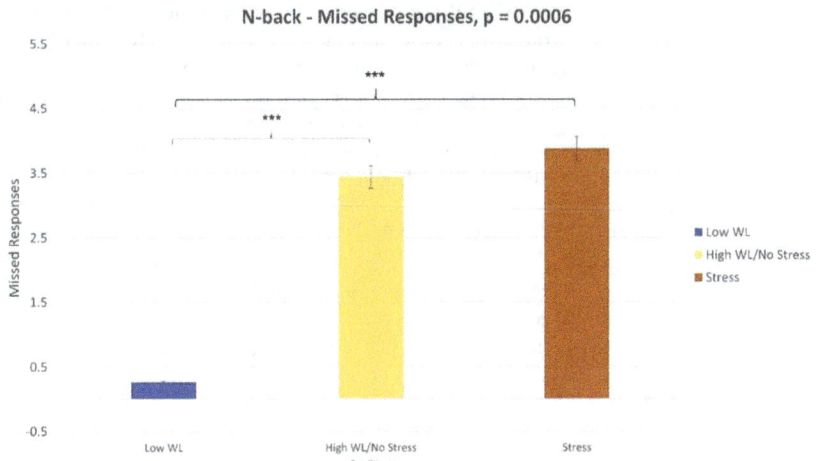

Figure 4. The number of missed responses was higher in high WL and stress conditions compared to the low WL condition ($p < 0.001$).

3.1.2. Doctor Game Task

The Wilcoxon signed-rank test revealed that the performance index significantly decreased ($p = 0.03$) during the high WL condition compared to the low WL one (Figure 5). The same was observed during the Stress condition when compared with the no stress one ($p = 0.02$).

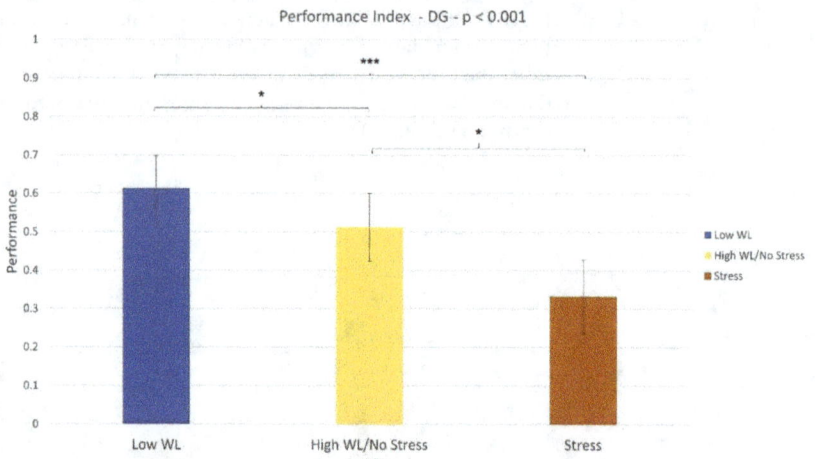

Figure 5. The performance index significantly decreased during the high WL condition compared to Low WL condition ($p = 0.03$). The same result was found in the stress vs. no stress comparison ($p = 0.001$).

3.2. Subjective Reports
3.2.1. N-back task

The Wilcoxon signed-rank test performed on the NASA-TLX demonstrated that participants perceived the High WL condition significantly more demanding ($p = 0.02$) than Low WL one (Figure 6). Additionally, at the end of the experiments they reported that the High WL condition resulted too difficult to be performed and that for this reason they did not or could not attend the task properly. Regarding the subjective stress evaluation, the combination of frustration and temporal demand parameters of the NASA-TLX was considered. These two parameters were selected accordingly with the relevant audio noise and the white-coat effect induced within the stress condition. The statistical analysis showed no significant difference ($p = 0.4$) in terms of perceived stress between no-stress and stress conditions.

3.2.2. Doctor Game Task

Looking at NASA-TLX total score, participants did not perceive the High WL condition to be significantly harder than Low WL condition ($p = 0.9$). Additionally, in this task we considered the frustration and temporal demand parameters of the NASA-TLX to assess the perceived stress, and no significant difference was found between the no-stress and stress conditions ($p = 0.8$).

3.2.3. Webcall Task

As showed in Table 2, during the positive condition participants rated mostly positive emotions than the negative ones. Instead, during negative conditions the rated emotions were mostly negative. However, some participants selected negative emotions during the positive calls while others positive emotions during the negative one.

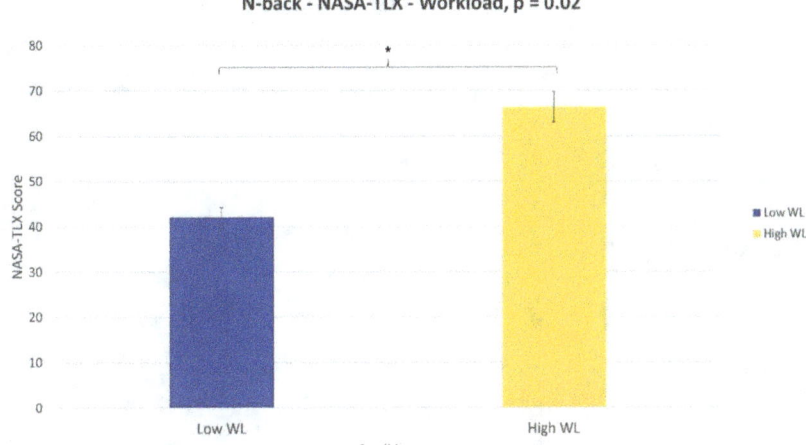

Figure 6. NASA-TLX total score during the low WL and high WL conditions ($p = 0.02$).

Table 2. Frequency of the emotions selected after positive and negative conditions of the Webcall.

Emotions (Geneva Emotion Wheel)	Positive Webcall	Negative Webcall
Admiration	1	
Contentment	1	1
Joy	12	
Love	3	2
Pleasure	6	
Pride	3	1
Relief		1
Interest	6	2
Embarrassment	1	
Compassion		1
Anger	1	2
Disappointment		4
Disgust		1
Fear		3
Guilt		3
Regret	1	1
Sadness	2	11
Shame	1	3

3.3. Neurophysiological Results

3.3.1. Methods comparisons

The statistical analysis revealed no significant difference in terms of EBR' between the consumer wearable and laboratory equipment during both NB ($p = 0.65$) and DG ($p = 0.69$). Similarly, the Wilcoxon signed-rank tests on the SCL' and HR' showed no significant differences in terms of SCL' (NB: $p = 0.09$; DG: $p = 0.4$) and HR' (NB: $p = 0.18$; DG: $p = 0.69$) estimation. Correlation analysis between the neurophysiological parameter estimated with wearable and laboratory devices was performed. All the parameters were significantly correlated ($p < 0.05$). EBR estimated with laboratory and wearable devices resulted highly and positively correlated ($R = 0.83$, $p < 10^{-47}$) (Figure 7). Correlation for SCL and HR resulted less strong but however significant. SCL correlation analysis (Figure 8) reported and R of 0.4 ($p < 10^{-6}$). Finally, R value for HR correlation (Figure 9) was 0.51 ($p < 10^{-14}$). To support correlation results, time dynamics of the investigated parameters acquired in a representative participant are depicted in Figures 10–12.

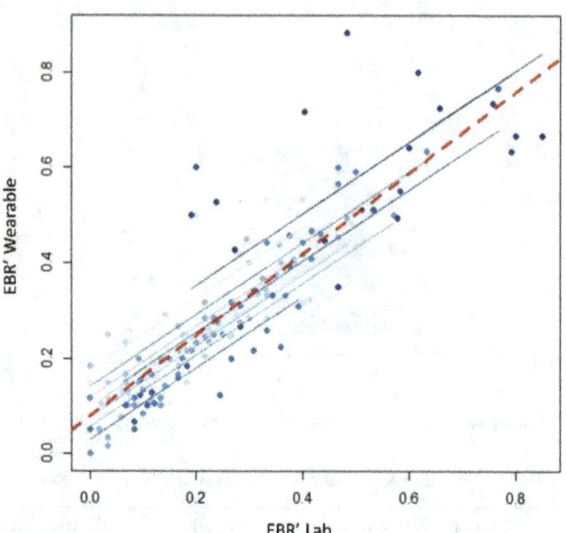

Figure 7. Pearson's repeated measure correlation for the Eyeblink Rate (EBR) estimated with laboratory and wearable devices. R = 0.83, $p < 10^{-47}$.

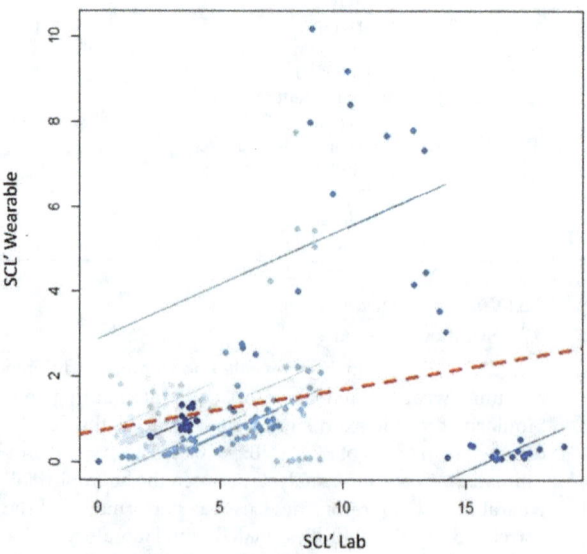

Figure 8. Pearson's repeated measure correlation for the Skin Conductance Level (SCL) estimated with laboratory and wearable devices. R = 0.4, $p < 10^{-6}$.

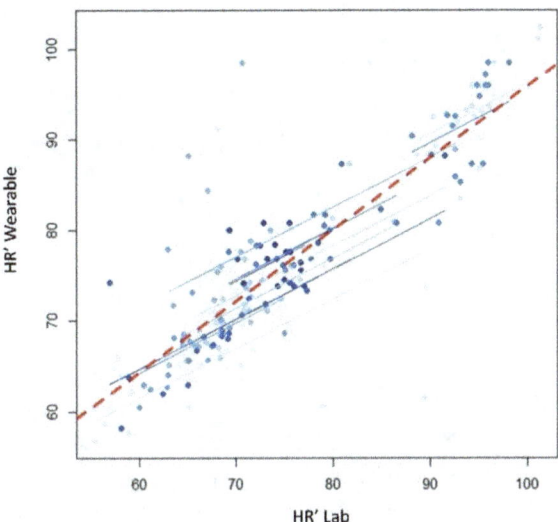

Figure 9. Pearson's repeated measure correlation for the Heart Rate (HR) estimated with laboratory and wearable devices. R = 0.51, $p < 10^{-14}$.

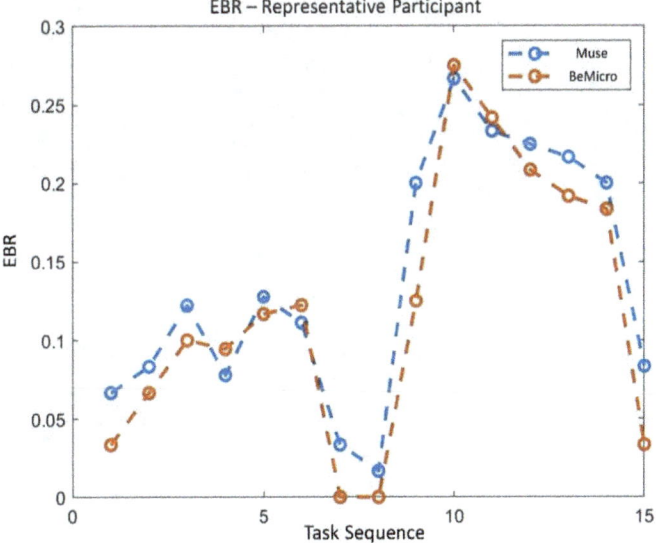

Figure 10. Time dynamics of EBR across all experimental task and conditions for both consumer wearable (blue) and laboratory device (red).

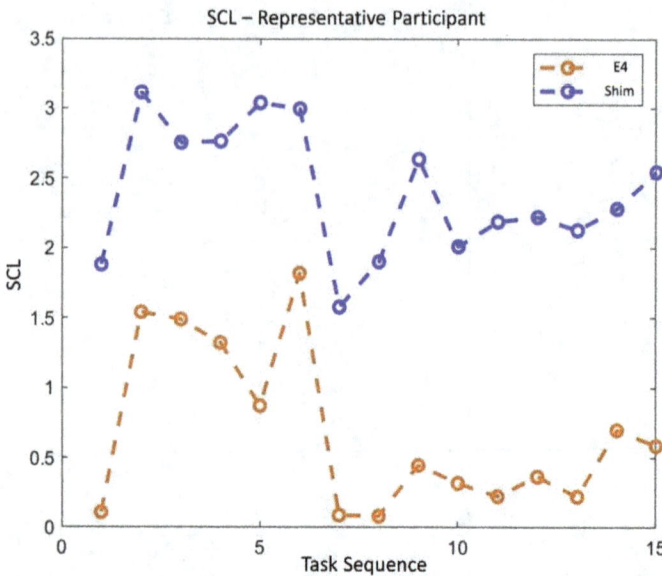

Figure 11. Time dynamics of SCL across all experimental task and conditions for both consumer wearable (red) and laboratory device (blue).

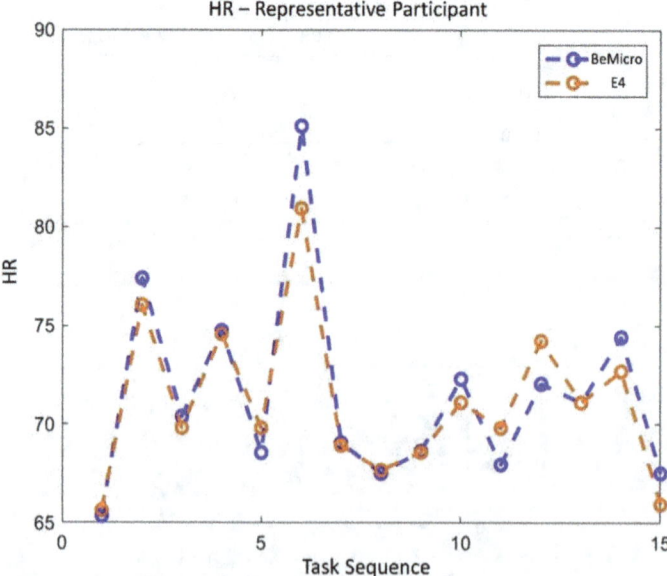

Figure 12. Time dynamics of EBR across all experimental task and conditions for both consumer wearable (red) and laboratory device (blue).

3.3.2. Mental workload

For both wearable and laboratory device the Wilcoxon signed-rank tests did not reveal significant differences (consumer wearable: $p = 0.64$; laboratory: $p = 0.96$) in terms of EBR' when comparing high WL vs. low WL conditions.

3.3.3. Stress

The Wilcoxon signed-rank tests on SCL' parameter estimated by the laboratory device and the wearable one returned significant difference showing higher values during the stress condition (all $p < 0.05$) both for the NB (Figure 13) and DG (Figure 14) task.

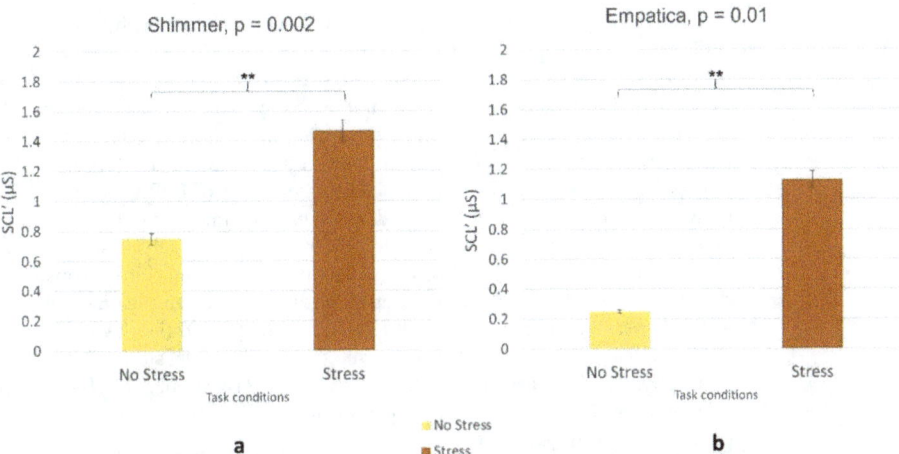

Figure 13. Increased SCL' in stress vs. no stress condition during NB task. Statistical analysis revealed significant difference between the conditions for both (**a**) laboratory equipment ($p = 0.002$) and (**b**) wearable device ($p = 0.1$).

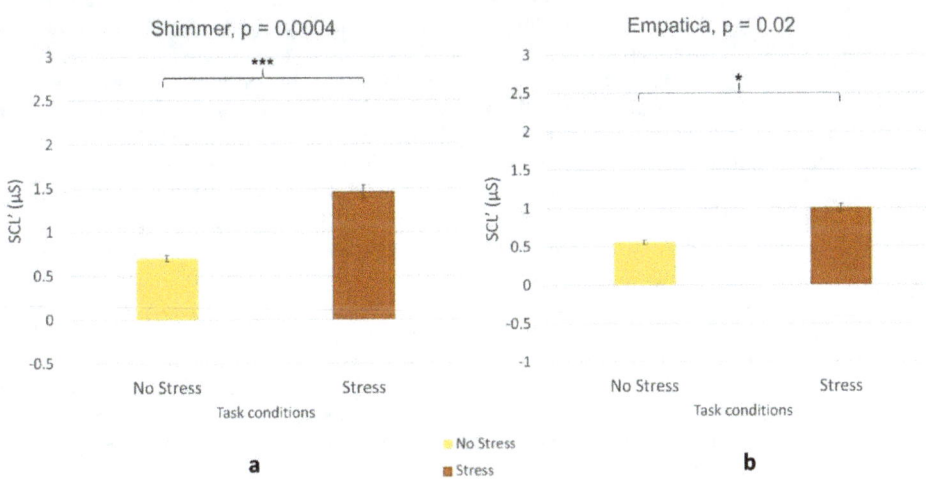

Figure 14. Increased SCL' in stress vs. no stress condition during DG task. Statistical analysis revealed significant difference between the conditions for both (**a**) laboratory equipment ($p = 0.0004$) and (**b**) wearable device ($p = 0.02$).

3.3.4. Emotional State

The Wilcoxon signed-rank test demonstrated no statistical differences (wearable: $p = 0.1$; laboratory: $p = 0.4$) in terms of EI between the positive and negative conditions.

4. Discussion

The objectives of the study consisted in assessing the reliability and capability of commercial wearable devices with respect to laboratory devices in estimating EBR, SCL and HR parameters and discriminating different levels of mental workload, stress, and emotional state.

4.1. Research Questions

Regarding the RQ1 (i.e., "Are the above-mentioned neurophysiological parameters (EBR, SCL and HR) gathered through consumer wearable devices comparable with those acquired with laboratory equipment?"), our results confirmed the feasibility to measure EBR, HR and SCL using consumer wearable devices. The parameters estimated with wearable and laboratory devices showed significant positive correlations as a demonstration that the two devices provided similar neurophysiological results (Figures 7–9). Additionally, no statistical differences were observed in terms of EBR, HR, and SCL estimation between the two technologies considered (i.e., consumer wearable and laboratory). In fact, for each of the parameters considered the statistical analysis showed no significant difference in the averaged. These results support the adoption of consumer wearable devices and the relative collected metrics to disentangle complex mental and emotional events in real-life environments. This aspect leads to the RQ2 (i.e., "Are consumer wearable devices reliable in assessing different levels of several mental states?"). EBR was used as a neurophysiological correlate of WL, and the Muse 2 (wearable) and BeMicro (laboratory) devices were compared. No difference was found in terms of mental workload variation during the NB and DG task.

4.2. Workload Assessment

Regarding the DG task, the absence of WL changes was probably due to the fact that the High WL condition was not so hard as expected. Indeed, even if performance decreased in the high WL condition compared to the low WL one, participants did not perceive the high WL condition to be harder. It is arguable that adding more items resulted in a similar WL demand between low and high WL conditions with no difference when comparing EBR' correlates.

Similarly, for the NB task, combining together performance and subjective reports, it could be argued that the absence of WL correlates was due to the difficulty of the task itself. In fact, NASA-TLX showed participants perceiving high WL condition to be harder than low WL one (Figure 6). However, at the end of the experimental session they reported that the High WL condition was too hard to be performed and for this reason they did not or could not attend the task properly. This finding is supported by performance analysis, where it was found number of missed responses significantly increased in high WL condition compared to low WL one (Figure 4). In this view, the absence of WL correlates could be a result of participants' abandoning the task. Alternatively, the lack of EBR' variations in both tasks could be motivated by EBR sensitivity. EBR parameter could be less sensitive to slight changes in task WL demand then other parameters (HR, HRV, PSD, ERP, etc.). This means that other parameters than EBR could have detected WL correlates in the same conditions. This points out directions for future works. The same paradigm could be tested using different neurophysiological correlates of WL to test their sensitivity and to support their adoption in different environments.

4.3. Stress Assessment

In terms of stress assessment, the SCL parameter was used as a neurophysiological correlate. The Empatica E4 (consumer wearable) and Shimmer (laboratory) evaluated an increased stress level during Stress condition compared to no stress one, both within NB (Figure 13) and DG (Figure 14) tasks. Even if stress correlates are accompanied with a decreased performance in both experimental tasks (Figure 3, Figure 5), participants were not able to perceive stress variations. In accordance with this, previous studies highlighted the limit in assessing perceived stress using subjective reports [34]. This study, therefore, confirmed the utility of using neurometrics to assess perceived stress [7]. It was also demonstrated that consumer wearable devices could substitute laboratory equipment to acquire such neurometrics. The possibility to detect stress in an obtrusive way is one of the most promising aspects of wearable devices.

4.4. Emotional State Assessment

Finally, regarding the possibility to discriminate between a positive EmS and a negative one using a combination of SCL and HR [55], both technologies were not able to differentiate these two conditions. Even if after positive condition participants selected mostly positive emotions (and negative ones after negative conditions), we found that after positive condition participants selected also some negative emotions and vice versa. It is arguable what arose from the two conditions was a blend of emotions, with no pure positive or negative connotations. Additionally, there is the possibility that two minutes interaction with a stranger in a simulated webcall was not enough to elicit a measurable neurophysiological change in the participants' emotional states. As exposed, considering performance and subjective evaluations, the reason for the absence of WL and EmS correlates could be the experimental design itself, which did not elicit the desired mental states. This limit points out direction for next works. Future studies should design an experiment to more accurately define WL and EmS conditions.

4.5. Limits and Future Directions

Although both the reliability of consumer wearable devices in estimating neurophysiological signals and their capability in discriminating different levels of stress is promising, some limitations must be discussed. An experimental design and tasks capable of eliciting the desired levels of the mental states must be implemented to better investigate the usability of wearable devices. For NB and DG, an improved design should elicit the proper level of workload while for the emotional state evaluations a longer duration of the task should be considered in order to elicit a stronger and measurable emotional, and therefore autonomic, response in the participants. Consumer wearable devices are user-friendly and non-invasive technologies, allowing their usage in dynamics condition in which laboratory equipment would not be adequate. The possibility to use these devices in dynamics environments must be supported by a good quality of the gathered signals. This is a challenging aspect for consumer wearable devices and their utilization must be carefully evaluated considering the recording settings and protocol in order to acquire a valid signal. In particular, after this preliminary evaluation of wearables reliability, their capability in differentiating between different mental states should will be tested in real-working conditions with attention to the processing and analysis of the data gathered with these devices and the results will be considered for the next study. Additionally, it should be underlined that one of the considered consumer wearable devices, the Empatica E4, can be classified as a high-level wearable device. The elevated cost of high-quality wearables could represent a limit in their adoption. For this reason, the possibility to estimate the considered signals and the related mental states using commercial and low-cost wearable devices should be also explored in order to broad the mental state monitoring in the consumer world, without limiting their adoption to the scientific research.

Furthermore, future works should investigate these and other mental states in a larger group of participants and investigate the impact of participants' movements on the quality of collected data with a particular attention to the devices/parameters affected by the movements and the intensity of the considered signals. Specifically, an important aspect that will be investigated in the next study is the comparison of the number of artifacts and the percentage of data loss found in consumer wearable devices with those of laboratory equipment. Additionally, reliability of investigated parameters in estimating mental states correlates in working-like tasks should be compared to other physiological signals (such as EEG and HRV) in order to detect the one that better fits to the recording conditions.

Consequently, the adoption of other physiological signals must be accompanied by an adequate task duration to provide reliable data. Once reliability of wearable devices has been confirmed, the possibility to discriminate mental states in real-time must be investigated. Finally, consumer wearable devices are optimal candidate for health and well-being monitoring [58,59]. When appropriate algorithms are applied it is possible to monitor patients' health by remote in real-time and prevent fatal and non-fatal occurrences. For this reason, it is important to investigate the acceptance of this wearable devices and their easiness to use [60]. This will be especially important for monitoring elderly population [61].

5. Conclusions

The study demonstrated that signal recorded with consumer wearable and laboratory devices showed a statistically positive correlation and no significant difference (RQ1). Additionally, it was demonstrated the capability in differentiating stress levels (RQ2). Within this experimental design it was impossible to differentiate between different levels of WL and EmS (RQ2).

The possibility to measure neurophysiological parameters at the same level laboratory devices do but with a limited invasiveness is one of the greatest points of strength of consumer wearable devices. On the other side, unobtrusiveness is achieved with reduced size which comports a limited duration of the battery, limiting these devices to short periods of testing. Furthermore, it is reported that the contact between wearable devices and the body id not always optimal, leading to missing or altered data [25]. This limits the use of consumer wearables to those case in which movement is compatible with data collecting.

Taken together, these findings support the adoption of low-cost wearable device to monitor operators' mental states in laboratory and real-life environments. The possibility to unobtrusively assess mental states has broad applications. It could be possible to monitor air-traffic controllers, medical operators, surgeons, while working without interfering with the performance. Hopefully, the ability to better differentiate between mental states will reduce the effect of tragic occurrences.

Author Contributions: Conceptualization: G.B. and V.R.; methodology: G.B. and V.R.; software: G.B., A.d.F., D.R., G.D.F., N.S., and V.R.; formal analysis: G.B., V.R., L.T., I.S., and A.G.; investigation: G.B. and V.R.; resources: G.B., P.A., A.G., A.V., and V.R.; data curation: G.B., V.R., and A.G.; writing—original draft preparation: A.G.; writing—review and editing: G.B., P.A., G.D.F., N.S., and A.V.; visualization: G.B. and A.G.; supervision: G.B.; funding acquisition: G.B. All authors have read and agreed to the published version of the manuscript.

Funding: This research was European Commission by Horizon2020 projects "WORKINGAGE: Smart Working environments for all Ages" (GA no. 826232); "SIMUSAFE: Simulator Of Behavioral Aspects For Safer Transport" (GA n. 723386); "SAFEMODE: Strengthening Synergies between Aviation and Maritime in the area of Human Factors towards Achieving more Efficient and Resilient MODE of Transportation" (GA no. 814961), "BRAINSAFEDRIVE: A Technology to Detect Mental States during Driving for Improving the Safety of the Road" (Italy-Sweden collaboration) with a grant of Ministero dell'Istruzione dell'Università e della Ricerca della Repubblica Italiana, "MINDTOOTH: Wearable device to decode human mind by neurometrics for a new concept of smart interaction with the surrounding environment" (GA no. 950998) and H2020-SESAR-2019-2 project: Transparent Artificial Intelligence and Automation to Air Traffic Management Systems, "ARTIMATION," GA no. 894238.

Institutional Review Board Statement: The study was conducted according to the guidelines of the Declaration of Helsinki and approved by the Sapienza University of Rome Ethical Committee in Charge for the Department of Molecular Medicine (protocol number: 2507/2020, approved on 4 August 2020).

Informed Consent Statement: Informed consent was obtained from all subjects involved in the study.

Data Availability Statement: The aggregated data presented in this study might be available on request from the corresponding author. The data are not publicly available because they were collected within the EU Project "WORKINGAGE: Smart Working environments for all Ages" (GA n.826232) and they are property of the Consortium.

Conflicts of Interest: The authors declare no conflict of interest.

References

1. Haghi, M.; Thurow, K.; Stoll, R. Wearable devices in medical internet of things: Scientific research and commercially available devices. *Healthc. Inform. Res.* **2017**, *23*, 4–15. [CrossRef]
2. Ranavolo, A.; Draicchio, F.; Varrecchia, T.; Silvetti, A.; Iavicoli, S. Wearable monitoring devices for biomechanical risk assessment at work: Current status and future challenges—A systematic review. *Int. J. Environ. Res. Public Health* **2018**, *15*, 2001. [CrossRef] [PubMed]
3. White, M.S.; Burns, C.; Conlon, H.A. The impact of an aging population in the workplace. *Work. Health Saf.* **2018**, *66*, 493–498. [CrossRef] [PubMed]
4. Borghini, G.; Astolfi, L.; Vecchiato, G.; Mattia, D.; Babiloni, F. Measuring neurophysiological signals in aircraft pilots and car drivers for the assessment of mental workload, fatigue and drowsiness. *Neurosci. Biobehav. Rev.* **2014**, *44*, 58–75. [CrossRef] [PubMed]
5. Young, M.S.; Brookhuis, K.A.; Wickens, C.D.; Hancock, P.A. State of science: Mental workload in ergonomics. *Ergonomics* **2015**, *58*, 1–17. [CrossRef]
6. Borghini, G.; Aricò, P.; Di Flumeri, G.; Cartocci, G.; Colosimo, A.; Bonelli, S.; Golfetti, A.; Imbert, J.P.; Granger, G.; Benhacene, R.; et al. EEG-based cognitive control behaviour assessment: An ecological study with professional air traffic controllers. *Sci. Rep.* **2017**, *7*, 1–16. [CrossRef]
7. Borghini, G.; Di Flumeri, G.; Aricò, P.; Sciaraffa, N.; Bonelli, S.; Ragosta, M.; Tomasello, P.; Drogoul, F.; Turhan, U.; Acikel, B.; et al. A multimodal and signals fusion approach for assessing the impact of stressful events on Air Traffic Controllers. *Sci. Rep.* **2020**, *10*, 1–18. [CrossRef]
8. Hansen, F. Human error: A concept analysis. *J. Air Transp.* **2006**, *11*, 61–77. Available online: https://ntrs.nasa.gov/search.jsp?R=20070022530 (accessed on 24 March 2021).
9. Arico, P.; Borghini, G.; Di Flumeri, G.; Colosimo, A.; Graziani, I.; Imbert, J.-P.; Granger, G.; Benhacene, R.; Terenzi, M.; Pozzi, S.; et al. Reliability over time of EEG-based mental workload evaluation during Air Traffic Management (ATM) tasks. In Proceedings of the 37th Annual International Conference of the IEEE Engineering in Medicine and Biology Society (EMBC), Milano, Italy, 25–29 August 2015; pp. 7242–7245. [CrossRef]
10. Aricò, P.; Reynal, M.; Di Flumeri, G.; Borghini, G.; Sciaraffa, N.; Imbert, J.-P.; Hurter, C.; Terenzi, M.; Ferreira, A.; Pozzi, S.; et al. How neurophysiological measures can be used to enhance the evaluation of remote tower solutions. *Front. Hum. Neurosci.* **2019**, *13*, 303. [CrossRef]
11. Borghini, G.; Aricò, P.; Astolfi, L.; Toppi, J.; Cincotti, F.; Mattia, D.; Cherubino, P.; Vecchiato, G.; Maglione, A.G.; Graziani, I.; et al. Frontal EEG theta changes assess the training improvements of novices in flight simulation tasks. In Proceedings of the 35th Annual International Conference of the IEEE Engineering in Medicine and Biology Society (EMBC); Institute of Electrical and Electronics Engineers, Osaka, Japan, 3–7 July 2013; Volume 2013, pp. 6619–6622.
12. Jahangiri, M.; Hoboubi, N.; Rostamabadi, A.; Keshavarzi, S.; Hosseini, A.A. Human error analysis in a permit to work system: A case study in a chemical plant. *Saf. Health Work* **2016**, *7*, 6–11. [CrossRef] [PubMed]
13. Kondrateva, O.; Kravchenko, M.; Loktionov, O. Development of the methods for assessing the risk of damage to health of the employees of the electric power industry. *Bezop. Promyshlennosti* **2019**, *2019*, 63–68. [CrossRef]
14. Bevilacqua, M.; Ciarapica, F.E. Human factor risk management in the process industry: A case study. *Reliab. Eng. Syst. Saf.* **2018**, *169*, 149–159. [CrossRef]
15. Babiloni, F. Mental workload monitoring: New perspectives from neuroscience. In *Communications in Computer and Information Science*; Springer: Cham, Switzerland, 2019; Volume 1107, pp. 3–19.
16. Arico, P.; Borghini, G.; Di Flumeri, G.; Bonelli, S.; Golfetti, A.; Graziani, I.; Pozzi, S.; Imbert, J.-P.; Granger, G.; Benhacene, R.; et al. Human factors and neurophysiological metrics in air traffic control: A critical review. *IEEE Rev. Biomed. Eng.* **2017**, *10*, 250–263. [CrossRef]
17. Wall, T.D.; Michie, J.; Patterson, M.; Wood, S.J.; Sheehan, M.; Clegg, C.W.; West, M. On the validity of subjective measures of company performance. *Pers. Psychol.* **2004**, *57*, 95–118. [CrossRef]
18. Sciaraffa, N.; Borghini, G.; Aricò, P.; Di Flumeri, G.; Colosimo, A.; Bezerianos, A.; Thakor, N.V.; Babiloni, F. Brain interaction during cooperation: Evaluating local properties of multiple-brain network. *Brain Sci.* **2017**, *7*, 90. [CrossRef]
19. Fairclough, S.H. Fundamentals of physiological computing. *Interact. Comput.* **2009**, *21*, 133–145. [CrossRef]
20. Cartocci, G.; Maglione, A.G.; Vecchiato, G.; Di Flumeri, G.; Colosimo, A.; Scorpecci, A.; Marsella, P.; Giannantonio, S.; Malerba, P.; Borghini, G.; et al. Mental workload estimations in unilateral deafened children. In Proceedings of the 37th Annual International Conference of the IEEE Engineering in Medicine and Biology Society (EMBC), Milano, Italy, 29–29 August 2015; Volume 2015, pp. 1654–1657. [CrossRef]

21. Patel, S.; Park, H.; Bonato, P.; Chan, L.; Rodgers, M. A review of wearable sensors and systems with application in rehabilitation. *J. Neuroeng. Rehabil.* **2012**, *9*, 21. [CrossRef]
22. Di Flumeri, G.; Aricò, P.; Borghini, G.; Sciaraffa, N.; Di Florio, A.; Babiloni, F. The dry revolution: Evaluation of three different EEG dry electrode types in terms of signal spectral features, mental states classification and usability. *Sensors* **2019**, *19*, 1365. [CrossRef] [PubMed]
23. Gradl, S.; Wirth, M.; Richer, R.; Rohleder, N.; Eskofier, B.M. An overview of the feasibility of permanent, real-time, unobtrusive stress measurement with current wearables. In Proceedings of the 13th EAI International Conference on Pervasive Computing Technologies for Healthcare, Trento, Italy, 20–23 May 2019; Volume 19, pp. 360–365.
24. E Dooley, E.; Golaszewski, N.M.; Bartholomew, J.B. Estimating accuracy at exercise intensities: A comparative study of self-monitoring heart rate and physical activity wearable devices. *JMIR mHealth uHealth* **2017**, *5*, e34. [CrossRef]
25. Lo, J.C.; Sehic, E.; Meijer, S.A. Measuring mental workload with low-cost and wearable sensors: Insights into the accuracy, obtrusiveness, and research usability of three instruments. *J. Cogn. Eng. Decis. Mak.* **2017**, *11*, 323–336. [CrossRef]
26. Menghini, L.; Gianfranchi, E.; Cellini, N.; Patron, E.; Tagliabue, M.; Sarlo, M. Stressing the accuracy: Wrist-worn wearable sensor validation over different conditions. *Psychophysiology* **2019**, *56*, e13441. [CrossRef]
27. Shcherbina, A.; Mattsson, C.M.; Waggott, D.; Salisbury, H.; Christle, J.W.; Hastie, T.; Wheeler, M.T.; Ashley, E.A. Accuracy in wrist-worn, sensor-based measurements of heart rate and energy expenditure in a diverse cohort. *J. Pers. Med.* **2017**, *7*, 3. [CrossRef]
28. McCarthy, C.; Pradhan, N.; Redpath, C.; Adler, A. Validation of the empatica E4 wristband. In Proceedings of the IEEE EMBS International Student Conference (ISC), Ottawa, ON, Canada, 29–31 May 2016; pp. 1–4.
29. Ragot, M.; Martin, N.; Em, S.; Pallamin, N.; Diverrez, J.-M. Emotion recognition using physiological signals: Laboratory vs. wearable sensors. *Adv. Intell. Syst. Comput.* **2018**, *608*, 15–22.
30. Setz, C.; Arnrich, B.; Schumm, J.; La Marca, R.; Tröster, G.; Ehlert, U. Discriminating stress from cognitive load using a wearable EDA device. *IEEE Trans. Inf. Technol. Biomed.* **2010**, *14*, 410–417. [CrossRef] [PubMed]
31. Krigolson, O.E.; Williams, C.C.; Norton, A.; Hassall, C.D.; Colino, F.L. Choosing MUSE: Validation of a low-cost, portable EEG system for ERP research. *Front. Neurosci.* **2017**, *11*, 109. [CrossRef] [PubMed]
32. Abujelala, M.; Abellanoza, C.; Sharma, A.; Makedon, F. Brain-EE: Brain enjoyment evaluation using commercial EEG headband. In Proceedings of the PETRA 2016, Corfu, Greece, 29 June–1 July 2016. [CrossRef]
33. Kirchner, W.K. Age differences in short-term retention of rapidly changing information. *J. Exp. Psychol.* **1958**, *55*, 352–358. [CrossRef] [PubMed]
34. Berka, C.; Levendowski, D.J.; Lumicao, M.N.; Yau, A.; Davis, G.; Zivkovic, T.; Olmstead, R.E.; Tremoulet, P.; Craven, P.L. EEG correlates of task engagement and mental workload in vigilance, learning, and memory tasks. *Aviat. Space Environ. Med.* **2007**, *78*, B231–B244. Available online: https://www.researchgate.net/publication/6289900_EEG_correlates_of_task_engagement_and_mental_workload_in_vigilance_learning_and_memory_tasks (accessed on 24 January 2021). [PubMed]
35. Skoluda, N.; Strahler, J.; Schlotz, W.; Niederberger, L.; Marques, S.; Fischer, S.; Thoma, M.V.; Spoerri, C.; Ehlert, U.; Nater, U.M. Intra-individual psychological and physiological responses to acute laboratory stressors of different intensity. *Psychoneuroendocrinology* **2015**, *51*, 227–236. [CrossRef] [PubMed]
36. De La Torre-Luque, A.; Caparros-Gonzalez, R.A.; Bastard, T.; Vico, F.J.; Buela-Casal, G. Acute stress recovery through listening to Melomics relaxing music: A randomized controlled trial. *Nord. J. Music Ther.* **2016**, *26*, 124–141. [CrossRef]
37. Ceccarelli, L.A.; Giuliano, R.J.; Glazebrook, C.M.; Strachan, S.M. Self-compassion and psycho-physiological recovery from recalled sport failure. *Front. Psychol.* **2019**, *10*, 1564. [CrossRef] [PubMed]
38. Konečni, V.J.; Brown, A.; Wanic, R.A. Comparative effects of music and recalled life-events on emotional state. *Psychol. Music* **2008**, *36*, 289–308. [CrossRef]
39. Hart, S.; Staveland, L. Development of NASA-TLX (Task Load Index) results of empirical and theoretical research. *Adv. Psychol.* **1988**, *52*, 139–183.
40. Coyne, A.K.; Murtagh, A.; McGinn, C. Using the Geneva Emotion Wheel to measure perceived affect in human-robot interaction. In Proceedings of the 2020 ACM/IEEE International Conference on Human-Robot Interaction, Cambridge, UK, 23–26 March 2020; pp. 491–498.
41. Zheng, B.; Jiang, X.; Tien, G.; Meneghetti, A.; Panton, O.N.M.; Atkins, M.S. Workload assessment of surgeons: Correlation between NASA TLX and blinks. *Surg. Endosc.* **2012**, *26*, 2746–2750. [CrossRef] [PubMed]
42. Grier, R.A. How High is High? A Meta-Analysis of NASA-TLX Global Workload Scores. *Proc. Hum. Factors Ergon. Soc. Annu. Meet.* **2015**, *59*, 1727–1731. [CrossRef]
43. Shuman, V.; Schlegel, K.; Scherer, K. Geneva Emotion Wheel Rating Study PROPEREMO View Project a Developmental Perspective of Emotion Regulation View Project. 2015. Available online: https://www.researchgate.net/publication/280850848 (accessed on 26 January 2021).
44. Faure, V.; Lobjois, R.; Benguigui, N. The effects of driving environment complexity and dual tasking on drivers' mental workload and eye blink behavior. *Transp. Res. Part F Traffic Psychol. Behav.* **2016**, *40*, 78–90. [CrossRef]
45. Di Flumeri, G.; Arico, P.; Borghini, G.; Colosimo, A.; Babiloni, F. A new regression-based method for the eye blinks artifacts correction in the EEG signal, without using any EOG channel. In Proceedings of the 38th Annual International Conference of the IEEE Engineering in Medicine and Biology Society (EMBC), Orlando, FL, USA, 16–20 August 2016; Volume 2016, pp. 3187–3190.

46. Abbas, S.N.; Abo-Zahhad, M. *Eye Blinking EOG Signals as Biometrics*; Springer: Cham, Switzerland, 2017; pp. 121–140.
47. Kleifges, K.; Bigdely-Shamlo, N.; Kerick, S.E.; Robbins, K.A. BLINKER: Automated extraction of ocular indices from eeg enabling large-scale analysis. *Front. Neurosci.* **2017**, *11*, 12. [CrossRef]
48. Borghini, G.; Ronca, V.; Vozzi, A.; Aricò, P.; Di Flumeri, G.; Babiloni, F. Monitoring performance of professional and oc-cupational operators. *Handb. Clin. Neurol.* **2020**, *168*, 199–205.
49. Bach, D.R. A head-to-head comparison of SCRalyze and Ledalab, two model-based methods for skin conductance analysis. *Biol. Psychol.* **2014**, *103*, 63–68. [CrossRef] [PubMed]
50. Benedek, M.; Kaernbach, C. A continuous measure of phasic electrodermal activity. *J. Neurosci. Methods* **2010**, *190*, 80–91. [CrossRef] [PubMed]
51. Braithwaite, J.J.; Derrick, D.; Watson, G.; Jones, R.; Rowe, M. A Guide for Analysing Electrodermal Activity (EDA) and Skin Conductance Responses (SCRs) for Psychological Experiments. 2015. Available online: https://www.birmingham.ac.uk/Documents/college-les/psych/saal/guide-electrodermal-activity.pdf (accessed on 24 March 2021).
52. Borghini, G.; Bandini, A.; Orlandi, S.; Di Flumeri, G.; Arico, P.; Sciaraffa, N.; Ronca, V.; Bonelli, S.; Ragosta, M.; Tomasello, P.; et al. Stress assessment by combining neurophysiological signals and radio communications of air traffic controllers. In Proceedings of the 42nd Annual International Conference of the IEEE Engineering in Medicine & Biology Society (EMBC); Institute of Electrical and Electronics Engineers (IEEE), online event (ex-Montreal). 20–24 July 2020; Volume 2020, pp. 851–854.
53. Goovaerts, H.G.; Ros, H.H.; Akker, T.J.V.D.; Schneider, H. A digital QRS detector based on the principle of contour limiting. *IEEE Trans. Biomed. Eng.* **1976**, *23*, 154–160. [CrossRef]
54. Pan, J.; Tompkins, W.J. A real-time QRS detection algorithm. *IEEE Trans. Biomed. Eng.* **1985**, *32*, 230–236. [CrossRef] [PubMed]
55. Russell, J.A.; Barrett, L.F. Core affect, prototypical emotional episodes, and other things called emotion: Dissecting the elephant. *J. Pers. Soc. Psychol.* **1999**, *76*, 805–819. [CrossRef]
56. Vecchiato, G.; Cherubino, P.; Maglione, A.G.; Ezquierro, M.T.H.; Marinozzi, F.; Bini, F.; Trettel, A.; Babiloni, F. How to measure cerebral correlates of emotions in marketing relevant tasks. *Cogn. Comput.* **2014**, *6*, 856–871. [CrossRef]
57. Bakdash, J.Z.; Marusich, L.R. Repeated measures correlation. *Front. Psychol.* **2017**, *8*, 456. [CrossRef] [PubMed]
58. Marakhimov, A.; Joo, J. Consumer adaptation and infusion of wearable devices for healthcare. *Comput. Hum. Behav.* **2017**, *76*, 135–148. [CrossRef]
59. Guk, K.; Han, G.; Lim, J.; Jeong, K.; Kang, T.; Lim, E.-K.; Jung, J. Evolution of wearable devices with real-time disease monitoring for personalized healthcare. *Nanomaterials* **2019**, *9*, 813. [CrossRef]
60. Tran, V.-T.; Riveros, C.; Ravaud, P. Patients' views of wearable devices and AI in healthcare: Findings from the ComPaRe e-cohort. *NPJ Digit. Med.* **2019**, *2*, 1–8. [CrossRef] [PubMed]
61. Stavropoulos, T.G.; Lazarou, I.; Strantsalis, D.; Nikolopoulos, S.; Kompatsiaris, I.; Koumanakos, G.; Frouda, M.; Tsolaki, M. Human factors and requirements of people with mild cognitive impairment, their caregivers and healthcare professionals for ehealth systems with wearable trackers. In Proceedings of the IEEE International Conference on Human-Machine Systems (ICHMS), Rome, Italy, 6–8 April 2020; pp. 1–6.

Article

Constructing an Emotion Estimation Model Based on EEG/HRV Indexes Using Feature Extraction and Feature Selection Algorithms

Kei Suzuki, Tipporn Laohakangvalvit *, Ryota Matsubara and Midori Sugaya

Shibaura Institute of Technology, Tokyo 135-8548, Japan; ma21072@shibaura-it.ac.jp (K.S.); ryota@sic.shibaura-it.ac.jp (R.M.); doly@shibaura-it.ac.jp (M.S.)
* Correspondence: tipporn@shibaura-it.ac.jp; Tel.: +81-3-5859-8517

Citation: Suzuki, K.; Laohakangvalvit, T.; Matsubara, R.; Sugaya, M. Constructing an Emotion Estimation Model Based on EEG/HRV Indexes Using Feature Extraction and Feature Selection Algorithms. *Sensors* **2021**, *21*, 2910. https://doi.org/10.3390/s21092910

Academic Editor: Alan Jović

Received: 31 March 2021
Accepted: 19 April 2021
Published: 21 April 2021

Publisher's Note: MDPI stays neutral with regard to jurisdictional claims in published maps and institutional affiliations.

Copyright: © 2021 by the authors. Licensee MDPI, Basel, Switzerland. This article is an open access article distributed under the terms and conditions of the Creative Commons Attribution (CC BY) license (https://creativecommons.org/licenses/by/4.0/).

Abstract: In human emotion estimation using an electroencephalogram (EEG) and heart rate variability (HRV), there are two main issues as far as we know. The first is that measurement devices for physiological signals are expensive and not easy to wear. The second is that unnecessary physiological indexes have not been removed, which is likely to decrease the accuracy of machine learning models. In this study, we used single-channel EEG sensor and photoplethysmography (PPG) sensor, which are inexpensive and easy to wear. We collected data from 25 participants (18 males and 7 females) and used a deep learning algorithm to construct an emotion classification model based on Arousal–Valence space using several feature combinations obtained from physiological indexes selected based on our criteria including our proposed feature selection methods. We then performed accuracy verification, applying a stratified 10-fold cross-validation method to the constructed models. The results showed that model accuracies are as high as 90% to 99% by applying the features selection methods we proposed, which suggests that a small number of physiological indexes, even from inexpensive sensors, can be used to construct an accurate emotion classification model if an appropriate feature selection method is applied. Our research results contribute to the improvement of an emotion classification model with a higher accuracy, less cost, and that is less time consuming, which has the potential to be further applied to various areas of applications.

Keywords: emotion recognition; electroencephalogram (EEG); photoplethysmography (PPG); machine learning; feature extraction; feature selection

1. Introduction

In recent years, there has been a number of studies on estimating human emotions in the engineering field, and there are a wide variety of fields where this technology is expected to be applied [1–3]. In human–robot interactions (HRI), emotion estimation technology is used to facilitate communication between humans and robots in real-life settings, such as schools [4], homes [5], ambient assisted living [6], hospitals [7], and in rehabilitation [8]. In the field of marketing, the best advertisements [9] for a customer are presented by estimating a customer's emotion. Furthermore, in the field of education, emotion analysis technology is used to improve the learning process and remote teaching [4]. In daily-living scenarios, such as in homes and ambient assisted living, several sensor technologies have been used to recognize emotions, aiming at improving emotional health and comfort, especially for older adults and people with disabilities [5,6]. In the medical field, mental healthcare is done by detecting unpleasant emotions, such as stress [10], and by assisting people who have communication difficulties due to handicaps [11].

Emotion estimation, which is applicable in various fields, can be divided into several methods. We divided them into two categories, based on the literature of Wang et al. [12] and Jianhua et al. [3]. The first is a method that analyzes facial expressions, posture, behavior, voice, etc. The second is a method that analyzes the autonomic nervous system using physiological indexes, such as electrocardiogram (ECG), respiration, heartbeat, electroencephalogram (EEG), electromyography (EMG), and eye movements. The former method is the result of the intervention of cognitive functions that people can express intentionally and has the advantage of being observable from the outside. However, it can be faked; for example, when a person expresses something different from his or her true intentions. This means that we may not be able to guarantee that an emotion can be estimated accurately [13]. The other is a method for estimating emotions based on direct physiological responses to stimuli, unlike faces and voices, and has received a great deal of attention in recent years [14,15]. Since physiological response to an external stimulus is difficult to change arbitrarily via human consciousness, the latter method has the advantage of being able to estimate emotions more objectively using physiological data [3,12,16].

In the early stages of emotion estimation by analyzing physiological data, the use of a single type of physiological index was the main method. For example, Krishna et al. employed EEG signals to classify basic emotions using a mixture classification technique [17]. However, in recent years, it is known that more complex emotion estimations with a high accuracy can be achieved by using multiple sources of physiological indexes [13].

To estimate emotions by analyzing physiological indexes, the Russell's circumplex model [18] and the Arousal–Valence space model [19] are often used (Figure 1). These models are among the most referenced emotion classification methods in the field of psychology, and represent basic human emotions on two axes, Arousal and Valence [3,14]. This model is also commonly used in studies to estimate emotions by analyzing physiological indexes and is regarded as a proven emotion classification model [2]. Several studies on emotion recognition using multimodal physiological signals have been reported, in which both basic and complex emotion recognition models have been proposed, combining physiological signals, especially EEG, ECG, and EMG [20]. Additionally, anxiety level recognition using blood volume pressure (BVP) and galvanic skin response (GSR), as well as skin temperature, has been proposed recently in areas of application like VR-based therapy [21].

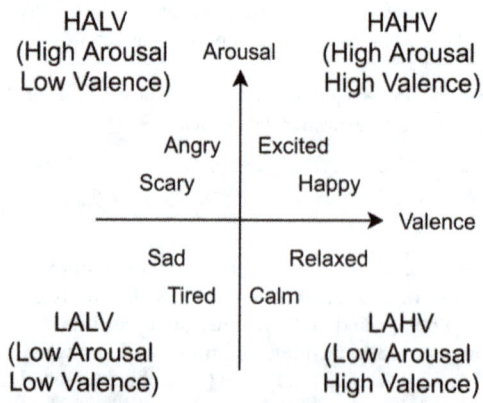

Figure 1. Arousal–Valence space model.

In emotion estimation studies using multimodal physiological indexes, the issue is how to combine physiological and psychological indexes. Ikeda et al. proposed an emotion estimation method that combines EEG and heart rate variability (HRV) indexes with psychological indexes based on Russell's circumplex model [16]. Ikeda et al. assigned EEG indexes to the Arousal axis of the psychological index (vertical axis of the Russell's circumplex model), and the HRV indexes to the Valence axis of the psychological index (horizontal axis of the Russell's circumplex model). Then, the correlation between EEG and HRV indexes were measured in real time and the psychological indexes were analyzed to classify emotions. It has been reported that EEG can be used to measure the state of concentration [22] and that it has a negative correlation with a subjectively evaluated level of arousal [2]. Therefore, we believe that there is a certain validity in mapping EEG indexes to Arousal. The HRV indexes have been considered reliable to detect stress as unpleasant emotions [23]. In addition, some HRV indexes can be used to estimate a relaxed state [2]. Therefore, we believe that there is a certain amount of validity in assigning the HRV indexes to Valence.

However, the method of Ikeda et al. does not take the individual differences that occur in physiological indexes when mapping EEG and HRV indexes to Arousal and Valence, respectively, into account. They mapped pNN50, one HRV index, to Valence. According to Francesco et al., the mean value of pNN50 is 0.3 [24]. In addition, Michael et al. reported that pNN50 is negatively correlated with stress level calculated using a self-assessment questionnaire [25]. Based on the above points, Ikeda et al. employed 0.3 as a threshold of pNN50: emotion is judged as having a high valence if pNN50 is above 0.3 and a low valence if it is below 0.3. However, for more general applications, it is necessary to deal with individual differences in physiological indexes, such as EEG and HRV indexes.

To address this issue, Urabe et al. proposed a machine learning method based on these physiological indexes and the ground-truth information acquired from a self-assessment [26]. They used deep learning with EEG and HRV indexes as features to construct an emotion estimation model for each individual, which enabled highly accurate emotion estimation. As a result of verifying the accuracy of emotion estimation using Urabe et al.'s method, it was reported that an average classification accuracy of 80% and a maximum classification accuracy of 100% were obtained in the four quadrants of the Arousal–Valence space model, HAHV, HALV, LALV, and LAHV, shown in Figure 1 [25].

However, when considering applications in medical fields, such as healthcare, an average accuracy of 80% may still be insufficient. In general, when constructing an estimation model using machine learning, it is suggested that the accuracy can be improved by discovering useful features for estimation and removing unnecessary ones through the calculation, extraction, and selection of features [27]. However, the number of features used in Urabe et al.'s study was only six; five for EEG indexes and one for HRV index, which supports the idea that that the lack of feature extraction and selection is one of the reasons for insufficient accuracy of their emotion estimation model.

Another study that used EEG and HRV indexes as features is that of Tong et al. [28]. They used a total of 34 physiological indexes: 9 HRV indexes from a photoplethysmogram (PPG) data and 25 EEG indexes from a five-channel EEG data. They reported that the machine learning accuracy using all indexes as features was 67% for binary classification of low and high arousal, and 65% for binary classification of low and high valence. However, they did not perform feature selection. By selecting features, we expected a higher accuracy in emotion estimation.

On the other hand, Katsigiannis et al. extracted 42 EEG-based features from 14-channel EEG data and 71 HRV-based features from ECG data [13]. They reported that the accuracy of emotion estimation using all of these features for the binary classification of both high/low arousal, as well as high/low valence, was about 62%.

Katsigiannis et al. extracted a larger number of features than Urabe et al. and Tong et al. However, feature selection was still not performed. In addition, there is an issue with the measurement equipment used for feature extraction. When wearing an EEG sensor, the electrodes need to touch the scalp, and hair needs to be avoided. In addition, some EEG sensors require saline solution or special gel to reduce the electrical resistance. To increase user comfort and ease of use, it is recommended to use fewer electrodes [14], but Katsigiannis et al. used 14 electrodes. In addition, although they used an ECG to calculate the HRV indexes, a PPG can be an alternative to measure the same indexes more inexpensively [2].

Therefore, our study used a simple single-electrode EEG sensor to increase user comfort and ease of use, and a PPG sensor to collect HRV data at a low cost, in order to verify whether emotion estimation technology can be performed more easily. In addition, we extracted and selected the features from EEG and HRV data, aiming at increasing the accuracy of emotion estimation model. In this paper, our method for feature extraction and selection, construction of deep-learning-based emotion estimation model, and validation of the model accuracy are presented.

The structure of this paper is as follows: Section 2 describes the EEG and HRV indexes to be used as features for model construction via machine learning; Section 3 describes the data collection method for model construction; Section 4 describes our proposed method, that is, the feature selection and its results; Section 5 describes the proposed emotion classification model and its accuracy validation results; and Section 6 summarizes the paper.

2. Feature Extraction from EEG/HRV Data

2.1. EEG Indexes

EEG is an electrical signal recorded in the brain using electrodes. The EEG signal is classified into several bands based on the frequency, each of which has different interpretations in psychological and brain activity states [29]. Generally, wide frequency bands such as α, β, and γ, are used as indexes to estimate human emotions. In addition, subdivided frequency bands such as low α and high α can be used to estimated more subtle human emotions. Therefore, we employed all of them as EEG indexes in this study.

In addition to the above EEG indexes, we used moving average of those EEG indexes with a window size of 15. Since EEG indexes have severe fluctuations by nature, which is considered to inhibit the effectiveness of the objective function minimization, and the threshold value calculation of the machine learning algorithm, calculating the moving average is considered to help reduce this inhibition, and may result in the increase of accuracy of emotion estimation model. Table 1 shows the EEG indexes and their corresponding frequency bands and interpretations used in this study [30–32].

Table 1. Electroencephalogram (EEG) indexes used in this study.

EEG Index/Band	Frequency Band (Hz)	Interpretation
δ	1–3	Deepest sleep without dreams, unconscious, non-REM sleep, cognitive task by frontal lobe
θ	4–7	Intuitive, creative, dream, recall, fantasy, imaginary, REM sleep
α [1]	8–12	Relaxed but not sleepy, tranquil, conscious
β [2]	13–30	Stress, wide awake, excited, conscious
γ [3]	31–50	Cognition, motor function, higher mental activity
Low α	8–9	Relaxed, peaceful, conscious
High α	10–12	Relaxed but focused
Low β	13–17	Thinking, accidents and environmental awareness, relaxed yet focused, integrated
High β	18–30	Alert, upset, agitation
Low γ	31–40	Memory, higher mental activity
Mid γ	41–50	Visual information processing
MA15 × [4] where x = {θ, δ, α, β, γ, Low α, High α, Low β, High β, Low γ, Mid γ}	Note [5]	Note [5]

[1] α is calculated from Low α + High α. [2] β is calculated from Low β + High β. [3] γ is calculated from Low γ + Mid γ. [4] Moving average of index x with window size of 15. [5] The frequency band and interpretation are corresponding to each EEG index/band x.

Urabe et al. evaluated the function of the frontal lobe in brain function in order to measure Arousal in the Arousal–Valence space model [25]. EEG signal acquired from the frontal lobe is often used for an integrated measurement of concentration and drowsiness. In addition, some studies reported that emotion estimation accuracy of 90% or more could be achieved only with a couple of electrodes placed in the frontal lobe [3]. Therefore, this study also measured EEG signals by placing an electrode near the left frontal lobe, namely the AF3 channel as defined by the International 10–20 EEG system, using Mindwave Mobile 2 manufactured by NeuroSky as EEG sensor, which is a simple and low-invasive single-channel EEG sensor with a sampling rate of 512 Hz. The output from this EEG sensor is acquired approximately once per second.

Although the EEG indexes α, β, and γ cannot be acquired directly from this EEG sensor, they can be calculated from the raw data: Low α + High α for α; Low β + High β for β; and Low γ + Mid γ for γ. Note that raw data acquired from this sensor represent the relative EEG powers calculated using NeuroSky's original algorithm and therefore has no units [33].

2.2. HRV Indexes

HRV is the physiological phenomenon of the variation in the time interval between adjacent heartbeats or inter-beat interval (IBI). We used pulse wave sensor manufactured by Switch Science that works with Arduino kit to acquire PPG signal. It has the sampling rate of 500 Hz and gives output approximately once per 0.5–1.5 s.

To extract HRV indexes, we employed two most widely used methods: time-domain and frequency-domain. Table 2 shows the HRV indexes and the corresponding interpretation employed in this study [34,35].

Table 2. Heart Rate Variability (HRV) indexes used in this study.

HRV Index	Definition	Interpretation
Inter-beat Interval (IBI)	Time interval between adjacent heartbeats	Sympathetic and parasympathetic nerves
Heart Rate (HR)	Number of beats per minute	Tension, Calm
pNNx [1] where x = {10, 20, 30, 40, 50}	Percentage of adjacent IBIs with absolute values greater than x ms	Parasympathetic nerve
SDNN [1]	Standard deviation of IBI	Sympathetic and parasympathetic nerves
RMSSD [1]	Root mean square of IBI difference	Parasympathetic nerve
SDNN/RMSSD [1]	Ratio of SDNN by RMSSD	Sympathetic nerve
CVNN [1]	Coefficient of variation of IBI	Sympathetic and parasympathetic nerves
LF [2]	Frequency-domain analysis of IBI power value of 0.04–0.15 Hz	Sympathetic and parasympathetic nerves
HF [2]	Frequency-domain analysis of IBI power value of 0.15–0.40 Hz	Parasympathetic nerve
LF/HF [2]	LF/HF	Sympathetic nerve

[1] Every time an IBI value is acquired, the value is calculated with the interval of 30. [2] Every time an IBI value is acquired, the value is calculated with an interval of 200 s.

HRV indexes are reported to be influenced by the sympathetic and parasympathetic nervous systems. LF and HF, which are frequency-domain HRV indexes, are decomposed from pulse wave signal into high-frequency (HF) and low-frequency (LF) domains using fast Fourier transform (FFT). LF is considered to the reflect sympathetic nerve, and HF is considered to reflect both parasympathetic and sympathetic nerves. Human emotions can be evaluated by using the ratio of LF and HF (LF/HF) [35]. We described the calculation method of LF and HF as a pseudocode, shown in Figure 2.

```
Declare array IBI_list

While experiment is not finished do
    Acquire pulsewave signal

    If new IBI_value is detected
        Append new IBI_value to IBI_list
        Remove oldest IBI_value from IBI_list
        Apply cubic spline interpolation to data in IBI_list
        Resample interpolated data in IBI_list to 1Hz
        Apply Hanning window to resampled data in IBI_list
        Perform Fast Fourier Transform with applied data in IBI_list
        Integrate power spectra of each frequency band of LF and HF
End
```

Figure 2. Pseudocode showing the calculation method of LF and HF.

In addition to LF and HF as frequency-domain HRV indexes, the standard deviation and coefficient of IBI variations can be used as time-domain HRV indexes for sympathetic and parasympathetic nerves. We calculated several indexes (i.e., pNNx, SDNN, RMSSD, SDNN/RMSSD, and CVNN) using 30 IBI datapoints as a sliding window size, meaning that these indexes are newly calculated each time the new IBI is acquired.

3. Data Collection

To prepare datasets for constructing emotion estimation model by machine learning, we needed to collect both EEG and HRV data and label them with corresponding emotions. This section describes an experimental method used to acquire these data. In addition, we describe how to prepare a dataset for machine learning using the collected data. The participants in this experiment were 25 adults who were in their 20s (16 Males; 6 Females) and 30s (2 Males; 1 Female). All of them are Japanese and were physically and emotionally healthy.

3.1. Emotional Stimulus

In this study, we used music as emotional stimulus employed from a music database created by researchers at Jyväskylä University under repeated consultation with professional musicians [30]. This database contains 110 film soundtracks, each of which is approximately 15 s long. All music was scored by professional musicians based on the dimensional and discrete emotion model into several emotions, such as valence, energy, tension, anger, fear, happy, sad, beauty, etc. For each quadrant of the Arousal–Valence space model, we selected two songs based on highest scores of corresponding emotions as follows: In HAHV, we used songs No.23 and No.24, which have the highest energy scores. In HALV, we used songs No.11 and No.68, which have the highest fear scores. In LALV, we used songs No.33 and No.109, which have the highest sad scores. In LAHV, we used songs No.41 and No.42, which have the highest beauty or tenderness scores (refer to [30] for a full details of the music database and their scores).

3.2. Emotion Estimation toward Stimulus

We performed subjective evaluation to estimate emotions as arousal and valence towards the eight selected songs using Self-Assessment Manikin (SAM). It is a non-verbal emotion evaluation method that can be performed by selecting one of nine mannequins that most closely resembles one's emotions (Figure 3). As SAM can be performed regardless of language, we expected that the influence by an individual difference on how one perceives the word can be reduced [36]. In this experiment, as some participants might not be accustomed to self-assessment of emotions using SAM; we asked them to practice using a simple experiment before starting the real experiment.

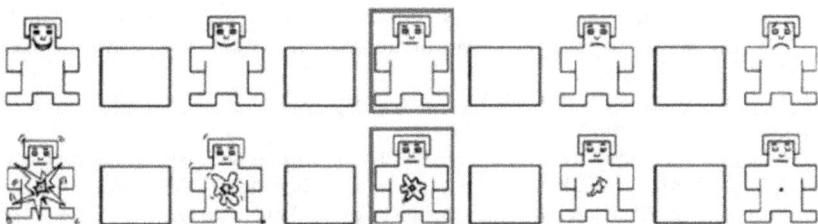

Figure 3. Self-Assessment Manikin (SAM) used for estimating emotions toward music stimuli. The upper scale is for the evaluation of the Valence level. The lower scale is for that of the Arousal level.

From the results of SAM, we determined emotion corresponding to each song based on the Arousal–Valence space model. A threshold of 5 was used as it is the mid-point on the SAM scale of 1 to 9, that is, an emotion evaluated with valence ≥ 5 is judged as high valence and vice versa. Similarly, an emotion evaluated with arousal ≥ 5 is judged as high arousal and vice versa. Based on these criteria, we divided the evaluated emotion-based Arousal–Valence space model into four classes, as follows:

- Emotions with Arousal > 5 and Valence $\geq$ 5 or Arousal = Valence = 5 belong to HAHV (the first quadrant);
- Emotions with Arousal $\leq$ 5 and Valence > 5 belong to HALV (the second quadrant);
- Emotions with Arousal < 5 and Valence $\leq$ 5 belong to LALV (the third quadrant);
- Emotions with Arousal $\geq$ 5 and Valence < 5 belong to LAHV (the fourth quadrant).

Based on the above thresholds, we generated categorical data by dividing them into four classes (i.e., HAHV, HALV, LALV, and LAHV): two classes of valence (low/high valence) and two classes of arousal (low/high arousal).

3.3. Experimental Procedure and Environment

The experimental procedure (Figure 4) is described as follows:

1. Participant sits on a chair and wears EEG sensor, pulse sensor, and earphone. Then, the recording of EEG and pulse wave data is started.
2. Participant practices the experiment by using simplified procedures of steps (3) to (4).
3. Participant waits for 10 min in a resting state (The first rest).
4. Participant listens to the music for 1 min (the same 15-s song is repeated 4 times) and then uses SAM to perform self-assessment of his/her emotion evoked by the music with no time limit. Then, he/she rests for 2 min.
5. Steps (3) and (4) are repeated until eight trials are finished. (Note that the music is changed for each trial). Then, the recording of EEG and pulse wave data is stopped.

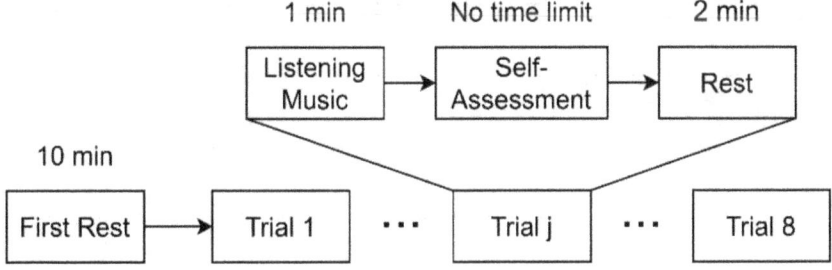

Figure 4. Experimental procedure.

In resting and music listening states, an image with a gray background and a black cross in the center was shown on the display placed in front of the participants. Participants were instructed to focus on the cross as much as possible in order to reduce unintentional visual noise. In addition, the experiment was conducted in a quiet room while the participants were wearing earphone at all time in order to reduce unintentional audio noise.

3.4. Dataset Construction

From the experiment, we determined sections (start/stop timestamps) when each music stimulus was presented in order to collect EEG and pulse wave data to calculate the EEG and HRV indexes. Since EEG and pulse wave sensors were unsynchronized, the data were fetched from the most recent EEG and pulse wave data, every second. Since each of the music stimulus was presented for about 60 s, approximate 60 EEGs and pulse wave data were generated for each. Subjective evaluation results were also assigned to the physiological data of the corresponding music. These steps were repeated eight times for eight selected songs. Finally, we constructed a dataset as input for machine-learning-based classification models using EEG and HRV indexes as input features and three types of classified emotions from Arousal and Valence scores as emotion labels of the input features. These three types were used for three types of emotion classification models: (1) four-class model for "HAHV/HALV/LALV/LAHV", (2) binary model for "Low arousal/High arousal", and (3) binary model for "Low valence/High valence".

As a result, the constructed dataset contained 3558, 2175, 2704, and 3312 datapoints for the four quadrants in the Arousal–Valence space model. The procedure of dataset construction is illustrated in Figure 5.

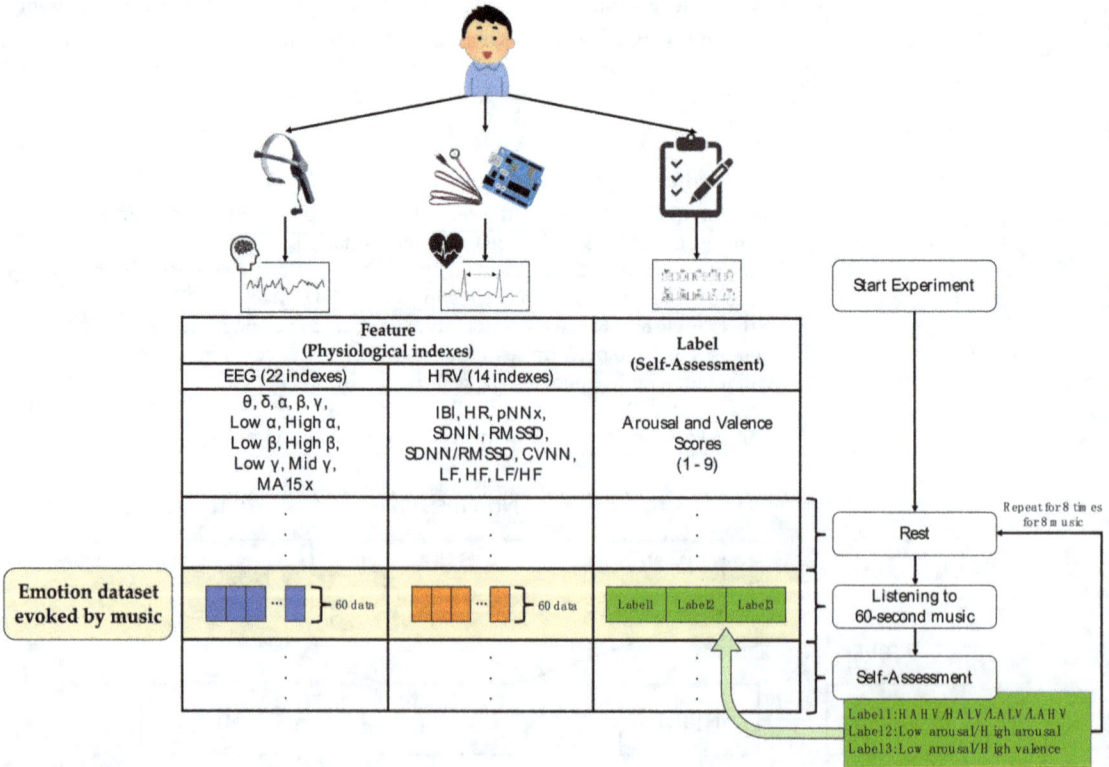

Figure 5. The illustration of the procedure to construct emotion dataset using EEG and HRV indexes as input features for machine-learning-based classification models and three types of classified emotions from self-assessment scores (Arousal and Valence) as three types of emotion labels.

4. Feature Selection

In this research, we proposed feature selection as a method to improve model accuracy, which was not employed in the research of Urabe et al. [26]. To select the features, we used the degree of contribution technique to generate the feature importance used for feature ranking from multiple feature selection algorithms; an ensemble approach. It was verified by Haq et al. that the ensemble feature selection method yielded a higher accuracy for emotion estimation compared with a single algorithm [37].

We used the following four feature selection algorithms: correlation ratio (CR), mutual information (MI), importance of random forest (RF), and weight of SVM L1 regularization (SVM L1). They were employed for two reasons: (1) they have already been proven, and (2) the feature importance can be calculated to make feature selection easier [38–40]. Each feature selection algorithm and the procedure to combine their results are described in the following sections.

4.1. Correlation Ratio (CR)

The correlation ratio is a value that quantifies the relationship between qualitative data and quantitative data. Categorical data from the SAM results were used to identify which quadrant in the Arousal–Valence space model the emotion belongs to. Correlation ratios were used to observe the relationship between the emotions in the four quadrants as qualitative data and the EEG/HRV indexes as quantitative data.

The calculation method is expressed by Equation (1). The definitions of the variables in the formula are as follows: η^2 denotes the correlation ratio; a denotes number of qualitative data types; n_i denotes number of features x data belonging to the i-th qualitative data; $\overline{x_i}$ denotes mean value of features x belonging to the i-th qualitative data; $\overline{x}$ denotes mean value of feature x; and $x_{i,j}$ denotes the value of the j-th feature x belonging to the i-th qualitative data.

$$\eta^2 = \frac{\sum_{i=1}^{a} n_i (\overline{x_i} - \overline{x})^2}{\sum_{i=1}^{a} \sum_{j=1}^{n_i} (x_{i,j} - \overline{x})} \tag{1}$$

4.2. Mutual Information (MI)

Mutual information is a quantified value of the relationship between two variables. In this study, we quantified the relationship between the emotions in the four quadrants and the EEG/HRV indexes.

The formula for calculating the amount of mutual information between qualitative data and quantitative data is as shown in Equation (2) [39]. The definitions of the variables in the formula are as follows: I(X; Y) denotes mutual information of X and Y; p(x) denotes probability of x; p(y) denotes probability of y; and p(x, y) denotes conditional probabilities of x and y.

$$I(X;Y) = \sum_{x,y} p(x, y) \log\left(\frac{p(x,y)}{p(x)p(y)}\right) \tag{2}$$

4.3. Importance of Random Forest (RF)

The importance of a random forest is a quantified value of the degree of contribution in estimating each feature, which is calculated by a machine learning algorithm. Random forest creates multiple decision trees, and the data are classified at the nodes in each decision tree. It is an algorithm that makes a final estimation by voting the classification results based on those decision trees.

The calculation method is expressed by Equations (3) and (4). The definitions of the variables in the formula is as follows: I_x denotes importance of feature x; N denotes number of nodes branched by feature x; $\Delta I_{x,n}$ denotes the amount of decrease in purity at the nth node branched by the feature x; G_{Parent} denotes impurity in the parent node of the nth node; $G_{Child\ Left}$ denotes impurity in the left child node in the nth node; $G_{Child\ Right}$ denotes impurity in the right child node in the nth node; m denotes number of data in the nth node;

m_{Left} denotes number of data in the left child node in the nth node; and m_{Right} denotes number of data of the right child node in the nth node.

$$I_x = \sum_{n=1}^{N} \Delta I_{x,n} \quad (3)$$

$$\Delta I_{x,n} = G_{Parent} - \frac{m_{Left}}{m} \times G_{Child\ Left} - \frac{m_{Right}}{m} \times G_{Chid\ Right} \quad (4)$$

At each node in multiple decision trees, the amount of decrease in impurity is calculated by classifying the ground-truth data as in Equation (3). The decrease in the impurity can be interpreted as an increase in the purity, which contributes to the classification and estimation. Therefore, the degree of contribution in estimation is quantified by taking the sum, as shown in Equation (4).

For the implementation of the random forest algorithm, we employed Scikit-learn Python-based machine-learning library. The parameter settings are as listed below.

- The number of trees in the forest: 1000
- Criterion: Gini impurity (default)
- The maximum depth of the tree: None (default)
- The minimum number of samples required to split an internal node: 2 (default)
- Bootstrap: True (default)
- All other required parameters are set as default by the library.

4.4. SVM L1 Regularization Weight (SVM L1)

Support vector machine (SVM) L1 regularization weight is the weight vector for each feature when the L1-norm regularization term is introduced into the SVM objective function. By introducing the regularization term, the weighting coefficients of the features that are not useful for estimation approach zero, and their influences are reduced, and thus the estimation accuracy is improved [41]. At this time, feature selection was performed by removing the features whose weighting coefficient was close to zero, considering as features not useful for estimation. The equation in which the L1-norm regularization term is introduced into the objective function of SVM is shown in Equation (5) [39]. The meaning of the variables in the formula is as follows: $||w||_1$ denotes L1-norm term; w denotes weight coefficient; and C denotes variable that controls the degree of influence of the L1-norm term.

$$\min_{w_0,w} \sum_{i=1}^{n} [1 - y_i(w_0 + \sum_{j=1}^{q} w_j x_{i,j})] + C||w||_1 \quad (5)$$

For the implementation of the SVM algorithm, we employed Scikit-learn Python-based machine-learning library. The parameter settings are as listed below.

- Kernel: Linear
- The norm used in the penalization: L1 (assigning coefficients/weights to the features)
- Regularization parameter (C): 1.0 (default)
- All other required parameters are set as default by the library.

4.5. Feature Selection Ensemble

To integrate the results from multiple feature selection algorithms, we performed the following steps (Figure 6):

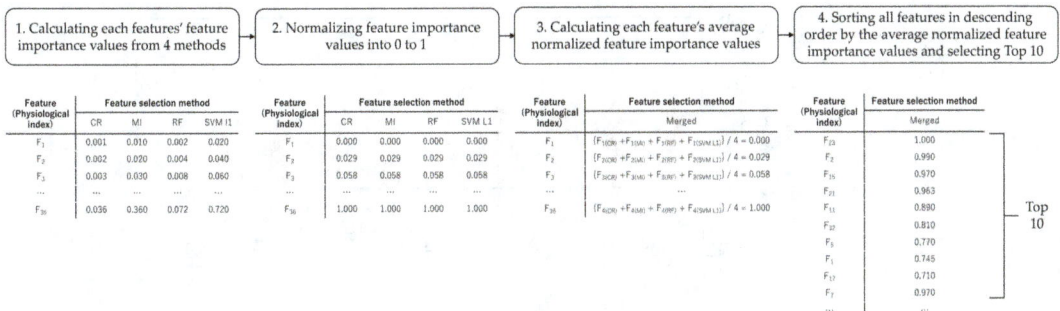

Figure 6. The illustration of the procedure of feature selection ensemble from the calculation of feature importance values by integrating the four feature selection methods to the selection of top 10 important features.

1. The feature importance of each feature was calculated for each feature selection algorithm. Note that the features are the physiological indexes consisting of 22 EEG indexes and 14 HRV indexes.
2. The feature importance values were normalized so that the maximum value was 1 and the minimum value was 0.
3. For each feature, the average normalized feature importance values were calculated from the values of the four feature selection algorithms.
4. All features were sorted in descending order by the average normalized feature importance values.
5. The indexes in the top 10 were selected as important features.

Figures 7 and 8 show the top 10 indexes that were judged as useful features for emotion estimation based on feature selection results. Figure 7 shows the result of feature selection for the classification of emotions into four classes: HAHV, HALV, LALV and LAHV. Figure 8 shows the classification of emotions into two classes: low arousal and high arousal. Figure 9 shows the classification of emotions into two classes: low valence and high valence.

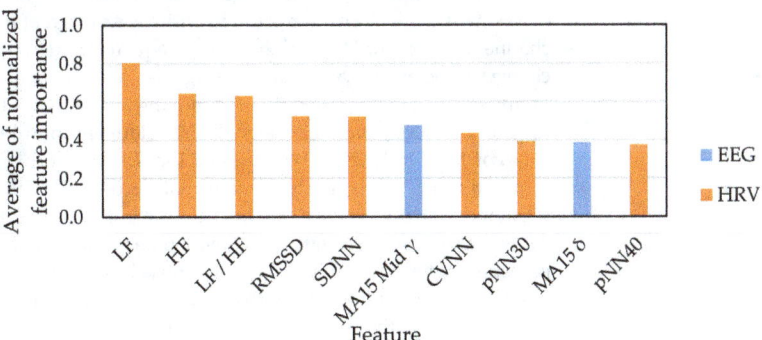

Figure 7. Feature selection result for HAHV, HALV, LALV and LAHV.

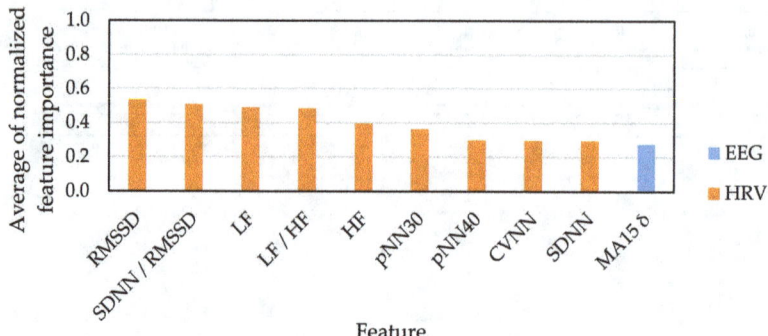

Figure 8. Feature selection result for low arousal and high arousal.

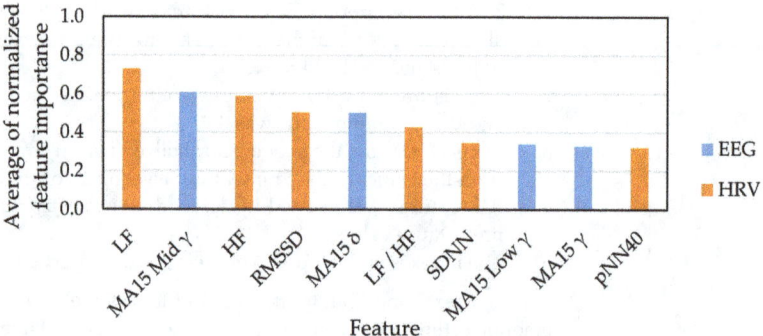

Figure 9. Feature selection result for low valence and high valence.

For EEG indexes, the feature selection results of the four emotion classifications of HAHV, HALV, LALV, and LAHV (Figure 7) suggest that the moving average of γ, that is the index acquired from the high-frequency-band EEG signal, relatively contributes to emotion estimation. This is consistent with the results reported by Wang et al. using a multi-channel EEG sensor [12] and that the γ frequency band is the most sensitive to emotional changes [3]. However, since the EEG signals were acquired only from the frontal lobe (AF4) in this study, it is suggested that the moving average of δ, that is the index acquired from the low-frequency-band EEG signal, also relatively contributes to emotion estimation.

For HRV indexes, it is suggested that LF, HF, and LF/HF, which were the indexes acquired from the frequency-domain analysis of HRV with long time intervals, contribute to emotion estimation. Since the analysis section was long, it was highly possible that these indexes may reflect the state at rest more than the state at which the emotional stimuli were presented, which make it difficult for those indexes to contribute to emotion estimation. However, our results were contrary to this presumption. Though the HRV indexes are related to sympathetic and parasympathetic nervous systems, there is a time lag between the time when the stimulus is presented and the time when the HRV index reflects the influence by the stimulus. From this point of view, the analysis interval is often set to 24 h or 5 min in order to calculate reliable HRV indexes that fully reflects the effects of sympathetic nerves and parasympathetic nerves. In this study, it is considered that LF, HF, and LF/HF have a relatively long analysis interval, which enhances the reliability of the indexes and, as a result, contributes to emotion estimation. Next, RMSSD, which has a high degree of contribution to emotion estimation, is a time-domain HRV index that has been reported to have the same reliability even in a short analysis section like five minutes [42] and is used for monitoring the athlete's condition. In addition, this index is suggested to have a high reliability for emotion estimation, despite the short analysis interval [43].

Among the top 10 features of the emotion classification for low and high arousal (Figure 8), the number of EEG indexes is one and the number of HRV indexes is nine. Since EEG indexes are used to measure concentration and arousal, we expected that the number of EEG indexes would be more than that of HRV indexes. However, the results differed from our expectations. Related studies suggested that concentration and arousal can be estimated by HRV [44–46], which resembles our result. Thus, we suggest that HRV is more useful than EEG for estimating low and high arousal.

On the other hand, among the top 10 features of the emotion classification low and high valence (Figure 9), the number of EEG indexes is four and the number of HRV indexes is six. Since HRV indexes are generally used to measure relaxation and stress, we expected that the number of HRV indexes would be more than that of EEG indexes. The result is the same as expected. In addition, some EEG indexes almost have the same feature importance as HRV indexes. Hence, there is a potential that the EEG indexes can also be used to estimate valence in addition to the HRV indexes. Related studies suggested that EEG is strongly correlated with valence and is useful for estimating low and high valence [3], which resembles our result.

In addition, there is a potential that the EEG indexes calculated from the AF3 node may be replaced by HRV indexes in the classification of low and high valence. This suggests that only HRV may be enough to estimate emotion even without EEG, which contributes to the simplification of emotion estimation technology.

5. Accuracy Verification and Discussion

In order to clarify the usefulness of applying our proposed feature selection method, multimodal physiological indexes for the emotion classification model were constructed in this study; accuracy verification was performed using a combination of several features. For accuracy verification, we employed several cross-validation methods with an emotion estimation model constructed using a deep learning algorithm.

5.1. Combination of Features

Table 3 shows 21 groups of feature combinations from EEG and/or HRV indexes. Three criteria to group feature combinations were applied as described below.

Table 3. Groups of feature combinations from EEG and/or HRV indexes.

Group No.	Group Name	Feature Combination
#1	EEG	θ, δ, Low α, High α, Low β, High β, Low γ, Mid γ, α, β, γ
#2	MA15 EEG	MA15 θ, MA15 δ, MA15 Low α, MA15 High α, MA15 Low β, MA15 High β, MA15 Low γ, MA15 Mid γ, MA15 α, MA15 β, MA15 γ
#3	TD HRV	IBI, HR, CVNN, SDNN, RMSSD, SDNN/RMSSD, pNN10, pNN20, pNN30, pNN40, pNN50
#4	FD HRV	LF, HF, LF/HF
#5	TD HRV + FD HRV	IBI, HR, CVNN, SDNN, RMSSD, SDNN/RMSSD, pNN10, pNN20, pNN30, pNN40, pNN50, LF, HF, LF/HF
#6	ALL	θ, δ, Low α, High α, Low β, High β, Low γ, Mid γ, α, β, γ, MA15 θ, MA15 δ, MA15 Low α, MA15 High α, MA15 Low β, MA15 High β, MA15 Low γ, MA15 Mid γ, MA15 α, MA15 β, MA15 γ, IBI, HR, CVNN, SDNN, RMSSD, SDNN/RMSSD, pNN10, pNN20, pNN30, pNN40, pNN50, LF, HF, LF/HF
#7	ENSEMBLE (HAHV, HALV, LALV, LAHV)	LF, HF, LF/HF, RMSSD, SDNN, MA15 Mid γ, CVNN, pNN30, MA15 δ, pNN40
#8	ENSEMBLE (Low/High Arousal)	RMSSD, SDNN/RMSSD, LF, LF/HF, HF, pNN30, pNN40, CVNN, SDNN, MA15 δ

Table 3. Cont.

Group No.	Group Name	Feature Combination
#9	ENSEMBLE (Low/High Valence)	LF, MA15 Mid γ, HF, RMSSD, MA15 δ, LF/HF, SDNN, MA15 Low γ, MA15 γ, pNN40
#10	CR (HAHV, HALV, LALV, LAHV)	MA15 Mid γ, LF/HF, MA15 γ, MA15 δ, MA15 Low γ, MA15 High β, SDNN/RMSSD, LF, MA15 High α, MA15 α
#11	CR (Low/High Arousal)	SDNN/RMSSD, LF/HF, MA15 δ, RMSSD, pNN10, MA15 Low α, MA15 Mid γ, MA15 Low β, Low α, pNN30
#12	CR (Low/High Valence)	MA15 Mid γ, MA15 γ, MA15 δ, MA15 Low γ, MA15 α, MA15 Low α, MA15 θ, pNN50, MA15 High α, γ
#13	MI (HAHV, HALV, LALV, LAHV)	RMSSD, LF, HF, SDNN, CVNN, LF/HF, β, High β, Mid γ, γ
#14	MI (Low/High Arousal)	RMSSD, LF, HF, SDNN, High α, δ, Low β, θ, β, CVNN
#15	MI (Low/High Valence)	RMSSD, LF, β, SDNN, HF, γ, High β, δ, Low β, CVNN
#16	RF (HAHV, HALV, LALV, LAHV)	LF, HF, LF/HF, RMSSD, CVNN, SDNN/RMSSD, SDNN, MA15 Low γ, MA15 Mid γ, MA15 High β
#17	RF (Low/High Arousal)	LF, LF/HF, HF, RMSSD, SDNN/RMSSD, MA15 High β, CVNN, MA15 δ, MA15 θ, SDNN
#18	RF (Low/High Valence)	LF, HF, LF/HF, RMSSD, MA15 Low γ, CVNN, MA15 High β, MA15 Mid γ, MA15 High α, SDNN/RMSSD
#19	SVM L1 (HAHV, HALV, LALV, LAHV)	SDNN, pNN30, LF, HF, pNN40, pNN20, CVNN, pNN10, pNN50, MA15 Mid γ
#20	SVM L1 (Low/High Arousal)	pNN30, pNN40, MA15 Low β, pNN20, pNN10, RMSSD, MA15 δ, HR, MA15 High β, MA15 Low γ
#21	SVM L1 (Low/High Valence)	LF, HF, MA15 Mid γ, pNN40, MA15 δ, RMSSD, pNN30, pNN20, LF/HF, HR,

1. The features were selected based on types of physiological indexes and calculation methods (Groups #1 to #5).
2. All features employed in this research were selected (Group #6).
3. The features were selected based on our proposed four feature selection methods (i.e., ensemble of the four feature selection methods, correlation ratio, mutual information, importance of random forest, and SVM L1 regularization weight) and the three emotion classification models (i.e., "HAHV, HALV, LALV, and LAHV", "Low/High Arousal", and "Low/High Valence") (Groups #7 to #21).

Based on the above criteria, the selected features and the selection method of each group are described as follows:

1. EEG group (#1) consists of all 11 EEG indexes employed in this study.
2. MA15 EEG group (#2) consists of 15-window-sized moving averages of all 11 EEG indexes.
3. TD HRV group (#3) consists of indexes calculated by all 11 HRV indexes calculated by time-domain analysis.
4. FD HRV group (#4) consists of indexes calculated by all 3 HRV indexes calculated by frequency-domain analysis.
5. TD HRV + FD HRV group (#5) consists of the combination of indexes from TD HRV (#3) and FD HRV (#4) groups.
6. ALL group (#6) consists of indexes that combines the indexes from EEG (#1), MA15 EEG (#2), TD HRV (#3), and FD HRV (#4).
7. ENSEMBLE (HAHV, HALV, LALV, and LAHV) group (#7) consists of the top 10 indexes that contribute to emotion estimation in the four-class emotion classification of HAHV, HALV, LALV, and LAHV.

8. ENSEMBLE (Low/High Arousal) group (#8) consists of the top 10 indexes that have the largest contribution of emotion estimation in the binary emotion classification into Low Arousal and High Arousal.
9. ENSEMBLE (Low/High Valence) group (#9) consists of the top 10 indexes that have the largest contribution in the binary emotion classification into Low Valence and High Valence.
10. CR (HAHV, HALV, LALV, and LAHV) group (#10) consists of the top 10 indexes from the correlation ratio as feature selection method that contribute to emotion estimation in the four-class emotion classification of HAHV, HALV, LALV, and LAHV.
11. CR (Low/High Arousal) group (#11) consists of the top 10 indexes from the correlation ratio as the feature selection method that contribute to emotion estimation in the four-class emotion classification of Low Arousal and High Arousal.
12. CR (Low/High Valence) group (#12) consists of the top 10 indexes from the correlation ratio as feature selection method that contribute to emotion estimation in the four-class emotion classification of Low Valence and High Valence.
13. MI (HAHV, HALV, LALV, and LAHV) group (#13) consists of the top 10 indexes from the mutual information as feature selection method that contribute to emotion estimation in the four-class emotion classification of HAHV, HALV, LALV, and LAHV.
14. MI (Low/High Arousal) group (#14) consists of the top 10 indexes from the mutual information as the feature selection method that contribute to emotion estimation in the four-class emotion classification of Low Arousal and High Arousal.
15. MI (Low/High Valence) group (#15) consists of the top 10 indexes from the mutual information as the feature selection method that contribute to emotion estimation in the four-class emotion classification of Low Valence and High Valence.
16. RF (HAHV, HALV, LALV, and LAHV) group (#16) consists of the top 10 indexes from the mutual information as the feature selection method that contribute to emotion estimation in the four-class emotion classification of HAHV, HALV, LALV, and LAHV.
17. RF (Low/High Arousal) group (#17) consists of the top 10 indexes from the importance of random forest as the feature selection method that contribute to emotion estimation in the four-class emotion classification of Low Arousal and High Arousal.
18. RF (Low/High Valence) group (#18) consists of the top 10 indexes from the importance of random forest as the feature selection method that contribute to emotion estimation in the four-class emotion classification of Low Valence and High Valence.
19. SVM L1 (HAHV, HALV, LALV, and LAHV) group (#19) consists of the top 10 indexes from the SVM L1 regularization weight as the feature selection method that contribute to emotion estimation in the four-class emotion classification of HAHV, HALV, LALV, and LAHV.
20. SVM L1 (Low/High Arousal) group (#20) consists of the top 10 indexes from the SVM L1 regularization weight as the feature selection method that contribute to emotion estimation in the four-class emotion classification of Low Arousal and High Arousal.
21. SVM L1 (Low/High Valence) group (#21) consists of the top 10 indexes from the SVM L1 regularization weight rest as the feature selection method that contribute to emotion estimation in the four-class emotion classification of Low Valence and High Valence.

5.2. Cross Validation

We selected the stratified K-fold (SKF) method to perform cross validation. It is a cross-validation method in which the ratio of the amount of data of each type of objective variable is equal when dividing training data and test data into K pieces [47]. In general, if there is a bias in the ratio of the amount of correct data for each of the training and test data, the amount of class 1 data will increase in the training data, while the number of class 1 data will decrease in the test data. The amount of data may result in unfair accuracy verification. Therefore, SKF was used to reduce these problems. For this cross-validation method, we set k to 10 which was used to divide data into 10 folds after merging the data of all participants. By using this method, the accuracy of emotion estimation model in which the data of all participants were included in the training data was calculated.

5.3. Accuracy Verification Indexes

We used Macro F1 as the accuracy verification index. Macro F1 is an extension of F1-score, which is an accuracy verification index used in binary classification to multi-label classification. The calculation method of F1-score is expressed by Equations (6)–(8).

$$\text{precision} = \frac{\text{TP}}{\text{TP} + \text{FP}} \quad (6)$$

$$\text{recall} = \frac{\text{TP}}{\text{TP} + \text{FN}} \quad (7)$$

$$F1 - \text{score} = \frac{2 \times \text{recall} \times \text{precision}}{\text{recall} + \text{precision}} \quad (8)$$

In the binary classification of positive and negative examples, the denotations of the variables in the equation is described as follows: TP denotes the amount of data for which the predicted value is a positive example and the prediction is correct; TN denotes the amount of data for which the predicted value is a negative example and the predicted value is correct; FP denotes the amount of data for which the predicted value is a positive example and the prediction is incorrect; FN denotes the amount of data for which the prediction is incorrect using the predicted value as a negative example; precision is an accuracy index that is emphasized when you want to reduce false positives; and recall is an accuracy index that is important when you want to avoid overlooking positive examples; F1-score is a balanced index by taking the harmonic mean of these accuracy indexes. Macro F1 is an accuracy index that calculates the above F1-score for each type of objective variable and their average value [47].

To construct a deep learning model, we used the same structure of the model constructed by Urabe et al. [26]: Intermediate layer: 256-dimensional three layers; intermediate layer activation function: ReLU; output layer activation function: Softmax; optimization algorithm: Stochastic Gradient Descent (SGD); and Dropout: 0.0.

5.4. Accuracy Verification Results

Figures 10–12 show the results of accuracy verification from the cross validations, the accuracy evaluation indexes, and the deep learning. The baseline accuracy of the classification model that returns a random prediction without learning is used as the baseline for accuracy comparison.

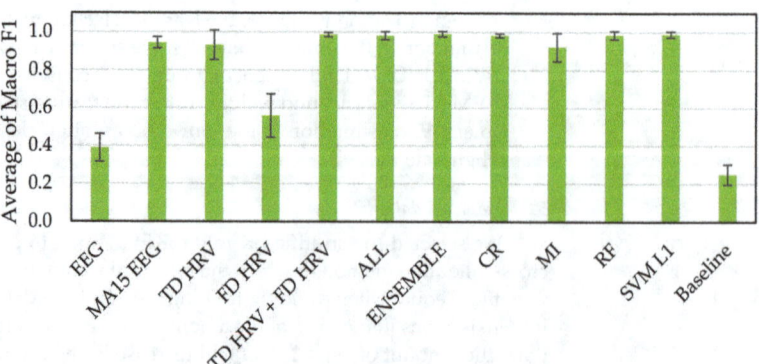

Figure 10. HAHV, HALV, LALV, LAHV (4 classes) emotion classification accuracies.

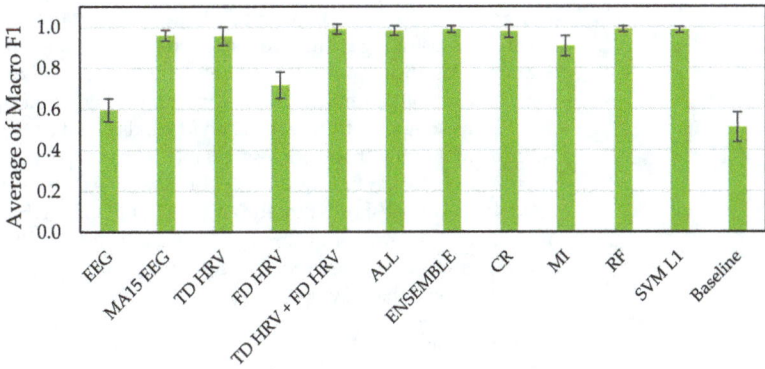

Figure 11. Low Arousal, High Arousal (2 classes) emotion classification accuracies.

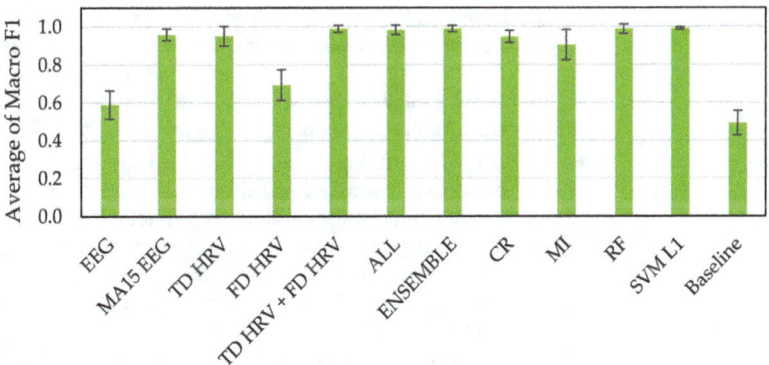

Figure 12. Low Arousal, High Valence (2 classes) emotion classification accuracies.

First, we compared the accuracies of every methods for feature selection with that of baseline. The results of the accuracy verification using Macro F1 scores as index showed that the accuracies range from 39% to 99% exceeding the baseline of 25% for the HAHV, HALV, LALV, and LAHV model (Figure 10), 59% to 99% exceeding the baseline of 51% for the Low and High Arousal classification model (Figure 11), and 59% to 99% exceeding the baseline of 49% for the Low and High Valence classification model (Figure 12).

Next, we compared the accuracies of our proposed methods (i.e., ENSEMBLE, CR, MI, RF, and SVM L1 groups) with that of all features (i.e., ALL group). The results show that all of them have high accuracies, ranging from 90% to 99% for all three classification models (i.e., "HAHV, HALV, LALV, and LAHV", "Low Arousal and High Arousal", and "Low Arousal and High Valence" models). These results indicate that even if all features were not used, the accuracy can reach 99%, which indicates the effectiveness of our proposed feature selection methods used in this study. Since a larger number of features makes the training time take longer in machine learning, we suggest reducing the time spent on training by reducing the number of features while the accuracy is still maintained.

Finally, we compared the accuracies of our proposed methods (i.e., ENSEMBLE, CR, MI, RF, and SVM L1 groups) with those of methods based on the types of physiological indexes and calculation methods (i.e., EEG, MA15 EEG, TD HRV, FD HRV, TD HRV + FD HRV groups). The results show that the accuracies of EEG and FD HRV groups are much lower than those of our proposed methods. In addition, even the accuracies of MA15 EEG, TD HRV, and TD HRV + FD HRV groups are almost the same as those of our proposed methods, they tended to have large variabilities indicating by the standard deviation illustrating as the error bars, especially for the "HAHV, HALV, LALV, and LAHV" emotion classification model. Therefore, we suggested that it is more effective to apply feature selection techniques for constructing the emotion classification model.

Even though the feature selection methods based on the types of physiological indexes and calculation methods are less reliable than our proposed method. By comparing the accuracies between EEG and MA15 EEG groups among the three emotion classification models, the result shows that the accuracy of EEG MA15 group is 56% increased at maximum from that of the EEG group. This result suggests that the accuracy was improved more than double when the moving average is applied to the indexes, suggesting the effectiveness of the moving average.

6. Discussion

In this research, we employed feature selection to improve the accuracy of an emotion classification model. We proposed four feature selection methods: correlation ratio (CR), mutual information (MI), importance of random forest (RF), and weight of SVM L1 regularization (SVM L1). In addition, we proposed the feature selection ensemble that combines the results from those four feature selection methods. Based on these, we obtained important features that were later used for model construction.

For accuracy verification, we constructed several emotion classification models using the feature combinations (Table 3) selected based on several criteria, including our proposed methods. As a result, we obtained the following findings:

- A model with high accuracy can be achieved even without using all features from physiological signals, suggesting that the accuracy is not always improved by combining large number of multimodal physiological indexes.
- The model using features only from specific physiological indexes, such as EEG or HRV, may produce a high accuracy; however, the variability tends to be large.
- The accuracy can be improved by applying the moving average to the normal values of physiological indexes.

Based on the above findings, we clarified that our proposed methods by using feature selection successfully improved the accuracy of the emotion classification model. In addition, as our proposed methods selected only top 10 important features, the training time for machine-learning based model can be reduced. Our research results contribute to the improvement of an emotion classification model with a higher accuracy, less cost, and that is less time consuming, which has potential to be further applied to various areas of applications.

This study has some limitations. First, we only collected the physiological signal data from a small number of participants that was unbalanced between males and females. In addition, we employed only eight music pieces (two for each of the four emotions in the Arousal–Valence space model), which might not be enough to fulfil the variety of music preferences among the participants and may result in not completely evoking target emotions. Therefore, we need to employ more music pieces and collect data from a larger number of participants in order to increase the reliability of our experimental results. In addition, as this is our first trial, we selected only four feature selection methods that can easily observe feature importance, and only one method for the cross validation in accuracy verification. Other feature selections, such as neural network, as well as cross validation methods, such as leave-one-subject-out (LOSO), should also be included and compared with our current proposed method in order to increase even higher accuracy for emotion classification model.

To construct the model for accuracy verification, we employed a deep learning algorithm which has shown great advantages in many research fields in recent year [48]. It has been proved to outperform the anomaly detection of medical images at a large scale [49]. Several techniques can be applied to improve the accuracy of deep learning models, such as data augmentation [50,51], the improvement of the capability to handle unseen data [52,53], and the adjustment of structures and parameters to train deep learning models which is typically an important process in every machine learning algorithm. Therefore, we will employ these promising techniques to increase the accuracy of our emotion classification model in order to enable the generalization capability.

7. Conclusions

Using an inexpensive and simple EEG and PPG sensors, we extracted and selected the features of the EEG and HRV indexes for the purpose of improving the accuracy of emotion estimation. We proposed feature selection as a method to improve the model accuracy. In order to verify the effectiveness of feature selection, several feature combinations of EEG and/or HRV indexes selected based on our criteria including our proposed feature selection have been used to construct emotion estimation models by deep learning algorithm. The accuracy verification was then performed with the stratified K-fold (SKF) cross-validation method. As a result, we suggest that it is possible to construct an emotion classification model using only a small number of features from physiological indexes. In addition, it was shown that the time spent on training can be shortened by reducing the features while maintaining an accuracy of 98% via appropriate feature selection methods.

For our future work, we will continue to improve our proposed feature selection method, as well as the model accuracy verification, which will enable the generalization of our emotion classification model.

Author Contributions: Conceptualization, K.S., T.L. and M.S.; methodology, K.S., T.L., R.M. and M.S.; software, K.S.; validation, K.S., R.M. and M.S.; writing—original draft preparation, K.S.; writing—review and editing, T.L. and M.S.; supervision, M.S. All authors have read and agreed to the published version of the manuscript.

Funding: This research received no external funding.

Institutional Review Board Statement: The study was conducted according to the guidelines of the Declaration of Helsinki, and approved by the Ethics Committee of Shibaura Institute of Technology.

Informed Consent Statement: Informed consent was obtained from all subjects involved in the study.

Data Availability Statement: Restrictions apply to the availability of the soundtrack datasets for music and emotion. The data were obtained from the University of Jyväskylä and are available on request.

Conflicts of Interest: The authors declare no conflict of interest.

References

1. Nocentini, O.; Fiorini, L.; Acerbi, G.; Sorrentino, A.; Mancioppi, G.; Cavallo, F. A Survey of Behavioral Models for Social Robots. *Robotics* **2019**, *8*, 54. [CrossRef]
2. Dzedzickis, A.; Kaklauskas, A.; Bucinskas, V. Human Emotion Recognition: Review of Sensors and Methods. *Sensors* **2020**, *20*, 592. [CrossRef] [PubMed]
3. Zhang, J.; Yin, Z.; Chen, P.; Nichele, S. Emotion recognition using multi-modal data and machine learning techniques: A tutorial and review. *Inf. Fusion* **2020**, *59*, 103–126. [CrossRef]
4. Conti, D.; Trubia, G.; Buono, S.; Di Nuovo, S.; Di Nuovo, A. Evaluation of a Robot-Assisted Therapy for Children with Autism and Intellectual Disability. In Proceedings of the Towards Autonomous Robotic Systems, Bristol, UK, 25–27 July 2018; Springer International Publishing: Cham, Switzerland, 2018; pp. 405–415.
5. Cavallo, F.; Aquilano, M.; Bonaccorsi, M.; Limosani, R.; Manzi, A.; Carrozza, M.C.; Dario, P. Improving Domiciliary Robotic Services by Integrating the ASTRO Robot in an AmI Infrastructure. In *Gearing Up and Accelerating Cross-Fertilization between Academic and Industrial Robotics Research in Europe*; Springer International Publishing: Cham, Switzerland, 2014; pp. 267–282.
6. Pudane, M.; Petrovica, S.; Lavendelis, E.; Ekenel, H.K. Towards Truly Affective AAL Systems. In *Enhanced Living Environments: Algorithms, Architectures, Platforms, and Systems*; Ganchev, I., Garcia, N.M., Dobre, C., Mavroustakis, C.X., Goleva, R., Eds.; Springer International Publishing: Cham, Switzerland, 2019; pp. 152–176. ISBN 9783030107529.
7. Sancarlo, D.; D'Onofrio, G.; Oscar, J.; Ricciardi, F.; Casey, D.; Murphy, K.; Giuliani, F.; Greco, A. MARIO Project: A Multicenter Survey About Companion Robot Acceptability in Caregivers of Patients with Dementia. In *Ambient Assisted Living*; Cavallo, F., Marletta, V., Monteriù, A., Siciliano, P., Eds.; Springer International Publishing: Cham, Switzerland, 2017; pp. 311–336.

The Effects of Individual Differences, Non-Stationarity, and the Importance of Data Partitioning Decisions for Training and Testing of EEG Cross-Participant Models

Alexander Kamrud *, Brett Borghetti and Christine Schubert Kabban

Department of Electrical and Computer Engineering, Air Force Institute of Technology,
Wright-Patterson AFB, OH 45433, USA; brett.borghetti@afit.edu (B.B.); christine.schubert@afit.edu (C.S.K.)
* Correspondence: alexander.kamrud.1@us.af.mil

Abstract: EEG-based deep learning models have trended toward models that are designed to perform classification on any individual (cross-participant models). However, because EEG varies across participants due to non-stationarity and individual differences, certain guidelines must be followed for partitioning data into training, validation, and testing sets, in order for cross-participant models to avoid overestimation of model accuracy. Despite this necessity, the majority of EEG-based cross-participant models have not adopted such guidelines. Furthermore, some data repositories may unwittingly contribute to the problem by providing partitioned test and non-test datasets for reasons such as competition support. In this study, we demonstrate how improper dataset partitioning and the resulting improper training, validation, and testing of a cross-participant model leads to overestimated model accuracy. We demonstrate this mathematically, and empirically, using five publicly available datasets. To build the cross-participant models for these datasets, we replicate published results and demonstrate how the model accuracies are significantly reduced when proper EEG cross-participant model guidelines are followed. Our empirical results show that by not following these guidelines, error rates of cross-participant models can be underestimated between 35% and 3900%. This misrepresentation of model performance for the general population potentially slows scientific progress toward truly high-performing classification models.

Keywords: EEG; deep learning; non-stationarity; individual differences; inter-subject variability; covariate shift; cross-participant; inter-participant

1. Introduction

EEG analysis has been a useful tool in neuroscience for decades in both clinical settings and the medical research community, proving to be useful for numerous applications such as classifying sleep patterns, epilepsy, identifying patterns of attention deficit hyperactivity disorder (ADHD), levels of mental workload [1,2], and emotion recognition [3]. EEG has also been useful for neural engineering with Brain–Machine Interfaces (BMIs), primarily due to EEG being used in combination with machine learning. Over the past decade, deep learning (DL) has been increasingly used to improve performance within models, allowing for automatic end-to-end processing and classification of the data, to include feature extraction using sequence models. Despite these improvements in model selection, the challenges of EEG's non-stationarity and inter-participant variability are still present [4,5] pp. 499–502.

One of the most significant challenges in building EEG classification models that are intended for use on any individual's EEG (cross-participant model) is accounting for the covariate shift that occurs due to EEG's non-stationarity and inter-participant variability [6–10]. Covariate shift in machine learning is a difference in the input distributions of the training and testing datasets [11]. This difference can significantly affect model performance, as a general guideline and assumption that is used in supervised machine learning is that these two input distributions are independent and identically distributed (i.i.d. assumption). Without this assumption, many theoretical guarantees and bounds on minimizing the test error are lost. For EEG cross-participant classification models, this covariate shift and its effects will always be present when the model classifies EEG data belonging to a participant that the model has not seen. However, models should be tested with data, which is representative of the data they will predict upon in the real world, and thus, EEG cross-participant models should be tested with unseen participants. Therefore, as a best practice in reporting accurate model performance for models intended to classify any individual's EEG, EEG cross-participant models should always be validated and tested using EEG data that comes from participants the model has not trained upon.

Despite previous work showing that EEG has inter-participant variability [5] pp. 499–502, and that this inter-participant variability leads to covariate shift when EEG models are tested with an unseen participant [6–10], the majority of EEG studies built to classify any individual's EEG do not follow this best practice of testing the model with unseen participants. In a recent literature review of deep learning-based EEG models by Roy et al., only 23 out of 108 cross-participant models utilized some method of proper dataset partitioning to ensure the model was tested with a participant that was not used for training [3]. This same literature review also compared the number of studies exploring models built for a specific individual (within-participant) versus cross-participant, and they found that since 2016, the growing trend has shifted toward building cross-participant models, with the latest ratio of studies researching cross-participant models to within-participant models being over 5:1 [3]. With this ever-growing popularity in EEG cross-participant models, it is critical that the body of research corrects its trend by properly using EEG data from unseen participants for validation and testing. By not following this best practice, the research pool may become increasingly diluted with studies reporting model performance metrics that are unrealistic and unrepresentative of the model's true ability. Additionally, data repositories that split data into training and testing datasets prior to being made available for download, such as Kaggle [12] and the University of California, Irvine (UCI) machine learning data repository [13], should also take this best practice into account. In this paper, we aim to present to the reader the importance of proper dataset partitioning.

This paper has the following structure. First, in Section 2, a well-established background is presented to ground the reader in regard to covariate shift and inter-participant variability within EEG; then, we fully articulate the problem of improper dataset partitioning using this background knowledge. Next, in Section 3, we demonstrate the effects of covariate shift and inter-participant variability both mathematically and in simple models, presenting evidence for the effects of these phenomena at a fundamental level. Finally, in Section 4, we utilize five publicly available datasets to present empirically the difference in model performance when following and not following this best practice of proper model validation and testing. We close with discussion in Section 5 and conclusions and future work in Section 6.

2. Background

2.1. Covariate Shift

For supervised machine learning, a standard guideline is that the training input distribution $P_{TR}(x)$ is equivalent to the test input distribution $P_{TE}(x)$ [11]. However, when these two distributions are not equivalent $P_{TR}(x) \neq P_{TE}(x)$, then there is typically a decrease in performance for most machine learning models. This form of dataset shift is referred to as covariate shift. This can happen for a number of reasons, such as the training and testing data being drawn from different populations, a lack of randomness in the number of trials/observations, an inadequate amount of them, or other biased sampling measures; in the case of EEG, covariate shift is due to individual differences and non-stationarity [10,14].

Below, in Figure 1, we see a simple example of covariate shift. Here, there is a classification boundary between two different classes, one represented by circles, and the other represented by triangles, with the classification boundary following the function

$y = -x^3$. The training dataset is marked in red and the test dataset is marked in blue. If we train a machine learning algorithm on only the training dataset and then test it on similar data such that $P_{TR}(x) = P_{TE}(x)$, then the model will be able to perform very well when tested, since the classification boundary is well defined between the two classes. In fact, many functions could easily define a reasonable boundary in this case; for example, $y = x^2/3$ or $y = 2|x|$ would yield good performance at discriminating the two classes of the training set shown in Figure 1. However, if we trained the model using only the red training data and tested with the blue testing data, the machine learning algorithm would have been trained with different data than it would be tested with ($P_{TR}(x) \neq P_{TE}(x)$), and it is unlikely that during training, the machine learning algorithm would have been able to discover the more complicated underlying discriminator function $y = -x^3$ having used only the red training data. Thus, the model trained only on the training data would perform poorly for classification of the test data, because the data distribution of the features from the training data and the distribution of the features from the test data are different.

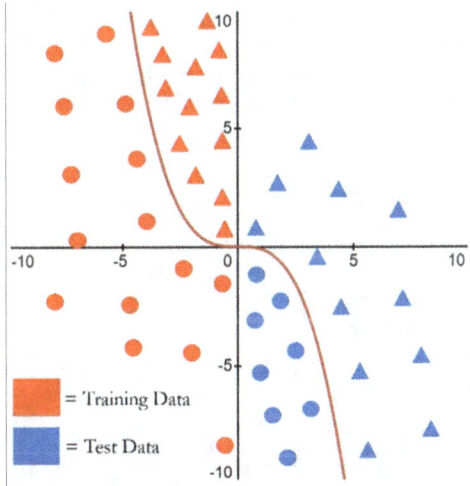

Figure 1. Simple example of covariate shift in classification data. Two classes of data are represented by circles and triangles, with the training dataset marked in red and the test dataset marked in blue. The true decision boundary between the two classes follows the function $y = -x^3$.

There are a number of different methods that can be used to detect if covariate shift is present due to the input distributions from two datasets being different. Given two datasets, $P_{TR}(x)$ and $P_{TE}(x)$, one method is to calculate *how* different the two probability distributions of the two datasets are,

$$D_{KL}(P_{TR}||P_{TE}) = \mathbb{E}_{x \sim P_{TR}}\left[\log \frac{P_{TE}(x)}{P_{TR}(x)}\right] = \mathbb{E}_{x \sim P_{TR}}[\log(P_{TR}(x)) - \log(P_{TE}(x))].$$

Another method for covariate shift detection is through visualization of the distributions in low-dimensional space using dimensionality reduction techniques. Manifold learning techniques such as t-Distributed Stochastic Neighbor Embedding (t-SNE), multi-dimensional scaling (MDS), IsoMap, and others, are useful for this as they capture non-linear information in the data [15] pp. 209–226. t-SNE is an unsupervised machine learning algorithm that is widely used for data visualization as it is particularly sensitive to local structure and reduces the tendency to crowd points toward the center of low-dimensional space [16]. As an unsupervised machine learning algorithm, t-SNE does not use labels of data for its learning, and it solely uses the features of each observation to perform its algorithm. It does this by first constructing a probability distribution for all pairs of observations in high-dimensional space such that similar observations (observations that are closer to one another in feature space) are assigned a higher probability of being neighbors, and dissimilar observations (observations that are further apart in feature space) are assigned a lower probability of being neighbors. Then, a new dataset is created with the same number of observations, but it is now spread randomly in low-dimensional feature space. It uses a Student's t-distribution to compute the similarity between all pairs of observations in low-dimensional space to create a second probability distribution and then uses gradient descent to iteratively shift the observations such that the KL divergence between the two different distributions is minimized. The main limitations of t-SNE are that it is computationally expensive and that the algorithm uses a non-convex objective function (KL divergence minimized using gradient descent, but initiated randomly), meaning multiple executions of the algorithm can lead to different embeddings (mappings of high-dimensional space to low-dimensional space). The dimensions of t-SNE are also difficult to interpret, as they are arbitrary distances that represent that closer neighboring points in low-dimensional space are likely to be neighbors in high-dimensional space [17].

Figure 2 shows an example of previous work utilizing t-SNE for high-dimensional data visualization outside of the EEG domain, with t-SNE performed on the well-known MNIST dataset, with the clusters corresponding to different input distributions within the data, and the colors corresponding to different classes [16,18].

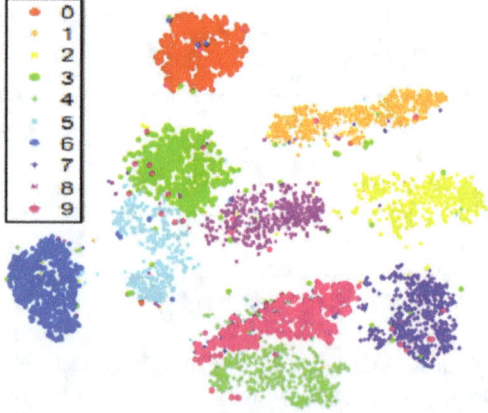

Figure 2. Example of 2D visualization using t-SNE on the MNIST dataset [16,18]. The dimensions of t-SNE are arbitrary distances that represent that closer neighboring points in low-dimensional space are likely to be neighbors in high-dimensional space.

t-SNE can also be used to visually detect covariate shift. A common example of covariate shift is when the testing data is partitioned from a subset of the clusters (i.e., participants for EEG), and the training data is partitioned from a different and separate subset of clusters; e.g., if in Figure 2 class 0 (red) was selected as the test data and classes 1–9 were selected as the training data. Cluster analysis algorithms such as k-means clustering or fuzzy c-means clustering can be utilized to identify if the training and testing data belong to separate clusters [19]; however, a simpler method to detect this is through visual inspection of the t-SNE graph. One can separately label the training and test data in the graph (e.g., with different colors) and then visually inspect to see if the training and test data correspond to separate clusters within the graph (covariate shift). Visual inspection for clusters involves identifying that for the majority of observations in one class, the majority of the nearest neighbors for those observations also belong to the same class, with a clear boundary between its class (cluster) and another class, meaning there is little to no overlap. This simple method of visual inspection also provides the benefit of visualizing the high-dimensional data in 2D.

2.2. Non-Stationarity and Individual Differences

One of the significant challenges associated with EEG analysis and classification is that EEG is both non-stationary [4] and that there are individual differences in EEG signals across individuals that result in inter-participant variability [5] pp. 499–502. EEG non-stationarity is due to a variety of internal and external causes, such as brain activity causing continual changes in states of neuronal assemblies [20], user attention levels, user fatigue, sensor equipment used, and scalp placement of electrodes [21]. Similar to non-stationarity, the individual differences in EEG signals are also due to a variety of factors, such as differences in variability in frequency peaks for individuals due to differences in personality traits [22], genetic variations [23–25], gamma–aminobutyric acid concentrations in the brain [26,27], and memory task performance [28].

These individual differences are underlying shifting covariates across participants, and they result in a change in the input distributions across all participants, while the conditional distribution of the output class y given the input feature vector x stays the same, resulting in a covariate shift for cross-participant machine learning models when they are tested upon EEG from participants that the model has not seen [6,7]. Thus, because of this inherent inter-participant variability in EEG signals, different strategies need to be used when performing EEG analysis [5] pp. 499–502 and training of cross-participant models [29].

2.3. Approaches to Data and Problem Formulation

When developing an EEG classification model, it is likely that it will belong to one of two main types of EEG models, either within-participant (a.k.a. intra-subject) or cross-participant (a.k.a. inter-subject) [3]. A within-participant model is one that intends to perform accurate classification of EEG for one individual and is thus built using only data from one participant. A cross-participant model is one that intends to perform classification on multiple individuals and is thus built using data from multiple participants. By training on data from multiple individuals, the goal is that the model becomes invariant to inter-participant variability, learning a function that accurately maps EEG input to the desired output label for most people. Additionally, cross-participant models can be built for different purposes and goals, such as for specific populations or for the general population. For example, the goal of a cross-participant BMI model could be to perform classification on only those specific individuals that use that specific BMI machinery. However, a more typical cross-participant model is one in which results are reported as though they are indicative of the model's ability to perform classification on the general population and thus any individual.

Each of these model types require different approaches to data partitioning across participants in order to report results that are accurate for their intended goal and target population. The within-participant model is more straightforward, as there is only one participant for both training, validation, and testing. However in cross-participant models, there are data from multiple participants, and because of the inter-participant variability that is inherent in EEG from individual to individual, how participants are used in cross-participant models for training, validation, and testing can have significant effects on model performance due to the differences in input distributions from individual to individual [6,7]. For example, if a cross-participant model is tested using data from an unseen participant, then the model's classification performance will be reduced due to the resulting covariate shift of this individual's unseen data. If a cross-participant model is only intended to perform classification on the same population that it is training upon and not also unseen individuals, as is in some BMI models, then ensuring the model is tested with unseen individuals is not necessary. However, for cross-participant models in which the model is intended for the general population and therefore unseen individuals, data should be prepared such that *participants* that are used for training are not also used for validation or testing, and *participants* used for validation are not also used for testing; otherwise, the model's performance will not accurately reflect its intended purpose of classification upon unseen individuals. This means that if participant A is used for training, then not even a single observation from participant A should be used for validation or testing, and if participant B is used for validation, then not even a single observation from participant B should be used for testing. An example of this method of proper vs. improper dataset partitioning for general population cross-participant models is depicted in Figure 3. It is also worth noting that proper validation of general population cross-participant models does not exclude the use of cross-validation (CV) as a performance evaluation technique. Instead, CV merely needs to be modified so that for each fold, *participants* used in training are not also used for validation, such as a Leave-One-Participant-Out approach or a Leave-N-Participants-Out approach.

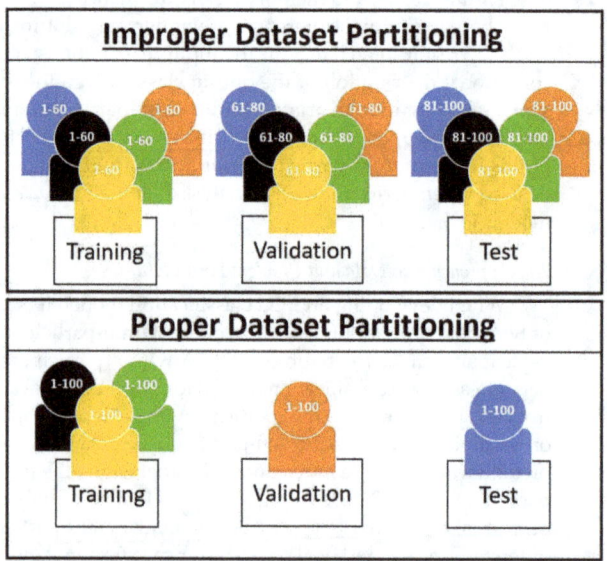

Figure 3. Two examples of creating the training, validation, and testing datasets with data from five participants. Numbers correspond to unique observations within each participant's dataset, with "1–60" referring to observations #1 through #60, "61–80" referring to observations #61 through #80, etc. The top illustrates improper dataset partitioning: data from each participant are used for all three datasets. In the top panel, while no unique observation is in more than one subset, each participants' data is still present in each subset. The bottom illustrates proper dataset partitioning: each participant's data are present in no more than one of the subsets.

Cross-participant models have significantly grown in popularity in recent years [3]; however, the majority of studies using cross-participant models do not follow this proper method of dataset partitioning. In Roy et al.'s literature review of deep learning-based EEG models, out of 108 studies using cross-participant models, only 23 utilized some method of proper dataset partitioning with a Leave-N-Participants-Out approach or a Leave-One-Participant-Out approach [3]. This results in the majority of studies having overestimated performance metrics—suggesting readers use models which, when used in scenarios involving the general population, may not perform as well as they were reported to have performed in the research. To obtain meaningful estimates of performance in the general population, cross-participant models need to follow proper dataset partitioning, as shown in Figure 3. Alternately, if the intent is not to use the model in the general population and is instead a tailored model designed for a specific population subset, the study should specifically state that the model's intended goal is only to perform classification upon the individuals it has been trained upon, to prevent the reader from incorrectly believing its efficacy would be similar in the general population.

In the following sections, we demonstrate in greater detail how covariate shift occurs, as well as its effects, in both simple model examples (Section 3), and in real-world, publicly available datasets (Section 4).

3. Initial Demonstration

To build understanding for how covariate shift manifests in any data, we utilize an initial demonstration of its effects in three settings: (1) first, we define covariate shift mathematically and illustrate how its effects on the expected loss of the test distribution can be accounted for; (2) next, we depict covariate shift using t-SNE, specifically using EEG data; and (3) finally, we demonstrate how we can affect covariate shift in EEG data by reducing the inter-participant variability through data transformations, thus increasing the model accuracy of properly validated EEG cross-participant models.

3.1. Defining and Estimating the Effects of Covariate Shift

In order to understand covariate shift at its fundamental level, we first define supervised learning. Supervised learning is the task of learning a function $f(x)$, which maps an input vector x to a labeled output y, typically done by estimating the conditional probability $p(y|x)$ [30] pp. 102–104. In order to estimate this function $f(x)$, a loss function $\ell(f(x),y)$ provides a measure of the difference between the true output y and the estimated $\hat{y}$ for the input vector x, with the loss function producing smaller values if $\hat{y}$ is correct and larger values if $\hat{y}$ is incorrect. Thus, the task of learning involves minimizing the expected loss of $\ell(f(x),y)$ over the probability density $p(x,y|\lambda)$ (parameterized by λ), i.e., minimizing the loss $\ell(f(x),y)$ over all possible inputs x [31],

$$E_{(x,y)\sim p(x,y|\lambda)}[\ell(f(x),y)] = \iint \ell(f(x),y)p(x,y|\lambda)dxdy. \tag{1}$$

However, in practice, the distribution $p(x,y|\lambda)$ is unknown and thus replaced by the empirical distribution, which can be estimated from training samples. If there is the set of samples L drawn from $p(x,y|\lambda)$, then Equation (1) becomes the objective of minimizing the empirical loss [31],

$$E_{(x,y)\sim L}[\ell(f(x),y)] = \frac{1}{|L|}\sum_{(x,y)\in L}\ell(f(x),y). \tag{2}$$

After minimizing the empirical loss and a prediction model is learned, the model is tested with the set of test samples T drawn from $p(x,y|\lambda)$, where T does not contain any samples from L that were used to minimize the empirical loss.

If the training data and testing data are independently and identically distributed (i.i.d.), meaning that every single observation of training and testing data are sampled independently and from the same distribution of $p(x,y|\lambda)$, then we expect that minimizing the expected training loss will in general also minimize the expected test loss [31]. This is an assumption that is common for many predictive models and is referred to as the i.i.d. assumption. However, many models are developed under conditions such as non-stationary signals or covariate shift. In these conditions, the i.i.d. assumption no longer holds, as the training and testing data come from different distributions, e.g., $p(x,y|\lambda)$ (parameterized by λ) for the training data, and $p(x,y|\theta)$ (parameterized by θ) for the testing data. As we no longer have the assumption of i.i.d. data, then we can no longer expect that minimizing the expected training loss also in general minimizes the expected test loss,

$$\underset{f}{\mathrm{argmin}}\ E_{(x,y)\sim p(x,y|\lambda)}[\ell(f(x),y)] \neq \underset{f}{\mathrm{argmin}}\ E_{(x,y)\sim p(x,y|\theta)}[\ell(f(x),y)]. \tag{3}$$

One method to address this lack of minimizing the expected test loss under covariate shift is through loss rescaling. Shimodaira proposed that if the training and test distributions are known, that the expected test loss could be minimized by appropriately weighting the training loss for each x with instance-specific weights $\frac{p(x|\theta)}{p(x|\lambda)}$ [31,32],

$$E_{(x,y)\sim\theta}[\ell(f(x),y)] = E_{(x,y)\sim\lambda}\left[\frac{p(x|\theta)}{p(x|\lambda)}\ell(f(x),y)\right]. \quad (4)$$

This loss rescaling results in larger loss values for instances of x where there are fewer training samples than test samples (weight ratio > 1), and smaller loss values for instances of x where there are more training samples than test samples (weight ratio < 1). Thus, in a dataset without covariate shift between training and test, more weight ratios' magnitudes would be close to unity because the features of the training data have a similar distribution to the features of the test data. Conversely, in a dataset with covariate shift between training and test, fewer ratios would be closer to 1.0, and more weight ratios would have magnitudes differing further from 1.0 because the training distribution and test distribution differ in their feature distributions.

While loss rescaling could be used to adjust machine learning performance outcomes, implementing loss rescaling can be difficult to achieve. As can be seen in Equation (4), for each instance of x with positive $p(x,y|\theta)$, there must also be a positive $p(x,y|\lambda)$; otherwise, there is a zero denominator, meaning this loss rescaling can only occur if the training distribution covers the entire support of the test distribution [31]. In high-dimensional data, it is more difficult to have this coverage due to the curse of dimensionality, i.e., that the sparsity of the data increases exponentially as the number of dimensions (e.g., number of features) increase. High-dimensional data are common in EEG datasets due to the nature of recording brain activity with high numbers of channels (i.e., scalp electrodes), and additionally, if spectral features are utilized, there are multiple frequency bands that could be extracted for each channel; it is not uncommon to collect spectral energy from five frequency bands across 64 electrodes for a total of 320 features in x.

While loss rescaling is unlikely to be useful for determining better estimates of performance in real-world EEG machine learning models, it can be useful for exploring effects of covariate shift in low-dimensional spaces. Next, we present a low-dimensional transformation of EEG datasets using Principal Components Analysis (PCA) in order to explore the performance differences between improper and proper partitioning of datasets for machine learning models.

We demonstrate the effects of these loss-rescaling weight ratio values $\frac{p(x|\theta)}{p(x|\lambda)}$ [31,32] using the spectral features of the Driver Fatigue dataset [33] described in Section 4.1. First, the input vectors are log transformed to reduce skew, and the dataset is partitioned into two separate training and test datasets using the proper and improper methods:

- For improper dataset partitioning, all participant data were shuffled together and one-twelfth of the data were randomly selected for the test set, with the remaining data selected for the training set.
- For proper dataset partitioning, one participant was selected for the test set, and the remaining 11 participants were selected for the training set.

Then, PCA was applied separately to the improper and proper datasets in order to reduce the dimensionality of the data to its first two principal components, with the amount of variance explained by the first two components being 0.72 for improper and 0.73 for proper. PCA dimensionality reduction is applied to both datasets so that the training distribution is more likely to cover the entire support of the test distribution [31]. Figure 4a,b depict the graphs for improper and proper dataset portioning: red dots representing training data observations, and blue dots representing test data observations. Note that in Figure 4a (improper), the test distribution is more uniformly spread throughout the training distribution, as all 12 participants are included in the test distribution, while in Figure 4b (proper), the test distribution is more clustered due to the entire test distribution belonging to a single participant.

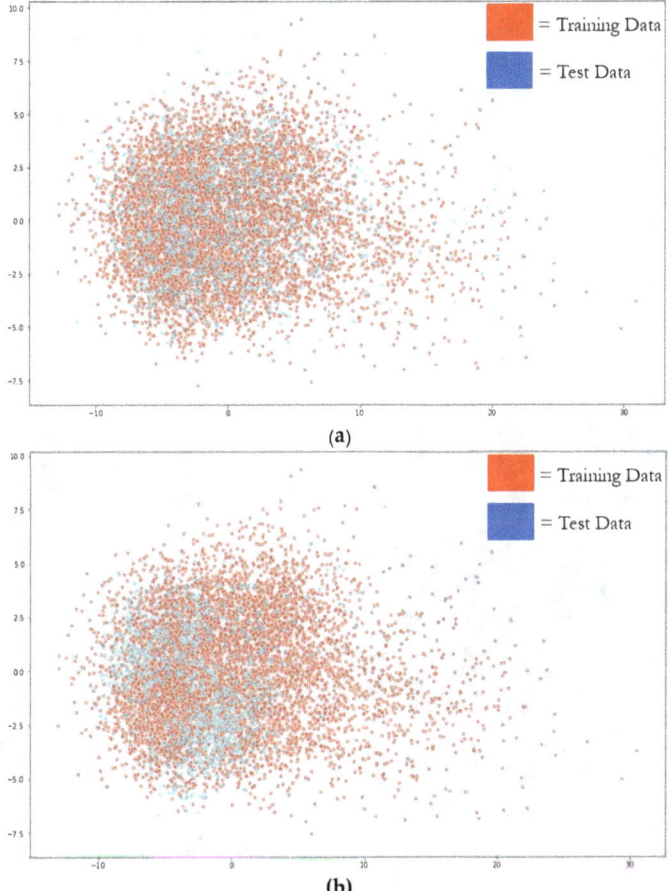

Figure 4. PCA projection of the first two principal components for (**a**) Improper and (**b**) Proper methods of dataset partitioning for spectral features of the Driver Fatigue dataset [33]. Red dots represent training data observations, and blue dots represent test data observations. Note that in the improper (**a**) that the test distribution is more uniformly spread throughout the training distribution, as all 12 participants are in the test distribution, while in the proper (**b**), the test distribution is more clustered due to the entire test distribution belonging to a single participant. These graphs are newly generated from the data obtained in the Driver Fatigue dataset [33].

Recall that the loss rescaling weight ratios represent a multiplier on the loss function in order to better estimate the expected real loss function from the loss estimate produced during evaluation of a model when there was a covariate difference between the test ($p(x,y \mid \theta)$) and training sets ($p(x,y \mid \lambda)$) used for machine learning. Ratios with values higher than 1 imply that there are more test data than training in this region; thus, the importance of the loss value in this region needs to be magnified; conversely, in regions with ratios smaller than 1, there is less test data than training data, meaning the loss values in this region are less important and their contribution to overall performance should be suppressed.

To calculate the loss rescaling weight ratio values $\frac{p(x \mid \theta)}{p(x \mid \lambda)}$ [31,32] within these datasets, some method of density estimation of the marginal input distributions is required; for the purposes of visualization and discussion, we utilize two-dimensional histogram estimators generated across a 7 × 7 grid of bins for each dataset (# of bins = 49). To help visualize this, imagine a 7 × 7 grid placed over the observations in each graph of Figure 4a and b, with the grid extending from the minimum values within the dataset, to the maximum values within the dataset, for both the X and Y axes. The number of training and testing observations within each histogram bin are calculated and normalized, providing our density estimation for the marginal input distributions, and subsequently the weight ratio values $\frac{p(x|\theta)}{p(x|\lambda)}$ for each bin. To better display the magnitude of difference in these weight ratio values, we display them in log scale, with a small value ($\varepsilon = 1.0 \times 10^{-5}$) added to the ratio values to avoid undefined values of log(0). This results in the log-transformed heat maps seen in Figure 5a–c, with Figure 5a being the log-transformed weight ratio values for the proper dataset ($\log(proper + \varepsilon)$), Figure 5b being the log-transformed weight ratio values for the improper dataset ($\log(improper + \varepsilon)$), and Figure 5c being the difference between the log transformed weight ratio values for proper minus improper ($\log(proper + \varepsilon) - \log(improper + \varepsilon)$).

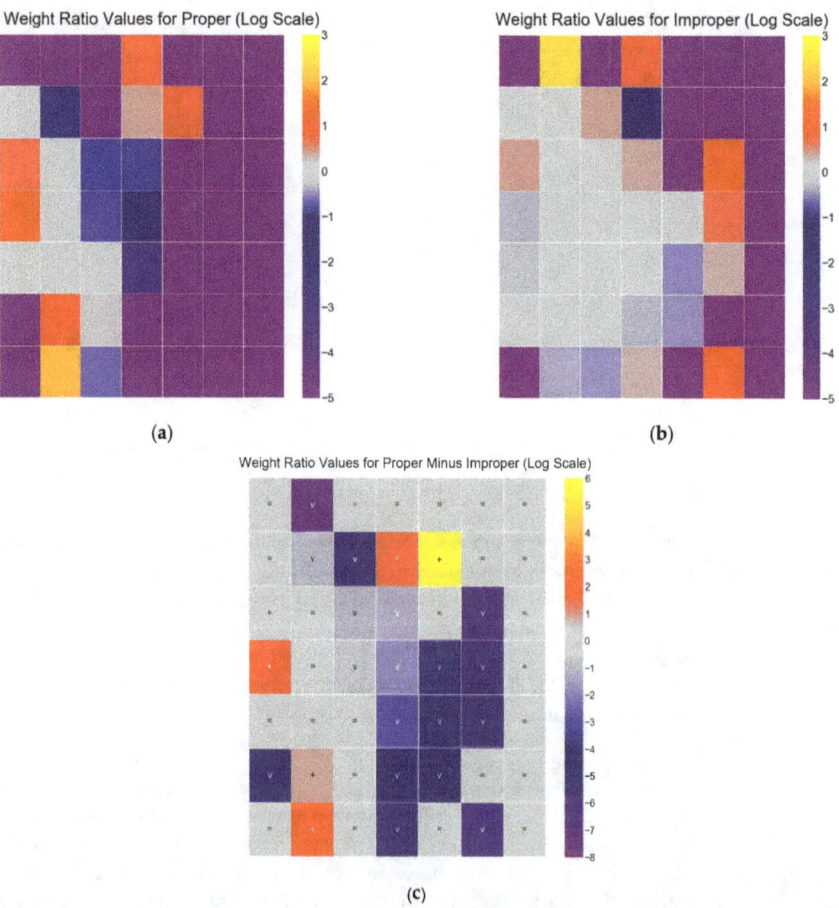

Figure 5. Heat maps for the log-transformed weight ratio values generated using two-dimensional histograms for (**a**) Proper (log(proper + ε)) and (**b**) Improper (log(improper + ε)) ($\varepsilon = 1.0 \times 10^{-5}$) methods of dataset partitioning for spectral features of the Driver Fatigue dataset [33]. Graph (**c**) depicts the difference in log-transformed weight ratio values between the proper and improper methods (log(proper + ε)—(log(improper + ε)), with labels for each bin indicating approximately equal weights (=), a significant negative delta (v), or a significant positive delta (+). These heat maps are newly generated from the data obtained in the Driver Fatigue dataset [33].

Figure 5a depicts that for the proper dataset partition, there are few bins (≈7) with a weight ratio close to 0, and many bins that are less than 0 (with many equal to -5, i.e., $\log(\varepsilon)$) or greater than 0. In contrast, Figure 5b depicts that for the improper dataset partition, there are more bins (≈14) with a weight ratio close to 0, and fewer bins that are less than 0 or greater than 0. Bins that are less than 0 for proper are also darker blue than bins that are less than 0 for improper, indicating the training data have a more similar distribution to the test for improper vs. proper. In Figure 5c, the difference of the log-transformed weight ratio values between the two heat maps (proper minus improper) indicates that approximately half of the bins have a delta of 0, and the other half of the bins have a delta that is significantly less than 1.0 or significantly greater than 1.0. This signifies that there can be significant differences in the weights required to rescale the loss depending on how the data are partitioned, with significantly more loss rescaling being required for the proper method of dataset partitioning vs. the improper method. This significant difference in loss rescaling between the two methods is indicative of proper dataset partitioning resulting in a covariate shift, and because the only difference in partitioning between the two methods is how participants are distributed, it is also indicative of an unseen participant resulting in covariate shift.

3.2. Covariate Shift in EEG

In Section 2.1, we discussed how t-SNE can be utilized in order to detect covariate shift in data, and in Section 2.2, we discussed how covariate shift is inherent in EEG models due to the nature of EEG's non-stationarity and the individual differences that result in inter-participant variability. Here, we utilize t-SNE to visually showcase why this inter-participant variability leads to the effect of covariate shift in EEG cross-participant models. As mentioned previously, t-SNE allows one to inspect for covariate shift in the data by first applying the unsupervised technique and then visually exploring the data in 2D space, examining it to see if the clusters of training data and testing data are isolated from one another through visual inspection.

We perform t-SNE on spectral features of the PTSD [34], Schizophrenia [35], and Driver Fatigue datasets [33], as well as entropy features for the Driver Fatigue data [33], with results shown in Figure 6. This is done to showcase that inter-participant variability is present across many tasks and participant populations and demonstrates it visually to complement the quantitative empirical results within Section 4. For each of the graphs in Figure 6, we see that the majority of the data are clustered by participant, meaning that most of the participant data belong to its own unique input distribution, with some overlap and similarity between participants. However, there are some limitations of t-SNE that are worth noting and that are not obvious, and without their understanding, they can lead to incorrect assumptions about the underlying structure of the data. One limitation is that the cluster sizes in a t-SNE plot do not relate to distance between points of the cluster, as the algorithm adapts "distance" to each of the local clusters in the dataset, meaning dense clusters are expanded and sparse clusters are contracted [17]. This means that the sparsity of the cluster cannot be implied to have meaning. Another limitation is that the global geometry of the plot is not reliable as a source of information, meaning that the distances between clusters may or may not be accurate methods of interpreting the high-dimensional data in 2D space. While it is possible to dial in the hyperparameters to the correct values so that the 2D space does accurately represent the global geometry of the data in high-dimensional space, this requires a priori knowledge of the underlying structure of the high-dimensional data, which is unavailable. The implication of these limitations is that when interpreting t-SNE plots, the focus should be on simply the number of clusters present in the data and how they relate to the training dataset and the testing dataset. Any other information within the plot should not be taken as evidence of the underlying structure of the data in high-dimensional space. These limitations are important in understanding the data presented in the next section.

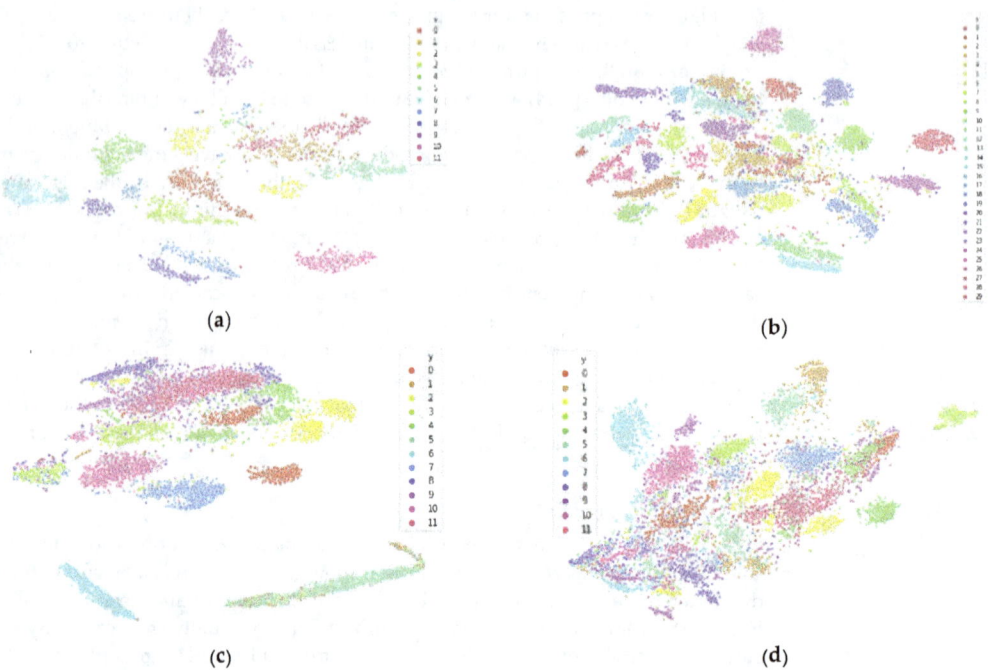

Figure 6. Example of using t-SNE for 2D dimensionality reduction and visualization of datasets utilized within this research, with colors corresponding to participants within the datasets, showcasing that inter-participant variability is present across different tasks and participant populations. Datasets depicted here are spectral features of the (**a**) PTSD, (**b**) Schizophrenia, (**c**) and Driver Fatigue datasets; and (**d**) Entropy features of the Driver Fatigue dataset. The dimensions of t-SNE are arbitrary distances that represent that closer neighboring points in low-dimensional space are likely to be neighbors in high-dimensional space.

3.3. Reducing Inter-Participant Variability

As mentioned in Section 2.2, current approaches to EEG modeling are classified as either within-participant or cross-participant. Due to inter-participant variability, cross-participant models tend to always have lower classification accuracies than within-participant models, despite the fact that more participants typically also result in a larger training dataset for the model.

In order to demonstrate these effects of inter-participant variability within cross-participant models, we study the phenomenon with synthetically altered data through transformation. To generate the data, we utilize two mutually exclusive, independent applied data transformations named *shifted Heaviside* (our own naming for the transformation for the purpose of discussion) and *shift to median*. The goal of these transformations is to reduce the inter-participant variability of the data while still preserving the local structure of each participant's EEG data. In this manner, it can then be seen that as inter-participant variability is reduced and participants become more similar and no longer have different input distributions, classification performance improves because the effect of the covariate shift has been reduced. The purpose of this exploration is to demonstrate this performance-affecting relationship of inter-participant variability and covariate shift; we do not recommend utilizing these transformations in practice for the purpose of improving model performance.

The apparent performance improvement that occurs when data are transformed to reduce inter-participant variability implies that there will likely be overestimated classification performance in cross-participant models that are improperly validated and tested. When a model uses the same participants for both training and validation or testing, the higher measured performance is due to the reduced inter-participant variability between the training dataset and the validation or testing dataset—essentially masking the true differences that would exist between the people the model was trained on and the people the model was intended to be used on in the future. Similarly, when we apply transformations to reduce inter-participant variability, the goal is to transform the data in a manner such that multiple participants appear as if they belong to a single participant, and we can induce the effect of masking the true differences.

The transformation *shifted Heaviside* is both participant-based and feature-based. As mentioned at the beginning of this section, the name *shifted Heaviside* is the name we use in this paper to refer to this transformation proposed by Arevalillo-Herraez et al. in [36], based on the Heaviside function, as this transformation was not named by its originators. It was proposed by Arevalillo-Herraez et al. specifically for the use of reducing inter-participant variability in EEG data, and it does so by using the median value for each feature of each participant in order to map the original feature vector into a binary feature vector of the same size [36]. The effect of this transformation can be thought of as having the effect of shifting the data to the different corners of a hypercube. To create the mapping, first, the median value of each feature of each participant is calculated. Then, the original feature vector data are converted to a binary encoded vector where each feature value is transformed to a 1 if the value is greater than the median of the feature vector, or a 0 if less than or equal to the median (akin to a shifted Heaviside function). Specifically, they formulate their algorithm as follows: for pth participant, for all feature vectors $x_{p,j}$, $j = 1, 2, \ldots, n_p$ in the set of training samples X_p, compute the median vector x'_p. Then, transform all feature vectors u for the same participant p according to Equation (5), where $[k]$ denotes the kth element (feature) of the corresponding vector.

$$\bar{u}[k] = \begin{cases} 1 & u[k] > x'_p[k], \\ 0 & u[k] \leq x'_p[k], \end{cases} \quad (5)$$

The *shift to median* transformation involves calculating a center point for each output class y across all participants in feature space and then shifting by class y each participant's data closer to those class center points so that each participant's data distribution moves closer together (toward the calculated class centers), while still preserving differences within each participant's individual data observations. The goal is to reduce inter-participant variability by shifting all participants to a similar range in feature space, while still preserving local structure within each participant, including class effect. The effect of this transformation can be thought of as shifting each participant's entire cluster of data by a certain amount so that it is re-centered on a new point (performed by class y). Using the same symbols in the previous paragraph, we have the following algorithm.

Shift to Median—Variables are defined as follows: y represents class, j represents the observation, p represents the participant, and N represents the total number of training samples.

1. $\forall y$ Calculate median vector $\widetilde{C}_y$ across all feature vectors $x_{p,y,j}$ of all participants $p = 1, \ldots, P$

   a. $\widetilde{C}_y = \begin{cases} x_{y, \frac{N+1}{2}} & N \text{ odd} \\ \frac{1}{2}\left(x_{y, \frac{N}{2}} + x_{y, \frac{N+1}{2}}\right) & N \text{ even} \end{cases}$

2. $\forall p \, \forall y \, \forall x_{p,j}$ Calculate median centroid $\widetilde{c}_{p,y}$ of p

   b. $\widetilde{c}_{p,y} = \begin{cases} x_{p,y, \frac{N+1}{2}} & N \text{ odd} \\ \frac{1}{2}\left(x_{p,y, \frac{N}{2}} + x_{p,y, \frac{N+1}{2}}\right) & N \text{ even} \end{cases}$

3. $\forall y \, \forall x_{p,j}$ Compute shifted vector $x'_{p,y,j} = x_{p,y,j} + \left(\widetilde{C}_y - \widetilde{c}_{p,y}\right)$

This results in three different datasets: original dataset, *shifted Heaviside* transformation, and *shift to median* transformation. Employing t-SNE on the datasets allows us to view the local clusters within the data. For EEG specifically, this typically allows us to identify clustering by participant, showcasing the inter-participant variability inherent across participants. To demonstrate this clustering as well as the EEG data transformations described above, we utilize the Driver Fatigue dataset [33] described in Section 4.1.

This dataset contains both entropy and spectral features. In information theory, the entropy of a time series quantifies its regularity and predictability over time [37], and the entropy features extracted for use include approximate entropy (AE), sample entropy (SE), and fuzzy entropy (FE) features [38]. The spectral features were extracted using Morlet wavelet transforms in MATLAB to determine the frequency-domain mean power of two of the five clinical frequency EEG bands: alpha (12–15 Hz) and beta (16–22 Hz) ([5] pp. 151–174). Two frequency-spectral-power features extracted from EEG were computed for each of the 30 channels. This results in 60 features for the spectral feature space and 90 features for the entropy feature space (three entropy measures across all 30 channels).

Figures 7a and 8a both illustrate the results of applying t-SNE to the untransformed Drive Fatigue datasets for the entropy and spectral feature spaces, respectively. It can be seen that in these high-dimensional data spaces of 90 and 60 features each that there is significant clustering by participant, with coloring corresponding to a participant's data. Note that this coloring has no effect on the t-SNE algorithm itself and is applied afterwards for visualization. As mentioned earlier in Section 3.2, due to the limitations of t-SNE, we cannot reliably interpret any information from the 2D plot outside of the number of clusters. Clusters found within t-SNE should only be treated as such: that they are localized clusters that exist within the high-dimensional data. After a data transformation, if t-SNE is unable to find local clustering despite hyperparameter tuning, then local clustering does not exist [17]. For these datasets, a lack of local clustering means that the inter-participant variability has been reduced to the point that t-SNE can no longer distinguish between participants in the feature space.

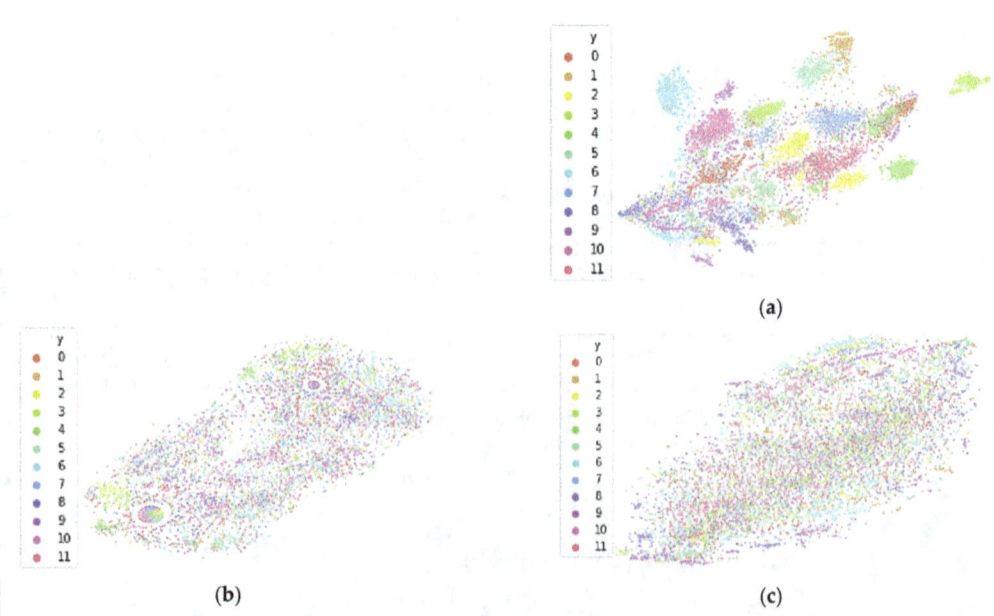

Figure 7. Results of visualizing the data using t-SNE for the entropy feature space before and after various data transformations: (**a**) Before any transformations; (**b**) After applying *shifted Heaviside* transformation; (**c**) After applying *shift to median* transformation. Colors correspond to different participants, with the same color applied to the same participant in each figure. Note in (**b**,**c**) that there is a lack of local clustering, implying that inter-participant variability has been reduced due to the transformations. The dimensions of t-SNE are arbitrary distances which represent that closer neighboring points in low-dimensional space are likely to be neighbors in high-dimensional space.

Figure 7b,c reveal the different data transformation's effects on local clustering within the entropy feature spaces and Figure 8b,c show the transformation's effects on the spectral feature spaces. For the entropy feature space, we see that each transformation has reduced the inter-participant variability to the point where t-SNE no longer finds local clustering within the data. Similarly, for the spectral feature space, we see that the *shifted Heaviside* transformation has the same result, while the *shift to median* transformation largely reduces local clustering within t-SNE, but not to the same effect as the *shifted Heaviside* transformation.

To demonstrate the effects of reducing inter-participant variability on classification accuracy in cross-participant models, cross-participant models were also built using each of these three datasets of data within both of the feature spaces (entropy and spectral). As this is the Driver Fatigue dataset, models were trained according to the methodology specified in Section 4.1. For each of the three subsets of data within both of the feature spaces of entropy and spectral features, separate models were trained and tested according to both the improper and proper methods of cross-participant model generation. For proper model generation, we follow the guidelines specified in Section 2.3, resulting in 12-fold LOPO CV. As mentioned in Section 4.1, for improper model generation, in order to match the number of folds (and data per fold) in LOPO CV, 12-fold CV was used with all participant data shuffled together and split across 12-folds. Together, this results in 12 models generated for each method.

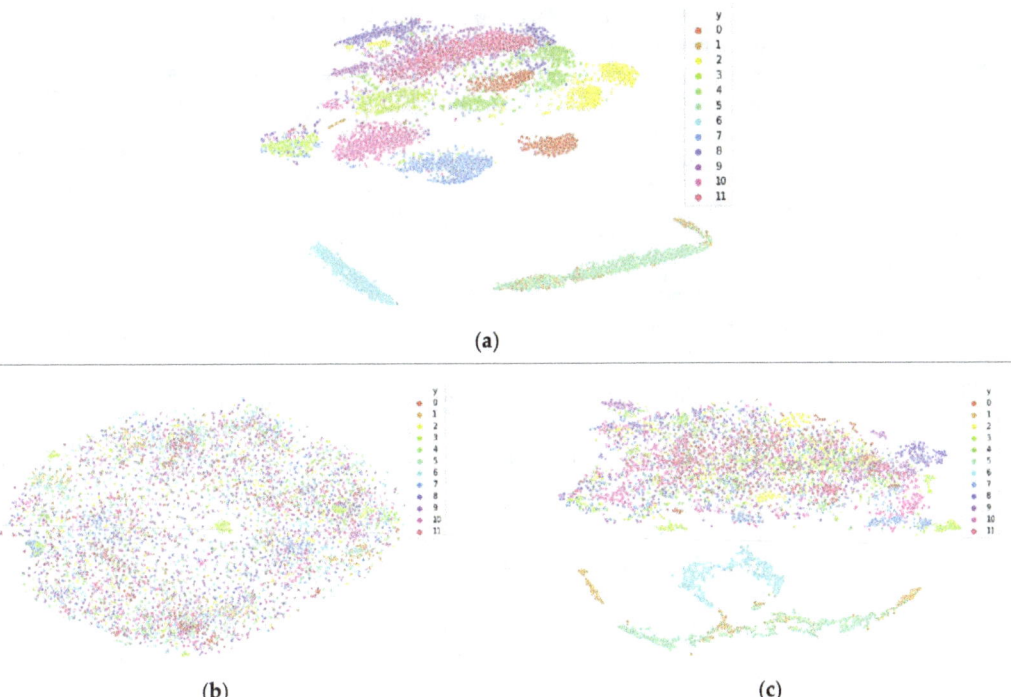

Figure 8. Results of visualizing the data using t-SNE for the spectral feature space before and after various data transformations: (**a**) Before any transformations; (**b**) After applying *shifted Heaviside* transformation; (**c**) After applying *shift to median* transformation. Colors correspond to different participants, with the same color applied to the same participant in each figure. The dimensions of t-SNE are arbitrary distances that represent that closer neighboring points in low-dimensional space are likely to be neighbors in high-dimensional space.

Table 1 contains the classification accuracy results for each of the 12 models. It can be seen that for both the entropy and spectral feature spaces that improper model testing did not benefit from the data transformations. Intuitively, this makes sense, as these models are tested improperly; thus, the model has seen each participant's input distribution, and therefore, a reduction of inter-participant variability is not impactful to the model. However, for proper model testing, we see that for both the entropy and spectral feature spaces that the *shift to median* transformation results in a dominance in accuracy of the 95% confidence interval (CI) from the transformation in comparison of the 95% CI's. While the *shifted Heaviside* transformation did result in a reduction of inter-participant variability for both feature spaces as shown in Figures 7b and 8b, this reduced inter-participant variability did not result in any significant effects on cross-participant model performance, suggesting that this transformation may be best suited for only certain datasets which its developers Arevalillo-Herraez et al. work with.

Table 1. Classification accuracies for the 12 models generated from transformed and non-transformed driver fatigue data. Improper models were generated with the improper method of cross-participant model generation utilizing 12-fold CV with all participant data shuffled together and split across 12 folds, and proper model generation utilized 12-fold LOPO CV. The purpose of this table is two-fold. One is to depict that improper model generation typically results in overestimated model accuracy as can be seen with increased accuracies for improper vs. proper. The other is to depict the results of the proper method on untransformed data versus the proper method on the two transformed datasets. **Bold** signifies dominance in accuracy of the 95% confidence interval from the transformation in comparison of the 95% confidence intervals.

	Entropy	Spectral
Improper		
Untransformed	0.91 (0.89, 0.93)	0.82 (0.79, 0.85)
Shifted Heaviside	0.72 (0.68, 0.76)	0.66 (0.62, 0.70)
Shift to Median	0.91 (0.89, 0.93)	0.82 (0.79, 0.85)
Proper		
Untransformed	0.50 (0.46, 0.54)	0.50 (0.46, 0.54)
Shifted Heaviside	0.50 (0.46, 0.54)	0.47 (0.43, 0.51)
Shift to Median	**0.80 (0.77, 0.83)**	**0.72 (0.68, 0.76)**

4. Empirical Demonstrations in Diverse EEG Case Studies

In this section, we utilize five publicly available datasets to empirically demonstrate the difference in machine learning performance results of using proper versus improper methods of dataset partitioning during training, validation and testing. These five datasets were selected to encompass diversity across the research activities using machine learning and EEG, to demonstrate the importance of following the proper methodology in many situations. The domains of the five datasets differ substantially in both tasks performed during data collection and subsequent classification using EEG, including both classification of different mental states within an individual: mental fatigue (*Driver Fatigue*), emotions (*Confused Students*), as well as determining of the existence of longer-term chronic conditions in individuals: mental disease (*Alcoholism*), psychological conditions (*PTSD*), and mental disorders (*Schizophrenia*). In the chronic condition datasets, each participant (and all of the observations corresponding to that participant) are either in the chronic condition class or the class representing normal. Summary details of these datasets can be seen in Table 2.

Table 2. Details for the publicly available datasets. All datasets are binary classification tasks, and all datasets are balanced except for the Alcoholism dataset. This gives chance accuracy for Alcoholism defined as 0.64 and 0.50 for all other datasets.

Dataset	Year Collected	Binary Classification Task	# of Participants
Driver Fatigue [33]	2017	Normal vs. Fatigue	12
Confused Students [12]	2013	Confused vs. Not Confused	10
Alcoholism [13]	1999	Alcoholic vs. Non-Alcoholic	122
PTSD [34]	2018	Pre-Treatment vs. Post-Treatment	12
Schizophrenia [35]	2014	Schizophrenia vs. Healthy Control	30

Model architectures used are selected based on research papers with top performance in their respective dataset and/or domain, with replication performed as closely as possible. In some cases, research papers were missing details about hyperparameters and other model details, and these details had to be selected using best practices of machine learning. With architecture and hyperparameters selected, two models are then created and evaluated separately using the same architecture and hyperparameter sweep (grid search utilized):

- Improper: trained, tuned, and evaluated during tests using all participant data.
- Proper: trained and tuned using data from a subset of the participants, then, during the test, evaluated using only data from participant(s) that were not used to train or tune the model.

Then, results of the two methods are contrasted and compared, with error rates displayed in a summary table in Section 5. It is also worth noting that the amount of data used for training and validation/testing is kept consistent across both the proper and improper methods, meaning that both models have the same quantity of observations to train upon, and additionally, both models are validated and tested with the same number of observations. This ensures that there is minimal difference between the two models in terms of architecture, hyperparameter sweeps, or the amount of data used for training, validation, or testing, and that the only difference between the models is the restriction surrounding which participants are used for training, validation, and testing for the proper method vs. the improper method.

The next five subsections are structured as case studies for each of the five datasets, and they are in the following order: *Driver Fatigue*, *Confused Students*, *Alcoholism*, *PTSD*, and *Schizophrenia*. Each case study first discusses the purpose of the experiment, how it was conducted, and what EEG data were collected (pre-processing details are provided in Appendix A). Then, information on the model architecture and its methodology are provided, as well as the results previous researchers had achieved using that methodology. Then, we detail our own methodology to include having to fill any gaps missing from their architecture or hyperparameter selection, as well as how we perform both improper and proper training, validation, and testing for the two different models. Finally, we state results achieved with both models and compare them.

4.1. Driver Fatigue

This dataset is available on Figshare [33] through a link provided in Min et al.'s paper, which details both the experiment and the subsequent deep learning performed [38]. Their experiment consisted of collecting EEG recordings during a driving simulator for the purpose of using these signals to develop a model that could detect driver fatigue using EEG signals. Twelve participants used the driving simulator for 1–2 h in a highway setting with low traffic density, with EEG recorded in two phases during the session. The first phase consisted of 20 min of continuous driving, with the last 5 min of this 20-min segment recorded and labeled as the *normal* state. The second phase consisted of driving that lasted for 40–100 min until the participant's self-reported questionnaire indicated that they were fatigued (surveys used were Lee's Subjective Fatigue Scale [39] and the Chalder Fatigue

Scale [40]), in which the last 5 min of driving were recorded in the EEG and labeled as the *fatigue* state. EEG was recorded using a 32-channel electrode cap, with two of the channels being reference channels linked to mastoid electrodes. The 5 min of EEG from each phase were epoched into 1 s segments for 300 epochs per phase per participant, resulting in a total of 3600 trials for the normal state and 3600 trials for the fatigue state. Then, the data were randomly split into training and testing datasets at a 50/50 ratio, without participants taken into account, thus resulting in improperly created datasets for cross-participant models. Feature extraction included several entropy measures, which were extracted for each trial and then normalized. In information theory, the entropy of a time series quantifies its regularity and predictability over time [37], with the measures extracted including approximate entropy, sample entropy, and fuzzy entropy [38].

In Min et al.'s work, these entropy features were then utilized for multiple classifiers, with the classifier that achieved the highest accuracy being an artificial neural network (ANN) [38]. The ANN had three layers, each with 20 hidden units and sigmoid activation functions. Gradient descent was used with mean squared error (MSE) for the loss the function, and the Levenberg–Marquardt function was used as the optimization function [41]. Leave-One-Out Cross-Validation (LOOCV) was utilized to report test classification accuracy, with their reported test accuracy being 0.968 or an error rate of 0.032.

The architecture above was followed for training both of our models; however, 12-fold CV was utilized, as there are 12 participants and Leave-One-Participant-Out (LOPO) CV results in 12-fold CV. Thus, for improper training and validation, 12-fold CV was used with all participant data shuffled together and split across 12-folds, and for proper training and validation, LOPO CV was used. Using this configuration, for improper testing of the cross-participant model, the best accuracy we obtained was 0.83, which was much lower than Min et al.'s reported test accuracy of 0.968 with their 50/50 training/testing split. In an effort to improve upon this, a hyperparameter sweep was conducted across hidden units (20, 30, 40, and 50), dropout rate (0.0, 0.1, 0.2), different learning rates (0.01, 0.001, 0.0001), and the *reduce_lr* callback of reducing the learning rate based on the number of epochs trained. The configuration with the highest classification accuracy for the improper method was one of 50 hidden units, 0.2 dropout rate, 0.001 learning rate, and *reduce_lr* callback was utilized. This hyperparameter sweep was also conducted for the proper method, with the configuration with the highest classification accuracy for the proper method being 40 hidden units, 0.2 dropout rate, 0.001 learning rate, and *reduce_lr* callback being utilized. Then, these configurations were used for improper and proper training and validation of the cross-participant models, respectively.

For improper training and validation of the cross-participant model using our configuration above, the reported classification accuracy using 12-fold CV was 0.91 (95% CI: 0.903, 0.917) or an error rate of 0.09 (95% CI: 0.083, 0.097). While this result is significantly lower than Min et al.'s error rate (0.09 vs. 0.032 [38]), our accuracy is still similar enough in magnitude for our goal of contrasting proper and improper methods of model evaluation. As such, when we built the model properly and trained and validated it using LOPOCV, the resulting accuracy was 0.540 (95% CI: 0.528, 0.552) or an error rate of 0.46 (95% CI: 0.448, 0.472). This error rate is over five times as that of the error rate of the improper method, illustrating how difficult classification of unseen participants is, and how significantly overestimated test accuracies can become by following an improper methodology, which does not account for the significance of inter-participant variability.

4.2. Confused Students

Participant data for this dataset are available on Kaggle [12] and come from an experiment involving college students. The purpose of the experiment was to collect EEG from college students while they were in a *confused* state and a *not confused* state and then build a model that could determine if the student was *confused* or *not confused* using the EEG signals. Researchers collected EEG while the students watched online education videos in a *confused* state and a *not confused* state [42]. Ten young adult college students watched two-minute online education videos (lectures) on various topics, which were assumed to not confuse an average college student, such as basic algebra and geometry, as well as topics that would be confusing, such as quantum mechanics and stem cell research. Each student watched five randomly selected videos from each category, and after each video, students self-rated their confusion on a scale of 1 (least confused) to 7 (most confused). EEG was recorded at a sampling rate of 512 Hz using a single-channel NeuroSky MindSet device, which has a single electrode that rests over the middle of the forehead, and two electrodes for ground and reference, each in contact with an ear. The first 30 s and last 30 s of each session's EEG recording were removed in case the student was not ready; the middle 60 s was available for analysis. Then, NeuroSky software was used to extract features from the signal at 2 Hz to include the mean of the raw signal, mean power for the five traditional frequency bands (to include alpha low/high, beta low/high, and gamma low/high), and MindSet's proprietary "attention" and "meditation" signals.

In addition to the experiment data, Kaggle also lists references with some of the latest classification results to use these data for the purpose of binary classification of whether a student is *confused* or *not confused*. The two references with the greatest classification accuracies both use bidirectional Long Short-Term Memory (LSTM) models as their neural network architecture [43,44], with the one we selected for replication being work from Ni et al., as their work provided the most detail for replication [44]. For Ni et al.'s work, each session consisted of a single trial as to provide sequence data for the recurrent neural network (RNN). Sessions from all nine participants were merged together for a cross-participant model, and 5-fold cross-validation was used across all participants (improper method). EEG features used consisted of proprietary measures from the MindSet EEG device labeled *Attention* (measure of mental focus) and *Meditation* (measure of calmness), the raw EEG signal values, and mean values of eight different frequency regions in the power spectrum. In addition to EEG signals, Ni et al. also opted to use the "Predefined Label" of whether a session was confusing or not as a feature. The bidirectional LSTM had 50 hidden units and used a tanh activation function, and it was followed by a fully connected layer with a sigmoid activation function. Before the bidirectional LSTM, batch normalization was used. No other architecture or hyperparameter methodology was provided. The CV test accuracy varied between 0.71 and 0.74 for their work, with an average 5-fold CV accuracy of 0.733.

To reproduce Ni et al.'s results for the improper model, the architecture above was followed along with the hyperparameters provided, and all of the EEG features were utilized, resulting in 11 total features used for training (in our replication of the research, the non-EEG "Predefined Label" feature was omitted; we do not recommend including a class label as a feature per standard practices of machine learning). In an effort to replicate their methodology of hyperparameter selection for the proper model, a hyperparameter grid search was performed across hidden units (40, 50, 60), dropout rate (0.0, 0.1, 0.2), and learning rate (0.001, 0.0001), with the highest performing proper model having hyperparameters of 50 hidden units, 0.0 dropout rate, and 0.0001 learning rate; the same hyperparameters Ni et al. and our improper model design used. This hyperparameter sweep ensures both the improper and proper models have selected their best hyperparameters for their input data. In an effort to increase the amount of training samples for the models, the EEG data were also segmented using a sliding sequence window of 15 samples in length and slides by 12 samples. Then, we built two separate cross-participant models using improper training and testing for one and proper training and testing for the other. The improper model utilized 5-fold CV for training and validation with all participant data shuffled together, resulting in every fold including some data from every participant (exact same method used by Ni et al.). The proper model also utilized 5-fold CV; however, it was Leave-Two-Participants-Out CV. Outside of this change in how the folds were formed for CV, all other variables remained the same between the models, to include architecture, features used, hyperparameters, and the number of observations used for both training and validation.

For improper training and validation of the cross-participant model using 5-fold CV, our replication of Ni et al.'s configuration [44] resulted in a test accuracy of 0.69 (95% CI: 0.654, 0.726), which was close to their reported test accuracy of 0.733, with a difference in error rates of 0.31 (95% CI: 0.274, 0.346) vs. 0.267. However, our proper training and validation of the proper cross-participant model using Leave-Two-Participants-Out CV resulted in an accuracy of 0.584 (95% CI: 0.552, 0.628) or an error rate of 0.416 (95% CI: 0.372, 0.448). The error rate of the proper method is over 33% greater than the error rate of the improper method, suggesting that improper training and testing of EEG data can lead to overestimation of model performance on unseen participants and thus the human population in general.

4.3. Alcoholism

Participant data for this dataset are available from both Kaggle [12] and the University of California, Irvine (UCI) machine learning data repository [13], with this research utilizing the *Full Dataset* from the UCI repository. The source of the data comes from one of a number of experiments sponsored by the National Institute on Alcohol Abuse and Alcoholism (NIAAA) in the early 1990s, which were conducted with the purpose of recording brain activity during a task that was expected to elicit differences in the neural activity of healthy participants and alcoholic participants [45,46]. In the control group, there were 45 male participants, and in the experimental group, there were 77 alcoholic male participants. The task used was a visual object recognition task: the participant was presented with a sequence of two images and had to determine whether the second image was the same as the first. Signals were recorded from 64 scalp EEG electrodes and 2 electrooculography (EOG) electrodes, at a sampling rate of 256 Hz, and were referenced to node site Cz during EEG measurement. This resulted in a sequence dataset with 64 features × 256 µV values for each of the (approximately) 100 observations per participant.

Recently, the *Full Dataset* from the UCI repository was utilized by Farsi et al. to train both ANN and LSTM classifiers, with their LSTM architecture having the best performance with a reported test accuracy of 0.93 [47]. They used improper dataset partitioning, mixing the participants data and selecting 80% of the data for training and 20% for testing. For improper training and validation of the cross-participant model, we used 5-fold CV to align with Farsi et al.'s 80% training 20% testing dataset preparation. For proper cross-participant model evaluation, we utilized 5-fold Leave-N-Participants-Out CV, with N equal to 24 or 25 depending on the fold. Although the paper provided an architecture, it did not explicitly identify their choice of best hyperparameters that were selected for their final LSTM model—they only provided a list of what hyperparameters were explored. Therefore, in an effort to recreate their work, we utilized the architecture they specified and performed a hyperparameter sweep across all of the hyperparameters that were explored by the authors. This resulted in a 3-layer LSTM with layers and hidden units as follows (100-(Dropout Layer)-32-1), and a hyperparameter sweep performed for activation function (Relu, tanh, Sigmoid), dropout rate (0.2, 0.4), optimizer (Adam, SGD), batch size (50, 150), learning rate (0.1, 0.0001), epochs (50, 100), and loss function (MSE, Binary Cross Entropy). The resulting models from these hyperparameter sweeps performed poorly for both improper and proper models, so we instead used a 3-layer LSTM architecture with descending hidden units (H) across the three layers (H, H-50, H-100), dropout and recurrent dropout activated for all three layers, with activation function tanh, recurrent activation function sigmoid, batch size 256, optimizer Adam, learning rate 0.0001, and loss function Binary Cross Entropy. Then, we performed a hyperparameter sweep for this architecture across hidden units (200, 250, 300, 350), dropout rate (0.2, 0.3, 0.4), and epochs (200, 300, 400, 500). This architecture and its hyperparameter sweep had better performance, so we opted to use it as our final architecture for both the improper and proper methods of model creation. The best configuration for the improper model had hyperparameters of hidden units 350, dropout rate 0.4, and epochs 500. The best configuration for the proper model had hyperparameters hidden units 300, dropout rate 0.4, and epochs 400.

The resulting improper model had a test accuracy of 0.84 (95% CI: 0.82, 0.86) or an error rate of 0.16 (95% CI: 0.12, 0.18). While this result is significantly lower than Farsi et al.'s error rate (0.16 vs. 0.07 [47]), our accuracy is still similar enough in magnitude for our goal of contrasting proper and improper methods of model evaluation. The resulting proper model had a test accuracy of 0.69 (95% CI: 0.67, 0.71) or an error rate of 0.31 (95% CI: 0.29, 0.33), which is close to chance accuracy of 0.64 or a chance error rate of 0.36, as this dataset was imbalanced with a majority class of alcoholics. The error rate of the properly data-partitioned model is almost twice as large as the error rate of the improper model, again suggesting that if the goal is to build a model that can be used to make accurate estimates on unseen individuals, then the EEG cross-participant model must be evaluated properly by evaluating it only using data from participants not used during training or validating the model.

4.4. Post-Traumatic Stress Disorder (PTSD)

This publicly available PTSD dataset can be found on Figshare [34] through an appendix and link provided in Rahmani et al.'s paper, which details the experiment used and their subsequent EEG analysis [34] (unrelated to machine learning). Researchers captured resting-state EEG from six healthy control (HC) participants and six combat-related PTSD participants, while they had an MRI taken, with the goal being to find differences between HCs and PTSD participants through analysis of the EEG. For this dataset, there were 33 channels of EEG recorded, with two of the 33 channels being used for ground and reference, and at a sampling rate of 5000 Hz. EEG preprocessing was performed in both the proprietary software BrainVision Analyzer2 and within EEGLAB. ICA was used to remove blink and saccade artifacts, and time periods containing motion artifacts from observed participant head motion were also removed. After artifact removal, the EEG was down-sampled to 250 Hz. Scans lasted 526 s, and the first 6 s were removed for steady-state signals, resulting in 520 s of raw voltage value data per participant. However, only the first continuous 50,000 data points without participant motion were used within Rahmani et al.'s analysis, and this was subsequently the case with the data uploaded and made available to the public, resulting in 200 s of raw EEG per participant being available for machine learning. Then, EEG signals were segmented into 1-s non-overlapping epochs, resulting in 200 observations per participant. For feature selection, spectral features were extracted for the 31 EEG channels using Morlet wavelet transforms in MATLAB to determine the frequency-domain mean power of the five traditional frequency bands: delta (2–4 Hz), theta (4–8 Hz), alpha (8–12 Hz), beta (15–30 Hz), and gamma (30–80 Hz) [5] pp. 151–174. The mean power of these five bands for all 31 channels results in a total of 155 features (31×5) for each of the 260 observations for each of the 12 participants.

Since this dataset has not yet been used for published research in the area of machine learning, there is no machine learning workflow we are attempting to replicate; instead, we utilize a standard fully connected multi-layer perceptron neural network (MLPNN) for our architecture, which is a common and most fundamental ANN.

A hyperparameter sweep was performed to find a good model. The sweep was conducted across the following hyperparameters: hidden layers (1, 2), hidden units (20, 30, 40, 50), dropout rate (0.0, 0.1, 0.2), and learning rates (0.01, 0.001, 0.0001) for both the improper and proper methods of model evaluation, and the hyperparameter configuration that resulted in the highest validation accuracy was selected for each method. The architecture used ReLU activation functions for dense layers, a Sigmoid activation function for the output layer, and 'Adam' for the optimizer; training was conducted for 50 epochs. For training and validation of the improper model, 12-fold CV was used with all participant data shuffled together and split across the 12-folds, and for training and validation of the proper model, 12-fold LOPO CV was used.

The best configuration for the improper model consisted of 1 hidden layer, 50 hidden units, a learning rate of 0.001, and a dropout rate of 0.2. This configuration resulted in a 12-fold CV accuracy of 0.995 (95% CI: 0.9922, 0.9978) or an error rate of 0.005 (95% CI:

0.0022, 0.0078). The best configuration for the proper model was similar in that it consisted of the same parameters for everything except the hidden units being 40 instead of 50. This configuration resulted in a 12-fold LOPO CV of 0.803 (95% CI: 0.7871, 0.8189) or an error rate of 0.197 (95% CI: 0.1811, 0.2129). This results in an error rate that is over 39 times larger for the proper method versus the improper method of training and validation, which is the 2nd largest difference between proper and improper partitioning within these case studies. Relying on the overly optimistic, extremely low error rate measured in the performance of the model trained using the improper training method would falsely drive overconfidence in the model's performance in future use. Once again, the evidence suggests that if the intent is to estimate performance on new people, proper segregation of participants in the partitioning of the training, validation, and test datasets is paramount.

4.5. Schizophrenia

This dataset is available on Kaggle [35] and was collected in an effort to study the difference in corollary discharge between participants with schizophrenia and those without schizophrenia (HCs) [48]. The participant's task was to either (1) press a button every 1–2 s to deliver an 80 dB tone, (2) passively listen to that same tone, or (3) press a button that did not produce a tone or any other effect other than the tactile response of depressing the button. Each event condition occurred a total of 100 times for each participant, resulting in 300 trials per participant. In total, in the dataset there were 32 HCs and 49 patients with schizophrenia; however, data from only 40 participants were available online (25 HCs and 15 diagnosed with schizophrenia).

Data were collected using a BioSemi ActiveTwo 64 + 2 electrode cap, with 64 scalp sites and 2 references electrodes placed over the mastoids [48]. Data were sampled at 1024 Hz and epoched at 3 s for each trial, with the start of each epoch being time-locked to 1.5 s before button press. The EEG data were uploaded to Kaggle [35] in two different formats, one in time-series as raw EEG voltage values, and the other with event-related potential (ERP) features. In order to generate richer features for machine learning, spectral features were extracted from the raw EEG voltage values for all 64 channels. This was done similarly as done in the PTSD dataset, using Morlet wavelet transforms in MATLAB to determine the frequency-domain mean power of the five traditional frequency bands: delta (2–4 Hz), theta (4–8 Hz), alpha (8–12 Hz), beta (15–30 Hz), and gamma (30–80 Hz) ([5] pp. 151–174). This resulted in 320 features for each observation (64 channels × 5 frequency bands = 320), with participants having between 280 and 290 observations each. Unfortunately, the dataset was heavily imbalanced, with 25 participants being HCs, and only 15 participants being diagnosed with schizophrenia. To alleviate this imbalance, only 15 of the 25 HCs were randomly selected to be used for machine learning.

For our architecture selection for this dataset, we use both a neural network, as well as a more traditional machine learning model—the random forest classifier. Buettner et al. achieved high levels of accuracy for EEG classification of HCs vs. participants with schizophrenia using an RFC [49] (albeit on a different EEG dataset), so they are a proven model type for this domain, with the neural network architecture implemented for additional investigation. The spectral features generated were utilized for both the MLPNN and the RFC, and both architectures followed both the proper and improper methods of model evaluation, resulting in four separate models generated. For improper training and validation, 30-fold CV was utilized with all participant data shuffled together and split across the 30-folds, and for proper training and validation, 30-fold LOPO CV was used. As with the PTSD dataset, we did not have a published neural network methodology to replicate for this dataset.

For the MLPNN architecture, a hyperparameter sweep was conducted across the following hyperparameters: hidden layers (1, 2), hidden units (20, 30, 40, 50), dropout rate (0.0, 0.1, 0.2), and learning rates (0.01, 0.001, 0.0001). This hyperparameter sweep was conducted for both the improper and proper methods of model evaluation, and the hyperparameter configuration that resulted in the highest validation accuracy was selected for each method. Other parameters of the architecture include using the ReLU activation function for dense layers, a Sigmoid activation function for the output layer, and 'Adam' for the optimizer; the number of training epochs set to 50.

RFC hyperparameters selected for hyperparameter tuning included the maximum depth of the trees and the number of features to consider. The number of estimators (trees) was determined by incrementally increasing the number of estimators by 5 from a low value of 50 until validation accuracy no longer improved. For this, maximum depth was set to its default sklearn value of 'None' so that there was no limit to depth, and the maximum features set to its typical recommended amount of $m = \sqrt{p}$ where p equals the 320 features, and thus, $m = \sqrt{320} = 18$ [50]. By incrementally increasing the number of estimators by 5 from 50 to 750 as described above, 110 was found to result in the best validation accuracy, and this amount was used for both proper and improper methods of model evaluation for the RFCs. From here, a hyperparameter sweep for the number of features and the maximum depth was conducted, utilizing values from 1 to 25 for each. These values were determined by going far above and below the typical recommended values for these parameters (e.g., the square root of features for the number of max_features m) [50]. This resulted in a hyperparameter sweep of $25^2 = 625$ models for both the improper and proper methods of model evaluation, resulting in 1250 models in total generated during hyperparameter search.

The best configuration for the MLPNN improper model consisted of 1 hidden layer, 50 hidden units, a learning rate of 0.001, and a dropout rate of 0.2. This configuration resulted in a 30-fold CV accuracy of 0.992 (95% CI: 0.990, 0.9939) or an error rate of 0.008 (95% CI: 0.0061, 0.01). For the proper MLPNN model, there was no significant difference between any of the configurations, and no model was able to perform better than random chance (50%), illustrating how severe the effect of covariate shift can be in EEG data, depending on the participants used. The best configuration for the RFC improper model was maximum features set to 15 and maximum depth set to 24, resulting in a 30-fold CV accuracy of 0.941 (95% CI: 0.936, 0.946) or an error rate of 0.059 (95% CI: 0.054, 0.064). For the proper RFC model, similar to the proper MLPNN model, there was no significant difference between any of the configurations, and no model was able to perform better than random chance (50%). This final case study showcases the most significant effect of covariate shift, resulting in models that are unable to perform better than random chance due to the significant inter-participant variability that exists between the participants.

5. Discussion

Our empirical results show that improper dataset evaluation can lead to unrealistic and overestimated accuracies for general population EEG cross-participant models. Table 3 specifies the extent of these differences in error rates between improper and proper methods, ranging from a 35% increase in error rate for the *confused students* dataset, all the way up to a 3900% increase in error rate in the case of the *schizophrenia* dataset. As mentioned in Section 4, the diversity of these datasets and the methods used provide evidence that performance overestimation due to improper data partitioning is indeed a phenomenon of EEG that is not unique to any one subset of experiment, task, participant, or equipment used, nor is it merely an aspect of only certain EEG features or types of machine learning models. Instead, the risk of performance overestimation is an inherent phenomenon of individual differences in EEG that should always be considered when developing general population EEG cross-participant models.

Table 3. Validation results for the five case studies (95% CI). All datasets are binary classification tasks, and all datasets are balanced except for the Alcoholism dataset. This gives chance error rate for Alcoholism defined as 0.36, and 0.50 for all other datasets. Results should be compared within datasets (left to right) between the improper and proper method. The proper method always reveals a significantly greater error rate than the improper method, suggesting the risks of overestimation of performance, which can result from using the improper method.

Dataset	Architecture Used	Error Rate–Improper Method	Error Rate–Proper Method
Driver Fatigue	MLPNN	0.09 (0.083, 0.097)	0.466 (0.448, 0.472)
Confused Students	Bi-LSTM	0.31 (0.274, 0.346)	0.416 (0.372, 0.448)
Alcoholism	LSTM	0.16 (0.12, 0.18)	0.31 (0.29, 0.33)
PTSD	MLPNN	0.005 (0.0022, 0.0078)	0.197 (0.1811, 0.2129)
Schizophrenia	MLPNN	0.008 (0.0061, 0.01)	0.50 (0.44, 0.56)
Schizophrenia	RFC	0.059 (0.054, 0.064)	0.50 (0.44, 0.56)

Proper care with EEG data preparation has been a subject of recent exploration by Li et al. as well [51]. Li et al. demonstrated that due to EEG's non-stationarity, proper guidelines for the design of the experiment much be followed in order obtain model results that are not overestimated, particularly in the block design of the experiment so that stimuli of different classes are intermixed. If not followed, models instead learn to classify through arbitrary temporal artifacts, giving the false appearance of high performance. Our findings are synergistic with Li's: we demonstrate the necessity of partitioning the data properly when performing machine learning on collected data *after* the experiment is complete; due to individual differences, proper care with EEG data partitioning by participant yields more accurate estimates of model results on future data. Together, both Li et al.'s guidelines for the design of the experiment and our guidelines for proper post-experiment dataset partitioning should be followed in order to obtain results for EEG cross-participant models that are representative of the model's performance on the general population.

In Section 3, we demonstrated how t-SNE can be used to visualize covariate shift between participants due to their inter-participant variability, and we also illustrated how the *shifted Heaviside* and the *shift to median* transformations could be utilized to reduce this inter-participant variability. Additionally, for the purpose of demonstrating the relationship between this inter-participant variability and covariate shift, we explored the effect of these transformations in improving cross-participant model accuracy for both improper and proper model creation across two different feature spaces (*entropy* and *spectral* features). As can be seen in Figures 7b,c and 8b,c, both transformations were successful in reducing inter-participant variability for both feature spaces; however, only the *shift to median* transformation resulted in a dominant increase in accuracy of the 95% confidence intervals for both feature spaces for proper model creation, with the *shifted Heaviside* transformation having no improvement in model accuracy. In contrast to the *shifted Heaviside* results, Arevalillo-Herraez et al. (the originators of the *shifted Heaviside* transformation) had improvement of model accuracy in three different datasets they utilized, all of which were affect recognition-based datasets with arousal and valence features [36]. In their research, they also followed proper dataset partitioning guidelines and utilized LOPO CV. This suggests that a transformation that results in a reduction or elimination of inter-participant variability does not necessarily imply an improvement in cross-participant model accuracy.

6. Conclusions

As mentioned in Section 2, five out of six EEG deep learning models in research today are cross-participant models, with only one out of those five models following some method of proper dataset partitioning to ensure the model was tested with unseen participants [3]. Our empirical results show that models that utilize improper dataset evaluation have overestimated and unrealistic accuracies for the general population, with the difference in error rates for improper versus proper dataset evaluation ranging from a 35% increase in error rate up to a 3900% increase in error rate. These empirical findings suggest that if this trend continues, the body of research for EEG cross-participant models will become diluted with research that claims overestimated and unrealistic performance metrics, both downplaying the true difficulty in creating a high-performing EEG cross-participant model, and also slowing scientific progress of researching methodologies, which results in cross-participant models that are truly high performing for the general population. Thus, it is absolutely critical that the body of research corrects this trend and follows the proper dataset partitioning guidelines described in this research. Specifically, it means that:

- Data from participants used for model training must not be used for model validation or testing.
- Participants that are utilized for validation must not be used for testing.

This ensures the model is tested with unseen participants and reflects its intended purpose.

These findings extend beyond individual researchers. In addition, it is also important that data contributors, and the owners and maintainers of dataset repositories (e.g., Kaggle [12] and the UCI machine learning data repository [13]) managing human data ensure these guidelines are followed as well. Specifically, for these repositories, we recommend that:

- Any EEG data that are made available for download should always have (de-identified) participant labels available so that users may properly partition the data themselves.
- If the data contributors or maintainers decide to pre-partition the data into separate training and test datasets (as is sometimes done for competitions of machine learning models), then proper dataset partitioning guidelines should be followed for preparing those training and test datasets before they are made available for download by the general public.

We also recommend that the repository include these guidelines of proper dataset partitioning with all hosted EEG datasets, as this would help spread the word in regard to proper dataset partitioning and inform users who are unaware of inter-participant variability and its effects.

Lastly, we strongly recommend that the "Neurotechnologies for Brain–Machine Interfacing" group of the Institute of Electrical and Electronics Engineers Standards Association (IEEE SA) consider and adopt these guidelines for all future proposals of standards. In this group's most recent *Standards Roadmap* [52], stakeholders and experts across government, academia, and industry identified the existing gap in the standardization of performance assessment and benchmarking for BMI as a clear priority for standardization [53]. Specifically, the proposal should identify these guidelines as a minimal reporting requirement for performance evaluation of EEG cross-participant models, leading to standardization in reporting how the data are partitioned, identifying their limitations, and curbing performance claims accordingly.

Author Contributions: A.K. is a PhD candidate performing this research as part of his dissertation research and is the investigator on the research as well as the primary author for the whole article. B.B. provided subject matter expertise on machine learning, and A.K. as research advisor mentored this student research and assisted with editing the whole article. C.S.K. has focused on the mathematical and theoretical mentorship with extra focus on Sections 2 and 3. All authors have read and agreed to the published version of the manuscript.

Funding: This research was sponsored and funded by James Lawton AFOSR/RTA, grant number F4FGA08305J006, "Information Acquisition Deficit Detection and Mitigation through Neurophysiological-sensed Operator Patterns".

Data Availability Statement: Publicly available datasets were utilized in this study. These datasets can be found at the following URL's. Driver Fatigue: https://figshare.com/articles/dataset/The_original_EEG_data_for_driver_fatigue_detection/5202739 (accessed on 4 May 2021). Confused Students: https://www.kaggle.com/wanghaohan/confused-eeg (accessed on 4 May 2021). Alcoholism: https://www.kaggle.com/nnair25/Alcoholics (accessed on 4 May 2021). PTSD: https://figshare.com/articles/dataset/Dynamical_Hurst_analysis_identifies_EEG_channel_differences_between_PTSD_and_healthy_ controls/6737795 (accessed on 4 May 2021). Schizophrenia: https://www.kaggle.com/broach/button-tone-sz (accessed on 4 May 2021).

Acknowledgments: We would like to thank our sponsor, James Lawton AFOSR/RTA, for supporting this research. The views and conclusions contained in this document are those of the authors and should not be interpreted as representing the official policies, either expressed or implied, of the United States Air Force or the U.S. Government.

Conflicts of Interest: The authors declare no conflict of interest.

Abbreviations

ANN	Artificial Neural Network
BMI	Brain–Machine Interface
CI	Confidence Interval
CV	Cross-Validation
DL	Deep Learning
DR	Dropout Rate
EEG	Electroencephalography
EOG	Electrooculography
GRU	Gated Recurrent Unit
HC	Healthy Control
HU	Hidden Unit
IEEE SA	Institute of Electrical and Electronics Engineers Standards Association
iid	Independent and Identically Distributed
KL	Kullback-Leibler
LOPO	Leave-One-Participant-Out
LOOCV	Leave-One-Out Cross-Validation
LR	Learning Rate
LSTM	Long Short-Term Memory
MLPNN	Multi-Layer Perceptron Neural Network
Opt	Optimizer
PCA	Principal Component Analysis
PTSD	Post-Traumatic Stress Disorder
ReLU	Rectified Linear Unit
RFC	Random Forest Classifier
RNNt-SNE	Recurrent Neural Networkt-Distributed Stochastic Neighbor Embedding
UCI	University of California, Irvine

Appendix A

In this appendix, we include any pre-processing details that were provided by the originators of the datasets used within this research.

Appendix A.1. Driver Fatigue Data

EEG was recorded using a 32-channel electrode cap, with two of the channels being reference channels linked to mastoid electrodes [38]. Scan 4.3 software of Neuroscan was used for preprocessing, with raw signals filtered by a 50 Hz notch filter and a 0.15 Hz to 45 Hz band pass filter in order to remove noise.

Appendix A.2. Confused Students Data

No known preprocessing information was provided by the originators.

Appendix A.3. Alcoholism Data

EEG correlates were sampled from 62 scalp electrodes and two EOG electrodes, at a sampling rate of 256 Hz [13]. Sampling started at 190 ms before onset of stimulus in order to record a pre-stimulus baseline, and EEG correlate durations provided in the dataset were 1 s in duration. Sensor values were provided in µV, resulting in a sequence of 256 temporally organized values for each EEG channel. Trials with excessive eye or body movements (>73.3 µV) were rejected online. Only artifact free EEG segments were used to include eye blink artifacts. EEG electrodes were referenced to node site Cz during EEG measurement.

Appendix A.4. PTSD Data

For this dataset, there were 33 channels of EEG recorded, with two of the 33 channels being used for ground and reference, and at a sampling rate of 5000 Hz [34]. EEG preprocessing was performed in the proprietary software BrainVision Analyzer2. MRI gradient artifacts and cardio ballistic artifacts were removed using the template subtraction method. Then, the EEG was down-sampled to 250 Hz and filtered with a 40 Hz low-pass filter. Then, ICA was applied to remove residual cardioballistic artifacts as well as blink and saccade artifacts. Time periods of head motion were removed.

Appendix A.5. Schizophrenia Data

Vertical EOG (VEOG) and Horizontal EOG (HEOG) were also collected for the purpose of capturing eye movement and blinks [35]. Due to the size of the raw EEG signals, preprocessing was already performed on the dataset prior to its upload for public use. This preprocessing included re-referencing to the averaged mastoid channels, applying a 0.1 Hz high-pass filter, interpolation of outlier channels, and rejection of outlier components and outlier trials due to EEG artifacts using the FASTER artifact rejection method [54].

References

1. Hefron, R.G.; Borghetti, B.J.; Christensen, J.C.; Kabban, C.M.S. Deep long short-term memory structures model temporal dependencies improving cognitive workload estimation. *Pattern Recognit. Lett.* **2017**, *94*, 96–104. [CrossRef]
2. Hefron, R.; Borghetti, B.; Kabban, C.S.; Christensen, J.; Estepp, J. Cross-participant EEG-based assessment of cognitive workload using multi-path convolutional recurrent neural networks. *Sensors* **2018**, *18*, 5. [CrossRef] [PubMed]
3. Roy, Y.; Banville, H.; Albuquerque, I.; Gramfort, A.; Falk, T.H.; Faubert, J. Deep learning-based electroencephalography analysis: A systematic review. *J. Neural Eng.* **2019**, *16*, 051001. [CrossRef] [PubMed]
4. Kaplan, A.Y.; Fingelkurts, A.A.; Borisov, S.V.; Darkhovsky, B.S. Nonstationary nature of the brain activity as revealed by EEG/MEG: Methodological, practical and conceptual challenges. *Signal Process.* **2005**, *85*, 2190–2212. [CrossRef]
5. Cohen, M.X. Analyzing Neural Time Series Data. In *Analyzing Neural Time Series Data*; The MIT Press: Cambridge, MA, USA, 2019; pp. 151–174, 499–502.
6. Sugiyama, M.; Krauledat, M.; Müller, K.R. Covariate shift adaptation by importance weighted cross validation. *J. Mach. Learn. Res.* **2007**, *8*, 985–1005.
7. Raza, H. Adaptive Learning for Modelling Non-Stationarity in EEG-Based Brain-Computer Interfacing. Ph.D. Thesis, Ulster University, Belfast, UK, 2016.
8. Raza, H.; Prasad, G.; Li, Y. Dataset shift detection in non-stationary environments using EWMA charts. In Proceedings of the 2013 IEEE International Conference on Systems, Man, and Cybernetics, Manchester, UK, 13–16 October 2013; pp. 3151–3156.
9. Raza, H.; Prasad, G.; Li, Y. EWMA based two-stage dataset shift-detection in non-stationary environments. In *IFIP Advances in Information and Communication Technology*; Springer: Berlin, Heidelberg, 2013; Volume 2, pp. 625–635.
10. Raza, H.; Prasad, G.; Li, Y. Adaptive learning with covariate shift-detection for non-stationary environments. In Proceedings of the 2014 14th UK Workshop on Computational Intelligence (UKCI), Bradford, UK, 8–10 September 2014.
11. Sugiyama, M.; Kawanabe, M. *Machine Learning in Non-Stationary Environments: Introduction to Covariate Shift Adaptation*; The MIT Press: Cambridge, MA, USA, 2012.
12. Begleiter, H.; Neurodynamics Laboratory. State University of New York Health Center at Brooklyn. Available online: http://www.downstate.edu/hbnl/ (accessed on 1 October 2020).
13. Dua, D.; Graff, C. UCI Machine Learning Repository. Available online: http://archive.ics.uci.edu/ml (accessed on 1 August 2019).
14. Raza, H.; Samothrakis, S. Bagging Adversarial Neural Networks for Domain Adaptation in Non-Stationary EEG. In Proceedings of the 2019 International Joint Conference on Neural Networks (IJCNN), Budapest, Hungary, 14–19 July 2019.
15. Géron, A. *Hands-On Machine Learning with Scikit-Learn, Keras, and TensorFlow: Concepts, Tools, and Techniques to Build Intelligent Systems*; O'Reilly Media: Sebastopol, CA, USA, 2019.
16. Van Der Maaten, L.; Hinton, G. Visualizing data using t-SNE. *J. Mach. Learn. Res.* **2008**, *9*, 2579–2625.
17. Wattenberg, M.; Viégas, F.; Johnson, I. How to Use t-SNE Effectively. Distill. 2016. Available online: http://doi.org/10.23915/distill.00002 (accessed on 1 September 2020).
18. Xiao, H.; Rasul, K.; Vollgraf, R. Fashion-MNIST: A Novel Image Dataset for Benchmarking Machine Learning Algorithms. *arXiv* **2017**, arXiv:1708.07747.

19. Birjandtalab, J.; Pouyan, M.B.; Nourani, M. An unsupervised subject identification technique using EEG signals. In Proceedings of the 2016 38th Annual International Conference of the IEEE Engineering in Medicine and Biology Society (EMBC), Orlando, FL, USA, 16–20 August 2016; pp. 816–819.
20. Rasoulzadeh, V.; Erkus, E.C.; Yogurt, T.A.; Ulusoy, I.; Zergeroğlu, S.A. A comparative stationarity analysis of EEG signals. *Ann. Oper. Res.* **2017**, *258*, 133–157. [CrossRef]
21. Li, Y.; Kambara, H.; Koike, Y.; Sugiyama, M. Application of covariate shift adaptation techniques in brain-computer interfaces. *IEEE Trans. Biomed. Eng.* **2010**, *57*, 1318–1324.
22. Matthews, G.; Amelang, M. Extraversion, arousal theory and performance: A study of individual differences in the eeg. *Pers. Individ. Dif.* **1993**, *14*, 347–363. [CrossRef]
23. Medrano, P.; Nyhus, E.; Smolen, A.; Curran, T.; Ross, R.S. Individual differences in EEG correlates of recognition memory due to DAT polymorphisms. *Brain Behav.* **2017**, *7*, e00870. [CrossRef] [PubMed]
24. Landolt, H.-P. Genetic determination of sleep EEG profiles in healthy humans. *Progress Brain Res.* **2011**, *193*, 51–61.
25. Smit, D.J.A.; Boomsma, D.I.; Schnack, H.G.; Hulshoff Pol, H.E.; De Geus, E.J.C. Individual Differences in EEG Spectral Power Reflect Genetic Variance in Gray and White Matter Volumes. *Twin Res. Hum. Genet.* **2012**, *15*, 384–392. [CrossRef] [PubMed]
26. Muthukumaraswamy, S.D.; Edden, R.A.E.; Jones, D.K.; Swettenham, J.B.; Singh, K.D. Resting GABA concentration predicts peak gamma frequency and fMRI amplitude in response to visual stimulation in humans. *Proc. Natl. Acad. Sci. USA* **2009**, *106*, 8356–8361. [CrossRef]
27. Muthukumaraswamy, S.D.; Singh, K.D. Visual gamma oscillations: The effects of stimulus type, visual field coverage and stimulus motion on MEG and EEG recordings. *Neuroimage* **2013**, *69*, 223–230. [CrossRef]
28. Cohen, M.X. Hippocampal-prefrontal connectivity predicts midfrontal oscillations and long-term memory performance. *Curr. Biol.* **2011**, *21*, 1900–1905.
29. Raza, H.; Rathee, D.; Zhou, S.M.; Cecotti, H.; Prasad, G. Covariate shift estimation based adaptive ensemble learning for handling non-stationarity in motor imagery related EEG-based brain-computer interface. *Neurocomputing* **2019**, *343*, 154–166. [CrossRef]
30. Goodfellow, I.; Bengio, Y.; Courville, A. *Deep Learning*; MIT Press: Cambridge, MA, USA, 2016.
31. Bickel, S. Learning under Differing Training and Test Distributions. Ph.D. Thesis, Universität Potsdam, Potsdam, Germany, 2008.
32. Shimodaira, H. Improving predictive inference under covariate shift by weighting the log-likelihood function. *J. Stat. Plan. Inference* **2000**, *90*, 227–244. [CrossRef]
33. Min, J.; Wang, P.; Hu, J. The Original EEG Data for Driver Fatigue Detection. Available online: https://figshare.com/articles/dataset/The_original_EEG_data_for_driver_fatigue_detection/5202739 (accessed on 12 February 2021).
34. Rahmani, B.; Wong, C.K.; Norouzzadeh, P.; Bodurka, J.; McKinney, B. Dynamical hurst analysis identifies eeg channel differences between ptsd and healthy controls. *PLoS ONE* **2018**, *13*, e0214527. [CrossRef]
35. Roach, B. EEG Data from Basic Sensory Task in Schizophrenia. Available online: https://www.kaggle.com/broach/button-tone-sz (accessed on 17 December 2020).
36. Arevalillo-Herráez, M.; Cobos, M.; Roger, S.; García-Pineda, M. Combining inter-subject modeling with a subject-based data transformation to improve affect recognition from EEG signals. *Sensors* **2019**, *19*, 2999. [CrossRef]
37. Donnelly, P.; Ellis, R.S. Entropy, Large Deviations, and Statistical Mechanics. *J. Am. Stat. Assoc.* **1987**, *82*, 399. [CrossRef]
38. Min, J.; Wang, P.; Hu, J. Driver fatigue detection through multiple entropy fusion analysis in an EEG-based system. *PLoS ONE* **2017**, *12*, e0188756.
39. Lee, K.A.; Hicks, G.; Nino-Murcia, G. Validity and reliability of a scale to assess fatigue. *Psychiatry Res.* **1991**, *36*, 291–298. [CrossRef]
40. Chalder, T.; Berelowitz, G.; Pawlikowska, T.; Watts, L.; Wessely, S.; Wright, D.; Wallace, E.P. Development of a fatigue scale. *J. Psychosom. Res.* **1993**, *37*, 147–153. [CrossRef]
41. Yu, H.; Wilamowski, B.M. Levenberg-marquardt training. *Ind. Electron. Handb.* **2011**, *5*, 1–16.
42. Wang, H.; Li, Y.; Hu, X.; Yang, Y.; Meng, Z.; Chang, K.M. Using EEG to improve massive open online courses feedback interaction. In Proceedings of the 16th Annual Conference on Artificial Intelligence in Education (AIED), Memphis, TN, USA, 9–13 July 2013.
43. Ni, Z.; Yuksel, A.C.; Ni, X.; Mandel, M.I.; Xie, L. Confused or not confused?: Disentangling Brain activity from EEG data using Bidirectional LSTM Recurrent Neural Networks. In Proceedings of the 8th ACM International Conference on Bioinformatics, Computational Biology, and Health Informatics, Boston, MA, USA, 20–23 August 2017.
44. Wang, H.; Wu, Z.; Xing, E.P. Removing confounding factors associated weights in deep neural networks improves the prediction accuracy for healthcare applications. In Proceedings of the Pacific Symposium on Biocomputing, Waimea, HI, USA, 3–7 January 2019.
45. Ingber, L. Statistical mechanics of neocortical interactions: Canonical momenta indicators of electroencephalography. *Phys. Rev. E* **1997**, *55*, 4578–4593. [CrossRef]
46. Zhang, X.L.; Begleiter, H.; Porjesz, B.; Litke, A. Electrophysiological Evidence of Memory Impairment in Alcoholic Patients. *Biol. Psychiatry* **1997**, *42*, 1157–1171. [CrossRef]
47. Farsi, L.; Siuly, S.; Kabir, E.; Wang, H. Classification of Alcoholic EEG Signals Using a Deep Learning Method. *IEEE Sens. J.* **2021**, *21*, 3552–3560. [CrossRef]
48. Ford, J.M.; Palzes, V.A.; Roach, B.J.; Mathalon, D.H. Did i do that? Abnormal predictive processes in schizophrenia when button pressing to deliver a tone. *Schizophr. Bull.* **2014**, *40*, 804–812. [CrossRef]

49. Buettner, R.; Hirschmiller, M.; Schlosser, K.; Rossle, M.; Fernandes, M.; Timm, I.J. High-performance exclusion of schizophrenia using a novel machine learning method on EEG data. In Proceedings of the 2019 IEEE International Conference on E-health Networking, Application & Services (HealthCom), Bogota, Colombia, 14–16 October 2019.
50. Casella, G.; Fienberg, S.; Olkin, I. *An Introduction to Statistical Learning*; Springer: New York, NY, USA, 2013.
51. Li, R.; Johansen, J.S.; Ahmed, H.; Ilyevsky, T.V.; Wilbur, R.B.; Bharadwaj, H.M.; Siskind, J.M. The Perils and Pitfalls of Block Design for EEG Classification Experiments. *IEEE Trans. Pattern Anal. Mach. Intell.* **2021**, *43*, 316–333.
52. Standards Roadmap: Neurotechnologies for Brain-Machine Interfacing, IEEE Standards Association, Piscataway, NJ, USA, Industry Connections Report IC17-007. Available online: https://standards.ieee.org/content/dam/ieee-standards/standards/web/documents/presentations/ieee-neurotech-for-bmi-standards-roadmap.pdf (accessed on 20 April 2021).
53. Chavarriaga, R.; Carey, C.; Contreras-Vidal, J.L.; Mckinney, Z.; Bianchi, L. Standardization of Neurotechnology for Brain-Machine Interfacing: State of the Art and Recommendations. *IEEE Open J. Eng. Med. Biol.* **2021**, *2*, 71–73. [CrossRef]
54. Nolan, H.; Whelan, R.; Reilly, R.B. FASTER: Fully Automated Statistical Thresholding for EEG artifact Rejection. *J. Neurosci. Methods* **2010**, *92*, 152–162. [CrossRef]

Review

A Review of EEG Signal Features and Their Application in Driver Drowsiness Detection Systems

Igor Stancin, Mario Cifrek and Alan Jovic *

Faculty of Electrical Engineering and Computing, University of Zagreb, Unska 3, 10000 Zagreb, Croatia; igor.stancin@fer.hr (I.S.); mario.cifrek@fer.hr (M.C.)
* Correspondence: alan.jovic@fer.hr

Abstract: Detecting drowsiness in drivers, especially multi-level drowsiness, is a difficult problem that is often approached using neurophysiological signals as the basis for building a reliable system. In this context, electroencephalogram (EEG) signals are the most important source of data to achieve successful detection. In this paper, we first review EEG signal features used in the literature for a variety of tasks, then we focus on reviewing the applications of EEG features and deep learning approaches in driver drowsiness detection, and finally we discuss the open challenges and opportunities in improving driver drowsiness detection based on EEG. We show that the number of studies on driver drowsiness detection systems has increased in recent years and that future systems need to consider the wide variety of EEG signal features and deep learning approaches to increase the accuracy of detection.

Keywords: drowsiness detection; EEG features; feature extraction; machine learning; drowsiness classification; fatigue detection; deep learning

1. Introduction

Many industries (manufacturing, logistics, transport, emergency ambulance, and similar) run their operations 24/7, meaning their workers work in shifts. Working in shifts causes misalignment with the internal biological circadian rhythm of many individuals, which can lead to sleeping disorders, drowsiness, fatigue, mood disturbances, and other long-term health problems [1–4]. Besides misalignment of the internal circadian rhythms with a work shift, sleep deprivation and prolonged physical or mental activity can also cause drowsiness [5–7]. Drowsiness increases the risk of accidents at the workplace [8–10], and it is one of the main risk factors in road and air traffic accidents per reports from NASA [11] and the US National Transportation Safety Board [12].

Drowsiness is the intermediate state between awareness and sleep [13–15]. Terms like tiredness and sleepiness are used as synonyms for drowsiness [16–18]. Some researchers also use fatigue as synonymous with drowsiness [19,20]. Definitions and differences between drowsiness and fatigue are addressed in many research papers [21–23]. The main difference between the two states is that short rest abates fatigue, while it aggravates drowsiness [24]. However, although the definitions are different, drowsiness and fatigue show similar behavior in terms of features measured from electroencephalogram (EEG) signal [25–28]. Because of this fact, in this review paper, we consider all the research papers whose topic was drowsiness, sleepiness, or fatigue, and we make no distinction among them.

The maximum number of hours that professional drivers are allowed to drive in a day is limited, yet drowsiness is still a major problem in traffic. A system for drowsiness detection with early warnings could address this problem. The most commonly used methods for drowsiness detection are self-assessment of drowsiness, driving events measures, eye-tracking measures, and EEG measures. Among these methods, drowsiness detection systems based on the EEG signal show the most promising results [18,29].

Brain neural network is a nonlinear dissipative system, i.e., it is a non-stationary system with a nonlinear relationship between causes and effects [30]. One way to analyze brain neural network is through feature extraction from the EEG signal. The most used techniques for feature extraction are linear, such as Fast Fourier Transform (FFT). Although it is a linear method, FFT also assumes that the amplitudes of all frequency components are constant over time, which is not the case with brain oscillations, since they are non-stationary. Because of the complexity of brain dynamics, there is a need for feature extraction methods that can properly take into account the nonlinearity and non-stationarity of brain dynamics. With an increase of computational power in recent years, many researchers work on improving the feature extraction methods, and there is a growing number of various features extracted from the EEG signal.

This paper aims to review the features extracted from the EEG signal and the applications of these features to the problem of driver drowsiness detection. We review the features since the large number of features described in the literature makes it difficult to understand their interrelationships, and also makes it difficult to choose the right ones for the given problem. To our knowledge, there is no similar review work that covers all the features discussed in this review. After the EEG features review, we continue with the review of driver drowsiness detection systems based on EEG. The main goal is to gain insight into the most commonly used EEG features and recent deep learning approaches for drowsiness detection, which would allow us to identify possibilities for further improvements of drowsiness detection systems. Finally, the main contributions of our work are the following: (1) Comprehensive review, systematization, and a brief introduction of the existing features of the EEG signal, (2) comprehensive review of the drowsiness detection systems based on the EEG signal, (3) comprehensive review of the existing similar reviews, and (4) discussion of various potential ways to improve the state of the art of drowsiness detection systems.

The paper is organized as follows: In Section 2, we present the overview of the existing review papers that are close to the topic of this paper, Section 3 provides the overview of the different features extracted from the EEG signal, Section 4 reviews the papers dealing with driver drowsiness detection systems, Section 5 provides a discussion about the features and drowsiness detection systems, and Section 6 brings the future directions of research and concludes the paper.

The search for the relevant papers included in our paper was done in the Web of Science Core Collection database. The search queries used were: (1) In Section 2.1—"{review, overview} {time, frequency, spectral, nonlinear, fractal, entropy, spatial, temporal, network, complex network} EEG features", (2) in Section 2.2—"{review, overview} driver {drowsiness, sleepiness, fatigue} {detection, classification}", (3) in Section 3—"<feature name> EEG feature", (4) in Section 4—"EEG driver {", deep learning, neural network} {drowsiness, sleepiness, fatigue} {detection, classification}". Beyond the mentioned queries, when appropriate, we also reviewed the papers cited in the results obtained through the query. Additional constraints for papers in Section 4 were: (1) They had to be published in a scientific journal, (2) they had to be published in 2010 or later, 2) at least three citations per year since the paper was published, (3) papers from 2020 or 2021 were also considered with less than three citations per year, but published in Q1 journals, and (4) the number of participants in the study experiment had to be greater than 10. The goal of these constraints was to ensure that only high quality and relevant papers were included in our study.

2. Related Work
2.1. Reviews of the EEG Signal Features

Stam [30] in his seminal review paper about the nonlinear dynamical analysis of the EEG and magnetoencephalogram (MEG) signals included more than 20 nonlinear and spatiotemporal features (e.g., correlation dimension, Lyapunov exponent, phase synchronization). The theoretical background of these features and dynamical systems were also covered. The paper gave an overview of the other research works that include explanations of the features from the fields of normal resting-state EEG, sleep, epilepsy, psychiatric diseases, normal cognition, distributed cognition, and dementia. The main drawback of the paper nowadays is that it is somewhat dated (from 2005) because additional approaches have been introduced in the meantime. Ma et al. [31] reviewed the most-used fractal-based features and entropies for the EEG signal analysis, and focused on the application of these features to sleep analysis. The authors concluded that using fractal or entropy methods may facilitate automatic sleep classification. Keshmiri [32], in a recent paper, provided a review on the usage of entropy in the fields of altered state of consciousness and brain aging. The author's work is mostly domain-specific, as it emphasizes incremental findings in each area of research rather than the specific types of entropies that were utilized in the reviewed research papers. Sun et al. [33] reviewed the complexity features in mild cognitive impairment and Alzheimer's disease. They described the usage of five time-domain entropies, three frequency-domain entropies, and four chaos theory-based complexity measures.

Motamedi-Fakhr et al. [34], in their review paper, provided an overview of more than 15 most-used features and methods (e.g., Hjorth parameters, coherence analysis, short-time Fourier transform, wavelet transform) for human sleep analysis. The features were classified into temporal, spectral, time-frequency, and nonlinear features. Besides these features, they also reviewed the research papers about sleep stages classification. Rashid et al. [35] reviewed the current status, challenges, and possible solutions for EEG-based brain-computer interface. Within their work, they also briefly discussed the most used features for brain–computer interfaces classified into time domain, frequency domain, time-frequency domain, and spatial domain.

Bastos and Schoffelen [36] provided a tutorial review of methods for functional connectivity analysis. The authors aimed to provide an intuitive explanation of how functional connectivity measures work and highlighted five interpretational caveats: The common reference problem, the signal-to-noise ratio, the volume conduction problem, the common input problem, and the sample size problem. Kida et al. [37], in their recent review paper, provided the definition, computation, short history, and pros and cons of the connectivity and complex network analysis applied to EEG/MEG signals. The authors briefly described the recent developments in the source reconstruction algorithms essential for the source-space connectivity and network analysis.

Khosla et al. [38], in their review, covered the applications of the EEG signals based on computer-aided technologies, ranging from the diagnosis of various neurological disorders such as epilepsy, major depressive disorder, alcohol use disorder, and dementia to the monitoring of other applications such as motor imagery, identity authentication, emotion recognition, sleep stage classification, eye state detection, and drowsiness monitoring. By reviewing these EEG signal-based applications, the authors listed features observed in these papers (without explanations), publicly available databases, preprocessing methods, feature selection methods, and used classification models. For the application of drowsiness monitoring, the authors reviewed only three papers, while other applications were better covered.

Ismail and Karwowski [39] overview paper dealt with a graph theory-based modeling of functional brain connectivity based on the EEG signal in the context of neuroergonomics. The authors concluded that the graph theory measures have attracted increasing attention in recent years, with the highest frequency of publications in 2018. They reviewed 20 graph theory-based measures and stated that the clustering coefficient and characteristic path length were mostly used in this domain.

Figure 1 shows the reviews presented in this section in chronological order of publication.

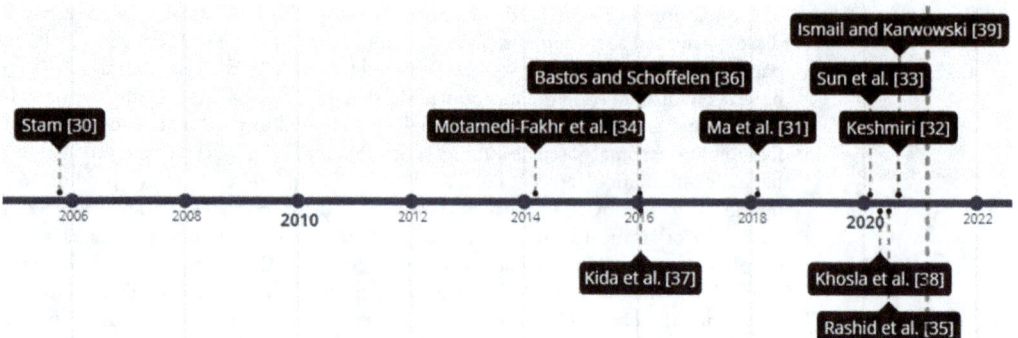

Figure 1. Chronologically ordered reviews of the EEG signal features.

2.2. Reviews of the Driver Drowsiness Detection

Lal and Craig [18], in their review of driver drowsiness systems, discussed the concept of fatigue and summarized the psychophysiological representation of driver fatigue. They concluded that most studies had found a correlation of theta and delta activity with the transition to fatigue.

Lenne and Jacobs [40], in their review paper, assessed the recent developments in the detection and prediction of drowsiness-related driving events. The driving events observed were the number of line crossings, the standard deviation of lateral position, the variability of lateral position, steering wheel variability, speed adjustments, and similar events. The authors concluded that these driving performance measures correlate with drowsiness in the experimental settings, although they stipulated that the new findings from on-road studies show a different impact on performance measures. Doudou et al. [41] reviewed the vehicle-based, video-based, and physiological signals-based techniques for drowsiness detection. They also reviewed the available commercial market solutions for drowsiness detection. When it comes to the EEG signal drowsiness detection, the authors included six papers that consider frequency-domain features in this field.

Sahayadhas et al. [42] reviewed vehicle-based measures, behavior-based measures, and physiological measures for driver drowsiness detection. The section on physiological measures included 12 papers with only frequency-domain features. Sikander and Anwar [43] reviewed drowsiness detection methods and categorized them into five groups—subjective reporting, driver biological features, driver physical features, vehicular features while driving, and hybrid features. When it comes to drowsiness detection using EEG signals, the authors focused more on explaining frequency-domain features used for drowsiness detection rather than presenting research that had already been done in this field.

Chowdhury et al. [44] reviewed different physiological sensors applied to driver drowsiness detection. Observed physiological methods for measuring drowsiness included electrocardiogram (ECG), respiratory belt, EEG, electrooculogram (EOG), electromyogram (EMG), galvanic skin response (GSR), skin temperature, and hybrid techniques. Related to EEG methods, the authors included papers based on the spectral power features, event-related potentials, and entropies. The authors also discussed different materials used for dry electrodes and the problem of measurement intrusiveness for the drivers.

Balandong et al. [45] split driver drowsiness detection systems into six categories based on the used technique—(1) subjective measures, (2) vehicle-based measures, (3) driver's behavior-based system, (4) mathematical models of sleep–wake dynamics, (5) human physiological signal-based systems, and (6) hybrid systems. The authors emphasized human physiological signal-based systems, but only the systems that rely on a limited number of EEG electrodes, as these kinds of systems are more practical for real-world applications. The authors concluded that the best results were obtained when the problem was observed as a binary classification problem and that the fusion of the EEG features with other physiological signals should lead to improved accuracy.

Other review papers of driver drowsiness systems are specialized for a certain aspect of the field, e.g., Hu and Lodewijsk [46] focused on differentiating the detection of passive fatigue, active fatigue, and sleepiness based on physiological signals, subjective assessment, driving behavior, and ocular metrics, Soares et al. [47] studied simulator experiments for drowsiness detection, Bier et al. [48] put focus on the monotony-related fatigue, and Philips et al. [49] studied operational actions (e.g., optimal staff, optimal schedule design) that reduce risk of drowsiness occurrence.

Figure 2 shows the reviews presented in this section in chronological order of publication.

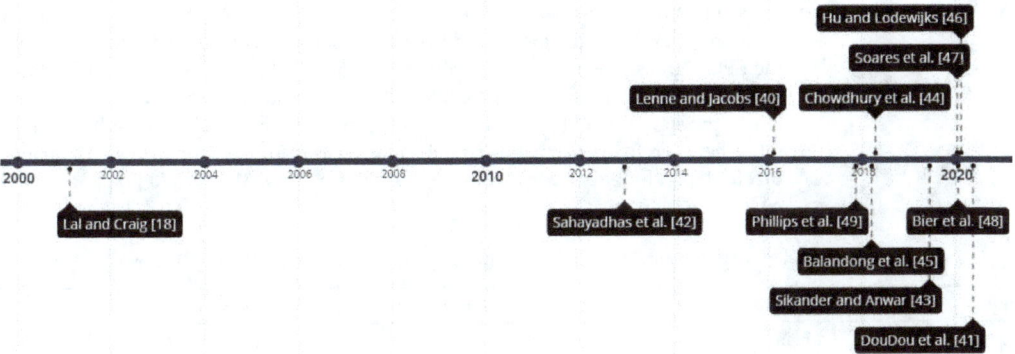

Figure 2. Chronologically ordered reviews of driver drowsiness detection methods.

3. EEG Features

The purpose of this section is to introduce features that researchers extract from the EEG signal. We will not go into the details of the computation for each feature. For the readers who are interested in the detailed computation for each feature, we suggest reading the cited papers. Instead, the main idea is to present, with a brief explanation, as many features as possible, which will later allow us to identify opportunities for further improvements in the area of driver drowsiness detection. Tables 1 and 2 show the list of all the features introduced in the following subsections. In the rest of this Section, we will use **bold** letters for the first occurrence of a particular feature name and *italic* letters for the first occurrence of a particular feature transformation or extraction method name.

3.1. Time, Frequency and Time-Frequency Domain Features

3.1.1. Time-Domain Features

The simplest features of the EEG signal are statistical features, like **mean**, **median**, **variance**, **standard deviation**, **skewness**, **kurtosis**, and similar [50]. **Zero-crossing rate (ZCR)** [51] is not a statistical feature, yet it is also a simple feature. It is the number of times that the signal crosses the x-axis. The *period-amplitude analysis* is based on the analysis of the half-waves, i.e., signals between two zero-crossings. With the period amplitude analysis, one can extract the **number of waves**, **wave duration**, **peak amplitude**, and **instantaneous frequency** (IF) (based only on the single observed half-wave) [52].

Hjorth parameters are features that are based on the variance of the derivatives of the EEG signal. **Mobility**, **activity**, and **complexity** [53] are the first three derivatives of the signal and the most-used Hjorth parameters. Mean absolute value of mobility, activity, and complexity can also be used as a features [54]. **K-complex** [55] is a characteristic waveform of the EEG signal that occurs in stage two of the non-rapid eye movement sleep phase. **Energy** (E) of the signal is the sum of the squares of amplitude.

3.1.2. Frequency-Domain Features

The power spectral density (PSD) of the signal, which is the base for calculation of the frequency domain features, can be calculated with several parametric and non-parametric methods. Non-parametric methods are used more often and include methods like Fourier transform (usually calculated with *Fast Fourier transform* algorithm, FFT [56]), *Welch's method* [57], or *Thompson multitaper method* [58]. Examples of parametric methods for the PSD estimation are the *autoregressive* (AR) models [59], *multivariate autoregressive* models [60], or the *autoregressive-moving average* (ARMA) models [61]. The non-parametric models have a more widespread usage, because there is no need for selecting parameters such as the model's order, which is the case for autoregressive models.

Statistical features like **mean**, **median**, **variance**, **standard deviation**, **skewness**, **kurtosis**, and similar are also used in the frequency domain. Relative powers of the certain frequency bands are the most used frequency-domain features in all fields of analysis of the EEG signals. The most commonly used frequency bands are **delta** (δ, 0.5–4 Hz), **theta** (θ, 4–8 Hz), **alpha** (α, 8–12 Hz), **beta** (β, 12–30 Hz), and **gamma** (γ, >30 Hz), band. There is also the **sigma band** (σ, 12–14 Hz) that is sometimes called **sleep spindles** [62]. Several ratios between frequency bands are widely used as features in the EEG signal analysis, i.e., θ/α [63], β/α [63], $(\theta + \alpha)/\beta$ [64], θ/β [64], $(\theta + \alpha)/(\alpha + \beta)$ [64], γ/δ [65] and $(\gamma + \beta)/(\delta + \alpha)$ [65].

Table 1. The list of time-domain, frequency domain and nonlinear features reviewed in this work.

Group	Feature Name	Abbr.	Group	Feature Name	Abbr.
Time-domain	Mean		Frequency-domain	θ/β	
	Median			$(\theta + \alpha)/(\alpha + \beta)$	
	Variance			γ/δ	
	Standard deviation			$(\gamma + \beta)/(\delta + \alpha)$	
	Skewness			Reflection coefficients	
	Kurtosis			Partial correlation coefficient	
	Zero-crossing rate	ZCR		Wavelet coefficients	
	Number of waves			Phase coupling	
	Wave duration		Nonlinear	Hurst exponent	H
	Peak amplitude			Renyi scaling exponent	
	Instantaneous frequency	IF		Renyi gener. dim. multifractals	
	Hjorth parameters			Capacity dimension D0	D0
	Mobility			Information dimension D1	D1
	Activity			Correlation dimension D2	D2
	Complexity			Katz fractal dimension	KFD
	K-complex			Petrosian fractal dimension	PFD
	Energy	E		Higuchi fractal dimension	HFD
Frequency-domain	Mean			Fractal spectrum	
	Median			Lyapunov exponents	LE
	Variance			Lempel-Ziv complexity	LZC
	Standard deviation			Central tendency measure	CTM
	Skewness			Auto-mutual information	AMI
	Kurtosis			Temporal irreversibility	
	Delta	δ		Recurrence rate	RR
	Theta	θ		Determinism	Det
	Alpha	α		Laminarity	Lam
	Beta	β		Average diagonal line length	L
	Gamma	γ		Maximum length of diagonal	Lmax
	Sigma	σ		Max. length of vertical lines	Vmax
	θ/α			Trapping time	TT
	β/α			Divergence	Div
	$(\theta + \alpha)/\beta$			Entropy of recurrence plot	ENTR

Table 2. The list of entropies, undirected and directed spatiotemporal (spt.), and complex network features reviewed in this work.

Group	Feature Name	Abbr.	Group	Feature Name	Abbr.
Entropies	Shannon entropy		Undirected spt.	Imaginary component of Coh	
	Renyi's entropy			Phase-lag index	PLI
	Tsallis entropy			Weighted phase lag index	wPLI
	Kraskov entropy	KE		Debiased weighted PLI	dwPLI
	Spectral entropy	SEN		Pairwise phase consistency	PPC
	Quadratic Renyi's SEN	QRSEN		Generalized synchronization	
	Response entropy	RE		Synchronization likelihood	SL
	State entropy	SE		Mutual information	MI
	Wavelet entropy	WE		Mutual information in freq.	MIF
	Tsallis wavelet entropy	TWE		Cross-RQA	
	Rényi's wavelet entropy	RWE		Correlation length	ξKLD
	Hilbert-Huang SEN	HHSE	Directed spt.	Granger causality	
	Log energy entropy	LogEn		Spectral Granger causality	
	Multiresolution entropy			Phase slope index	PSI
	Kolmogorov's entropy		Complex networks	Number of vertices	
	Nonlinear forecasting entropy			Number of edges	
	Maximum-likelihood entropy			Degree	D
	Coarse-grained entropy			Mean degree	
	Correntropy	CoE		Degree distribution	
	Approximate entropy	ApEn		Degree correlation	r
	Sample entropy	SampEn		Kappa	k
	Quadratic sample entropy	QSE		Clustering coefficient	
	Multiscale entropy	MSE		Transitivity	
	Modified multiscale entropy	MMSE		Motif	
	Composite multiscale entropy	CMSE		Characteristic path length	
	Permutation entropy	PE		Small worldness	
	Renyi's permutation entropy	RPE		Assortativity	
	Permutation Rényi entropy	PEr		Efficiency	
	Multivariate PE	MvPE		Local efficiency	
	Tsallis permutation entropy	TPE		Global efficiency	
	Dispersion entropy	DisE		Modularity	
	Amplitude-aware PE	AAPE		Centrality degree	
	Bubble entropy	BE		Closeness centrality	
	Differential entropy	DifE		Eigenvalue centrality	
	Fuzzy entropy	FuzzyEn		Betweenness centrality	
	Transfer entropy	TrEn		Diameter	d
Undirected spt.	Coherence			Eccentricity	Ecc
	Partial coherence			Hubs	
	Phase coherence			Rich club	
	Phase-locking value	PLV		Leaf fraction	
	Coherency	Coh		Hierarchy	Th

The frequency domain of the signal can also be obtained using *wavelet decomposition* [66,67] and *matching pursuit decomposition* [68,69] methods. Unlike Fourier transform, which decomposes a signal into sinusoids, wavelet decomposition uses an underlying mother wavelet function for decomposition, and matching pursuit decomposition uses the dictionaries of signals to find the best fit for the signal.

From autoregressive models, one can extract features such as **reflection coefficients** or **partial correlation coefficients**. **Wavelet coefficients** obtained after applying wavelet decomposition can also be used as features. PSD is usually used to obtain the second-order statistics of the EEG signal. However, one can also consider the higher-order spectrum. For example, **phase coupling** [70] of different frequency components can be obtained with the higher-order spectral analysis.

3.1.3. Time-Frequency Features

The analysis of the EEG signal in the domains of time and frequency simultaneously is a powerful tool, since the EEG signal is a non-stationary signal [71,72]. The most important component of time-frequency domain analysis is the possibility to observe changes in the frequency over time. Short-time Fourier transform (STFT) is the simplest function that uses uniform separation of the observed signal and calculates its frequency components. A *spectrogram* [71] can be obtained with the application of STFT. Wavelet transform [73] is the usual alternative method to spectrogram that also provides coefficients as features from the time-frequency domain. The main advantage of wavelet transform compared to spectrogram is a variable window size, dependent on spectrum frequencies.

3.2. Nonlinear Features

Brain dynamics constitute a complex system. A system is complex when it is constructed from many nonlinear subsystems that cannot be separated into smaller subsystems without changing their dynamical properties. Fractal systems are often used for describing the brain dynamics measured with the EEG signal. To explain fractal systems, first, we need to introduce the scaling law. The scaling law is describing (asymptomatically) a self-similar function F as a function of the scale parameter s, i.e., $F(s) \sim s^\alpha$. When applied to a self-affine signal, each axis should be scaled by a different power factor to obtain statistically equivalent changes in both directions. If s is used in the x-axis direction, then $s' = s^H$ should be used in the y-axis direction. The power factor H is called the **Hurst exponent** [74,75]. The Hurst exponent is a measure of long-term memory of the signal and is related to the fractal dimension with the equation $D0 = 2 - H$ for self-similar time-series, where fractal dimension $D0$ is defined in the next paragraph. Time-series q is monofractal if it is linearly interdependent with its **Renyi scaling exponent** $\tau(q)$, otherwise, it is multifractal. The **Renyi generalized dimension of multifractals** is defined as $D(q) = \tau(q)/(q-1)$. For more detailed explanations about fractality and multifractality of the time-series, we refer the reader to [76–78].

In EEG signal analysis, all fractal dimensions are estimated based on the underlying attractor (a geometric structure towards which stationary dissipative system gravitates in its state space) of the signal [79]. In a strict mathematical sense, most time-series have the one-dimensional **support fractal dimension $D0$** (or capacity dimension or Hausdorff dimension) if there are no missing values. Regardless of the value of the $D0$, the **information dimension $D1$** and **correlation dimension $D2$** [79–81] can be calculated. The correlational dimension $D2$ can be calculated with both monofractal and multifractal approaches. The **Katz fractal dimension** (KFD) [82], the **Petrosian fractal dimension** (PFD) [83], and the **Higuchi fractal dimension** (HFD) [84] are different approaches to the estimation of the fractal dimension. With multifractal time-series analysis, a **fractal spectrum** consisting of multiple fractal dimensions can be obtained [85,86].

Methods for fractal time-series analysis can be classified [76] into stationary analysis methods (such as *Fluctuation Analysis* [87], *Hurst's Rescaled-Range Analysis* [74], and similar), non-stationary analysis (such as *Detrended Fluctuation Analysis* [88], *Centered Moving Average Analysis* [89], *Triangle Total Areas* [90], and similar), and multifractal analysis (such as *Wavelet Transform Modulus Maxima* [91], *Multifractal Detrended Fluctuation Analysis* [92], and similar). Each of these methods provides its own estimation of fractal dimension or scaling exponent features.

Lyapunov exponents (LE) [93] are measures of the attractor's complexity. If a system has at least one positive Lyapunov exponent, then the system can be characterized as a chaotic dynamical system. A positive Lyapunov exponent points to exponential divergence of the two nearby trajectories in the attractor over time [94]. **Lempel-Ziv complexity** (LZC) [95] is a measure of complexity that binarizes time-series and then searches for the occurrence of consecutive binary characters or "words" and counts the number of times a new "word" is encountered. The **Central tendency measure** (CTM) [96] is a measure of the variability of the observed time-series and represents the percentage of points on the scatter plot that fall into a given radius. **Auto-mutual information** (AMI) [97] is a mutual information measure applied to time-delayed versions of the same EEG time-series. **Temporal irreversibility** [98] of a time-series implies the influence of nonlinear dynamics, non-Gaussian noise, or both. It is a statistical property that differs based on the direction in which time proceeds, e.g., any sequence of measurements has a different probability of occurrence than its time reverse.

A *recurrence plot* [99] is a graphical method for the detection of reoccurring patterns in the time-series. *Recurrence quantification analysis (RQA)* [100] is a group of algorithms for the automatic quantification of recurrence plots. RQA is a noise resistant method, meaning it gives good results even when the signal-to-noise ratio of considered signals is unfavorable [101]. The **recurrence rate** (RR) is the probability that a specific state of a time-series will reoccur. **Determinism** (Det) is the percentage of points that form diagonal lines on the recurrence plot and **laminarity** (Lam) is the percentage of points forming vertical lines in the recurrence plot. The **average diagonal line length** (L), **maximum length of diagonal** (Lmax), and **maximum length of vertical lines** (Vmax) are also used as RQA-based features. **Trapping time** (TT) is the average vertical line length and it relates to the predictability of the time-series. **Divergence** (Div) is the reciprocal value of the maximal diagonal line length and it can have a trend similar to the positive Lyapunov exponents. **Entropy of the recurrence plot** (ENTR) reflects the complexity of the deterministic structure of the system.

3.3. Entropies

Entropy was first introduced to the field of information theory by Shannon in 1948 [102,103]. **Shannon's information entropy** is calculated based on the expression $-\sum_j p_j \log(p_j)$, where p_j is the probability distribution of the observed data. It is used to measure uncertainty or randomness in the observed time-series. There are many derived variations of information entropy used in EEG analysis. The entropies may be considered as nonlinear features, but we describe them in a separate subsection due to their specific calculation.

Rényi's entropy [104] is defined with the expression $-\frac{\alpha}{1-\alpha}\sum \log p_k^\alpha$, where $\alpha > 0$ and $\alpha \neq 1$. It is a generalization of Shannon's entropy in the case of a limited value of $\alpha \to 1$. **Quadratic Rényi's entropy** (or just Rényi's entropy) is the case where $\alpha = 2$. **Tsallis entropy** (q-entropy) [105] is a generalization of the Boltzman–Gibbs entropy from statistical thermodynamics and is defined with the expression $\frac{k}{q-1}\left(1 - \sum_i p_i^q\right)$, where k is a positive constant and q is the non-extensity parameter. For $q > 1$, the entropy has a more significant reaction to the events that occur often, whereas for $0 < q < 1$, the entropy has a more significant reaction to rare events.

The three aforementioned entropies can be calculated from the raw EEG signal. Besides that, they are a base for calculating several other entropies in the field of EEG analysis. **Kraskov entropy** (KE) [50] is an unbiased estimator of Shannon's entropy for a d-dimensional random sample. **Spectral entropy** (SEN) [106] is calculated with the expression for Shannon's entropy based on the normalized PSD of the EEG signal. **Quadratic Renyi's spectral entropy** (QRSEN) [107] is calculated with the usage of Renyi's entropy expression, and the difference compared to the spectral entropy is that it gives the higher weights to the lower frequencies. Commercial M-Entropy Module [108] uses two different components of spectral entropy—**response entropy** (RE) and **state entropy** (SE). State entropy includes the spectrum between 0.8 and 32 Hz, while response entropy includes the spectrum between 0.8 and 47 Hz.

Wavelet entropy (WE) [109,110] is somewhat similar to spectral entropy. The difference is that it is calculated based on the coefficients of the wavelet decomposition of the given time-series. There are two generalizations of wavelet entropy—**Tsallis wavelet entropy** (TWE) and **Rényi's wavelet entropy** (RWE) [111]. **Hilbert–Huang spectral entropy** (HHSE) [112] applies Shannon's entropy to the Hilbert–Huang spectrum, which is obtained by the *Hilbert–Huang transform* [111,113]. **Log energy entropy** (LogEn) [114] is similar to the wavelet entropy, but only uses summation of logarithms of the probabilities. **Multiresolution entropy** [115] uses the combination of windowing and wavelet transform for the detection of changes in parameters that define the observed process (i.e., the parameters of brain dynamics).

Kolmogorov's entropy [116] is an embedding entropy and is defined as the sum of positive Lyapunov exponents. It represents the rate of information loss and a degree of predictability (regularity) of the attractor. Accurate computation of Kolmogorov's entropy is computationally expensive, so several entropies are used for the estimation of Kolmogorov's entropy based on the less computationally expensive methods. **Nonlinear forecasting entropy** [117] is the estimation of Kolmogorov's entropy for time-series with too few points. It is based on the forecasting of the time-series data, i.e., on the correlation coefficient of the forecasted points with actually observed points. The estimation method is independent of the forecasting method used. **Maximum-likelihood entropy** [118] is also the estimation of Kolmogorov entropy. It is derived with the application of maximum-likelihood to the correlation integral, which is treated as a probability distribution. **Coarse-grained entropy** [119] is an estimation of the attractor' entropy for cases where standardly used dimensions, Lyapunov exponents, and Kolmogorov's entropy are not suitable due to the high dimensionality of the observed process. **Correntropy** (CoE) [120] is an estimation of nonlinear autocorrelation.

Approximate entropy (ApEn) [121] is derived from Kolmogorov's entropy and its use in the analysis of the EEG signal (and other physiological signals) is widespread. It addresses the irregularity of a time-series. Predictable time-series, i.e., time-series with many repetitive patterns will have a small value of approximate entropy. **Sample entropy** (SampEn) [122] was introduced as an improvement to approximate entropy. It reduces the error of the approximate entropy by eliminating its two disadvantages—(1) self-matches and (2) dependence on the time-series length. Sample entropy is also an approximation of signal complexity. **Quadratic sample entropy** (QSE) [123] is SampEn insensitive to the data radius parameter r. It allows r to vary as needed to achieve confident estimates of the conditional probability. **Multiscale entropy** (MSE) [124] is a generalization of an entropy measure (such as sample entropy) to different time scales. **Modified multiscale entropy** (MMSE) [125] uses the same procedure as MSE, but replaces coarse-graining with a moving average procedure. **Composite multiscale entropy** (CMSE) [126] is a modification of the MSE that tackles the problem of increased variance and error estimation for short time-series.

Permutation entropy (PE) [127] estimates signal variability based on the repetition of the ordinal patterns. The algorithm requires parameter m (permutation order) to obtain ordinal patterns and their probabilities of occurrence. These probabilities are then applied in Shannon's entropy expression. Moreover, **Renyi's permutation entropy** (RPE) [128], **permutation Rényi entropy** (PEr) [129], **multivariate permutation entropy** (MvPE) [130], and **Tsallis permutation entropy** (TPE) [111] can be calculated for the ordinal patterns. **Dispersion entropy** (DisE) [131] is a modification of permutation entropy that tackles the problem of amplitude information loss (since permutation entropy only considers the order of the amplitude values but not the values themselves). **Amplitude-aware permutation entropy** (AAPE) [132] is based on the similar idea of using the value of the signal with the permutation entropy. **Bubble entropy** (BE) [133] is similar to permutation entropy with the main difference in the method used for ranking vectors in the embedding space. Namely, permutation entropy uses repetition of the ordinal patterns and bubble entropy uses the number of steps needed to sort a vector with the bubble sort algorithm. **Differential entropy** (DifE) [134] calculation is based on Shannon's entropy expression and the estimation of the underlying probability density function of time-series. **Fuzzy entropy**

(FuzzyEn) [135] is based on the concept of fuzzy sets, first introduced by Zadeh [136]. It is similar to sample entropy, but instead of using the Heaviside function for distance calculation, it uses a fuzzy membership function. **Transfer entropy** (TrEn) [137] uses concepts similar to mutual information (see Section 3.4) with the ability to quantify the exchange of information between two systems. It is an asymmetric measure for information transfer from process X to process Y, which measures the effect of the past values of processes X and Y on the present value of process Y.

3.4. Spatiotemporal Features

Features that were introduced above are all calculated based on a single EEG channel. Since EEG recording devices can have hundreds of channels nowadays, features that describe the relationship between different channels bring further insight into the understanding of brain functions. This is the main idea behind the usage of the spatiotemporal features—to describe the relationship between different brain regions for particular states or events. Spatiotemporal features can be divided into two groups—directed and non-directed. The non-directed ones relate to the synchronization of two or more channels without any knowledge of the direction, while the directed ones include the causation between them, i.e., they measure functional connectivity.

3.4.1. Non-Directed Spatiotemporal Features

Coherence [138] is a cross-correlation equivalent in the frequency-domain, i.e., the cross-correlation of the PSD from two different channels. It reflects the synchronization of the changes of frequency components between the observed channels. **Partial coherence** [139] is an adjusted coherence with removed common signal's linear effect based on the third channel, which is not physically close to the two observed channels. **Phase coherence** [140] is the coherence of the phases of the signals. It was introduced to overcome the problem of detection of nonlinear dependencies between the two channels.

The **phase-locking value** (PLV) [141] represents the measure of the transient phase locking that is completely independent of the signal's amplitude, which is not the case for the coherence measure. **Coherency** [142] is calculated similar to coherence, but without applying the magnitude operator to the cross-spectral density of two channels. The obtained complex-valued quantity is called coherency. The **imaginary component of coherency** (iCoh) [143] reflects the nonlinear interaction between the two underlying time-series. **Phase-lag index** (PLI) [144] is a measure of the asymmetry of the distribution of phase differences between two signals. It brings improvement compared to the imaginary component of coherency by removing the effect of amplitude information. The **weighted phase lag index** (wPLI) [145] uses weights to reduce a phase lag index's sensitivity to noise, while the **debiased weighted phase lag index** (dwPLI) [145] additionally reduces a sample-size bias. **Pairwise phase consistency** (PPC) [146] is a measure similar to PLV, but it quantifies the distribution of all pairwise phase differences across observations.

Generalized synchronization [147] incorporates the nonlinear property of the dynamical systems into its calculation. The idea is to observe two dynamical systems, a response system and a driving system, where the response system is a function of the driving system. Authors propose a numerical method called *mutual false nearest neighbors* for distinguishing between synchronized and unsynchronized behavior of the systems. *Arnhold's measure* [148] is another algorithm for measuring such interdependence between two dynamical systems. **Synchronization likelihood** (SL) [149] brings several improvements into these methods—it is sensitive to linear and nonlinear brain dynamics and is suitable for an analysis of the non-stationary systems. It is calculated based on the similarity of the time-delayed embeddings in the state space.

Mutual information (MI) [150] quantifies the amount of information obtained about one time-series through observing the other time-series. It is a commonly used measure in the information theory and is calculated based on Shannon's entropy. **Mutual information**

in frequency (MIF) [151] is a recently developed measure that calculates the mutual information between the PSDs of two time-series. Its interpretation is similar to coherence.

Cross-recurrence quantification analysis [101] is similar to RQA, but instead of observing the self-similarity of a single signal, the similarity of two different channels is observed. The features extracted are the same as in the case of single-channel RQA (see Section 3.2). The **correlation length** (ξ_{KLD}) [152] is a measure of the spatio-temporal disorder based on the Karhunen–Loeve decomposition.

3.4.2. Directed Spatiotemporal Features

Granger causality [153] is a well-known statistical test, which tests whether one time-series forecasts (causes) the other time-series, and vice-versa. It is based on the autoregressive forecast models of the two time-series. **Spectral Granger causality** [154] can also be calculated and it is based on the estimation of the spectral transfer matrix and the covariance of the autoregressive model's residuals. The **phase slope index** (PSI) [155] is a robust estimation of the information flow direction. It is insensitive to the mixtures of the independent sources, which is the main problem for Granger causality. Transfer entropy, which is explained in Section 3.3, can also be considered a directed spatiotemporal feature.

3.5. Complex Networks

The features introduced in Section 3.1, Section 3.2, and Section 3.3 were based only on a single channel of the EEG signal. Section 3.4 introduced features calculated based on the pairwise interactions between the two channels. In this section, the main goal is to introduce the features that observe the interactions between more than two channels. Complex networks are a graph-theory-based approach to EEG signal analysis. A connectivity matrix obtained by observing all pairwise connections between channels is used to obtain a graph. Any method explained in Section 3.4 can be used to determine connectivity matrix, and popular choices are correlation, PLI, or MI. Graphs can be weighted based on the values of the connectivity matrix or unweighted by applying thresholding to the connectivity matrix. A minimum spanning tree can also be used as a method for obtaining an acyclic graph with all vertices included. For more details about graph construction and complex networks, we refer the reader to papers [156,157]. In continuation of this section, we introduce features that are calculated based on the obtained graph. These features are functional connectivity features.

Once the graph is obtained, the **number of vertices** and the **number of edges** can be used as features. The **degree** (D) [158] of a vertex is the number of edges connected to the vertex. The **mean degree** of the network is a metric of density. The **degree distribution** is a probability distribution of the degrees and it provides information about the structure of the graph. **Degree correlation** (r) [159] is the correlation coefficient of degrees of pairs of neighbors in a graph. **Kappa** (k) [159] is a measure of the degree diversity and it measures the broadness of the degree distribution. The **clustering coefficient** [160] is a measure of the vertices connectedness in a graph and it can be local (for a sub-graph) or global. If the local clustering coefficient is equal to one, it means that the corresponding local sub-graph is fully connected. The global clustering coefficient is sometimes called **transitivity** [161]. A **motif** [162] is a generalized version of the clustering coefficient and a pattern of local connectivity. The average of all pairwise shortest path lengths is called **characteristic path length** [160]. **Small worldness** [163] is a second-order graph statistic and its calculation is based on the trade-off between high local clustering and short path length. **Assortativity** [164] is the measure of vertex tendency to link with other vertices with a similar number of edges.

Efficiency [165] is a measure of the efficiency of the information exchange in the graph. **Local efficiency** [165] is the inverse of the shortest path lengths between vertices on the observed sub-graph, where the sub-graph consists of all neighbors of the observed vertex. **Global efficiency** [165] is the average efficiency of the graph divided by the average efficiency of a fully connected graph. **Modularity** [166] describes the structure of the graph and represents the degree to which a graph is subdivided into non-overlapping clusters.

Each vertex in the graph has a measure of **centrality degree** [167], which represents the number of shortest paths in the graph that the observed vertex is involved in. Similarly, each vertex in the graph has a measure of **closeness centrality** [168], which represents the average distance of the observed vertex from all other vertices in the graph. **Eigenvalue centrality** [169] is a measure of the ease of accessibility of a vertex to other vertices. It is computed based on the relative vertex scores, with the basic idea that the high-scoring connections should contribute more to vertex influence than the low-scoring vertices. **Betweenness centrality** [170] is a measure of the importance of the vertex in a graph. It is computed based on the number of times a vertex occurs along the shortest path between two other vertices.

Diameter (d) [159] is the longest shortest path of a graph. **Eccentricity** (Ecc) [159] is the longest shortest path from a referenced vertex to any other vertex in the graph. **Hubs** [171] are vertices with high centrality. Hubs tend to be connected and this property is called assortativity. **Rich club** [172] is a sub-graph of highly interconnected hubs. **Leaf fraction** [159] of a graph is the number of vertices with exactly one edge. **Hierarchy** (T_H) [159] captures the ratio between a small diameter on one hand and overloading of the hub nodes on the other hand.

4. Driver Drowsiness Detection Systems

The aim of this Section is to review the work on drowsiness detection focusing on the features used. The inclusion criteria for the papers are stated in Section 1. Tables 3 and 4 show a summary of the reviewed work on driver drowsiness detection, and the rest of the Section briefly presents each work.

Balam et al. [173] used a convolutional neural network (CNN) for the classification based on the raw EEG signal from the Cz-Oz channel. They used data from the Sleep-EDF Expanded Database and their ground truth for drowsiness was the S1 sleep stage. Since the authors used a publicly available database, they compared their deep learning (DL) approach with the other feature-based approaches, and they concluded that this approach resulted in at least 3% better results. Chaabene et al. [174] used frequency-domain features for defining the ground truth. They used CNN with raw EEG signal from seven electrodes as input and achieved 90% drowsiness detection accuracy.

Yingying et al. [175] used a Long Short-Term Memory (LSTM) network to classify sleepiness in two classes and their final classification accuracy achieved was 98%. Their ground truth labels for classification were based on the alpha-blocking phenomenon and the alpha wave attenuation-disappearance phenomenon. The authors claimed that these two phenomena represent two different sleepiness levels, relaxed wakefulness and sleep onset, respectively. The authors used only the O2 channel of the EEG signal and performed a continuous wavelet transform to obtain the PSD. Zou et al. [176] used multiscale PE, multiscale SampEn, and multiscale FuzzyEn. Their ground truth labels were based on Li's subjective fatigue scale and the accuracy achieved was 88.74%. Chaudhuri and Routray [177] used only three entropies as features—ApEn, SampEn, and modified SampEn. Their experiment was designed to slowly increase the fatigue level of the participants because of the effects of physical and mental workload, along with the effects of sleep deprivation. The experiment was divided into 11 stages and stages 7 and later were labeled as the fatigue state. The authors used SVM and achieved 86% accuracy.

Budak et al. [178] used MIT/BIH Polysomnographic EEG database in their study. Their ground truth for binary classification was based on sleep stages labeled by an expert. The awake stage was labeled the awake state and stage I of sleep was labeled the drowsy state. The authors used ZCR, E, IF, and SEN as traditional features, and also used AlexNet on the spectrogram images to obtain additional 4096 features (layers fc6 and fc7 of AlexNet). The accuracy of the binary classification was 94.31%, which is the best result achieved on this dataset, according to the authors. Mehreen et al. [179] used δ, δ/α, θ, θ/φ, $\delta/\alpha+\beta+\gamma$, and δ/θ EEG features, along with blink features and head movement features and achieved 92% accuracy of drowsiness detection. Based on EEG features only, the accuracy was 76%. The authors used subjective evaluation with Karolinska Sleepiness Scale (KSS) as the ground truth. It is unclear how the authors converted nine levels of KSS into a two-level ground truth. Chen et al. [180] used the clustering coefficient and characteristic path length of the graph obtained for δ, θ, α, and β frequency bands. The graph was obtained using the phase lag index. The ground truth labels were binary. The first three minutes of participants' driving were labeled as alert state and the last three minutes as fatigue state. SVM was selected for classification and achieved 94.4% accuracy. The authors conclude that the functional connectivity of the brain differs significantly between the alert and fatigue state, particularly in the α and β bands.

Table 3. The summary of metadata of the reviewed driver drowsiness detection papers.

Author	Year	Participants	Electrodes
Chaabene et al. [174]	2021	12	14 channels
Balam et al. [173]	2021	23	Pz-Oz
Yingying et al. [175]	2020	12	O1 and O2
Zou et al. [176]	2020	16	32 channels
Chaudhuri and Routray [177]	2020	12	19 Channels
Budak et al. [178]	2019	16	C3-O1, C4-A1, and O2-A1
Chen et al. [179]	2019	14	14 channels
Mehreen et al. [180]	2019	50	AF7, AF8, TP9 and TP10
Martensson et al. [181]	2019	86	Fz-A1, Cz-A2 and Oz-Pz
Barua et al. [182]	2019	30	30 channels
Ogino and Mitsukura [183]	2018	29	Fp1
Chen et al. [184]	2018	15	30 channels
Chen et al. [185]	2018	15	30 channels
Chen et al. [186]	2018	12	40 channels
Hu and Min [187]	2018	22	30 channels
Dimitrakopoulos et al. [188]	2018	40	64 channels
Hong et al. [189]	2018	16	Ear channel
Li and Chung [190]	2018	17	O1 and O2
Min et al. [191]	2017	12	32 channels
Awais et al. [192]	2017	22	19 channels
Nguyen et al. [193]	2017	11	64 channels
Hu [194]	2017	28	32 channels
Chai et al. [195]	2017	43	32 channels
Chai et al. [196]	2017	43	32 channels
Mu et al. [197]	2017	11	27 channels
Fu et al. [198]	2016	12	O1 and O2
Ahn et al. [199]	2016	11	64 channels
Huang et al. [200]	2016	12	30 channels
Li et al. [201]	2015	20	O1 and O2
Chen et al. [202]	2015	16	9 channels
Sauvet et al. [203]	2014	14	C3-M2 and O1-M2
Lee et al. [204]	2014	20	Fpz-Cz and Pz-Oz
Garces Correa et al. [205]	2014	18	C3-O1, C4-A1 and O2-A1
Zhang et al. [110]	2014	20	O1 and O2
Hu et al. [206]	2013	40	Fz-A1, Cz-A2 and Oz–Pz
Picot et al. [207]	2012	20	F3, C3, P3 and O1
Zhao et al. [208]	2011	13	32 channels
Khushaba et al. [20]	2011	31	Fz, T8 and Oz
Liu et al. [209]	2010	50	13 channels

Table 4. The summary of reviewed driver drowsiness detection papers. The meanings of the abbreviations are: TD—time-domain, FD—frequency-domain, N—nonlinear, EN—entropies, CN—complex networks, SIG—signal-based labeling, Li's—Li's subjective fatigue scale, SD—sleep deprivation, NREM1—labels based on the sleep stages, BE3—first and last three minutes as two labels, BE5—first and last five minutes as two labels, BIH—behavior-based labeling, WIE—Wierwille scale, RT—reaction time based labeling, EXP—expert labeling, LSTM—long-short term memory, KNN—k nearest neighbor, SVM—support vector machine, RF—random forest, ELM—extreme learning machine, GBDT—gradient boosting decision tree, NN—neural network, FLDA—Fisher linear discriminant analysis, SDBN—sparse deep belif network, HMM—hidden Markov model, and Thres.—thresholding-based algorithm.

Author	Features	Target	Algorithm	No. Classes	Acc.
Chaabene et al. [174]	Raw	SIG	CNN	2	90.14
Balam et al. [173]	Raw	NREM1	CNN	2	94.00
Yingying et al. [175]	FD	SIG	LSTM	2	98.14
Zou et al. [176]	EN	Li's	KNN		88.74
Chaudhuri and Routray [177]	EN	SD	SVM	2	86.00
Budak et al. [178]	TD, FD, EN and special	NREM1	LSTM	2	94.31
Chen et al. [179]	CN	BE3	SVM	2	94.40
Mehreen et al. [180]	FD	KSS	SVM	2	92.00
Martensson et al. [181]	FD, N and EN	KSS	RF	2	93.50
Barua et al. [182]	TD, FD and EN	KSS	SVM	2 and 3	93.00 and 79.00
Ogino and Mitsukura [183]	FD and EN	KSS	SVM	2	67.00
Chen et al. [184]	CN	KSS			
Chen et al. [185]	CN	KSS	KNN	2	98.60
Chen et al. [186]	CN	BE3	ELM	2	95.00
Hu and Min [187]	EN	BE5	GBDT	2	94.00
Dimitrakopoulos et al. [188]	CN	BE5	SVM	2	92.10
Hong et al. [189]	FD, N and EN	EBE	SVM	5	99.50
Li and Chung [190]	FD	WIE	SVM	5	93.87
Min et al. [191]	FD and EN	BE5	NN	2	98.30
Awais et al. [192]	TD, FD and EN	BIH	SVM	2	80.00
Nguyen et al. [193]	FD	SIG	FLDA	2	79.20
Hu [194]	EN	BE5	AdaBoost	2	97.50
Chai et al. [195]	FD	BE5	SDBN	2	90.60
Chai et al. [196]	FD	BE5	NN	2	88.20
Mu et al. [197]	EN	Li's	SVM	2	97.00
Fu et al. [198]	FD	KSS	HMM	3	AUC 0.841
Ahn et al. [199]	FD	SD	FLDA	2	75.90
Huang et al. [200]	FD	RT			
Li et al. [201]	FD	BIH	SVM	2	93.16
Chen et al. [202]	FD, N and EN	SIG	ELM	2	95.60
Sauvet et al. [203]	FD	EXP	Threshold	2	98.30
Lee et al. [204]	TD and FD	NREM1	SVM	4	98.50
Garces Correa et al. [205]	TD and FD	NREM1	NN	2	87.40
Zhang et al. [110]	N and EN	SIG	NN	4	96.50
Hu et al. [206]	FD	KSS	SVM	2	75.00
Picot et al. [207]	FD	SIG	Threshold	5	80.60
Zhao et al. [208]	FD	Li's	SVM	3	81.60
Khushaba et al. [20]	FD	WIE	LDA	5	95.00
Liu et al. [209]	EN	KSS and Li's	HMM	2	84.00

Martensson et al. [181] used θ, α, $\theta/(\theta + \alpha)$, $\alpha/(\theta + \alpha)$, $(\theta + \alpha)/\beta$, α/β, $(\theta + \alpha)/(\theta + \beta)$, θ/β, SampEn, and HFD from three EEG channels together with features from EOG and ECG signals. The authors performed a sequential forward floating feature selection method for dimensionality reduction and six EEG features were selected—HFD, θ, $\alpha/(\theta + \alpha)$, θ/β, $\theta/(\theta + \alpha)$ and α. Random forest was selected as the best model and achieved 93.5% accuracy on the test set and 84% on the leave-one-subject-out validation scheme. The ground truth was obtained with the KSS. The severely sleepy class was for a KSS score greater than seven and the sufficiently alert class was for a KSS score of less than seven.

KSS scores equal to seven were discarded as outlined. Barua et al. [182] used δ, θ, α, β, γ, (θ + α)/β, α/β, (θ + α)/(α + β), and θ/β from 30 EEG channels along with features from EOG and contextual information (e.g., time awake, duration of last sleep, and the like). The authors achieved the best accuracy of 93% for binary classification and 79% for classification into three classes. Self-evaluation with KSS score was used as ground truth and KSS score was classified into three classes—alert class for KSS scores below six, somewhat sleepy class for KSS scores below eight, and sleepy for KSS scores equal to eight or nine. In the binary classification, the authors used two methods (fuzzy centroid redistribution and SVM predicted redistribution) for redistribution of somewhat sleepy classes into the alert and sleepy classes. Ogino and Mitsukura [183] used δ, θ, α, β, and γ as frequency domain features, and parameters of the autoregressive model and MSE were also added to the feature set. Only the Fp1 channel was used and the authors achieved 67% accuracy by using SVM. The ground truth labels were based on the KSS score, where the alert class was for a KSS score less than four and the drowsy class was for a KSS score greater than six.

Chen et al. [184] analyzed the difference in complex network features for each frequency band (δ, θ, α, and β) between alert and drowsy states. The authors used the features: Number of vertices, number of edges, D, leaf fraction, d, Ecc, betweenness centrality, k, Th, and r. Their ground truth was based on the KSS score. A significant difference was found in the four features of the δ-band and five features of the θ-band. In addition, the authors suggested a more linear graph configuration in alert states and a more star-shaped graph configuration in drowsy states. Chen et al. [185] used the same experiment for drowsiness classification in a related study. Three complex network features (degree, degree correlation, and kappa) were extracted for each frequency band (δ, θ, α, and β). The ground truth was based on the KSS score and they performed binary classification. The highest accuracy of 98.6% was achieved using the k nearest neighbor (KNN) algorithm. Chen et al. [186] used phase synchronization, phase coherence, k, betweenness centrality, and Th as features. The first three minutes of participants' driving were labeled as an alert state and the last three minutes as a fatigue state. The highest accuracy achieved was 95% using the extreme learning machine (ELM) algorithm. Dimitrakopoulos et al. [187] used 64 channels and computed three complex network features—clustering coefficient, characteristic path length, and small-worldness. The authors achieved 92.1% accuracy for drowsiness classification. The network values of the first and the last 5-min windows were used to indicate the states of maximum alertness and maximum fatigue, respectively.

Hong et al. [188] used δ, θ, α, β, ratio indices, frequency domain statistics, the generalized Hurst exponent, HFD, SEN, and PE from the ear channel together with photoplethysmography (PPG) and ECG. The highest accuracy achieved was 99.5%. The ground truth labels were divided into five levels and were labeled by experts based on behavioral expressions. The authors ranked the features using four different methods, and in each method, at least four of the seven best-ranked features were nonlinear features. Hu and Min [189] used 30 channels and four entropies from each channel—SEN, ApEn, SampEn, and FuzzyEn. The authors achieved 94% accuracy in drowsiness classification. They used a ground truth based on self-reported fatigue. If the measurement lasted longer than 30 min before the participant self-reported fatigue, the signals from the 5th to 10th minute were used as the normal state and the signals from the last five minutes before the end of the experiment were used as the fatigued state. Li and Chung [190] used θ, α, and β features from O1 and O2 channels along with gyroscope-based head movement measurement. The subjective Wierwille scale was used to obtain five-level ground truth. The achieved accuracy for five-level classification was 93% and for binary classification it was 96%. Awais et al. [191] used mean, variance, minimum, maximum, E, SampEn, δ, θ, α, β, and γ from 19 channels along with ECG signal. SVM was used for classification and they achieved 80% accuracy for binary classification. When only EEG features were used, the accuracy was 76%. The authors used video-based facial features including eye blink duration, facial expressions, facial tone, eye blinking rate, and movements such as head-nodding and yawning for establishing ground truth. When a drowsy event began, five minutes before it were marked as the alert state and five minutes after it were marked as the drowsy state.

Min et al. [192] used SEN, ApEn, SampEn, and FuzzyEn for fatigue detection. These four entropies gave better results than AR coefficients. An experiment was terminated based on the subjective report of fatigue. To confirm these fatigue reports, the authors utilized the Chalder Fatigue Scale and Li's Subjective Fatigue Scale before and after the experiment. The first five minutes of the recording were labeled as the normal state and the last five minutes of the recording were labeled as the fatigued state. The authors achieved an accuracy of 98.3%. Nguyen et al. [193] used δ, θ, α, β, and γ features from 64 channels along with near-infrared spectroscopy (NIRS). EOG and ECG signals were also measured, but they were only used to establish the ground truth labels. Fisher linear discriminant analysis (FLDA) was used for binary classification with 79.2% accuracy when EEG and NIRS were used. The accuracy when only EEG features were used was 70.5%. The authors introduced the drowsiness detection index, a variable derived for drowsiness detection, and they reported that it predicts the onset of drowsiness on average 3.6 s earlier. Hu [194] used SEN, ApEn, SampEn, and FuzzyEn features from 32 channels of the EEG signal. An experiment was terminated based on the EOG parameter associated with fatigue and self-reported fatigue. The first five minutes were labeled as the normal state and the last five minutes were labeled as the fatigue state. The AdaBoost classification algorithm was used and achieved 97.5% accuracy. Chai et al. [195] used AR coefficients as features. The ground truth labels were binary, with the first five minutes of driving labeled as the alert state and the last five minutes of driving labeled as the fatigued state. An experiment was terminated when the participant drove of the road for 15 s or when consistent signs of fatigue (such as head nodding and prolonged eye closure) were detected. The authors used NN for classification and achieved 88.2% accuracy. Chai et al. [196] used AR features from 32 channels. The first five minutes of data were used as an alert state and the last five minutes as a drowsy state. The authors used a sparse deep belief network as a classification algorithm and achieved 90% accuracy. Mu et al. [197] used FuzzyEn from Fp1 and Fp2 channels and achieved 97% accuracy using the SVM algorithm. The ground truth labels were binary with the first 10 min labeled as the normal state and the last 10 min labeled as the fatigued state. The stopping criteria of the experiment were based on Li's subjective fatigue scale and Borg's CR-10 scale.

Fu et al. [198] used θ, α, and β features from O1 and O2 channels along with EMG and respiration. The ground truth was set based on the KSS score, where level one was KSS score equal to one or two, level two was KSS score equal to three or four, and level three was KSS score equal to five or six. The reported average area under the curve (AUC) was 0.841. When only EEG features were used, the average AUC was 0.644. Ahn et al. [199] used δ, θ, α, β, and γ along with EOG, ECG, and fNIRS. FLDA was used for binary classification with 79.2% accuracy using all the available sensors. The accuracy based only on the EEG signal features was 59.7%. Binary ground truth was used with the well-rested group and the sleep-deprived group. Huang et al. [200] used only the α feature. The system developed in this study did not use a classification algorithm. It was based on measuring the response times of the subjects. Drowsiness was labeled for the moments when the response time was 2.5 times greater than the mean response time, which helped the authors to determine a threshold for α feature value indicating drowsiness. An auditory warning system was developed to help subjects to remain alert.

Li et al. [201] used θ, α, and β features from O1 and O2 channels. The ground truth alert and drowsy data were labeled based on the percentage of eyelid closure (PERCLOS) and the number of adjustments on the steering wheel. The best accuracy of 93.16% was achieved using the SVM classifier and only θ and β features. The authors used the probability of prediction instead of the discrete class label to develop an early warning system with a probability threshold of 0.424. Chen et al. [202] used δ, θ, α, β, γ, ApEn, SampEn, Rényi's entropy, and RQA features, along with the EOG. Two neurologists manually labeled binary ground truth values based on the EOG features and frequency domain features. ELM was used for classification based on the nonlinear features only and achieved 95.6% accuracy. Sauvet et al. [203] used θ, α, β, (θ + α)/β, and fuzzy fusion of these features. Feature thresholding was applied for classification and an accuracy of 98.3% was achieved. The ground truth was based on expert scoring, but it is unclear how this scoring was performed.

Lee et al. [204] used δ, θ, α, β, time-domain statistics, ZCR, and several ratio indices from Fpz-Cz and Pz-Oz EEG channels. The ground truth was classified into four classes: Awake, slightly drowsy, moderately drowsy, and extremely drowsy. These classes were determined by experienced physicians, with the first three classes being derived from the awake-sleep stage and the extremely drowsy class corresponding to the N1 sleep stage. SVM was used for classification and the best accuracy achieved was 98.5%. Garces Correa et al. [205] used MIT-BIH Polysomnographic Database in their research. Eighteen subjects were selected and δ, θ, α, β, γ, time-domain statistics, and frequency domain statistics features were extracted. The ground truth alert and drowsy labels were determined based on the awake and S1 sleep stages, respectively. A neural network was used for classification and it achieved 87.4% accuracy. Zhang et al. [110] used LZC and peak-to-peak versions of ApEn and SampEn. Peak-to-peak means that instead of using all the data points of the features, the authors used only the difference between the maximum and minimum values in the sliding window. Four levels of ground truth labels were used, referred to as normal state, mild fatigue, mood swing, and excessive fatigue. These labels were determined based on the various entropy patterns used in the paper, but it is unclear exactly how the labels were determined. A neural network was used for classification and it achieved 96.5% accuracy.

Hu et al. [206] used δ, θ, α, β, and frequency domain statistics along with EOG signal features. The authors achieved a final drowsiness detection accuracy of 75%. Binary ground truth labels were used. The alert state was defined with a KSS score less than 8 and Karolinska drowsiness score (KDS) equal to 0, while drowsiness was defined with a KSS score greater than 7 and a KDS score equal to or greater than 50. The KDS is an EEG/EOG-based drowsiness scoring experiment where the final score is between 0% (alert) and 100% (drowsy) [210]. Picot et al. [207] used only α and β features from the P3 channel together with the EOG signal. The ground truth was labeled by experts based on the EEG and EOG signal. Five levels were used in labeling the ground truth, but three levels were used to evaluate the drowsiness detection system. The drowsiness detection system was based on the statistical test to compare the two populations and thresholding, and achieved an accuracy of 80.6%. Zhao et al. [208] used multivariate autoregressive coefficients as features along with the EOG signal. The accuracy achieved with the SVM classifier was 81.6%. The ground truth labels were based on Li's subjective fatigue scale. Khushaba et al. [20] introduced a hybrid type of EEG features called fuzzy mutual information-based wavelet-packet features, and achieved a drowsiness detection accuracy of 95%. Their ground truth had five levels and was based on Wierewille and Ellsworth criteria. Wierwille and Ellsworth criteria [211] is a textual description of the drowsiness continuum based on behavioral and facial signs that should prepare raters to rate participants' drowsiness based on observations of the video while driving. Liu et al. [209] used ApEn and Kolmogorov entropy of the δ, θ, α, and β frequency bands. The ground truth was binary with pre-task time as the alert state and post-task time as the fatigue state. The authors confirmed a statistically significant increase in fatigue level based on the five different subjective scales—KSS, Stanford sleepiness scale, Samn–Perelli checklist, Li's subjective fatigue scale, and Borg's CR-10 scale. A hidden Markov model was used for classification and achieved 84% accuracy.

5. Discussion

Section 3 presented 147 features that were classified into 7 categories, as shown in Tables 1 and 2. As mentioned, Tables 3 and 4 show a summary of 39 reviewed papers on drowsiness detection. The year with the most papers meeting the inclusion criteria is 2018 with eight included papers. Figure 3 shows the number of included papers and the number of papers as a result of the search query: "EEG driver drowsiness detection". Based on both trends, it can be seen that the number of papers on this topic is increasing.

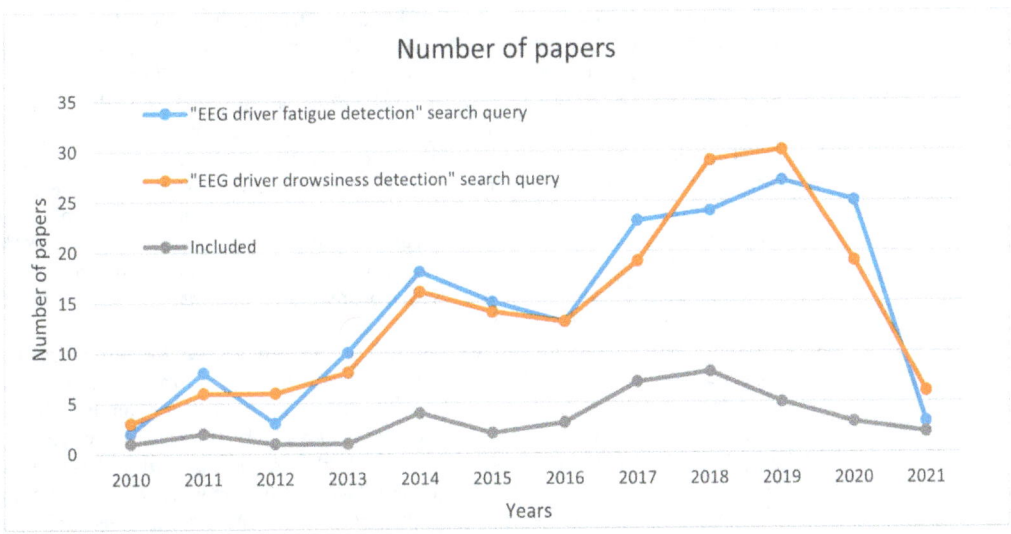

Figure 3. The number of papers included in the study and the number of papers obtained as a result of the "EEG driver drowsiness detection" and "EEG driver fatigue detection" search query, data until April 2021.

From 2013 to 2016, there were only two papers that used entropies and eight papers that used only frequency domain statistics. Although there is a higher number of published papers in recent years, there are fewer papers that rely only on frequency-domain features. Nonlinear features, entropies, and complex network features have been increasingly used in recent years. Reported drowsiness detection accuracies have remained more or less the same over the years and are usually between 80% and 99%. There is an increasing body of work that has been done with higher numbers of participants (30 or more), and it is reasonable to assume that the accuracies from these works are the most reliable.

Although we often refer to accuracy as a quality measure for the developed system, it must be noted that it is not possible to fairly compare the accuracy of different works because most of the works have been performed with a private dataset based on different experimental designs.

Besides the different datasets used, we observe that the methodology used for validation of the drowsiness detection systems is also a common problem. As mentioned earlier, EEG signal is a non-stationary and nonlinear signal with high inter-individual differences. Because of these properties, the only proper way for model validation is the validation on the signals from an unseen subject. Empirical tests show that there is a large difference in the accuracies between validation on the unseen subjects and validation on the unseen parts of the signal [212]. Reporting of validation with improper methodology can create overexpectation of the model performance, bad generalization on the unseen subjects, and can lead other researchers in the wrong direction. This effect is visible through the examples of papers that use validation on the unseen subjects, but also report about validation on the unseen parts of the signal in order to be comparable with existing research [173]. The fourth inclusion constraint defined in Section 1 was used to eliminate the papers that have a low probability of achieving good generalization due to a low number of participants.

The highest accuracy achieved was 99.5% in the work of Hong et al. [188]. It is interesting to note that the authors included features from three different categories. The authors used standard frequency bands and ratio indices, the nonlinear generalized Hurst exponent and HFD, and the entropies SEN and PE. Although this is not a large number of features, it is reasonable to assume that their diversity leads to the high accuracy of drowsiness detection. It is difficult to say how reliable the given accuracy is because only 16 participants took part in the experiment and there may be a high sampling bias in the data. The study by Martensson et al. [181] also used features from three different categories. The features used were standard frequency domain features and ratio indices, entropy SampEn, and nonlinear HFD. This study had the largest number of participants (86), and the accuracy achieved was 93.5%. These two studies suggest that using different types of features should result in high accuracy of drowsiness detection.

Complex network features for EEG signal analysis have become very popular in recent years, and this is also true for drowsiness detection systems. There are four papers [179,184–186] that include complex network features. One of them only provides analysis without classification and the remaining three have high accuracy—93%, 94%, and 98%. Complex networks are a promising approach, but confirming the reliability of such a system, especially when combined with features from other categories, requires studies with a large number of participants.

There is also a growing body of research on drowsiness detection using deep learning models. Deep learning models are known for their high ability to learn hidden structures in the data, but they often require a large amount of data for proper training. They can be used with the raw data as input, but also with features, or both. There are five papers using deep learning that met our inclusion criteria. In the first one, the authors used the LSTM network with raw data and different types of features and achieved 94.4% accuracy [178]. Their research was based on only 16 participants. The second one also used LSTM, but for prediction of the underlying alpha phenomena that is the base for determining drowsiness level [175]. The other three papers used CNN as a classification method. The highest accuracy achieved was 94% and the model used only raw data, without any pre-computed EEG signal features [173].

The reported accuracies for these deep learning models are in line with the accuracies of other models but, as we stated earlier, a direct comparison of the accuracies may lead to the wrong conclusions. Balam et al. [173] provided a proper comparison of different approaches. The authors used a publicly available dataset, so they were able to provide a fair comparison of different approaches. Their CNN approach was compared with one research based on the LSTM network and seven feature-based research studies. The best accuracy was obtained with their proposed method, while the LSTM method had a slightly lower accuracy. All seven feature-based approaches had more than 5% lower accuracy on average. A similar comparison was provided in Budak et al. [178] on a different publicly available dataset. Furthermore, the difference was that the authors used features and raw data for their LSTM model. The comparison was made with one deep learning approach and six other feature-based approaches. Again, the feature-based approaches had a lower performance by about 7%, on average.

These two pieces of research suggest that the deep learning approach is more appropriate and has higher performance for drowsiness detection than the feature-based approach. Nevertheless, it must be noted that all of the feature-based approaches that had lower accuracy used only time-domain and/or frequency-domain features. As shown and discussed earlier, the addition of different types of features could lead to an improvement of these models. From the inspected literature, it is currently unclear whether the inclusion of additional features would outperform deep learning models. In addition, it would be interesting to examine what effect would the addition of the features that are a measure of signal's memory (like Hurst exponent) have, since the LSTM model also relies on the previous values of the signal. However, we can speculate that the addition of the memory-based features would increase the accuracy of these feature-based models, but probably not enough to outperform LSTM models. The reason for this is because deep models have a higher capacity for learning hidden structures than the memory-based features, but additional research should be made to support the speculation.

A larger amount of data is needed for proper training of deep learning models compared to non-deep learning models. Acquiring the data is often a problem when it comes to EEG-based drowsiness detection. Authors of research studies that use deep learning approaches often employ generative adversarial networks for the augmentation of the dataset [175]. This process often leads to an improved performance of the model. Regardless of the possibilities for augmentation of the dataset, researchers should strive to gather as much as possible real EEG signals. The larger number of participants would ensure greater diversity of the dataset, reduce the influence of inter-individual differences in EEG signals, make models more robust, and allow enough data for proper validation of models.

As we discussed earlier, there is evidence that different types of features improve drowsiness detection models. In the papers that met our inclusion criteria, about 50 different features were used, while we introduced 147 EEG-based features in our review. Approximately 100 unused features provide much room for further research. In particular, spatiotemporal features were only used to obtain a graph for complex network features [184].

Another way to improve such systems is to set better ground truth labels. Currently, many works use subjective self-evaluation as ground truth. The KSS is used most often for this purpose. The KSS is a nine-level scale, with the first four levels describing alertness, the 5th neutral level, and the last four levels describing sleepiness. The four levels for alertness and sleepiness have detailed descriptions, and they are very similar. It is also hard to tell if the scale is linear with the same distances between adjacent levels. Since it is a subjective scale with small differences between adjacent levels, it may lead to subjectivity bias and inconsistencies in the ground truth labels, which was confirmed in [191], where the authors state after the statistical test results: "Subjective measures were not reliable for detecting drowsiness alone, and that solely relying on self-reported measures may not provide a meaningful measure of a person's actual physiological state." Future research on how to provide a unified definition and description of drowsiness is needed to combat this subjectivity bias.

For future research, we recommend the development of a drowsiness detection system that consider raw data, features from all seven categories, and deep learning models. Ground truth labels should be based on the unified, standard definition and description of drowsiness. If there is not yet research providing such a unified definition of drowsiness, then ground truth should be confirmed with multiple independent sources to reduce subjectivity bias (even expert labels are prone to subjectivity). Because electrophysiological signals have high interindividual differences, a large number of participants (about 100 or more [181]) is needed to reduce sample bias and increase the chances of a model to have good generalization.

6. Conclusions

With this review paper, we bring four contributions: (1) Comprehensive review, systematization, and a brief description of the existing features of the EEG signal, (2) comprehensive review of the drowsiness detection systems, (3) comprehensive review of the existing similar reviews, and (4) discussion of various potential ways to improve the state of the art of drowsiness detection systems. In continuation, we summarize our suggestions for the general improvement of the field of drowsiness detection systems.

A higher number of participants in the experiments (about 100 or more) is needed to ensure diversity of a dataset, reduce the influence of inter-individual differences of EEG signals, make models more robust, and allow enough data for proper validation of models. Validation of EEG-based driver drowsiness detection should always be done based on the data from unseen subjects (for example, using leave-one-subject-out cross-validation). Whenever possible, datasets should be published publicly to allow fair comparison of different approaches. Based only on the papers from this review, without additional research, we were not able to identify a single feature or a feature category that guarantees the best performance of the drowsiness detection system. What we can conclude is that a higher number of features from at least four different categories should lead to more reliable drowsiness detection systems with lower sampling bias and higher generalization ability. Deep learning models exhibit higher performance for drowsiness detection than the considered non-deep learning models based on time and frequency-domain features. Nevertheless, the use of pre-computed EEG signal features together with deep learning models should always be considered (in addition to raw EEG data modeling), since in some cases, the addition of pre-computed features to deep learning models additionally boosted performance.

For future research that would have a strong impact on the field of drowsiness detection systems, we suggest the development of a unified, standard definition and description of drowsiness, which would lead to a reduction in subjective bias and easier comparison of different studies.

Author Contributions: Conceptualization, I.S. and A.J.; methodology, I.S. and A.J.; validation, I.S.; M.C. and A.J.; formal analysis, I.S. and A.J.; investigation, I.S.; resources, I.S.; data curation, I.S.; writing—original draft preparation, I.S.; writing—review and editing, M.C. and A.J.; visualization, I.S.; supervision, A.J.; project administration, M.C. and A.J.; funding acquisition, M.C. All authors have read and agreed to the published version of the manuscript.

Funding: This work has been carried out within the project "Research and development of the system for driver drowsiness and distraction identification—DFDM", funded by the European Regional Development Fund in the Republic of Croatia under the Operational Programme Competitiveness and Cohesion 2014–2020.

Institutional Review Board Statement: Not applicable.

Informed Consent Statement: Not applicable.

Data Availability Statement: Not applicable.

Conflicts of Interest: The authors declare no conflict of interest.

References

1. Eastman, C.I.; Martin, S.K. How to use light and dark to produce circadian adaptation to night shift work. *Ann. Med.* **1999**, *31*, 87–98. [CrossRef]
2. Chellappa, S.L. Circadian misalignment: A biological basis for mood vulnerability in shift work. *Eur. J. Neurosci.* **2020**, *52*, 3846–3850. [CrossRef]
3. Kang, J.-H.; Miao, N.-F.; Tseng, I.-J.; Sithole, T.; Chung, M.-H. Circadian Activity Rhythms and Sleep in Nurses Working Fixed 8-hr Shifts. *Biol. Res. Nurs.* **2015**, *17*, 348–355. [CrossRef]
4. Arendt, J. Shift work: Coping with the biological clock. *Occup. Med.* **2010**, *60*, 10–20. [CrossRef]
5. Brown, I.D. Driver Fatigue. *Hum. Factors J. Hum. Factors Ergon. Soc.* **1994**, *36*, 298–314. [CrossRef]
6. Soleimanloo, S.S.; Wilkinson, V.E.; Cori, J.M.; Westlake, J.; Stevens, B.; Downey, L.; Shiferaw, B.A.; Rajaratnam, S.M.W.; Howard, M.E. Eye-Blink Parameters Detect On-Road Track-Driving Impairment Following Severe Sleep Deprivation. *J. Clin. Sleep Med.* **2019**, *15*, 1271–1284. [CrossRef] [PubMed]
7. Vicente, J.; Laguna, P.; Bartra, A.; Bailón, R. Drowsiness detection using heart rate variability. *Med. Biol. Eng. Comput.* **2016**, *54*, 927–937. [CrossRef] [PubMed]
8. Chellappa, S.L.; Morris, C.J.; Scheer, F.A.J.L. Effects of circadian misalignment on cognition in chronic shift workers. *Sci. Rep.* **2019**, *9*, 1–9. [CrossRef] [PubMed]
9. Folkard, S. Shift work, safety and productivity. *Occup. Med.* **2003**, *53*, 95–101. [CrossRef] [PubMed]
10. Ross, J.K. Offshore industry shift work–health and social considerations. *Occup. Med.* **2009**, *59*, 310–315. [CrossRef]
11. Orasanu, J.; Parke, B.; Kraft, N.; Tada, Y.; Hobbs, A.; Anderson, B.; Dulchinos, V. *Evaluating the Effectiveness of Schedule Changes for Air Traffic Service (ATS) Providers: Controller Alertness and Fatigue Monitoring Study*; Technical Report; Fedaral Aviation Administration, National Technical Information Service (NTIS): Alexandria, VA, USA, 2012.
12. National Transportation Safety Board. *Most Wanted List of Transportation Safety Improvements: Reduce Fatigue-Related Accidents*; National Transportation Safety Board: Washington, DC, USA, 2018.
13. Corsi-Cabrera, M.; Arce, C.; Ramos, J.; Lorenzo, I.; Guevara, M.A. Time Course of Reaction Time and EEG While Performing a Vigilance Task During Total Sleep Deprivation. *Sleep* **1996**, *19*, 563–569. [CrossRef]
14. Jackson, M.; Kennedy, G.A.; Clarke, C.; Gullo, M.; Swann, P.; Downey, L.; Hayley, A.C.; Pierce, R.J.; Howard, M.E. The utility of automated measures of ocular metrics for detecting driver drowsiness during extended wakefulness. *Accid. Anal. Prev.* **2016**, *87*, 127–133. [CrossRef] [PubMed]

15. Oken, B.S.; Salinsky, M.C.; Elsas, S.M. Vigilance, alertness, or sustained attention: Physiological basis and measurement. *Clin. Neurophysiol.* **2006**, *117*, 1885–1901. [CrossRef] [PubMed]
16. Kamran, M.A.; Mannan, M.M.N.; Jeong, M.Y. Drowsiness, Fatigue and Poor Sleep's Causes and Detection: A Comprehensive Study. *IEEE Access* **2019**, *7*, 167172–167186. [CrossRef]
17. Papadelis, C.; Chen, Z.; Kourtidou-Papadeli, C.; Bamidis, P.D.; Chouvarda, I.; Bekiaris, E.; Maglaveras, N. Monitoring sleepiness with on-board electrophysiological recordings for preventing sleep-deprived traffic accidents. *Clin. Neurophysiol.* **2007**, *118*, 1906–1922. [CrossRef]
18. Lal, S.K.; Craig, A. A critical review of the psychophysiology of driver fatigue. *Biol. Psychol.* **2001**, *55*, 173–194. [CrossRef]
19. Lin, C.-T.; Wu, R.-C.; Liang, S.-F.; Chao, W.-H.; Chen, Y.-J.; Jung, T.-P. EEG-based drowsiness estimation for safety driving using independent component analysis. *IEEE Trans. Circuits Syst. I Regul. Pap.* **2005**, *52*, 2726–2738. [CrossRef]
20. Khushaba, R.N.; Kodagoda, S.; Lal, S.; Dissanayake, G. Driver Drowsiness Classification Using Fuzzy Wavelet-Packet-Based Feature-Extraction Algorithm. *IEEE Trans. Biomed. Eng.* **2011**, *58*, 121–131. [CrossRef]
21. Neu, D.; Linkowski, P.; Le Bon, O. Clinical complaints of daytime sleepiness and fatigue: How to distinguish and treat them, especially when they become 'excessive' or 'chronic'? *Acta Neurol. Belg.* **2010**, *110*, 15–25. [PubMed]
22. Neu, D.; Mairesse, O.; Verbanck, P.; Linkowski, P.; Le Bon, O. Non-REM sleep EEG power distribution in fatigue and sleepiness. *J. Psychosom. Res.* **2014**, *76*, 286–291. [CrossRef]
23. Phillips, R.O. A review of definitions of fatigue—And a step towards a whole definition. *Transp. Res. Part F Traffic Psychol. Behav.* **2015**, *29*, 48–56. [CrossRef]
24. Johns, M.W.; Chapman, R.J.; Crowley, K.E.; Tucker, A. A new method for assessing the risks of drowsiness while driving. *Somnologie Schlafforschung Und Schlafmed.* **2008**, *12*, 66–74. [CrossRef]
25. Simon, M.; Schmidt, E.A.; Kincses, W.E.; Fritzsche, M.; Bruns, A.; Aufmuth, C.; Bogdan, M.; Rosenstiel, W.; Schrauf, M. EEG alpha spindle measures as indicators of driver fatigue under real traffic conditions. *Clin. Neurophysiol.* **2011**, *122*, 1168–1178. [CrossRef]
26. Craig, A.; Tran, Y.; Wijesuriya, N.; Nguyen, H. Regional brain wave activity changes associated with fatigue. *Psychophysiology* **2012**, *49*, 574–582. [CrossRef]
27. Aeschbach, D.; Matthews, J.R.; Postolache, T.T.; Jackson, M.A.; Giesen, H.A.; Wehr, T.A. Dynamics of the human EEG during prolonged wakefulness: Evidence for frequency-specific circadian and homeostatic influences. *Neurosci. Lett.* **1997**, *239*, 121–124. [CrossRef]
28. Borghini, G.; Astolfi, L.; Vecchiato, G.; Mattia, D.; Babiloni, F. Measuring neurophysiological signals in aircraft pilots and car drivers for the assessment of mental workload, fatigue and drowsiness. *Neurosci. Biobehav. Rev.* **2014**, *44*, 58–75. [CrossRef]
29. Kundinger, T.; Sofra, N.; Riener, A. Assessment of the Potential of Wrist-Worn Wearable Sensors for Driver Drowsiness Detection. *Sensors* **2020**, *20*, 1029. [CrossRef] [PubMed]
30. Stam, C. Nonlinear dynamical analysis of EEG and MEG: Review of an emerging field. *Clin. Neurophysiol.* **2005**, *116*, 2266–2301. [CrossRef] [PubMed]
31. Ma, Y.; Shi, W.; Peng, C.-K.; Yang, A.C. Nonlinear dynamical analysis of sleep electroencephalography using fractal and entropy approaches. *Sleep Med. Rev.* **2018**, *37*, 85–93. [CrossRef]
32. Keshmiri, S. Entropy and the Brain: An Overview. *Entropy* **2020**, *22*, 917. [CrossRef] [PubMed]
33. Sun, J.; Wang, B.; Niu, Y.; Tan, Y.; Fan, C.; Zhang, N.; Xue, J.; Wei, J.; Xiang, J. Complexity Analysis of EEG, MEG, and fMRI in Mild Cognitive Impairment and Alzheimer's Disease: A Review. *Entropy* **2020**, *22*, 239. [CrossRef] [PubMed]
34. Motamedi-Fakhr, S.; Moshrefi-Torbati, M.; Hill, M.; Hill, C.M.; White, P.R. Signal processing techniques applied to human sleep EEG signals—A review. *Biomed. Signal Process. Control.* **2014**, *10*, 21–33. [CrossRef]
35. Rashid, M.; Sulaiman, N.; Majeed, A.P.P.A.; Musa, R.M.; Nasir, A.F.A.; Bari, B.S.; Khatun, S. Current Status, Challenges, and Possible Solutions of EEG-Based Brain-Computer Interface: A Comprehensive Review. *Front. Neurorobot.* **2020**, *14*. [CrossRef] [PubMed]
36. Bastos, A.M.; Schoffelen, J.-M. A Tutorial Review of Functional Connectivity Analysis Methods and Their Interpretational Pitfalls. *Front. Syst. Neurosci.* **2016**, *9*, 175. [CrossRef] [PubMed]
37. Kida, T.; Tanaka, E.; Kakigi, R. Multi-Dimensional Dynamics of Human Electromagnetic Brain Activity. *Front. Hum. Neurosci.* **2016**, *9*. [CrossRef]
38. Khosla, A.; Khandnor, P.; Chand, T. A comparative analysis of signal processing and classification methods for different applications based on EEG signals. *Biocybern. Biomed. Eng.* **2020**, *40*, 649–690. [CrossRef]
39. Ismail, L.E.; Karwowski, W. A Graph Theory-Based Modeling of Functional Brain Connectivity Based on EEG: A Systematic Review in the Context of Neuroergonomics. *IEEE Access* **2020**, *8*, 155103–155135. [CrossRef]
40. Lenné, M.G.; Jacobs, E.E. Predicting drowsiness-related driving events: A review of recent research methods and future opportunities. *Theor. Issues Ergon. Sci.* **2016**, *17*, 533–553. [CrossRef]
41. Doudou, M.; Bouabdallah, A.; Berge-Cherfaoui, V. Driver Drowsiness Measurement Technologies: Current Research, Market Solutions, and Challenges. *Int. J. Intell. Transp. Syst. Res.* **2019**, *18*, 297–319. [CrossRef]
42. Sahayadhas, A.; Sundaraj, K.; Murugappan, M. Detecting Driver Drowsiness Based on Sensors: A Review. *Sensors* **2012**, *12*, 16937–16953. [CrossRef]
43. Sikander, G.; Anwar, S. Driver Fatigue Detection Systems: A Review. *IEEE Trans. Intell. Transp. Syst.* **2019**, *20*, 2339–2352. [CrossRef]

44. Chowdhury, A.; Shankaran, R.; Kavakli, M.; Haque, M. Sensor Applications and Physiological Features in Drivers' Drowsiness Detection: A Review. *IEEE Sens. J.* **2018**, *18*, 3055–3067. [CrossRef]
45. Balandong, R.P.; Ahmad, R.F.; Saad, M.N.M.; Malik, A.S. A Review on EEG-Based Automatic Sleepiness Detection Systems for Driver. *IEEE Access* **2018**, *6*, 22908–22919. [CrossRef]
46. Hu, X.; Lodewijks, G. Detecting fatigue in car drivers and aircraft pilots by using non-invasive measures: The value of differentiation of sleepiness and mental fatigue. *J. Saf. Res.* **2020**, *72*, 173–187. [CrossRef]
47. Soares, S.; Ferreira, S.; Couto, A. Driving simulator experiments to study drowsiness: A systematic review. *Traffic Inj. Prev.* **2020**, *21*, 29–37. [CrossRef] [PubMed]
48. Bier, L.; Wolf, P.; Hilsenbek, H.; Abendroth, B. How to measure monotony-related fatigue? A systematic review of fatigue measurement methods for use on driving tests. *Theor. Issues Ergon. Sci.* **2018**, *21*, 22–55. [CrossRef]
49. Phillips, R.O.; Kecklund, G.; Anund, A.; Sallinen, M. Fatigue in transport: A review of exposure, risks, checks and controls. *Transp. Rev.* **2017**, *37*, 742–766. [CrossRef]
50. Jiang, D.; Lu, Y.-N.; Ma, Y.; Wang, Y. Robust sleep stage classification with single-channel EEG signals using multimodal decomposition and HMM-based refinement. *Expert Syst. Appl.* **2019**, *121*, 188–203. [CrossRef]
51. Michielli, N.; Acharya, U.R.; Molinari, F. Cascaded LSTM recurrent neural network for automated sleep stage classification using single-channel EEG signals. *Comput. Biol. Med.* **2019**, *106*, 71–81. [CrossRef] [PubMed]
52. Geering, B.A.; Achermann, P.; Eggimann, F.; Borbély, A.A. Period-amplitude analysis and power spectral analysis: A comparison based on all-night sleep EEG recordings. *J. Sleep Res.* **1993**, *2*, 121–129. [CrossRef]
53. Hjorth, B. EEG analysis based on time domain properties. *Electroencephalogr. Clin. Neurophysiol.* **1970**, *29*, 306–310. [CrossRef]
54. Wang, X.-W.; Nie, D.; Lu, B.-L. EEG-Based Emotion Recognition Using Frequency Domain Features and Support Vector Machines. In *International Conference on Neural Information Processing, ICONIP 2011*; Springer: Berlin/Heidelberg, Germany, 2011; pp. 734–743. [CrossRef]
55. Oliveira, G.H.; Coutinho, L.R.; da Silva, J.C.; Pinto, I.J.; Ferreira, J.M.; Silva, F.J.; Santos, D.V.; Teles, A.S. Multitaper-based method for automatic k-complex detection in human sleep EEG. *Expert Syst. Appl.* **2020**, *151*, 113331. [CrossRef]
56. Nussbaumer, H.J. *The Fast Fourier Transform*; Springer: Berlin/Heidelberg, Germany, 1981; pp. 80–111. [CrossRef]
57. Welch, P. The use of fast Fourier transform for the estimation of power spectra: A method based on time averaging over short, modified periodograms. *IEEE Trans. Audio Electroacoust.* **1967**, *15*, 70–73. [CrossRef]
58. Thomson, D. Spectrum estimation and harmonic analysis. *Proc. IEEE* **1982**, *70*, 1055–1096. [CrossRef]
59. Akaike, H. Fitting autoregressive models for prediction. *Ann. Inst. Stat. Math.* **1969**, *21*, 243–247. [CrossRef]
60. Neumaier, A.; Schneider, T. Estimation of parameters and eigenmodes of multivariate autoregressive models. *ACM Trans. Math. Softw.* **2001**, *27*, 27–57. [CrossRef]
61. Said, S.E.; Dickey, D.A. Testing for unit roots in autoregressive-moving average models of unknown order. *Biometrika* **1984**, *71*, 599–607. [CrossRef]
62. De Gennaro, L.; Ferrara, M. Sleep spindles: An overview. *Sleep Med. Rev.* **2003**, *7*, 423–440. [CrossRef]
63. Eoh, H.J.; Chung, M.K.; Kim, S.-H. Electroencephalographic study of drowsiness in simulated driving with sleep deprivation. *Int. J. Ind. Ergon.* **2005**, *35*, 307–320. [CrossRef]
64. Jap, B.T.; Lal, S.; Fischer, P.; Bekiaris, E. Using EEG spectral components to assess algorithms for detecting fatigue. *Expert Syst. Appl.* **2009**, *36*, 2352–2359. [CrossRef]
65. da Silveira, T.L.; Kozakevicius, A.J.; Rodrigues, C.R. Automated drowsiness detection through wavelet packet analysis of a single EEG channel. *Expert Syst. Appl.* **2016**, *55*, 559–565. [CrossRef]
66. Adeli, H.; Zhou, Z.; Dadmehr, N. Analysis of EEG records in an epileptic patient using wavelet transform. *J. Neurosci. Methods* **2003**, *123*, 69–87. [CrossRef]
67. Stéphane, M. *A Wavelet Tour of Signal Processing*; Elsevier: Amsterdam, The Netherlands, 2009. [CrossRef]
68. Franaszczuk, P.; Bergey, G.K.; Durka, P.; Eisenberg, H.M. Time–frequency analysis using the matching pursuit algorithm applied to seizures originating from the mesial temporal lobe. *Electroencephalogr. Clin. Neurophysiol.* **1998**, *106*, 513–521. [CrossRef]
69. Durka, P.; Ircha, D.; Blinowska, K. Stochastic time-frequency dictionaries for matching pursuit. *IEEE Trans. Signal Process.* **2001**, *49*, 507–510. [CrossRef]
70. Eiselt, M.; Schelenz, C.; Witte, H.; Schwab, K. Time-variant Parametric Estimation of Transient Quadratic Phase Couplings during Electroencephalographic Burst Activity. *Methods Inf. Med.* **2005**, *44*, 374–383. [CrossRef]
71. Cohen, L. *Time-Frequency Analysis*; Prentice Hall: Hoboken, NJ, USA, 1995; Volume 778.
72. Abbate, A.; DeCusatis, C.M.; Das, P.K. Time-Frequency Analysis of Signals. In *Wavelets and Subbands*; Birkhäuser Boston: Boston, MA, USA, 2002; pp. 103–187. [CrossRef]
73. Meyer, Y. *Wavelets and Operators*; Cambridge University Press: Cambridge, UK, 1993. [CrossRef]
74. Hurst, H.E. THE PROBLEM OF LONG-TERM STORAGE IN RESERVOIRS. *Int. Assoc. Sci. Hydrol. Bull.* **1956**, *1*, 13–27. [CrossRef]
75. Lloyd, E.H.; Hurst, H.E.; Black, R.P.; Simaika, Y.M. Long-Term Storage: An Experimental Study. *J. R. Stat. Soc. Ser. A (Gen.)* **1966**, *129*, 591. [CrossRef]
76. Kantelhardt, J.W. Fractal and Multifractal Time Series. In *Encyclopedia of Complexity and Systems Science*; Springer: New York, NY, USA, 2009; pp. 3754–3779. [CrossRef]
77. Barnsley, M.F. *Fractals Everywhere*; Elsevier: Amsterdam, The Netherlands, 1993. [CrossRef]

78. Kantz, H.; Schreiber, T. *Nonlinear Time Series Analysis*; Cambridge University Press: Cambridge, UK, 2003.
79. Pritchard, W.; Duke, D. Measuring Chaos in the Brain—A Tutorial Review of EEG Dimension Estimation. *Brain Cogn.* **1995**, *27*, 353–397. [CrossRef]
80. Grassberger, P.; Procaccia, I. Estimation of the Kolmogorov entropy from a chaotic signal. *Phys. Rev. A* **1983**, *28*, 2591–2593. [CrossRef]
81. Grassberger, P.; Procaccia, I. Measuring the strangeness of strange attractors. *Phys. D Nonlinear Phenom.* **1983**, *9*, 189–208. [CrossRef]
82. Dash, D.P.; Kolekar, M.H.; Jha, K. Multi-channel EEG based automatic epileptic seizure detection using iterative filtering decomposition and Hidden Markov Model. *Comput. Biol. Med.* **2020**, *116*, 103571. [CrossRef]
83. Moctezuma, L.A.; Molinas, M. Towards a minimal EEG channel array for a biometric system using resting-state and a genetic algorithm for channel selection. *Sci. Rep.* **2020**, *10*, 1–14. [CrossRef]
84. Ferenets, R.; Lipping, T.; Anier, A.; Jantti, V.; Melto, S.; Hovilehto, S. Comparison of Entropy and Complexity Measures for the Assessment of Depth of Sedation. *IEEE Trans. Biomed. Eng.* **2006**, *53*, 1067–1077. [CrossRef] [PubMed]
85. Zorick, T.; Mandelkern, M.A. Multifractal Detrended Fluctuation Analysis of Human EEG: Preliminary Investigation and Comparison with the Wavelet Transform Modulus Maxima Technique. *PLoS ONE* **2013**, *8*, e68360. [CrossRef] [PubMed]
86. Muzy, J.F.; Bacry, E.; Arneodo, A. Multifractal formalism for fractal signals: The structure-function approach versus the wavelet-transform modulus-maxima method. *Phys. Rev. E* **1993**, *47*, 875–884. [CrossRef]
87. Bunde, A.; Havlin, S. (Eds.) *Fractals in Science*; Springer: Berlin/Heidelberg, Germany, 1994. [CrossRef]
88. Peng, C.-K.; Buldyrev, S.; Havlin, S.; Simons, M.; Stanley, H.E.; Goldberger, A.L. Mosaic organization of DNA nucleotides. *Phys. Rev. E* **1994**, *49*, 1685–1689. [CrossRef]
89. Álvarez-Ramírez, J.; Rodriguez, E.; Echeverria, J.C. Detrending fluctuation analysis based on moving average filtering. *Phys. A Stat. Mech. Its Appl.* **2005**, *354*, 199–219. [CrossRef]
90. Lotfalinezhad, H.; Maleki, A. TTA, a new approach to estimate Hurst exponent with less estimation error and computational time. *Phys. A Stat. Mech. Its Appl.* **2020**, *553*, 124093. [CrossRef]
91. Muzy, J.F.; Bacry, E.; Arneodo, A. Wavelets and multifractal formalism for singular signals: Application to turbulence data. *Phys. Rev. Lett.* **1991**, *67*, 3515–3518. [CrossRef] [PubMed]
92. Kantelhardt, J.W.; Zschiegner, S.A.; Koscielny-Bunde, E.; Havlin, S.; Bunde, A.; Stanley, H. Multifractal detrended fluctuation analysis of nonstationary time series. *Phys. A Stat. Mech. Its Appl.* **2002**, *316*, 87–114. [CrossRef]
93. Shevchenko, I.I. Lyapunov exponents in resonance multiplets. *Phys. Lett. A* **2014**, *378*, 34–42. [CrossRef]
94. Shen, C.; Yu, S.; Lu, J.; Chen, G. Designing Hyperchaotic Systems With Any Desired Number of Positive Lyapunov Exponents via A Simple Model. *IEEE Trans. Circuits Syst. I Regul. Pap.* **2014**, *61*, 2380–2389. [CrossRef]
95. Lempel, A.; Ziv, J. On the Complexity of Finite Sequences. *IEEE Trans. Inf. Theory* **1976**, *22*, 75–81. [CrossRef]
96. Cohen, M.; Hudson, D.; Deedwania, P. Applying continuous chaotic modeling to cardiac signal analysis. *IEEE Eng. Med. Boil. Mag.* **1996**, *15*, 97–102. [CrossRef]
97. Abásolo, D.; Escudero, J.; Hornero, R.; Gómez, C.; Espino, P. Approximate entropy and auto mutual information analysis of the electroencephalogram in Alzheimer's disease patients. *Med. Biol. Eng. Comput.* **2008**, *46*, 1019–1028. [CrossRef]
98. Daw, C.S.; Finney, C.E.A.; Kennel, M.B. Symbolic approach for measuring temporal "irreversibility". *Phys. Rev. E* **2000**, *62*, 1912–1921. [CrossRef] [PubMed]
99. Eckmann, J.-P.; Kamphorst, S.O.; Ruelle, D. Recurrence Plots of Dynamical Systems. *Europhys. Lett. (EPL)* **1987**, *4*, 973–977. [CrossRef]
100. Webber, C.L.; Zbilut, J.P. Dynamical assessment of physiological systems and states using recurrence plot strategies. *J. Appl. Physiol.* **1994**, *76*, 965–973. [CrossRef]
101. Zbilut, J.P.; Giuliani, A.; Webber, C.L. Detecting deterministic signals in exceptionally noisy environments using cross-recurrence quantification. *Phys. Lett. A* **1998**, *246*, 122–128. [CrossRef]
102. Shannon, C.E. A Mathematical Theory of Communication. *Bell Syst. Tech. J.* **1948**, *27*, 379–423. [CrossRef]
103. Shannon, C.E. A Mathematical Theory of Communication. *Bell Syst. Tech. J.* **1948**, *27*, 623–656. [CrossRef]
104. Rényi, A. *Probability Theory*; North-Holland: Amsterdam, The Netherlands, 1970.
105. Tsallis, C.; Mendes, R.; Plastino, A. The role of constraints within generalized nonextensive statistics. *Phys. A Stat. Mech. Its Appl.* **1998**, *261*, 534–554. [CrossRef]
106. Fell, J.; Röschke, J.; Mann, K.; Schäffner, C. Discrimination of sleep stages: A comparison between spectral and nonlinear EEG measures. *Electroencephalogr. Clin. Neurophysiol.* **1996**, *98*, 401–410. [CrossRef]
107. Kannathal, N.; Choo, M.L.; Acharya, U.R.; Sadasivan, P. Entropies for detection of epilepsy in EEG. *Comput. Methods Programs Biomed.* **2005**, *80*, 187–194. [CrossRef]
108. Viertio-Oja, H.; Maja, V.; Sarkela, M.; Talja, P.; Tenkanen, N.; Tolvanenlaakso, H.; Paloheimo, M.P.J.; Vakkuri, A.P.; Ylihankala, A.M.; Merilainen, P. Description of the Entropytm algorithm as applied in the Datex-Ohmeda S/5tm Entropy Module. *Acta Anaesthesiol. Scand.* **2004**, *48*, 154–161. [CrossRef]
109. Särkelä, M.O.K.; Ermes, M.J.; van Gils, M.J.; Yli-Hankala, A.M.; Jäntti, V.H.; Vakkuri, A.P. Quantification of Epileptiform Electroencephalographic Activity during Sevoflurane Mask Induction. *Anesthesiology* **2007**, *107*, 928–938. [CrossRef]

110. Zhang, C.; Wang, H.; Fu, R. Automated Detection of Driver Fatigue Based on Entropy and Complexity Measures. *IEEE Trans. Intell. Transp. Syst.* **2013**, *15*, 168–177. [CrossRef]
111. Eliang, Z.; Ewang, Y.; Esun, X.; Eli, D.; Voss, L.J.; Sleigh, J.W.; Ehagihira, S.; Eli, X. EEG entropy measures in anesthesia. *Front. Comput. Neurosci.* **2015**, *9*, 16. [CrossRef]
112. Huang, N.E.; Shen, Z.; Long, S.R.; Wu, M.C.; Shih, H.H.; Zheng, Q.; Yen, N.-C.; Tung, C.C.; Liu, H.H. The empirical mode decomposition and the Hilbert spectrum for nonlinear and non-stationary time series analysis. *Proc. R. Soc. A Math. Phys. Eng. Sci.* **1998**, *454*, 903–995. [CrossRef]
113. Li, X.; Li, D.; Liang, Z.; Voss, L.J.; Sleigh, J.W. Analysis of depth of anesthesia with Hilbert–Huang spectral entropy. *Clin. Neurophysiol.* **2008**, *119*, 2465–2475. [CrossRef] [PubMed]
114. Aydın, S.; Saraoğlu, H.M.; Kara, S. Log Energy Entropy-Based EEG Classification with Multilayer Neural Networks in Seizure. *Ann. Biomed. Eng.* **2009**, *37*, 2626–2630. [CrossRef]
115. Torres, M.E.; Gamero, L.G.; Flandrin, P.; Abry, P. Multiresolution entropy measure. In *Wavelet Applications in Signal and Image Processing V*; Aldroubi, A., Laine, A.F., Unser, M.A., Eds.; Optical Science, Engineering and Instrumentation: San Diego, CA, USA, 1997; Volume 3169, pp. 400–407. [CrossRef]
116. Schuster, H.G.; Just, W. *Deterministic Chaos*; Wiley: Hoboken, NJ, USA, 2005. [CrossRef]
117. Wales, D.J. Calculating the rate of loss of information from chaotic time series by forecasting. *Nat. Cell Biol.* **1991**, *350*, 485–488. [CrossRef]
118. Schouten, J.C.; Takens, F.; Bleek, C.M.V.D. Maximum-likelihood estimation of the entropy of an attractor. *Phys. Rev. E* **1994**, *49*, 126–129. [CrossRef]
119. Paluš, M. Coarse-grained entropy rates for characterization of complex time series. *Phys. D Nonlinear Phenom.* **1996**, *93*, 64–77. [CrossRef]
120. Santamaria, I.; Pokharel, P.; Principe, J. Generalized correlation function: Definition, properties, and application to blind equalization. *IEEE Trans. Signal Process.* **2006**, *54*, 2187–2197. [CrossRef]
121. Pincus, S.M.; Gladstone, I.M.; Ehrenkranz, R.A. A regularity statistic for medical data analysis. *J. Clin. Monit.* **1991**, *7*, 335–345. [CrossRef] [PubMed]
122. Richman, J.S.; Moorman, J.R. Physiological time-series analysis using approximate entropy and sample entropy. *Am. J. Physiol. Circ. Physiol.* **2000**, *278*, H2039–H2049. [CrossRef] [PubMed]
123. García-Martínez, B.; Martínez-Rodrigo, A.; Cantabrana, R.Z.; García, J.M.P.; Alcaraz, R. Application of Entropy-Based Metrics to Identify Emotional Distress from Electroencephalographic Recordings. *Entropy* **2016**, *18*, 221. [CrossRef]
124. Courtiol, J.; Perdikis, D.; Petkoski, S.; Müller, V.; Huys, R.; Sleimen-Malkoun, R.; Jirsa, V.K. The multiscale entropy: Guidelines for use and interpretation in brain signal analysis. *J. Neurosci. Methods* **2016**, *273*, 175–190. [CrossRef]
125. Wu, S.-D.; Wu, C.-W.; Lee, K.-Y.; Lin, S.-G. Modified multiscale entropy for short-term time series analysis. *Phys. A Stat. Mech. Its Appl.* **2013**, *392*, 5865–5873. [CrossRef]
126. Wu, S.-D.; Wu, C.-W.; Lin, S.-G.; Wang, C.-C.; Lee, K.-Y. Time Series Analysis Using Composite Multiscale Entropy. *Entropy* **2013**, *15*, 1069–1084. [CrossRef]
127. Cuesta-Frau, D.; Murillo-Escobar, J.P.; Orrego, D.A.; Delgado-Trejos, E. Embedded Dimension and Time Series Length. Practical Influence on Permutation Entropy and Its Applications. *Entropy* **2019**, *21*, 385. [CrossRef] [PubMed]
128. Zhao, X.; Shang, P.; Huang, J. Permutation complexity and dependence measures of time series. *EPL (Europhys. Lett.)* **2013**, *102*, 40005. [CrossRef]
129. Mammone, N.; Duun-Henriksen, J.; Kjaer, T.W.; Morabito, F.C. Differentiating Interictal and Ictal States in Childhood Absence Epilepsy through Permutation Rényi Entropy. *Entropy* **2015**, *17*, 4627–4643. [CrossRef]
130. He, S.; Sun, K.; Wang, H. Multivariate permutation entropy and its application for complexity analysis of chaotic systems. *Phys. A Stat. Mech. Its Appl.* **2016**, *461*, 812–823. [CrossRef]
131. Rostaghi, M.; Azami, H. Dispersion Entropy: A Measure for Time-Series Analysis. *IEEE Signal Process. Lett.* **2016**, *23*, 610–614. [CrossRef]
132. Azami, H.; Escudero, J. Amplitude-aware permutation entropy: Illustration in spike detection and signal segmentation. *Comput. Methods Programs Biomed.* **2016**, *128*, 40–51. [CrossRef]
133. Manis, G.; Aktaruzzaman; Sassi, R. Bubble Entropy: An Entropy Almost Free of Parameters. *IEEE Trans. Biomed. Eng.* **2017**, *64*, 2711–2718. [CrossRef]
134. Cover, T.M.; Thomas, J.A. *Elements of Information Theory*; Wiley: Hoboken, NJ, USA, 2005.
135. Chen, W.; Wang, Z.; Xie, H.; Yu, W. Characterization of Surface EMG Signal Based on Fuzzy Entropy. *IEEE Trans. Neural Syst. Rehabil. Eng.* **2007**, *15*, 266–272. [CrossRef]
136. Zadeh, L.A. Fuzzy sets. *Inf. Control* **1965**, *8*, 338–353. [CrossRef]
137. Schreiber, T. Measuring Information Transfer. *Phys. Rev. Lett.* **2000**, *85*, 461–464. [CrossRef]
138. Randolph, P.H. Spectral Analysis and Its Applications. *Technometrics* **1970**, *12*, 174. [CrossRef]
139. Kuś, R.; Kamiński, M.; Blinowska, K.J. Determination of EEG Activity Propagation: Pair-Wise Versus Multichannel Estimate. *IEEE Trans. Biomed. Eng.* **2004**, *51*, 1501–1510. [CrossRef]
140. Mormann, F.; Lehnertz, K.; David, P.; Elger, C.E. Mean phase coherence as a measure for phase synchronization and its application to the EEG of epilepsy patients. *Phys. D Nonlinear Phenom.* **2000**, *144*, 358–369. [CrossRef]

141. Lachaux, J.-P.; Rodriguez, E.; Martinerie, J.; Varela, F.J. Measuring phase synchrony in brain signals. *Human Brain Mapp.* **1999**, *8*, 194–208. [CrossRef]
142. Nunez, P.L.; Srinivasan, R.; Westdorp, A.F.; Wijesinghe, R.S.; Tucker, D.M.; Silberstein, R.B.; Cadusch, P.J. EEG coherency. *Electroencephalogr. Clin. Neurophysiol.* **1997**, *103*, 499–515. [CrossRef]
143. Nolte, G.; Bai, O.; Wheaton, L.; Mari, Z.; Vorbach, S.; Hallett, M. Identifying true brain interaction from EEG data using the imaginary part of coherency. *Clin. Neurophysiol.* **2004**, *115*, 2292–2307. [CrossRef] [PubMed]
144. Stam, C.J.; Nolte, G.; Daffertshofer, A. Phase lag index: Assessment of functional connectivity from multi channel EEG and MEG with diminished bias from common sources. *Hum. Brain Mapp.* **2007**, *28*, 1178–1193. [CrossRef] [PubMed]
145. Vinck, M.; Oostenveld, R.; van Wingerden, M.; Battaglia, F.; Pennartz, C.M.A. An improved index of phase-synchronization for electrophysiological data in the presence of volume-conduction, noise and sample-size bias. *NeuroImage* **2011**, *55*, 1548–1565. [CrossRef]
146. Vinck, M.; van Wingerden, M.; Womelsdorf, T.; Fries, P.; Pennartz, C. The pairwise phase consistency: A bias-free measure of rhythmic neuronal synchronization. *NeuroImage* **2010**, *51*, 112–122. [CrossRef]
147. Rulkov, N.F.; Sushchik, M.M.; Tsimring, L.S.; Abarbanel, H.D.I. Generalized synchronization of chaos in directionally coupled chaotic systems. *Phys. Rev. E* **1995**, *51*, 980–994. [CrossRef]
148. Arnhold, J.; Grassberger, P.; Lehnertz, K.; Elger, C.E. A robust method for detecting interdependences: Application to intracranially recorded EEG. *Phys. D Nonlinear Phenom.* **1999**, *134*, 419–430. [CrossRef]
149. Stam, C.; Van Dijk, B. Synchronization likelihood: An unbiased measure of generalized synchronization in multivariate data sets. *Phys. D Nonlinear Phenom.* **2002**, *163*, 236–251. [CrossRef]
150. Pereda, E.; Quiroga, R.Q.; Bhattacharya, J. Nonlinear multivariate analysis of neurophysiological signals. *Prog. Neurobiol.* **2005**, *77*, 1–37. [CrossRef] [PubMed]
151. Young, J.; Dragoi, V.; Aazhang, B. Precise measurement of correlations between frequency coupling and visual task performance. *Sci. Rep.* **2020**, *10*, 1–14. [CrossRef] [PubMed]
152. Zoldi, S.M.; Greenside, H.S. Karhunen-Loève Decomposition of Extensive Chaos. *Phys. Rev. Lett.* **1997**, *78*, 1687–1690. [CrossRef]
153. Granger, C.W.J. Investigating Causal Relations by Econometric Models and Cross-spectral Methods. *Econometrica* **1969**, *37*, 424–438. [CrossRef]
154. Geweke, J. Measurement of Linear Dependence and Feedback Between Multiple Time Series. *J. Am. Stat. Assoc.* **1982**, *77*, 304. [CrossRef]
155. Nolte, G.; Ziehe, A.; Nikulin, V.V.; Schlögl, A.; Krämer, N.; Brismar, T.; Müller, K.-R. Robustly Estimating the Flow Direction of Information in Complex Physical Systems. *Phys. Rev. Lett.* **2008**, *100*, 234101. [CrossRef]
156. Stam, C.J. Modern network science of neurological disorders. *Nat. Rev. Neurosci.* **2014**, *15*, 683–695. [CrossRef]
157. Zou, Y.; Donner, R.V.; Marwan, N.; Donges, J.F.; Kurths, J. Complex network approaches to nonlinear time series analysis. *Phys. Rep.* **2019**, *787*, 1–97. [CrossRef]
158. Rubinov, M.; Sporns, O. Complex network measures of brain connectivity: Uses and interpretations. *NeuroImage* **2010**, *52*, 1059–1069. [CrossRef]
159. Stam, C.J.; van Straaten, E.C.W. The organization of physiological brain networks. *Clin. Neurophysiol.* **2012**, *123*, 1067–1087. [CrossRef] [PubMed]
160. Watts, D.J.; Strogatz, S. Collective dynamics of 'small-world' networks. *Nat. Cell Biol.* **1998**, *393*, 440–442. [CrossRef]
161. Newman, M.E.J. The Structure and Function of Complex Networks. *SIAM Rev.* **2003**, *45*, 167–256. [CrossRef]
162. Milo, R.; Shen-Orr, S.; Itzkovitz, S.; Kashtan, N.; Chklovskii, D.; Alon, U. Network Motifs: Simple Building Blocks of Complex Networks. *Science* **2002**, *298*, 824–827. [CrossRef]
163. Humphries, M.D.; Gurney, K. Network 'Small-World-Ness': A Quantitative Method for Determining Canonical Network Equivalence. *PLoS ONE* **2008**, *3*, e0002051. [CrossRef]
164. Fallani, F.D.V.; Astolfi, L.; Cincotti, F.; Mattia, D.; Tocci, A.; Salinari, S.; Marciani, M.; Witte, H.; Colosimo, A.; Babiloni, F. Brain Network Analysis From High-Resolution EEG Recordings by the Application of Theoretical Graph Indexes. *IEEE Trans. Neural Syst. Rehabil. Eng.* **2008**, *16*, 442–452. [CrossRef] [PubMed]
165. Latora, V.; Marchiori, M. Efficient Behavior of Small-World Networks. *Phys. Rev. Lett.* **2001**, *87*, 198701. [CrossRef] [PubMed]
166. Leicht, E.; Newman, M.E.J. Community Structure in Directed Networks. *Phys. Rev. Lett.* **2008**, *100*, 118703. [CrossRef]
167. Newman, M. *Networks*; Oxford University Press: Oxford, UK, 2010.
168. Sabidussi, G. The centrality index of a graph. *Psychometrika* **1966**, *31*, 581–603. [CrossRef] [PubMed]
169. Batool, K.; Niazi, M.A. Towards a Methodology for Validation of Centrality Measures in Complex Networks. *PLoS ONE* **2014**, *9*, e90283. [CrossRef] [PubMed]
170. Freeman, L.C. Centrality in social networks conceptual clarification. *Soc. Netw.* **1978**, *1*, 215–239. [CrossRef]
171. Iakovidou, N.D. Graph Theory at the Service of Electroencephalograms. *Brain Connect.* **2017**, *7*, 137–151. [CrossRef] [PubMed]
172. Heuvel, M.V.D.; Sporns, O. Rich-Club Organization of the Human Connectome. *J. Neurosci.* **2011**, *31*, 15775–15786. [CrossRef]
173. Balam, V.P.; Sameer, V.U.; Chinara, S. Automated classification system for drowsiness detection using convolutional neural network and electroencephalogram. *IET Intell. Transp. Syst.* **2021**, *15*, 514–524. [CrossRef]
174. Chaabene, S.; Bouaziz, B.; Boudaya, A.; Hökelmann, A.; Ammar, A.; Chaari, L. Convolutional Neural Network for Drowsiness Detection Using EEG Signals. *Sensors* **2021**, *21*, 1734. [CrossRef]

175. Jiao, Y.; Deng, Y.; Luo, Y.; Lu, B.-L. Driver sleepiness detection from EEG and EOG signals using GAN and LSTM networks. *Neurocomputing* **2020**, *408*, 100–111. [CrossRef]
176. Zou, S.; Qiu, T.; Huang, P.; Bai, X.; Liu, C. Constructing Multi-scale Entropy Based on the Empirical Mode Decomposition(EMD) and its Application in Recognizing Driving Fatigue. *J. Neurosci. Methods* **2020**, *341*, 108691. [CrossRef]
177. Chaudhuri, A.; Routray, A. Driver Fatigue Detection Through Chaotic Entropy Analysis of Cortical Sources Obtained From Scalp EEG Signals. *IEEE Trans. Intell. Transp. Syst.* **2019**, *21*, 185–198. [CrossRef]
178. Budak, U.; Bajaj, V.; Akbulut, Y.; Atilla, O.; Sengur, A. An Effective Hybrid Model for EEG-Based Drowsiness Detection. *IEEE Sens. J.* **2019**, *19*, 7624–7631. [CrossRef]
179. Chen, J.; Wang, H.; Wang, Q.; Hua, C. Exploring the fatigue affecting electroencephalography based functional brain networks during real driving in young males. *Neuropsychologia* **2019**, *129*, 200–211. [CrossRef] [PubMed]
180. Mehreen, A.; Anwar, S.M.; Haseeb, M.; Majid, M.; Ullah, M.O. A Hybrid Scheme for Drowsiness Detection Using Wearable Sensors. *IEEE Sens. J.* **2019**, *19*, 5119–5126. [CrossRef]
181. Martensson, H.; Keelan, O.; Ahlstrom, C. Driver Sleepiness Classification Based on Physiological Data and Driving Performance From Real Road Driving. *IEEE Trans. Intell. Transp. Syst.* **2019**, *20*, 421–430. [CrossRef]
182. Barua, S.; Ahmed, M.U.; Ahlström, C.; Begum, S. Automatic driver sleepiness detection using EEG, EOG and contextual information. *Expert Syst. Appl.* **2019**, *115*, 121–135. [CrossRef]
183. Ogino, M.; Mitsukura, Y. Portable Drowsiness Detection through Use of a Prefrontal Single-Channel Electroencephalogram. *Sensors* **2018**, *18*, 4477. [CrossRef]
184. Chen, J.; Wang, H.; Hua, C.; Wang, Q.; Liu, C. Graph analysis of functional brain network topology using minimum spanning tree in driver drowsiness. *Cogn. Neurodyn.* **2018**, *12*, 569–581. [CrossRef]
185. Chen, J.; Wang, H.; Hua, C. Assessment of driver drowsiness using electroencephalogram signals based on multiple functional brain networks. *Int. J. Psychophysiol.* **2018**, *133*, 120–130. [CrossRef] [PubMed]
186. Chen, J.; Wang, H.; Hua, C. Electroencephalography based fatigue detection using a novel feature fusion and extreme learning machine. *Cogn. Syst. Res.* **2018**, *52*, 715–728. [CrossRef]
187. Hu, J.; Min, J. Automated detection of driver fatigue based on EEG signals using gradient boosting decision tree model. *Cogn. Neurodyn.* **2018**, *12*, 431–440. [CrossRef]
188. Dimitrakopoulos, G.N.; Kakkos, I.; Dai, Z.; Wang, H.; Sgarbas, K.; Thakor, N.; Bezerianos, A.; Sun, Y. Functional Connectivity Analysis of Mental Fatigue Reveals Different Network Topological Alterations Between Driving and Vigilance Tasks. *IEEE Trans. Neural Syst. Rehabil. Eng.* **2018**, *26*, 740–749. [CrossRef]
189. Hong, S.; Kwon, H.; Choi, S.H.; Park, K.S. Intelligent system for drowsiness recognition based on ear canal electroencephalography with photoplethysmography and electrocardiography. *Inf. Sci.* **2018**, *453*, 302–322. [CrossRef]
190. Li, G.; Chung, W.-Y. Combined EEG-Gyroscope-tDCS Brain Machine Interface System for Early Management of Driver Drowsiness. *IEEE Trans. Hum. Mach. Syst.* **2017**, *48*, 50–62. [CrossRef]
191. Min, J.; Wang, P.; Hu, J. Driver fatigue detection through multiple entropy fusion analysis in an EEG-based system. *PLoS ONE* **2017**, *12*, e0188756. [CrossRef]
192. Awais, M.; Badruddin, N.; Drieberg, M. A Hybrid Approach to Detect Driver Drowsiness Utilizing Physiological Signals to Improve System Performance and Wearability. *Sensors* **2017**, *17*, 1991. [CrossRef]
193. Nguyen, T.; Ahn, S.; Jang, H.; Jun, S.C.; Kim, J.G. Utilization of a combined EEG/NIRS system to predict driver drowsiness. *Sci. Rep.* **2017**, *7*, 43933. [CrossRef]
194. Hu, J. Automated Detection of Driver Fatigue Based on AdaBoost Classifier with EEG Signals. *Front. Comput. Neurosci.* **2017**, *11*, 72. [CrossRef] [PubMed]
195. Chai, R.; Ling, S.H.; San, P.P.; Naik, G.R.; Nguyen, T.N.; Tran, Y.; Craig, A.; Nguyen, H. Improving EEG-Based Driver Fatigue Classification Using Sparse-Deep Belief Networks. *Front. Neurosci.* **2017**, *11*, 103. [CrossRef] [PubMed]
196. Chai, R.; Naik, G.R.; Nguyen, T.N.; Ling, S.H.; Tran, Y.; Craig, A.; Nguyen, H. Driver Fatigue Classification With Independent Component by Entropy Rate Bound Minimization Analysis in an EEG-Based System. *IEEE J. Biomed. Health Inform.* **2017**, *21*, 715–724. [CrossRef]
197. Mu, Z.; Hu, J.; Yin, J. Driving Fatigue Detecting Based on EEG Signals of Forehead Area. *Int. J. Pattern Recognit. Artif. Intell.* **2017**, *31*, 1750011. [CrossRef]
198. Fu, R.; Wang, H.; Zhao, W. Dynamic driver fatigue detection using hidden Markov model in real driving condition. *Expert Syst. Appl.* **2016**, *63*, 397–411. [CrossRef]
199. Ahn, S.; Nguyen, T.; Jang, H.; Kim, J.G.; Jun, S.C. Exploring Neuro-Physiological Correlates of Drivers' Mental Fatigue Caused by Sleep Deprivation Using Simultaneous EEG, ECG, and fNIRS Data. *Front. Hum. Neurosci.* **2016**, *10*, 219. [CrossRef] [PubMed]
200. Huang, K.-C.; Huang, T.-Y.; Chuang, C.-H.; King, J.-T.; Wang, Y.-K.; Lin, C.-T.; Jung, T.-P. An EEG-Based Fatigue Detection and Mitigation System. *Int. J. Neural Syst.* **2016**, *26*, 1650018. [CrossRef] [PubMed]
201. Li, G.; Lee, B.-L.; Chung, W.-Y. Smartwatch-Based Wearable EEG System for Driver Drowsiness Detection. *IEEE Sens. J.* **2015**, *15*, 7169–7180. [CrossRef]
202. Chen, L.-L.; Zhao, Y.; Zhang, J.; Zou, J.-Z. Automatic detection of alertness/drowsiness from physiological signals using wavelet-based nonlinear features and machine learning. *Expert Syst. Appl.* **2015**, *42*, 7344–7355. [CrossRef]

203. Sauvet, F.; Bougard, C.; Coroenne, M.; Lely, L.; Van Beers, P.; Elbaz, M.; Guillard, M.; Leger, D.; Chennaoui, M. In-Flight Automatic Detection of Vigilance States Using a Single EEG Channel. *IEEE Trans. Biomed. Eng.* **2014**, *61*, 2840–2847. [CrossRef] [PubMed]
204. Lee, B.G.; Lee, B.L.; Chung, W.-Y. Mobile Healthcare for Automatic Driving Sleep-Onset Detection Using Wavelet-Based EEG and Respiration Signals. *Sensors* **2014**, *14*, 17915–17936. [CrossRef] [PubMed]
205. Correa, A.G.; Orosco, L.; Laciar, E. Automatic detection of drowsiness in EEG records based on multimodal analysis. *Med. Eng. Phys.* **2014**, *36*, 244–249. [CrossRef] [PubMed]
206. Hu, S.; Zheng, G.; Peters, B. Driver fatigue detection from electroencephalogram spectrum after electrooculography artefact removal. *IET Intell. Transp. Syst.* **2013**, *7*, 105–113. [CrossRef]
207. Picot, A.; Charbonnier, S.; Caplier, A. On-Line Detection of Drowsiness Using Brain and Visual Information. *IEEE Trans. Syst. Man Cybern. Part A Syst. Hum.* **2011**, *42*, 764–775. [CrossRef]
208. Zhao, C.; Zheng, C.; Zhao, M.; Tu, Y.; Liu, J. Multivariate autoregressive models and kernel learning algorithms for classifying driving mental fatigue based on electroencephalographic. *Expert Syst. Appl.* **2011**, *38*, 1859–1865. [CrossRef]
209. Liu, J.; Zhang, C.; Zheng, C. EEG-based estimation of mental fatigue by using KPCA–HMM and complexity parameters. *Biomed. Signal Process. Control.* **2010**, *5*, 124–130. [CrossRef]
210. Gillberg, M.; Kecklund, G.; Åkerstedt, T. Sleepiness and performance of professional drivers in a truck simulator—comparisons between day and night driving. *J. Sleep Res.* **1996**, *5*, 12–15. [CrossRef] [PubMed]
211. Wierwille, W.W.; Ellsworth, L.A. Evaluation of driver drowsiness by trained raters. *Accid. Anal. Prev.* **1994**, *26*, 571–581. [CrossRef]
212. Kamrud, A.; Borghetti, B.; Kabban, C.S. The Effects of Individual Differences, Non-Stationarity, and the Importance of Data Partitioning Decisions for Training and Testing of EEG Cross-Participant Models. *Sensors* **2021**, *21*, 3225. [CrossRef]

An Improved Deep Residual Network Prediction Model for the Early Diagnosis of Alzheimer's Disease

Haijing Sun [1,2], Anna Wang [1,*], Wenhui Wang [1] and Chen Liu [1]

1. College of Information Science and Engineering, Northeastern University, Shenyang 110819, China; seamirror@126.com (H.S.); wenhuiwang@stumail.neu.edu.cn (W.W.); liuchenne@gmail.com (C.L.)
2. College of Information Engineering, Shenyang University, Shenyang 110044, China
* Correspondence: wanganna@mail.neu.edu.cn

Abstract: The early diagnosis of Alzheimer's disease (AD) can allow patients to take preventive measures before irreversible brain damage occurs. It can be seen from cross-sectional imaging studies of AD that the features of the lesion areas in AD patients, as observed by magnetic resonance imaging (MRI), show significant variation, and these features are distributed throughout the image space. Since the convolutional layer of the general convolutional neural network (CNN) cannot satisfactorily extract long-distance correlation in the feature space, a deep residual network (ResNet) model, based on spatial transformer networks (STN) and the non-local attention mechanism, is proposed in this study for the early diagnosis of AD. In this ResNet model, a new Mish activation function is selected in the ResNet-50 backbone to replace the Relu function, STN is introduced between the input layer and the improved ResNet-50 backbone, and a non-local attention mechanism is introduced between the fourth and the fifth stages of the improved ResNet-50 backbone. This ResNet model can extract more information from the layers by deepening the network structure through deep ResNet. The introduced STN can transform the spatial information in MRI images of Alzheimer's patients into another space and retain the key information. The introduced non-local attention mechanism can find the relationship between the lesion areas and normal areas in the feature space. This model can solve the problem of local information loss in traditional CNN and can extract the long-distance correlation in feature space. The proposed method was validated using the ADNI (Alzheimer's disease neuroimaging initiative) experimental dataset, and compared with several models. The experimental results show that the classification accuracy of the algorithm proposed in this study can reach 97.1%, the macro precision can reach 95.5%, the macro recall can reach 95.3%, and the macro F1 value can reach 95.4%. The proposed model is more effective than other algorithms.

Keywords: residual network; Mish; spatial transformer networks; non-local attention mechanism; Alzheimer's disease

1. Introduction

Alzheimer's disease (AD) is a common, irreversible, progressive neurological disease characterized by cognitive impairment, whereby the patient's memory and thinking ability are slowly damaged over time [1,2]. AD is characterized by an insidious onset, slow progression, and irreversible course. Currently, there is no effective treatment that can reverse the damage caused by Alzheimer's disease [3,4]. At present, most patients with clinically diagnosed AD are in the middle or advanced stage, which means that the optimal time for treatment has already passed. Mild cognitive impairment (MCI) is an intermediate state between normal function and AD. It refers to a mild impairment of cognitive and memory functions rather than dementia [5,6]. According to statistics, the conversion rate of people with MCI to AD is significantly higher than that of healthy people [7]. Accurate diagnosis early in the course of the disease may allow patients to initiate preventive and intervention measures to slow or stop the progression of the disease before irreversible brain damage takes place. Therefore, the early and accurate diagnosis of AD has important research significance [8,9].

At present, there are the following three categories of methods for the early diagnosis of AD: diagnostic methods based on clinical symptoms and cognitive function examination scales, biomarker-based detection methods, and neuroimaging-based detection methods [10–12]. The diagnostic method, based on clinical symptoms and a cognitive function examination scale, can be used in the quantitative assessment of cognitive impairment, and has the advantages of easy operation, low cost, and standardized diagnosis. However, due to the lack of objective evidence, it is easy for the diagnosis to be detrimentally influenced by non-pathological subjective factors, which inevitably lead to clinical misdiagnosis. [13–15]. A biomarker-based detection method is used to diagnose the disease and judge the disease stage by measuring biomarker levels in patients. For example, β-amyloid$_{1-42}$ (Aβ_{1-42}), total tau protein (T-tau), and hyperphosphorylated tau (P-tau), the core biomarkers of AD that are mostly used in clinical practice, are derived from CSF and have shown high sensitivity and specificity in the identification of AD patients. Through providing effective diagnosis of AD in its early or asymptomatic stages, this approach may buy time for patients, increasing the effectiveness of treatment and reducing the disease incidence. However, this method cannot be used as a routine detection method due to the difficulty and traumatic nature of obtaining samples for determination of these biochemical indicators [16,17]. This problem can be circumvented when using neuroimage-based diagnostic methods. High-quality medical images, such as those acquired using positron emission computed tomography (PET) and magnetic resonance imaging (MRI), can provide doctors with more sufficient and subtle disease information, help doctors make diagnoses more quickly and accurately, and greatly reduce the misdiagnosis efficiency [18,19]. PET scans are performed after a patient is injected with a radioactive substance to see if there are lesions. However, PET has the disadvantages of poor specificity, low resolution, inaccurate anatomical positioning, and high cost [20]. MRI can clearly show the structure and anatomy of the human brain, which is conducive to the measurement and study of changes during brain atrophy in AD [21,22]. At present, the MRI diagnosis of AD is mainly based on subjective image reading by imaging doctors. This method is time consuming, laborious, and subjective, which will affect the accuracy in making judgments regarding the disease course. Hence, how to address these issues by using a computer to automatically and accurately classify MRI, and then identify MCI and AD has become a hot research topic in recent years [23,24].

In the past ten years, deep learning and machine learning methods have achieved great success in the fields of speech recognition, computer vision, and image and video analysis [25]. More and more studies have applied convolutional neural network (CNN) combined with MRI imaging for the early diagnosis of AD [26]. The traditional CNN network is usually composed of an input layer, hidden layer, and output layer in series. The input layer is responsible for receiving input data [27]. The hidden layer is generally composed of multiple convolutional layers and pooling layers. Its function is to extract the layered features of the input images. This hierarchical structure can gradually extract the high-level features in the image. However, these methods have the following disadvantages: given the depth of the layers in the traditional CNN network structure, excessively deep networks can actually reduce the accuracy of classification to a certain extent [27,28]. Moreover, traditional CNN lacks invariance to the affine transformation of the image. This defect is caused by the CNN default sampling method (matrix sampling). The convolutional layer of traditional CNN cannot satisfactorily extract the long-distance correlation in the feature space. In order to solve the above problems, an improved deep residual network (ResNet) model, combining spatial transformer networks (STN) and a non-local attention mechanism, is proposed for the early diagnosis of AD [29–31].

In this study, our key contributions are given below:

1. We propose a new ResNet model where a new Mish activation function is selected in the ResNet-50 backbone to replace the Relu function;

2. The STN is introduced between the input layer and the improved ResNet-50 backbone. This enhances the spatial invariance of the model;
3. A non-local attention mechanism is introduced between the fourth and fifth stages of the improved ResNet-50 backbone.

2. Related Work

In this section, we review studies related to the early diagnosis of AD. With the increasing attention given to MCI, more and more researchers have proposed new MCI prediction methods [32].

There are diagnostic methods based on the clinical symptom and cognitive function scale. Several AD screening scales commonly used in clinical practice include the clock-drawing test (CDT), mini-mental state examination (MMSE), Montreal cognitive assessment (MOCA), and Alzheimer's disease assessment scale (ADAS-COG), among others. [33–35]. Brodaty H. et al. [36] argued that a clock map is a very effective test screening measure for detecting mild or moderate AD in the clinical population, with very low false-negative and false-positive rates. Pozueta A. et al. [37] proposed that a combination of MMSE and CVLT-LDTR could distinguish PR-AD and S-MCI at the baseline. The analysis of these two neuropsychological predictors is relatively short and may be easily accomplished in a non-specialist clinical setting. Zainal N. et al. [38] proposed that ADAS-COG, which is widely used in clinical trials, may be suitable for an Asian cohort, and is useful for detecting MCI and mild AD. Roman F. et al. [39] proposed that Argentina-type MBT and MMSE were significantly correlated with memory cells and that they were effective tools for detecting MCI. The working characteristics of the MBT are very suitable, more so than those of other commonly used tests for detecting MCI. Carlew A. et al. [40] proposed that detection by MMSE is significantly affected by the disease course, while in the case of MOCA, severe MCI results in insignificant changes. Although statistically significant, the actual clinical significance of the changes in MOCA is unclear. The growing use of MOCA requires further research to understand what constitutes clinically significant changes and whether it is appropriate to track cognitive trajectories.

There are diagnostic methods based on biomarker detection; cerebrospinal fluid (CSF) biomarkers $A\beta_{1-42}$, T-tau, and P-tau are well-validated, and are being increasingly used in clinical practice as tools for the affirmative diagnosis of AD [41]. The long-term stability of core CSF biomarkers in patients with AD provides further support for their use in clinical studies and treatment monitoring in clinical trials [42]. Michael E. et al. [43] proposed that CSF $A\beta_{1-42}$ showed the best diagnostic accuracy among the CSF biomarkers. At a sensitivity of 85%, the specificity in differentiating AD dementia from other diagnoses ranged from 42% to 77%. Geijselaers S. et al. [44] provided further evidence of the relationship between brain insulin signaling and AD pathology. This also highlights the need to consider sex and the APOE ε4 genotype during assessment. Gs A. et al. [45] proposed that blood, urine, saliva, and tears have yielded promising results, and several new molecules have been identified as potential brain biomarkers thanks to the development of new ultra-sensitive techniques. In this review, the authors discuss the advantages and limitations of classic CSF biomarkers for AD, as well as the latest prospects for new CSF candidate biomarkers and alternative substrates. Fossati S. et al. [46] found that plasma tau is higher in AD independently from CSF-tau. Importantly, adding plasma tau to CSF tau or P-tau improves the diagnostic accuracy, suggesting that plasma tau may represent a useful biomarker for AD, especially when added to CSF tau measures. Abe K. et al. [47] found that the present serum biomarker set provides a new, rapid, non-invasive, highly quantitative, and low-cost clinical application for dementia screening, and also suggests an alternative pathway or mechanism by which AD causes neuroinflammation and neurovascular unit damage. Nabers A. et al. [48] used immune infrared sensors to measure the secondary structure distribution of amyloid beta (Aβ) and tau in plasma and cerebrospinal fluid as structure-based biomarkers of AD. In the first diagnostic screening step, structure-based Aβ blood biomarkers support AD recognition with a sensitivity of 90%. In the second diagnostic validation step, the combination of structure-based cerebrospinal fluid biomarkers Aβ and tau allowed the exclusion of false positives, with an overall specificity of 97%.

There are also neuroimage-based detection methods. Basheera S. et al. [49] used a CNN model with inception blocks to extract depth features from gray matter slices for the early prediction of AD. Ji H. et al. [50] mainly studied the early diagnosis of AD using convolutional neural networks. The gray matter and white matter image slices of MRI were used as classification inputs. After a convolution operation combined with the output of deep learning classifier, an ensemble learning method was adopted to improve classification. Tofail B. et al. [51] proposed constructing multiple deep two-dimensional convolutional neural networks (2D-CNNs) to learn various features from local brain images and combine these features with the final classification for AD diagnosis. Subramoniam M. et al. [52] proposed a method for the prediction of AD from MRI based on deep neural networks. The state of image classification networks, such as VGG, residual network (ResNet), etc., with transfer learning, show promising results. The performance of pretrained versions of these networks can be improved by transfer learning. A ResNet-based architecture with a large number of layers was found to give the best result in terms of predicting different stages of the disease. Hussain et al. [53] proposed a model based on 12-layer CNN to use brain MRI data for the dichotomization and detection of AD.

Among the abovementioned methods available for the early diagnosis of AD, the diagnosis method based on MRI has the advantages of non-invasiveness and non-radioactivity, and has become an indispensable technical tool in the clinical and scientific research of AD. In this study, ResNet-50 is used as the backbone network because of its simpler structure, and since the increase in identity mapping does not reduce network performance. The proposed method can extract more information from layers by deepening the network structure through deep ResNet [54,55].

3. Materials and Methods

3.1. Data Selection

The data used in this study come from ADNI (Alzheimer disease neuroimaging initiative) (http://adni.loni.usc.edu (accessed on 16 February 2020)) [56]. Generally, the dataset is divided into the following 3 categories: normal control (NC), mild cognitive impairment (MCI), and Alzheimer's disease (AD). MCI is a major step in the transition from a normal to AD state. We screened a total of 515 samples, which were divided into 55 AD samples, 255 NC samples, and 205 MCI samples. The proportion of men and women in each category was roughly equal. MMSE mainly relies on experienced doctors to ask patients to obtain scale scores. The scale score is a continuous integer from 0 to 30. The higher the score, the healthier the patient, while the lower the score, the more severe the dementia. For NC, the MMSE score is 24–30 and the ADAS-Cog score is <12. For MCI, the MMSE score is 23–30 and the ADAS-Cog score is 7–17. For AD, its MMSE score is 20–26 and the ADAS-Cog score is 12–29 [57]. Information on the collected data is shown in Table 1.

Table 1. Information of subjects from ADNI dataset used in this study.

Dataset	ADNI		
Diagnosis	NC	MCI	AD
Number of samples	255	205	55
Number of female samples	127	103	27
Number of male samples	128	102	28
Age	70.6 ± 5.1	73.8 ± 7.5	78.9 ± 8.6
ADAS-Cog	<12	7–17	12–29
MMSE	24–30	23–30	20–26

3.2. Deep Residual Neural Network

ResNet was proposed by 4 Chinese scientists, including Kaiming He, from the former Microsoft Research Institute, and the proposal of deep ResNet is a milestone event in the history of CNN images. The residual module in the deep ResNet is shown in Figure 1 [58].

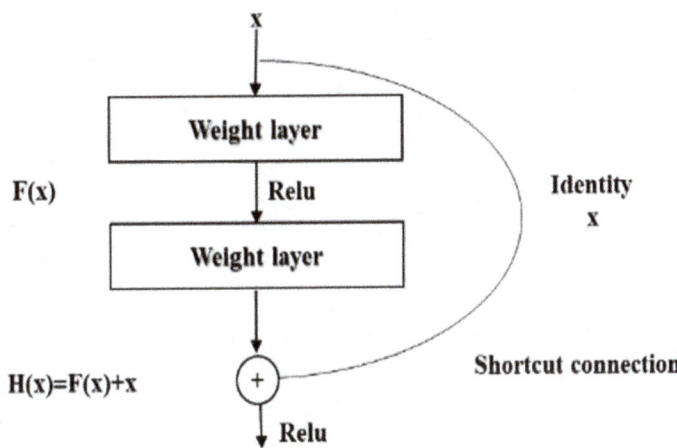

Figure 1. The residual block of the residual network.

In the figure, x is weighted by the first layer, then F(x) + x is obtained after the nonlinear variation in the Relu function and the weighting of the second layer. This is a linear stack, and the two layers constitute a residual learning module. The network composed of residual modules is called ResNet. The difference between the ResNet and the ordinary network is that the jump connection is introduced, which can help the information of the previous residual block flow into the next residual block without obstruction. The problem of vanishing gradient and degradation caused by too deep a network is avoided [58,59].

Since the Relu function often causes the permanent inactivation of neurons, these inactivated neurons will be occupied. Due to the computational resources involved, the ability to extract image features still needs to be improved. In order to make up for the deficiency of Relu, the new activation function Mish was selected to replace the function of Relu in the model. The Mish activation function is expressed as in Equation (1) [60], as follows:

$$f(x) = xtanh(ln(1 + e^x))$$ (1)

The positive value of the Mish activation function can reach any height, avoiding saturation due to capping. Due to the smoothness of the Mish activation curve, better information can be penetrated into the neural network, resulting in better accuracy and generalization. As the depth of the network increases, Mish can better maintain accuracy.

In the deep ResNet-50, the bottleneck residual module is stacked with a 1 × 1 convolution, 3 × 3 convolution, and 1 × 1 convolution. The two 1 × 1 convolutions play the role of decreasing and increasing dimensions, respectively. The bottleneck residual module can greatly improve the computational efficiency and significantly increase the depth of the residual block. The introduction of more Mish activation functions can improve the representation ability of ResNet. The bottleneck residuals module of different layers for the ResNet-50 architecture is expressed in Figure 2 [58–60].

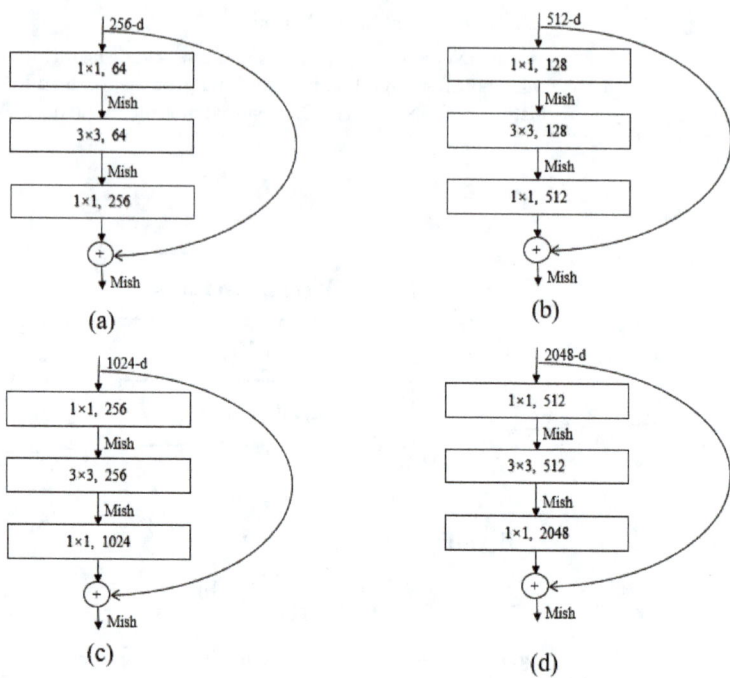

Figure 2. Bottleneck residuals module of different layers for the ResNet-50 architecture. (**a**) Stage 2, (**b**) stage 3, (**c**) stage 4, (**d**) stage 5.

3.3. Spatial Transformer Networks (STN)

STN can adaptively perform spatial transformation. In the case of large spatial differences in the input data, this network can be added to the existing convolutional network to improve the accuracy of classification. The STN network consists of a localization network, a grid generator, and a sampler, as shown in Figure 3 [61].

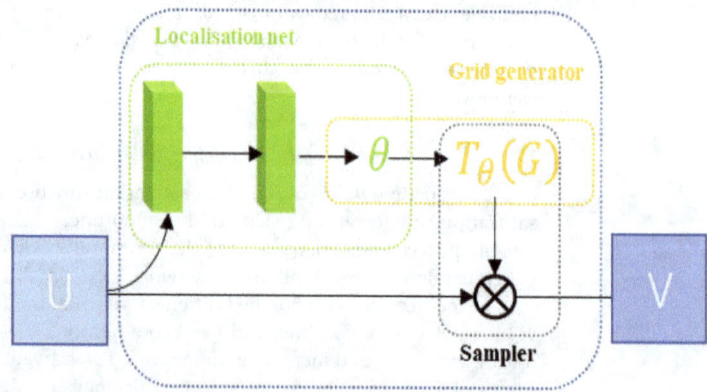

Figure 3. The STN module.

Localization net: localization net is traditional CNN and this is the network used for the regression transformation parameter θ.

Grid generator: the grid generator generates a coordinate network corresponding to each pixel of the output image in the input image.

Sampler: a sampler uses the sampling network and the input element graph as an input, then inputs, then obtains the result after transforming the element graph.

After the input picture is passed through the STN module, the transformed picture is obtained, and the transformed picture is then input into the CNN network. Loss is calculated through the loss function, and the gradient is then calculated to update the θ parameter. Finally, the STN module will learn how to correct the picture [61,62].

3.4. Non-Local Attention Mechanism

The attention mechanism is a general mechanism for information acquisition, which is applied to scenarios where a large number of sources are used to obtain specific critical information and avoid processing all the data. The non-local attention mechanism directly captures remote dependencies by calculating the interaction between any two locations, rather than being limited to adjacent points. The non-local attention mechanism is shown in Figure 4 [63].

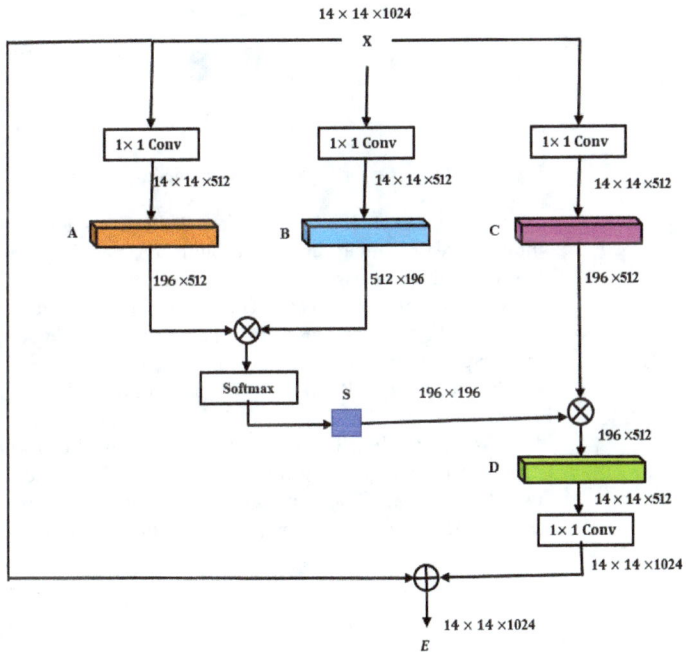

Figure 4. Non-local attention mechanism.

Three feature images, A, B, and C, can be obtained through three 1 × 1 convolutional layers. A and B are multiplied to obtain S using softmax. Then, the product of S and C can be multiplied by the scale coefficient to obtain D, D can be reshaped to the original shape, and then X is added to obtain the final output E. We can see that the value of each position of E is a weighted sum of the original feature and each position. E_j can be written as Equation (2) [63,64].

$$E_j = \alpha \sum_{i=1}^{N}(S_{ji}C_i) + X_i \tag{2}$$

3.5. Proposed Method

In this paper, a new deep ResNet learning method that combines STN and the non-local attention mechanism is proposed. The model uses MRI slices of a large number of subjects to train the network, automatically learns image features, avoiding manual extraction, and then classifies the input images based on these features to obtain diagnosis results for the subject's state. In this study, a new activation function Mish was selected to replace Relu in the traditional ResNet-50 model. This method could solve the problem of local information loss in ordinary CNN and can satisfactorily extract the long-distance correlation in feature space. The framework of the proposed method is shown in Figure 5 [58–65].

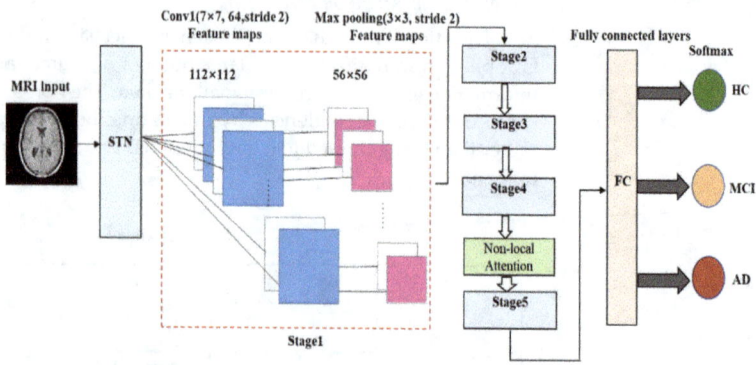

Figure 5. The framework of the proposed method.

A local network is a network used in regression of transformation parameter θ. Its input is a feature image and its output is the spatial transformation of parameter θ through a series of hidden network layers. If a 2D affine transformation is required, θ is the output of a 6-dimensional (2 × 3) vector. The size of θ depends on the type of transformation applied.

A grid generator is used to build a sampling grid according to the predicted transformation parameters. It is the output of a group of points in the input image after sampling and transformation. What the grid generator actually obtains is a kind of mapping relation T_θ [62].

Assuming that the coordinate of each pixel of input image is (x_i^s, y_i^s), the coordinate of each pixel of output image is (x_i^t, t_i^t). The space transformation function T_θ is a two-dimensional affine transformation function. The corresponding relationship between (x_i^s, y_i^s) and (x_i^t, y_i^t) can be written as Equation (3), as follows:

$$\begin{pmatrix} x_i^s \\ y_i^s \end{pmatrix} = T_\theta(G_i) = A_\theta \begin{pmatrix} x_i^t \\ y_i^t \\ 1 \end{pmatrix} = \begin{bmatrix} \theta_{11} & \theta_{12} & \theta_{13} \\ \theta_{21} & \theta_{22} & \theta_{23} \end{bmatrix} \begin{pmatrix} x_i^t \\ y_i^t \\ 1 \end{pmatrix} \quad (3)$$

In Equation (3), S represents the coordinate point of the input feature image, T represents the coordinate point of the output feature image, and A_θ is the output of the local network.

The sampler in STN uses the sampling grid and the input feature map as the input to produce the output. Additionally, it obtains the result after the feature map is transformed. Further, n and m will traverse all coordinates of the original graph U, and U_{nm} refers to the pixel values of a point in the original graph U. Then, x_i^s, y_i^s denotes the coordinates of the corresponding point in the U graph to be found at the ith point in V. The denoted coordinates are those on the U graph. K denotes filling by different methods, usually using bilinear interpolation. The following Equation (4) is obtained [61,62]:

$$V_i = \sum_n \sum_m U_{nm} max(0, 1 - |x_i^s - m|) max(0, 1 - |y_i^s - n|) \quad (4)$$

Integrating the STN module between the input and ResNet allows the network to automatically learn how to transform the feature map, thus helping to reduce the overall cost of network training. We locate the output value in the network, indicating how to transform each item of training data [61–64].

The non-local attention mechanism is embedded as a component in ResNet-50, and new weights are learned in transfer learning so that pretrained weights are not unavailable due to the introduction of new modules [63,65].

The architecture of the proposed method is shown in Table 2 [58].

Table 2. The architecture of the proposed method.

Layer Name	Output Size	Layer
STN	224 × 224	Localization network, grid generator, sampler
Conv1	112 × 112	7 × 7, 64, stride 2
Max pooling	56 × 56	3 × 3, stride 2
Stage 2	56 × 56	$\begin{bmatrix} 1\times1, & 64 \\ 3\times3, & 64 \\ 1\times1, & 256 \end{bmatrix} \times 3$, Mish
Stage 3	28 × 28	$\begin{bmatrix} 1\times1, & 128 \\ 3\times3, & 128 \\ 1\times1, & 512 \end{bmatrix} \times 4$, Mish
Stage 4	14 × 14	$\begin{bmatrix} 1\times1, & 256 \\ 3\times3, & 256 \\ 1\times1, & 1024 \end{bmatrix} \times 6$, Mish
Non-local attention module	14 × 14	Attention × 1
Stage 5	7 × 7	$\begin{bmatrix} 1\times1, & 512 \\ 3\times3, & 512 \\ 1\times1, & 2048 \end{bmatrix} \times 3$, Mish
Average pooling	1 × 1	7 × 7, stride 1
FC, softmax		1000-d

The environment of this experiment is a Linux system, which is designed and realized by the Keras framework, and the model is trained using the Adam optimization algorithm. The experiment steps are as follows:

(1) The experiment uses two-dimensional slices as training data, so it is necessary to slice the three-dimensional MRI coronal plane. In order to ensure that the input image size of the classifier is consistent, this experiment unifies these slices into a size of 224 × 224. The experiment uses the CAT12 toolkit of the SPM12 software to preprocess the images. Image preprocessing includes format conversion, skull stripping, grayscale normalization, MRI slicing, and uniform sizing, etc. The detailed preprocessing process is shown in Figure 6;
(2) The Keras experimental platform was built and the STN + ResNet + attention network model was designed;
(3) The K-fold (K = 5) cross validation method was used to randomly divide the dataset, with 80% used as the training set and 20% used as the test set;
(4) The training set was input into the network for training and the training results were obtained;
(5) The optimal model parameters were saved and tested in the model using the test set data.

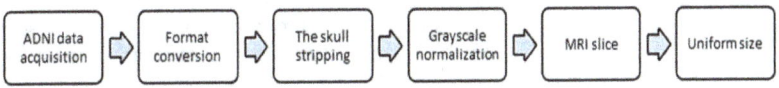

Figure 6. Preprocessing flow chart.

The flow chart with detailed steps is shown in Figure 7.

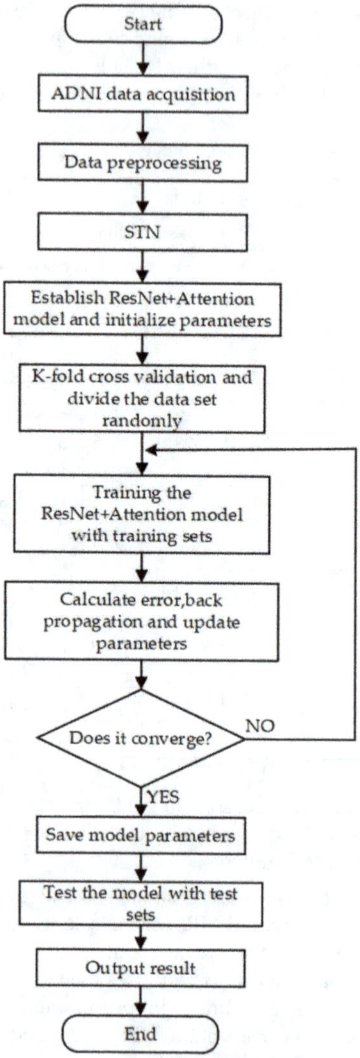

Figure 7. The detailed step flow chart.

4. Experimental Results and Discussion

We considered our result in the context of multi-class classification. The multi-classification data were transformed into two classification problems and a one-vs-rest strategy was adopted—that is, one category comprised positive samples and the other categories comprised negative samples [66–70].

TP_i: the prediction is category i, the reality is category i.
TN_i: the prediction is other classes of category i, the reality is other classes of category i.
FP_i: the prediction is category i, the reality is other classes of category i.
FN_i: the prediction is other classes of category i, the reality is category i.

Each category was taken as a positive sample to calculate the total accuracy, precision, and recall values for each category. The accuracy can be expressed using Equation (5), as follows:

$$Accuracy = \frac{Number\ of\ samples\ correctly\ classified}{Number\ of\ samples\ for\ all\ categories} \quad (5)$$

The precision of a certain category can be understood as predicting the accuracy of the sample, expressed as Equation (6), as follows:

$$Precision_i = \frac{TP_i}{TP_i + FP_i} \quad (6)$$

The recall of a certain category can be understood as the extent to which the sample of category i, which was correctly predicted, covers the sample of category i in the sample set, expressed as Equation (7), as follows:

$$Recall_i = \frac{TP_i}{TP_i + FN_i} \quad (7)$$

To investigate the merits and demerits of classifiers under different categories, a macro average should be introduced. Macro-averaging refers to the mathematical average of the values of each statistical index of all types. Their calculation equations are expressed in Equations (8)–(10), as follows:

$$Precision_{macro} = \frac{\sum_{i=1}^{N} Precision_i}{N} \quad (8)$$

$$Recall_{macro} = \frac{\sum_{i=1}^{N} Recall_i}{N} \quad (9)$$

$$F1_{macro} = \frac{2 Precision_{macro} Recall_{macro}}{Precision_{macro} + Recall_{macro}} \quad (10)$$

The total confusion matrix is obtained by adding the values of each folded confusion matrix. For the convenience of calculating the $Precision_{macro}$, $Recall_{macro}$, and $F1_{macro}$, we use the average confusion matrix of multiple classifications. We divide the value of the total confusion matrix by five to get the average confusion matrix. The model proposed in this study was used for training and testing on the selected ADNI dataset, and the test results are shown in Table 3 [70].

Table 3. Average confusion matrix and experimental results.

Confusion Matrix		Predicted Class			Recall	
		NC	MCI	AD		
Actual Class	NC	51	0	0	1.000	
	MCI	1	39	1	0.951	$Recall_{macro} = 0.953$
	AD	0	1	10	0.909	
Precision		0.981	0.975	0.909	Acc = 0.971	$F1_{macro} = 0.954$
		$Precision_{macro} = 0.955$				

For the purpose of illustrating the effectiveness of the method proposed in this paper, ResNet50 baseline, ResNet50 + Mish, and STN + ResNet50 + Mish were selected to conduct experiments using the same dataset. The $Accuracy$, $Precision_{macro}$, $Recall_{macro}$, and $F1_{macro}$ of each model were, respectively, calculated as shown in Table 4.

Table 4. Performance comparison of the proposed classification method.

Model	Accuracy	Precision$_{macro}$	Recall$_{macro}$	F1$_{macro}$
ResNet50 baseline	0.913 ± 0.035	0.871 ± 0.033	0.887 ± 0.032	0.879
ResNet50 + Mish	0.932 ± 0.032	0.893 ± 0.030	0.924 ± 0.028	0.908
STN + ResNet50 + Mish	0.951 ± 0.021	0.940 ± 0.023	0.939 ± 0.021	0.939
Proposed method	0.971 ± 0.016	0.955 ± 0.015	0.953 ± 0.018	0.954

In this paper, the Accuracy, Precision$_{macro}$, Recall$_{macro}$, and F1$_{macro}$ value of the above models were successively compared and analyzed, as shown in Figure 8.

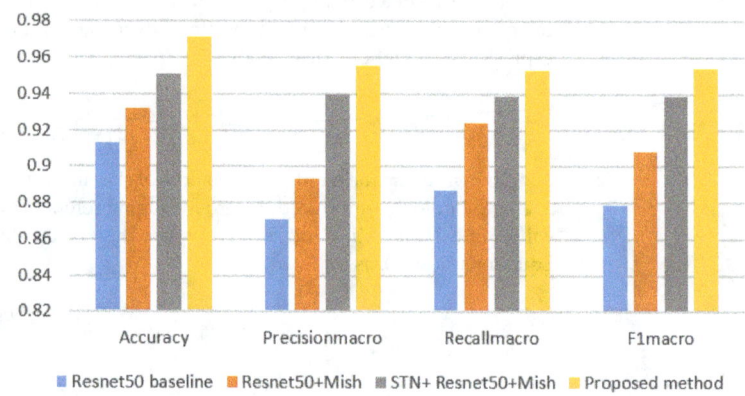

Figure 8. Comparison of the Accuracy, Precision$_{macro}$, Recall$_{macro}$, and F1$_{macro}$ value.

The experimental results show that the method proposed in this article is compared with the other three methods in classification accuracy. There is a big improvement, and the standard deviation of the experimental results is smaller. The experiments show that the Mish activation function is used to replace the Relu function in the model, and the accuracy is increased by 1.9% compared with the baseline. After the introduction of the STN and attention mechanism, the accuracy of the model increased by 5.8%.

5. Conclusions

In this research article, we propose a deep learning model based on ResNet-50 for the early diagnosis of Alzheimer's disease. In the model, a new Mish activation function is selected in the ResNet-50 backbone to replace the Relu function, the STN is introduced between the input layer and the improved ResNet-50 backbone, and a non-local attention mechanism is introduced between the fourth and fifth stages of the improved ResNet-50 backbone. The Mish activation function is boundless (that is, the positive value can reach any height) to avoid saturation due to capping. Theoretically, the slight bias toward the negative values allows for better gradient flows in comparison with the hard zero boundary, as in Relu. Integrating the STN module into the ResNet-50 network allows the network to automatically learn how to transform the feature map, thus helping to reduce the overall cost of network training. The addition of a non-local block attention mechanism module provides a solid improvement. The proposed method was validated using the ADNI experimental dataset and compared with the ResNet-50 baseline, ResNet-50 + Mish, and STN + ResNet-50 + Mish models. The experimental results show that the proposed model is more effective and provides a better robustness for clinical application. The integration with STN enhances the ability of this model to extract network features by improving the spatial invariance of the network. This demonstrates its good recognition effect. The introduction of a non-local block attention mechanism can enhance model robustness. In the end, the experiment results found using the ADNI dataset show that the classification accuracy of the algorithm proposed in this paper reached 97.1%, the macro precision reached 95.5%, the macro recall reached 95.3%, and the macro F1 value reached 95.4%, thus verifying the advantages of the proposed model. The proposed method has high significance in the practical application of AD. The combination of AD susceptibility gene detection and pattern recognition is our future research direction [71].

Author Contributions: Methodology, H.S.; software, H.S.; writing—original draft preparation, H.S.; writing—review and editing, A.W., W.W., and C.L.; supervision, A.W. All authors have read and agreed to the published version of the manuscript.

Funding: This research received no external funding.

Acknowledgments: In this work, the sample data are all derived from the Alzheimer's disease neuroimaging initiative (ADNI) database (http://adni.loni.usc.edu (accessed on 16 February 2020)).

Conflicts of Interest: The authors declare no conflict of interest.

References

1. Lukiw, W.J.; Vergallo, A.; Lista, S.; Hampel, H.; Zhao, Y. Biomarkers for Alzheimer's Disease (AD) and the Application of Precision Medicine. *J. Pers. Med.* **2020**, *10*, 138. [CrossRef] [PubMed]
2. Sabbagh, M.N.; Blennow, K. Peripheral Biomarkers for Alzheimer's Disease: Update and Progress. *Neurol. Ther.* **2019**, *8*, 33–36. [CrossRef]
3. Husain, M. Blood tests to screen for Alzheimer's disease. *Brain* **2021**, *144*, 355–356. [CrossRef] [PubMed]
4. Lane, C.A.; Hardy, J.; Schott, J.M. Alzheimer's disease. *Eur. J. Neurol.* **2018**, *25*, 59–70. [CrossRef] [PubMed]
5. Rma, B.; At, C.; Rrc, D. Alzheimer's disease and other neurodegenerative dementias in comorbidity: A clinical and neuropathological overview. *Clin. Biochem.* **2019**, *73*, 26–31.
6. Delmastro, F.; Di Martino, F.; Dolciotti, C. Cognitive Training and Stress Detection in MCI Frail Older People Through Wearable Sensors and Machine Learning. *IEEE Access* **2020**, *8*, 65573–65590. [CrossRef]
7. Liu, S.Q.; Liu, S.D.; Cai, W.D. Early diagnosis of Alzheimer's disease with deep learning. In Proceedings of the 2014 IEEE 11th International Symposium on Biomedical Imaging (ISBI), Beijing, China, 29 April–2 May 2014; pp. 1015–1018.
8. Brugnolo, A.; Girtler, N.; Pardini, M.; Doglione, E.; Orso, B.; Massa, F.; Donegani, M.I.; Bauckneht, M.; Morbelli, S.; Arnaldi, D.; et al. Brain Resources: How Semantic Cueing Works in Mild Cognitive Impairment due to Alzheimer's Disease (MCI-AD). *Diagnostics* **2021**, *11*, 108. [CrossRef] [PubMed]
9. Guo, M.; Li, Y.; Zheng, W.; Huang, K.; Zhou, L.; Hu, X.; Yao, Z.; Hu, B. A novel conversion prediction method of MCI to AD based on longitudinal dynamic morphological features using ADNI structural MRIs. *J. Neurol.* **2020**, 1–15. [CrossRef] [PubMed]
10. Counts, S.E.; Ikonomovic, M.D.; Mercado, N.; Vega, I.E.; Mufson, E.J. Biomarkers for the Early Detection and Progression of Alzheimer's Disease. *Neurotherapeutics* **2017**, *14*, 35–53. [CrossRef] [PubMed]
11. Hampel, H. Biomarkers for Alzheimer's disease: Academic, industry and regulatory perspectives. *Nat. Rev. Drug Discov.* **2010**, *9*, 560–574. [CrossRef]
12. Zhao, A.; Li, Y.; Yan, Y.; Qiu, Y.; Li, B.; Xu, W.; Wang, Y.; Liu, J.; Deng, Y. Increased prediction value of biomarker combinations for the conversion of mild cognitive impairment to Alzheimer's dementia. *Transl. Neurodegener.* **2020**, *9*, 1–10. [CrossRef] [PubMed]
13. Lonie, J.A.; Tierney, K.M.; Ebmeier, K.P. Screening for mild cognitive impairment: A systematic review. *Int. J. Geriatr. Psychiatry* **2009**, *24*, 902–915. [CrossRef]
14. Choe, Y.M.; Lee, B.C.; Choi, I.-G.; Suh, G.-H.; Lee, D.Y.; Kim, J.W. MMSE Subscale Scores as Useful Predictors of AD Conversion in Mild Cognitive Impairment. *Neuropsychiatr. Dis. Treat.* **2020**, *16*, 1767–1775. [CrossRef]
15. Milian, M.; Leiherr, A.-M.; Straten, G.; Müller, S.; Leyhe, T.; Eschweiler, G.W. The Mini-Cog versus the Mini-Mental State Examination and the Clock Drawing Test in daily clinical practice: Screening value in a German Memory Clinic. *Int. Psychogeriatr.* **2011**, *24*, 766–774. [CrossRef]
16. Inmaculada, L.F.; Inmaculada, C.I.; Aitana, S.E. Transmembrane Amyloid-Related Proteins in CSF as Potential Biomarkers for Alzheimer's Disease. *Front. Neurol.* **2015**, *6*, 125.
17. Delaby, C.; Muñoz, L.; Torres, S. Impact of CSF storage volume on the analysis of Alzheimer's disease biomarkers on an automated platform. *Clin. Chim. Acta* **2019**, *490*, 98–101. [CrossRef] [PubMed]
18. Mohanty, R.; Mårtensson, G.; Poulakis, K.; Rodriguez-Vieitez, E.; Grothe, M.; Nordberg, A.K.; Ferreira, D.; Westman, E. Towards harmonizing subtyping methods for PET and MRI studies of Alzheimer's disease. *Alzheimer's Dement.* **2020**, *16*, e042807. [CrossRef]
19. Ottoy, J.; Niemantsverdriet, E.; Verhaeghe, J.; De Roeck, E.; Struyfs, H.; Somers, C.; Wyffels, L.; Ceyssens, S.; Van Mossevelde, S.; Bossche, T.V.D.; et al. Association of short-term cognitive decline and MCI-to-AD dementia conversion with CSF, MRI, amyloid- and 18F-FDG-PET imaging. *NeuroImage Clin.* **2019**, *22*, 101771. [CrossRef] [PubMed]
20. Pagani, M.; Nobili, F.; Morbelli, S.; Arnaldi, D.; Giuliani, A.; Öberg, J.; Girtler, N.; Brugnolo, A.; Picco, A.; Bauckneht, M.; et al. Early identification of MCI converting to AD: A FDG PET study. *Eur. J. Nucl. Med. Mol. Imaging* **2017**, *44*, 2042–2052. [CrossRef]

21. Choi, B.-K.; Madusanka, N.; Choi, H.-K.; So, J.-H.; Kim, C.-H.; Park, H.-G.; Bhattacharjee, S.; Prakash, D. Convolutional Neural Network-based MR Image Analysis for Alzheimer's Disease Classification. *Curr. Med. Imaging Rev.* **2020**, *16*, 27–35. [CrossRef] [PubMed]
22. Lin, L. Effects of mind body exercise on brain structure and function a systematic review on MRI studies. *Brain Sci.* **2021**, *11*, 205.
23. Ren, F.; Yang, C.; Qiu, Q.; Zeng, N.; Cai, C.; Hou, J.; Zou, Q. Exploiting Discriminative Regions of Brain Slices Based on 2D CNNs for Alzheimer's Disease Classification. *IEEE Access* **2019**, *7*, 181423–181433. [CrossRef]
24. Sumanth, S.; Suresh, A. Survey on identification of Alzheimer disease using magnetic resonance imaging (MRI) images. *Int. J. Innov. Technol. Explor. Eng.* **2019**, *8*, 3564–3570.
25. D'Angelo, G.; Palmieri, F. GGA: A modified Genetic Algorithm with Gradient-based Local Search for Solving Constrained Optimization Problems. *Inf. Sci.* **2020**, *547*, 136–162. [CrossRef]
26. Mehmood, A.; Maqsood, M.; Bashir, M.; Shuyuan, Y. A Deep Siamese Convolution Neural Network for Multi-Class Classification of Alzheimer Disease. *Brain Sci.* **2020**, *10*, 84. [CrossRef] [PubMed]
27. Al-Shoukry, S.; Rassem, T.H.; Makbol, N.M. Alzheimer's Diseases Detection by Using Deep Learning Algorithms: A Mini-Review. *IEEE Access* **2020**, *8*, 77131–77141. [CrossRef]
28. Amini, M.; Pedram, M.; Moradi, A.; Ouchani, M. Diagnosis of Alzheimer's Disease Severity with fMRI Images Using Robust Multitask Feature Extraction Method and Convolutional Neural Network (CNN). *Comput. Math. Methods Med.* **2021**, *2021*, 5514839. [CrossRef] [PubMed]
29. Yang, Q.; Zhou, P. Representation and Classification of Auroral Images Based on Convolutional Neural Networks. *IEEE J. Sel. Top. Appl. Earth Obs. Remote Sens.* **2020**, *13*, 523–534. [CrossRef]
30. Wang, L.; Wang, B.; Zhao, P.; Liu, R.; Liu, J.; Miao, Q. Malware Detection Algorithm Based on the Attention Mechanism and ResNet. *Chin. J. Electron.* **2020**, *29*, 1054–1060. [CrossRef]
31. Yang, M.; Li, D.; Zhang, W. Spatial non-local attention for thoracic disease diagnosis and visualisation in weakly supervised learning. *IET Image Process.* **2019**, *13*, 1922–1930. [CrossRef]
32. Xiao, R.; Cui, X.; Qiao, H.; Zheng, X.; Zhang, Y.; Zhang, C.; Liu, X. Early diagnosis model of Alzheimer's disease based on sparse logistic regression with the generalized elastic net. *Biomed. Signal Process. Control* **2021**, *66*, 102362. [CrossRef]
33. Fortea, J.; Vilaplana, E.; Carmona-Iragui, M. Clinical and biomarker changes of Alzheimer's disease in adults with Down syndrome: A cross-sectional study. *Lancet* **2020**, *395*, 1988–1997. [CrossRef]
34. Cid, R.C.; Crocco, E.; Kitaigorodsky, M.; Beaufils, L.; Peña, P.; Grau, G.; Visser, U.; Loewenstein, D. A Novel Computerized Cognitive Stress Test to Detect Mild Cognitive Impairment. *J. Prev. Alzheimer's Dis.* **2021**, *8*, 135–141. [CrossRef]
35. Suda, S.; Muraga, K.; Ishiwata, A.; Nishimura, T.; Aoki, J.; Kanamaru, T.; Suzuki, K.; Sakamoto, Y.; Katano, T.; Nagai, K.; et al. Early Cognitive Assessment Following Acute Stroke: Feasibility and Comparison between Mini-Mental State Examination and Montreal Cognitive Assessment. *J. Stroke Cerebrovasc. Dis.* **2020**, *29*, 104688. [CrossRef] [PubMed]
36. Brodaty, H.; Moore, C.M. The Clock Drawing Test for dementia of the Alzheimer's type: A comparison of three scoring methods in a memory disorders clinic. *Int. J. Geriatr. Psychiatry* **1997**, *12*, 619–627. [CrossRef]
37. Pozueta, A.; Rodríguez-Rodríguez, E.; Vazquez-Higuera, J.L. Detection of early Alzheimer's disease in MCI patients by the combination of MMSE and an episodic memory test. *BMC Neurol.* **2011**, *11*, 78. [CrossRef] [PubMed]
38. Zainal, N.H.; Silva, E.; Lim, L.L. Psychometric Properties of Alzheimer's Disease Assessment Scale-Cognitive Subscale for Mild Cognitive Impairment and Mild Alzheimer's Disease Patients in an Asian Context. *Ann. Acad. Med. Singap.* **2016**, *45*, 273. [PubMed]
39. Roman, F.; Iturry, M.; Rojas, G.; Barceló, E.; Buschke, H.; Allegri, R.F. Validation of the Argentine version of the Memory Binding Test (MBT) for Early Detection of Mild Cognitive Impairment. *Dement. Neuropsychol.* **2016**, *10*, 217–226. [CrossRef]
40. Carlew, A.; Goette, W.; Womack, K. A-02 Comparing Rate of Change in MoCA and MMSE Scores over Time in an MCI and AD sample. *Arch. Clin. Neuropsychol.* **2020**, *35*, 6.
41. Solje, E.; Benussi, A.; Buratti, E.; Remes, A.; Haapasalo, A.; Borroni, B. State-of-the-Art Methods and Emerging Fluid Biomarkers in the Diagnostics of Dementia—A Short Review and Diagnostic Algorithm. *Diagnostics* **2021**, *11*, 788. [CrossRef]
42. Liguori, C.; Paoletti, F.P.; Placidi, F.; Ruffini, R.; Sancesario, G.M.; Eusebi, P.; Mercuri, N.B.; Parnetti, L. CSF Biomarkers for Early Diagnosis of Synucleinopathies: Focus on Idiopathic RBD. *Curr. Neurol. Neurosci. Rep.* **2019**, *19*, 3. [CrossRef] [PubMed]
43. Michael, E. CSF biomarkers for the differential diagnosis of Alzheimer's disease: A large-scale international multicenter study. *Alzheimer's Dement.* **2015**, *11*, 1306–1315.
44. Geijselaers, S.L.; Aalten, P.; Ramakers, I.H.; De Deyn, P.P.; Heijboer, A.C.; Koek, H.L.; OldeRikkert, M.G.; Papma, J.M.; Reesink, F.E.; Smits, L.L.; et al. Association of Cerebrospinal Fluid (CSF) Insulin with Cognitive Performance and CSF Biomarkers of Alzheimer's Disease. *J. Alzheimer's Dis.* **2017**, *61*, 309–320. [CrossRef]
45. Gs, A.; Sb, B. AD biomarker discovery in CSF and in alternative matrices. *Clin. Biochem.* **2019**, *72*, 52–57.
46. Fossati, S.; Cejudo, J.R.; Debure, L. Plasma tau complements CSF tau and P-tau in the diagnosis of Alzheimer's disease. *Alzheimer's Dement. Diagn. Assess. Dis. Monit.* **2019**, *11*, 483–492. [CrossRef] [PubMed]
47. Abe, K.; Shang, J.; Shi, X.; Yamashita, T.; Hishikawa, N.; Takemoto, M.; Morihara, R.; Nakano, Y.; Ohta, Y.; Deguchi, K.; et al. A New Serum Biomarker Set to Detect Mild Cognitive Impairment and Alzheimer's Disease by Peptidome Technology. *J. Alzheimer's Dis.* **2020**, *73*, 217–227. [CrossRef]

48. Nabers, A.; Hafermann, H.; Wiltfang, J. Aβ and tau structure-based biomarkers for a blood- and CSF-based two-step recruitment strategy to identify patients with dementia due to Alzheimer's disease. *Alzheimer's Dement. Diagn. Assess. Dis. Monit.* **2019**, *11*, 257–263. [CrossRef]
49. Basheera, S.; Ram, M.S.S. A novel CNN based Alzheimer's disease classification using hybrid enhanced ICA segmented gray matter of MRI. *Comput. Med. Imaging Graph.* **2020**, *81*, 101713. [CrossRef]
50. Ji, H.; Liu, Z.; Yan, W.Q.; Klette, R. Early diagnosis of Alzheimer's disease using deep learning. In *ACM International Conference Proceeding Series*; Association for Computing Machinery: New York, NY, USA, 2019; pp. 87–91.
51. Bin Tufail, A.; Ma, Y.-K.; Zhang, Q.-N. Binary Classification of Alzheimer's Disease Using sMRI Imaging Modality and Deep Learning. *J. Digit. Imaging* **2020**, *33*, 1073–1090. [CrossRef]
52. Subramoniam, M.; Aparna, T.R.; Anurenjan, P.R.; Sreeni, K.G. Deep learning based prediction of Alzheimer's disease from magnetic resonance images. *arXiv* **2020**, arXiv:2101.04961v1.
53. Hussain, E.; Hasan, M.; Hassan, S.Z.; Azmi, T.H.; Rahman, A.; Parvez, M.Z. Deep Learning Based Binary Classification for Alzheimer's Disease Detection Using Brain MRI Images. In Proceedings of the 2020 15th IEEE Conference on Industrial Electronics and Applications (ICIEA), Kristiansand, Norway, 9–13 November 2020; pp. 1115–1120.
54. Li, B.; He, Y. An Improved ResNet Based on the Adjustable Shortcut Connections. *IEEE Access* **2018**, *6*, 18967–18974. [CrossRef]
55. Wen, L.; Li, X.; Gao, L. A transfer convolutional neural network for fault diagnosis based on ResNet-50. *Neural Comput. Appl.* **2020**, *32*, 6111–6124. [CrossRef]
56. Available online: http://adni.loni.usc.edu (accessed on 16 February 2020).
57. Liu, M.; Li, F.; Yan, H.; Wang, K.; Ma, Y.; Shen, L.; Xu, M. A multi-model deep convolutional neural network for automatic hippocampus segmentation and classification in Alzheimer's disease. *NeuroImage* **2020**, *208*, 116459. [CrossRef]
58. He, K.; Zhang, X.; Ren, S.; Sun, J. Deep residual learning for image recognition. In Proceedings of the IEEE Conference on Computer Vision and Pattern Recognition, Las Vegas, NV, USA, 27–30 June 2016; pp. 770–778.
59. Zhang, L.; Schaeffer, H. Forward Stability of ResNet and Its Variants. *J. Math. Imaging Vis.* **2020**, *62*, 328–351. [CrossRef]
60. Misra, D. Mish: A self regularized non-monotonic neural activation function. *arXiv* **2019**, arXiv:1908.08681.
61. Lin, C.H.; Lucey, S. Inverse Compositional Spatial Transformer Networks. In Proceedings of the 2017 IEEE Conference on Computer Vision and Pattern Recognition (CVPR), Honolulu, HI, USA, 21–26 July 2017; pp. 2252–2260.
62. Jaderberg, M.; Simonyan, K.; Zisserman, A.; Kavukcuoglu, K. Spatial transformer networks. In *Advances in Neural Information Processing Systems*; MIT Press: Cambridge, MA, USA, 2015; pp. 2017–2025.
63. Wang, X.; Girshick, R.; Gupta, A.; He, K. Non-local Neural Networks. In Proceedings of the 2018 IEEE/CVF Conference on Computer Vision and Pattern Recognition, Salt Lake City, UT, USA, 18–23 June 2018; pp. 7794–7803.
64. Vaswani, A.; Shazeer, N.; Parmar, N. Attention Is All You Need. In *Advances in Neural Information Processing Systems*; MIT Press: Cambridge, MA, USA, 2017; pp. 5998–6008.
65. Li, M.; Li, O.; Liu, G.; Zhang, C. An Automatic Modulation Recognition Method with Low Parameter Estimation Dependence Based on Spatial Transformer Networks. *Appl. Sci.* **2019**, *9*, 1010. [CrossRef]
66. Syed, A.T.; Merugu, S.; Koppula, V.K. Plant recognition using spatial transformer network. *Int. J. Recent Technol. Eng.* **2019**, *7*, 334–336.
67. Chen, D.; Chen, P.; Yu, X.; Cao, M.; Jia, T. Deeply-Learned Spatial Alignment for Person Re-Identification. *IEEE Access* **2019**, *7*, 143698–143692. [CrossRef]
68. Wang, Y.; Liu, X.; Yu, C. Assisted Diagnosis of Alzheimer's Disease Based on Deep Learning and Multimodal Feature Fusion. *Complexity* **2021**, *2021*, 6626728. [CrossRef]
69. Xu, M.; Liu, Z.; Wang, Z.; Sun, L.; Liang, Z. The Diagnosis of Alzheimer's Disease Based on Enhanced Residual Neutral Network. In Proceedings of the 2019 International Conference on Cyber-Enabled Distributed Computing and Knowledge Discovery (CyberC), Guilin, China, 17–19 October 2019; pp. 405–411.
70. Zhu, X.; Cheng, D.; Zhang, Z.; Lin, S.; Dai, J. An Empirical Study of Spatial Attention Mechanisms in Deep Networks. In Proceedings of the 2019 IEEE/CVF International Conference on Computer Vision (ICCV), Seoul, Korea, 27 October–2 November 2019; pp. 6687–6696.
71. D'Angelo, G.; Palmieri, F. Discovering genomic patterns in SARS-CoV-2 variants. *Int. J. Intell. Syst.* **2020**, *35*, 1680–1698. [CrossRef]

Article

Event-Centered Data Segmentation in Accelerometer-Based Fall Detection Algorithms

Goran Šeketa , Lovro Pavlaković, Dominik Džaja, Igor Lacković * and Ratko Magjarević

Faculty of Electrical Engineering and Computing, University of Zagreb, 10000 Zagreb, Croatia; goran.seketa@fer.hr (G.Š.); lovropavlakovic@gmail.com (L.P.); dominik.dzaja@fer.hr (D.D.); ratko.magjarevic@fer.hr (R.M.)
* Correspondence: igor.lackovic@fer.hr

Abstract: Automatic fall detection systems ensure that elderly people get prompt assistance after experiencing a fall. Fall detection systems based on accelerometer measurements are widely used because of their portability and low cost. However, the ability of these systems to differentiate falls from Activities of Daily Living (ADL) is still not acceptable for everyday usage at a large scale. More work is still needed to raise the performance of these systems. In our research, we explored an essential but often neglected part of accelerometer-based fall detection systems—data segmentation. The aim of our work was to explore how different configurations of windows for data segmentation affect detection accuracy of a fall detection system and to find the best-performing configuration. For this purpose, we designed a testing environment for fall detection based on a Support Vector Machine (SVM) classifier and evaluated the influence of the number and duration of segmentation windows on the overall detection accuracy. Thereby, an event-centered approach for data segmentation was used, where windows are set relative to a potential fall event detected in the input data. Fall and ADL data records from three publicly available datasets were utilized for the test. We found that a configuration of three sequential windows (pre-impact, impact, and post-impact) provided the highest detection accuracy on all three datasets. The best results were obtained when either a 0.5 s or a 1 s long impact window was used, combined with pre- and post-impact windows of 3.5 s or 3.75 s.

Keywords: fall detection; event-centered data segmentation; wearable sensors; accelerometer; window duration

1. Introduction

Falls among the elderly population are a major public health problem. Statistics from the World Health Organization (WHO) indicate that around 30% of adults over 65 years of age experience at least one fall per year [1]. Falls are one of the main causes of death in the elderly population [2]. Non-fatal falls also pose a problem because they leave a negative impact on both the physical and psychological health of elderly persons.

Negative consequences of a fall event can be reduced by shortening the time interval during which a person remains involuntary on the ground after the fall [3]. For this purpose, automatic fall detection systems can be used. Although fall detection systems are unable to prevent falls from happening, they can ensure that immediate assistance is provided to the faller by automatically detecting fall events and sending alarms to health professionals or caregivers. Because the faller might be unable to activate an alarm or search for help, it is important that such fall detection systems are automated [4].

Based on the sensor type used to detect falls, automatic fall detection systems are categorized as wearable or non-wearable. Wearable systems are placed on a person's body with sensors that can track motion and gestures. On the other hand, non-wearable systems use sensors placed in a person's environment, such as optical sensors, cameras, and floor sensors, to detect a fall. A review of different fall detection approaches can be found in [5]. A multitude of researchers have focused on wearable systems equipped with accelerometer sensors as they offer several advantages in terms of cost, power efficiency, ease of use, and portability [6]. Our work is also based on wearable accelerometer-based fall detection system records.

The process of accelerometer-based fall detection comprises three stages: data segmentation, feature extraction, and classification. The main goal of the data segmentation stage is to divide a continuous stream of data acquired from the accelerometer into segments, because features for classification can be extracted only from data segments of finite duration. Features are extracted from those data segments and passed to a classifier to discriminate whether the segment contains data from a fall event or from a regular Activity of Daily Living (ADL).

Different features [7] and classification techniques [8] have been explored for use in fall detection systems. In our previous work, we analyzed the performance of fall detection systems using different classification techniques: threshold-based classification [9,10] and different Machine Learning (ML) classifiers [11]. However, only a few research publications so far have focused on the data segmentation stage, although it significantly affects the systems performance in terms of power efficiency and detection accuracy [12,13].

Two approaches for data segmentation are used in fall detection research. In the first approach, a sliding window of a fixed duration (with or without overlap) is applied to the input data stream. The sliding window duration defines boundaries of a data segment from which further feature extraction and classification is performed. A description of fall detection systems that utilize sliding windows for data segmentation can be found in [14–17]. In the second approach, a trigger is initially set to detect a potential fall event in an input data stream by searching for acceleration peaks above a predefined threshold value. When a potential fall event is detected, one or multiple window(s) placed around this event determine data segments for further feature extraction and classification. Because a sudden change in acceleration is sensed in most falls at the moment a person hits the ground, with this approach, features are extracted from data segments centered around that potential impact point. This type of segmentation is thus called event-centered data segmentation.

Studies have shown advantages of using event-centered data segmentation over sliding windows. In [18], the performance of event-centered data segmentation with one window around a potential fall event was compared to sliding window segmentation for different window sizes. They found that the event-centered data segmentations performed slightly better than the sliding window based data segmentation. Putra et al. [19] proposed a fall detection system based on event-centered data segmentation with three windows. To evaluate the performance of the proposed system, they also measured performance when two different sliding window segmentation methods were used (with and without overlapping windows). They found that the event-centered segmentation outperformed sliding window segmentation while significantly reducing the computational cost.

The same as in [18], researchers in [20–22] also employed a single window for event-centered data segmentation. Another approach was used in [19,23–26], where data segmentation was based on multiple windows. Using more than one segmentation window is justified by an idea that in spite of the variable and irregular nature and typology of falls, they can be decomposed as a sequence of typical "stages" or phases. With this approach, the intention is to align data segmentation windows with different fall phases and thus extract more specific features for use in the classification stage.

Although event-centered data segmentation is regularly implemented in fall detection systems, no research so far has explored how different configurations of data segmentation windows affect the performance of the system in terms of detection accuracy. The aim of this paper is to fill this gap by comparing fall detection classifier performance in the case of implementation of either one, two, or three windows for event-centered data segmentation and to propose the optimal duration for each of these windows.

The remainder of the paper is organized as follows: Section 2 describes the methodology, followed by results in Section 3. A discussion of the results is provided in Section 4.

Finally, Section 5 concludes the paper and points out the important practical implications of this study.

2. Materials and Methods

In our research, we implemented a fall detection testing environment, as shown in Figure 1. We used three publicly available datasets with fall and ADL records gathered from young participants in a controlled environment while wearing an acceleration sensor attached to the waist. Consequently, each record from the datasets contains only one fall or ADL activity. We first take fall and ADL data records from selected datasets and search for potential fall events. For each detected potential fall event, a part of the record before and after the event is extracted. Data segmentation with different window configurations is then applied to this event-centered data record. From there, data segments are obtained, and a set of features is calculated for each segment. Finally, a classifier is used to distinguish fall from ADL events, and its performance in terms of detection accuracy is evaluated. These steps are described in more detail in the following sections. For all the calculation and analyses in this study we used Matlab R2020b.

Figure 1. Architecture of the implemented testing environment for fall detection.

2.1. Fall Model

Although falls are diverse in etiologies (causes), circumstances, characteristics, and clinical consequences, a fall can generally be defined as "an unexpected event in which the person comes to rest on the ground, floor, or lower level" [27]. For research purposes, falls are usually described as a sequence of multiple phases. Models with different numbers of phases have been proposed [28–30], but a model with three phases is most widely accepted.

A fall starts when a person loses balance and starts an uncontrolled descent towards the ground that can no longer be recovered by protective strategies. The period between the start of the fall and the body impact on a lower surface is often called the pre-impact or falling phase. During this phase, the acceleration towards the ground is in most cases less than 9.81 $\frac{m}{s^2}$ (1 g), but it can be influenced by balance recovery attempts such as stepping strategies or grabbing on to other objects. The total duration of this phase depends on the circumstances and the balance recovery strategies employed by the faller.

The moment when a person hits the ground or some other lower surface for the first time is considered the beginning point of the impact phase. This moment usually causes an abrupt change of the acceleration direction. The magnitude of acceleration change depends on falling dynamics and type of ground surface.

At the end of the impact phase, the person is lying or sitting on the ground or other lower surface. This phase is called the rest phase. If the person is unable to move due to the fall, no significant changes in acceleration magnitude can be observed in this phase. However, this is not the case if the person makes attempts to recover from the fall.

An example of a fall event measured with a tri-axial accelerometer is shown in Figure 2. The figure displays measurements from three accelerometer axes combined into a single value called *Acceleration Vector Magnitude (AVM)*. AVM is calculated according to Equation (1):

$$AVM[i] = \sqrt{(a_x[i])^2 + (a_y[i])^2 + (a_z[i])^2}, \quad (1)$$

where i is the current data sample and a_x, a_y, and a_z represent, respectively, the acceleration signals in the x, y, and z axes of the sensor. Accelerations and the *AVM* value are thereby expressed in g units (1 g = 9.81 $\frac{m}{s^2}$).

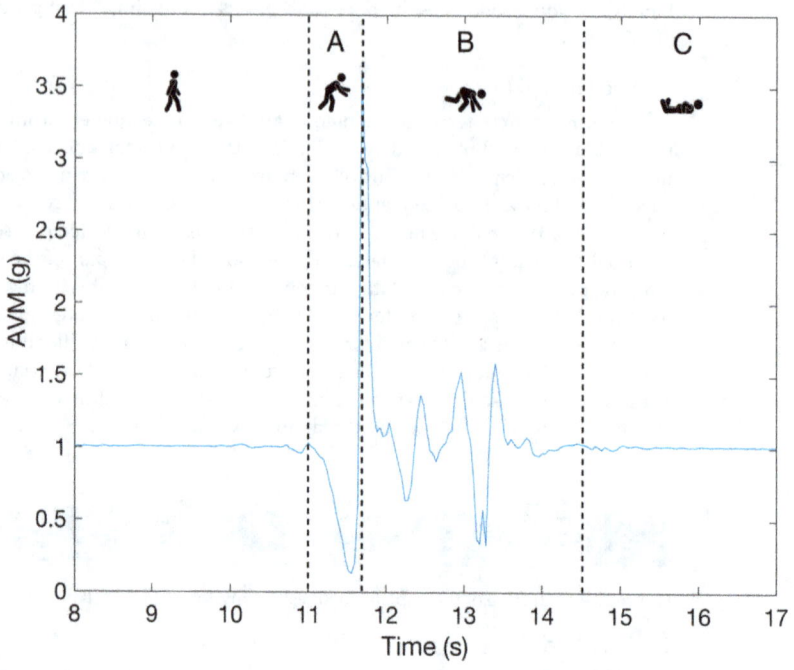

Figure 2. An example of a fall signal with three phases: A is the pre-fall phase, B is the impact phase, and C is the rest phase.

2.2. Datasets

Three publicly available datasets that contain acceleration measurements of falls and ADL were used in this research: ErciyesUni [17], FallAllD [31], and SisFall [32]. For all three datasets, young subjects performed a variety of simulated falls and ADL in a controlled environment while wearing accelerometer sensors attached to different body parts. In this study, we used only records from the waist sensor because this position was used by all three datasets.

Fall detection systems are mainly intended for use by elderly populations, but recording unintentional falls from elderly people in real life is a complex task. Because real-life falls are rare events, recording them is both time consuming and costly [33]. The FARSEEING consortium, consisting of 10 partners from 5 EU countries, succeeded in recording 300 real-world fall events with inertial sensors over 4 years (from January 2012 to December 2015) [34]. From this collaborative project, a subset of 20 falls is publicly available. So far, no open datasets are available that contain a significant number of real life elderly falls. Therefore, the majority of studies still use data from simulated falls of young healthy subjects recorded in a safe environment [35].

A separate record was created for each performed ADL or fall. In this way, each record stored in the dataset contains only one type of fall or ADL and is uniquely labeled with an anonymized subject identifier, activity type (e.g., frontal fall to the knees, ADL sitting down on a chair, etc.), and trial number. Besides these common characteristics, datasets were created by different research groups and with distinct experimental protocols.

The ErciyesUni dataset contains sensor measurements from 17 subjects (age: 19–27, weight: 47–92 kg, height: 157–184 cm), acquired while they performed a set of scripted ADL and simulated falls. In total, the dataset contains 1360 ADL and 1700 fall records. Every subject performed 16 types of ADL and 20 different types of falls with 5 repetitions while wearing 6 sensing units (Xsens MTw Motion Tracking Kit, Xsens, Enschede, The Netherlands). Those sensing units measured accelerations of different body parts by accelerometers (measurement range ±16 g, sampling frequency 25 Hz). They were worn by the subjects attached to different body parts: head, chest, waist, wrist, tight, and ankle. In this work, we used data from the waist worn sensing unit in order to process signals from the same sensor position because signals from that position are present in all three selected datasets.

FallAllD is a dataset of falls and ADL records simulated by 15 volunteering participants. Each participant performed 35 types of simulated falls and 44 types of ADL. The average age, height, and weight of participants were 32 years, 171 cm, and 67 kg, respectively. The participants were asked to wear a sensing unit around their neck and wrist, and attached to the waist while performing predefined movements. Each sensing unit was equipped with four sensors: an accelerometer, a gyroscope, a magnetometer, and a barometer. For our study, we used acceleration data from the sensing unit attached to the waist. The measurement range of the employed accelerometer was ± 8 g and the sampling frequency was 238 Hz.

The SisFall dataset was acquired by SISTEMIC group (University of Antioquia, Medellin, Colombia). This dataset contains measurements from a group of 15 elderly subjects and a group of 23 young adults. For this study, we used fall and ADL data collected from young subjects only (age 25.0 ± 8.6 years, height 165.7 ± 9.3 cm, weight 57.7 ± 15.5 kg) because the elderly group did not perform simulated falls. Acceleration and angular velocity measurements were acquired with an inertial sensor unit (Shimmer sensing, Ireland) while subjects wore the sensor attached to their waist and performed a set of 15 different types of falls and 19 types of ADL. In total, 2707 ADL data records and 1798 fall data records were acquired. Acceleration was measured with two accelerometers embedded on the Shimmer sensing unit: ADXL345 (measurements range ± 16 g) and MMA851Q (measurements range ± 8 g). A sampling frequency of 200 Hz was employed for acceleration measurements. For this study, we selected data from the accelerometer ADXL345 due to the larger measurement range.

From all three datasets, we excluded data records that contained physically not interpretable data and were therefore most likely caused by a measurement/sensor error. All falls and ADL data with the maximal value of AVM larger than 30 g and all falls data with maximal peak value lower than 1.1 g were excluded from further analysis. The constraint of 30 g was chosen because the accelerometer measurement range in the employed datasets was ± 16 g (SisFall and ErciyesUni) and ± 8 g (FallAllD). So, even if acceleration values from the top of these ranges (16 g and 8 g) would have been recorded during a fall or ADL in all three axes, the value of AVM calculated according to Equation (1) would be less than 30 g. We chose the value of 1.1 g to discard all fall records in which potentially no fall was recorded because this value is just slightly larger than AVM recorded during rest (1 g) and at the same time far enough from the minimal recorded acceleration peak of 1.6 g, which was found in a study on real world falls [36]. We discarded 7 falls and 3 ADL from the ErciyesUni dataset due to these criteria. Example of such signals are shown in Figure 3.

Additionally, to ensure that the time span of the records was long enough for data segmentation, only fall records with the largest AVM peak recorded more than 5 s before the end of the signal record were taken into consideration. In total, 49 fall records from the SisFall dataset did not satisfy this criteria and they were not used in this research. From the FallAllD dataset, all records satisfied the criteria.

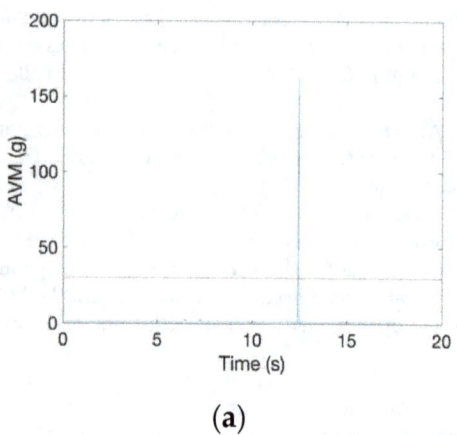 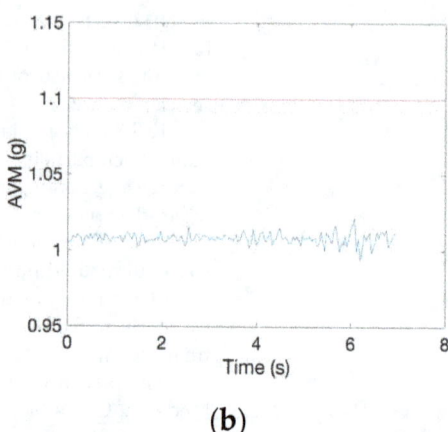

(a) (b)

Figure 3. Examples of fall records in the ErciyesUni dataset excluded from further analysis due to: (**a**) the maximal *AVM* peak value larger than 30 g and (**b**) the maximal *AVM* peak value lower than 1.1 g.

2.3. Potential Fall Event Detection

The main goal of potential fall event detection is to detect changes in acceleration that might come from a fall. By detecting a potential fall event, only a preselection of data is made; all potential fall events are further processed for the decision as to whether they actually come from a fall or from some fall-like ADL. A potential fall event detection algorithm has to be simple, fast, and able to accurately identify all fall events while rejecting ADL as much as possible. This way, the computational cost of the system is reduced because the more complex ML based algorithm is utilized only for fall-like events while most of the ADL is already rejected. Another benefit of this approach is that it provides a center point for data segmentation based on extracting features from specific fall phases.

Potential fall event detection is based on detecting a sudden and large increase of acceleration magnitude in the input signal that can be observed during fall impact [26]. The impact is the most prominent part of a fall signal measured with accelerometer sensors. In the impact phase, when the faller hits the ground or some other lower level surface, an abrupt change of the direction in acceleration signals occurs. This change is due to the breaking acceleration opposite to the initial fall direction.

During a fall, multiple high acceleration peaks may be produced as a result of the protective actions the person performs to avoid or reduce the consequences of the impact. Examples are protective arm movements, falling to knees to break the fall in two parts, or holding on to objects to slow down the fall [28]. During a fall, a person can also hit other objects. The presence of multiple acceleration peaks in a fall signal may cause detection of multiple possible fall events, thus making the alignment of fall phases more difficult. Examples of two acceleration signals measured during a broken fall to the knees from the ErciyesUni dataset are presented in Figure 4. The figure shows records of the same type of fall simulated by two subjects. In these falls, subjects first fell to their knees and then continued to fall until their chest touched the ground. In the first example, the maximal *AVM* peak occurred during the initial impact to the knees, while in the second example, a larger *AVM* peak, was measured when the upper part of the body impacted with ground.

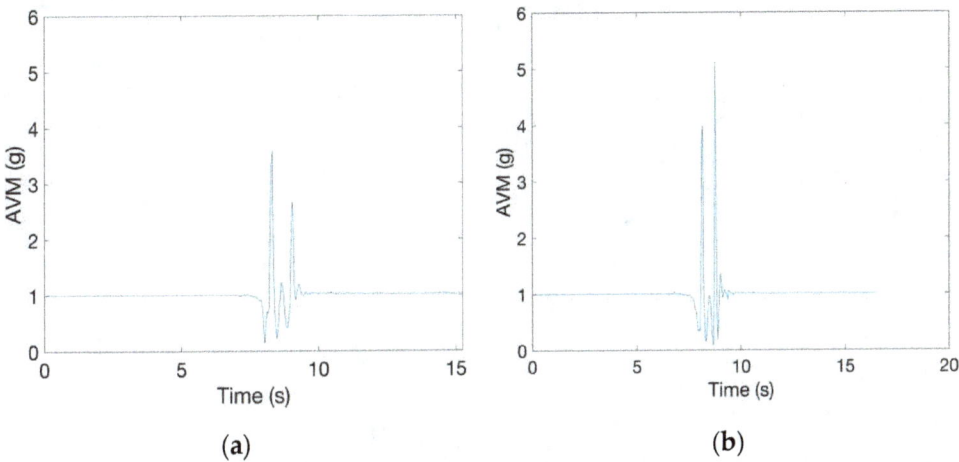

Figure 4. Examples of the same fall type from the ErciyesUni dataset simulated by two subjects: (**a**) the impact to the knees produces larger AVM peak than the impact of the body to the ground; (**b**) the AVM peak is larger when the upper part of the body impacts the ground.

Methods for event detection that avoid multiple-peak problems have been proposed in the literature [19,20,37,38]. They are all based on similar reasoning. Because falling down is a single event that happens suddenly, a fall-like event should not have traits of repetitiveness and can be characterized as an acceleration peak higher than a predefined threshold followed by a period without peaks larger than the threshold. We implemented a potential fall event detector following this idea.

Firstly, we calculated the AVM for each data sample. If the AVM value exceeded a fixed threshold, we analyzed further data in the period after the sample that was larger than the threshold. Then, if the AVM value of all data points in that period were lower than the threshold, a potential fall event was detected.

We had to choose the duration of the period in which we looked for further peaks after the AVM acceleration peak. A similar method for event detection was used in a previous study [37] and yielded good results with a time period of 2.5 s, so we chose 2.5 s as the time period in which we look for further peaks after the acceleration peak. In order to find the best thresholds for each dataset, we tested the method of potential fall detection with a range of threshold values for all fall records. The threshold values were varied from 0 to 5 g with a step of 0.005 g. Only those potential fall events detected after the largest AVM peak in fall records were labeled as true fall events. This criterion was set because the FallAllD and SisFall datasets contain ADL activities in fall records prior to the fall event. An example of a fall record where a potential fall event is detected during ADL before the fall is shown in Figure 5. By using that additional criterion, we ensure that a potential fall event detected in the ADL part of a fall record is correctly labelled as a false fall event.

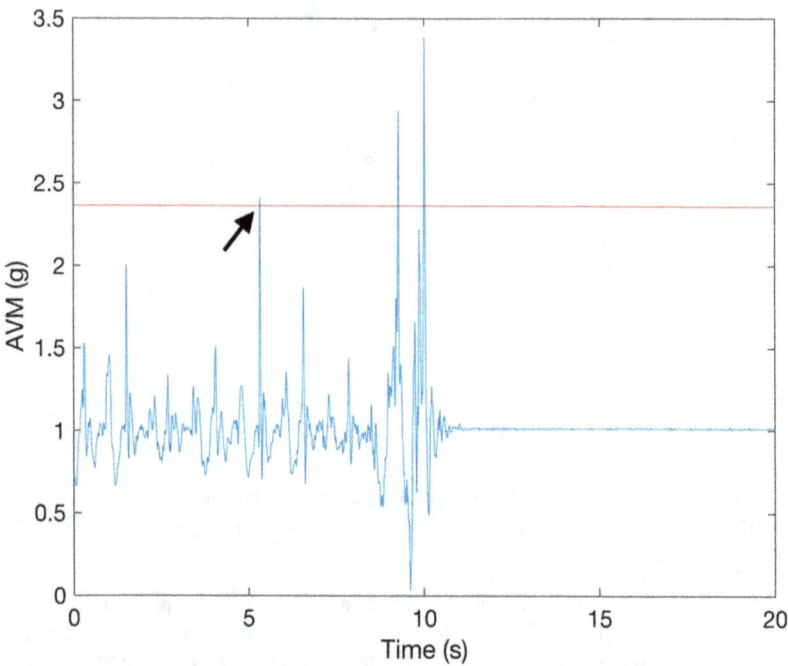

Figure 5. An example of a fall record from the FallAllD dataset that contains an ADL before the fall. The arrow indicates the point in the signal where the ADL causes detection of a false potential fall event.

We selected the largest threshold for which in all fall records at least one true positive event was detected. Choosing the largest threshold minimizes the number of false alarms with ADL data. The thresholds chosen for each dataset are as follows:

- ErciyesUni: 1.330 g;
- FallAllD: 2.360 g;
- SisFall: 1.775 g.

Using this method, we detected potential fall events from ADL and fall records. We then extracted data of each potential fall event containing 4 s of data both before and after the event into a new record (event-centered data record). All event-centered data records that were taken from ADL dataset records were labeled as ADL. Additionally, all parts of the records from fall signals occurring before the largest peak were labeled as ADL (because they were triggered by an activity before the fall, as discussed previously). Only event-centered data records from falls that are detected after the largest AVM peak were labeled as falls.

The maximal period of 4 s was chosen for data extraction because of the limitations in data from the public datasets used in this study. Namely, those datasets provide records of falls and ADL with limited duration. For this research, it is beneficial to have as much data as possible available before and after each potential fall event in both fall and ADL records. The duration of 4 s was chosen to provide a fair amount of time for data segmentation analysis while preventing too many ADL and fall records being discarded due to a lack of data (to short signal records) being available for analysis.

The final number of event-centered data records chosen for further processing is listed in Table 1. For comparison, Table 1 also contains the number of records that would be available if all potential fall events were used, neglecting the criterion of minimal time for analysis (limit 0 s). The number of data records that would be available with a time limit of 5 s is also given. Raising the limit from 4 s to 5 s would lead to a significant reduction of available data from the SisFall dataset and therefore we found it not acceptable in our study.

Table 1. The number of event-centered data records referred to the minimal time available before and after a potential fall event.

Dataset	Minimal Time Available (s)	Number of Fall Records	Number of ADL Records
ErciyesUni	0	1460	914
	4	1454	904
	5	1448	883
FallAllD	0	314	472
	4	301	368
	5	300	335
SisFall	0	1823	1308
	4	1649	945
	5	1433	667

2.4. Event-Centered Data Segmentation

When a potential fall event is detected, a single window or multiple windows before and after the event are used to define boundaries of the data segments from which features for classification are calculated. So defined data segments should contain characteristics of the entire fall or of specific fall phases. There are, however, multiple window configurations that can be used to extract these data segments. The aim of this research was to explore how these window configurations in the data segmentation stage influence performance of the fall detection system and to find the best performing one. Performance was thereby measured by the ability of the system to correctly detect falls when they really occurred while avoiding raising false alarms for ADL.

We used the model presented in Figure 6 to create different configurations of windows with varying durations.

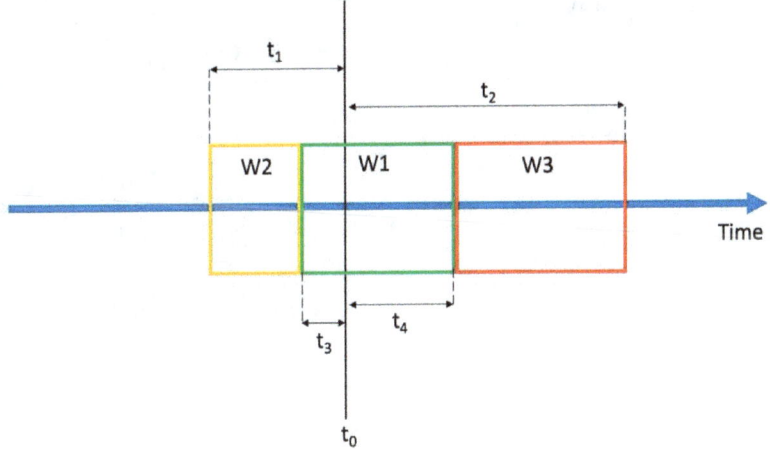

Figure 6. The model for testing different window configurations in event-centered data segmentation; t_0 marks the occurrence of a potential fall event. Parameters t_{1-4} determine the time between t_0 and the beginning or the end of a window.

The model consists of three sequential and coupled windows labeled W1, W2, and W3, and 4 timing parameters labeled t_1, t_2, t_3, and t_4. Each window spans a segment of input data. Parameters t_{1-4} determine the time between the beginning or the end of a window and the detected potential fall event at time, t_0. The impact window, W1, spans between $(t_0 - t_3)$ and $(t_0 + t_4)$, the pre-impact window, W2, spans between $(t_0 - t_3)$ and $(t_0 - t_1)$, and finally the post-impact window, W3, spans between $(t_0 + t_4)$ and $(t_0 + t_2)$. By varying the criteria for parameter inclusion and duration, different configurations of windows can be created, as shown in Table 2.

Table 2. Criteria for parameters to form specific data segmentation window configurations for testing.

Number of Windows in Configuration	Window Configurations	Criteria for Parameters
1	W1	$t_1 = t_3$ AND $t_2 = t_4$
2	W1 & W2	$t_2 = t_4$ AND $t_1 > t_3$ AND ($t_3 > 0$ OR $t_4 > 0$)
	W1 & W3	$t_1 = t_3$ AND $t_2 > t_4$ AND ($t_3 > 0$ OR $t_4 > 0$)
	W2 & W3	$t_3 = 0$ AND $t_4 = 0$ AND $t_1 > 0$ AND $t_2 > 0$
3	W1 & W2 & W3	$t_1 > 0$ AND $t_2 > 0$ AND $t_1 > t_3$ AND $t_2 > t_4$ AND ($t_3 > 0$ OR $t_4 > 0$)

Parameters t_1 and t_2 were varied from 0 to 4 s, with a step size of 0.5 s. For each value of t_1, parameter t_3 was changed from 0 to t_1, with steps of 0.25 s. Similarly, t_4 was varied in range from 0 to t_2 for each value of t_2 in steps of 0.25 s. All possible combinations of parameter values $t_{1;4}$ were tested. The maximal window duration is limited to 4 s due to the available duration of data in the event-centered data records. This issue was discussed in Section 2.3.

2.5. Feature Extraction

We calculated a set of features from each data segment provided by event-centered data segmentation. Features should gather distinctive parameters that are used by the classifier to differentiate between falls and ADL. The set of features we chose for this work is commonly used in fall detection research [18]. In total, eight features were calculated for each segment from tri-axial acceleration data (a_x, a_y, a_z) or AVM according to Equations (2)–(9). All features and variables used to calculate them were expressed in g units (1 g = 9.81 $\frac{m}{s^2}$).

$$\overline{AVM} = \frac{1}{N}\sum_{i=1}^{N} AVM[i] \quad (2)$$

$$AVM_{max} = \max_{i=1,2,...N} AVM[i] \quad (3)$$

$$AVM_{min} = \min_{i=1,2,...N} AVM[i] \quad (4)$$

$$AVM_{range} = AVM_{max} - AVM_{min} \quad (5)$$

$$s_N = \sqrt{\frac{1}{N}\sum_{i=1}^{N}(AVM[i] - \overline{AVM})^2} \quad (6)$$

$$SMA = \sum_{i=1}^{N}(|a_x[i]| + |a_y[i]| + |a_z[i]|) \quad (7)$$

$$AAMV = \frac{1}{N}\sum_{i=1}^{N}|AVM[i+1] - AVM[i]| \quad (8)$$

$$AVM_{rms} = \sqrt{\sum_{i=1}^{N}\left(a_x[i]^2 + a_y[i]^2 + a_z[i]^2\right)} \quad (9)$$

where N is the number of samples in a data record, $\overline{AVM}$ is the mean, and s_N is the standard deviation of all AVM samples in a record. The maximal and the minimal values and the difference between the maximal and minimal values (range) of AVM samples in a record are given by Equations (3)–(5), respectively. The *Summed Magnitude Area* (SMA) is the sum of the absolute values of the acceleration components in all three axes in a record, and it is calculated according to Equation (7). The *Average Absolute Acceleration Magnitude* (AAMV) is calculated according to Equation (8) as a difference between two consecutive AVM samples. Finally, AVM_{rms} is calculated as a square root of the sum of squared acceleration values in all three axes (Equation (9)).

Although orientation of the sensor can be estimated from tri-axial accelerometer data, features based on orientation were not used in this study. Estimation of orientation assumes a known orientation of the accelerometer sensor axes with respect to the wearer's body. In a real life application of a fall detection system, this would require a user to always wear the sensor at a predefined orientation. This reduces the usability of the system and therefore we preferred solutions that do not depend on posture information.

2.6. Classification and Performance Evaluation

For the training of the machine learning algorithm, segments from each event-centered data record were individually labeled as either a fall or an ADL.

We used the fitcsvm function from MATLAB's Statistics and Machine Learning Toolbox to implement an SVM classifier. Previous works in the field of fall detection systems have shown good performance results for the SVM classifier [11,39]. Basically, SVM tries to find the best hyperplane that maximizes the margins between each of the classes. Several hyperparameters affect the classification result with the SVM classifier: *C*, *gamma*, and *kernel*. We standardized the features and used the radial basis function *kernel*. Hyperparameter value *C* for the SVM classifier was set to 1. The parameter *gamma* was automatically set to an appropriate value by the software using a heuristic procedure.

We employed five-fold cross validation to evaluate the performance of the classifier. All data records were randomly partitioned into five portions. Then four portions were utilized as training data and one portion as testing data. This was repeated five times until each portion was used as the testing set. Averaged test results over all iterations were taken.

The following metrics were used to evaluate the test results:

$$F_{score} = \frac{2TP}{2TP + FP + FN} \tag{10}$$

$$AMR_{type} = \frac{FN_{type}}{FN + TP} \tag{11}$$

$$AFPR_{type} = \frac{FP_{type}}{FP + TN} \tag{12}$$

where TP, FP, FN, TN, FN_{type}, and FP_{type} are defined as follows:

- TP = number of all true positive records; a data record is determined as a TP if it is labeled and detected as a fall;
- FP = number of all false positive records; a data record is determined as an FP if it is labeled as an ADL and detected as a fall;
- FN = number of all false negative records; a data record is determined as an FN if it is labeled as a fall and detected as an ADL;
- TN = number of all true negative records; a data record is determined as a TN if it is labeled as an ADL and detected as an ADL;
- FN_{type} = number of FN records for a particular type of fall;
- FP_{type} = number of FP records for a particular type of ADL.

F_{score} is a harmonic mean of sensitivity and precision and is often used as a single standard measure for evaluation of fall detection systems [33,40,41]. AMR_{type} (from Activity Miss Rate) and $AFPR_{type}$ (from Activity False Positive Rate) express percentage of records from a particular ADL or fall type that are misclassified. Thereby, AMR_{type} is the percentage of falls of one type that are not detected and $AFPR_{type}$ is the percentage of ADL of a single type that are detected as falls.

3. Results

The performance of the SVM classifier was evaluated with different configurations of windows in the data segmentation process. A total of 6560 classification results per dataset were obtained for all combinations of window parameter values t_{1-4}.

The highest classifier performances achieved when using one, two, and three windows for data segmentation are listed in Table 3. Firstly, subsets of all results relevant to each window combination were extracted. The criteria for parameters t_{1-4} given in Table 2 were used to obtain each subset. For example, to acquire the subset of all results when one window is used, all combinations were selected for which t_1 is equal to t_3 and t_2 is equal to t_4. This subset then contains results of classification when window W1 with different durations, defined by t_3 and t_4, are used. The highest classifier performance reported in Table 3 is then simply the maximal value of the F_{score} achieved in the subset.

Table 3. The maximal F_{score} achieved for each configuration of data segmentation window.

Number of Windows in Configuration	Window Configurations	Max F_{score} ErciyesUni (%)	Max F_{score} FallAllD (%)	Max F_{score} SisFall (%)
1	W1	99.2	89.5	94.2
2	W1 & W2	99.5	94.0	97.3
	W1 & W3	99.6	93.0	97.1
	W2 & W3	99.3	92.5	96.5
3	W1 & W2 & W3	99.7	96.1	98.4

The results show that the highest classification performance is achieved when all three windows, W1–W3, were used for data segmentation. This combination has the highest maximal achieved F_{score} in all three datasets (99.7% in the ErciyesUni dataset, 96.1% in the FallAllD dataset, and 98.4% in the SisFall dataset). Generally, the lowest scores in all three datasets are obtained when only one window is used.

The values of parameters t_{1-4}, for which maximal F_{score} are achieved with data segmentation based on three windows, are listed in Table 4. Because the results differ between datasets, we explored whether a range of parameters can be found that performs well in all datasets.

Table 4. Values of parameters t_{1-4} for which the best performance is achieved for each dataset when three windows are used for segmentation.

Dataset	t_1 (s)	t_2 (s)	t_3 (s)	t_4 (s)
ErciyesUni	4	3.5	0.5	0.5
FallAllD	3	4	0.5	0.25
SisFall	4	3.5	0.5	0.25

The size of each window for data segmentation is determined by a pair of parameters: W1 (t_3, t_4), W2 (t_2, t_4), W3 (t_1, t_3). The maximal F_{score} for all tested combinations of parameter pairs were calculated for every dataset. An average of scores from all three datasets is shown in Figure 7. All scores are color coded to facilitate the analysis, where darker green is showing better scores while darker red is showing low values in scoring.

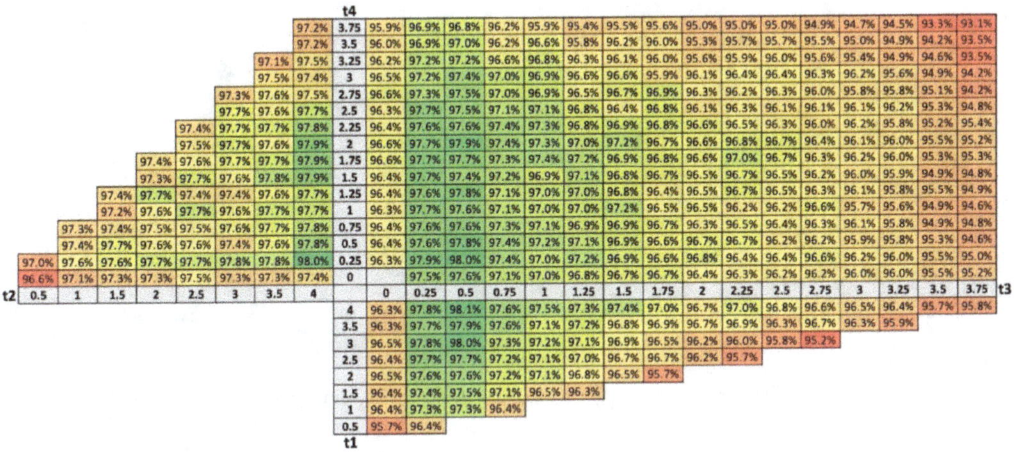

Figure 7. The average of maximal F_{score} from all datasets for each pair of parameters (t_3, t_4), (t_2, t_4), (t_1, t_3). Scores are color coded where darker green is showing higher scores while darker red is showing lower scores.

The best results in the three window-based data segmentation approaches were obtained when parameters t_1 and t_2 were set to the maximal value tested, 4 s, and when the t_3 and t_4 values were either 0.25 s or 0.5 s. Because these parameters define the duration of the segmentation windows, as stated in Section 2.4, we can express these results in terms of window duration. Thus, the best results were obtained for a shorter duration of the impact window, W1 (0.5 s or 1 s), and a longer duration of the pre-impact and post-impact windows, W2 and W3 (3.5 s or 3.75 s).

4. Discussion

In this study, we implemented a testing environment for a fall detection system in order to explore how the configuration of windows used in event-centered data segmentation affects the detection accuracy. Configurations of one to three windows with varying window durations were used at the data segmentation stage. Performance of an SVM classifier was evaluated with F_{score} metrics for all configurations.

The results from Table 3 show that the highest F_{score} is achieved when three windows are used for event-centered data segmentation. In the ErciyesUni dataset, the difference between the performances achieved with one, two, and three windows was small, and all of the scores were higher than 99%. In the FallAllD and SisFall datasets, the difference was more prominent and the highest achieved scores were lower than in the ErciyesUni dataset. Overall performances differ between datasets due to the heterogeneity of fall and ADL types present in each dataset. Figures 8 and 9 show the AMR_{type} and $AFPR_{type}$ of activities for the configuration where the highest F_{score} is achieved with three windows for data segmentation. Similar activities were grouped together for a better overview. Some of the ADL types that caused false positive alarms in the FallAllD and SisFall dataset, such as turning in bed, failed attempt to get up from a chair, and walking up stairs, are not present in the ErciyesUni dataset. ErciyesUni does not contain any falls that follow an ADL (such as falls during walking, jogging, or sitting). The lack of ADL and fall types that are more difficult for classification in ErciyesUni may be the cause of the better scores achieved compared to the FallAllD and SisFall datasets. Heterogeneity of data between datasets has been the focus of some previous studies [2,35,42–44], which have shown that the type of activities contained in datasets for fall detection differs significantly. Moreover, difference between falls and ADL types contained in the datasets is one of the factors that explains the difference in the threshold values for potential fall event detection presented in Section 2.3.

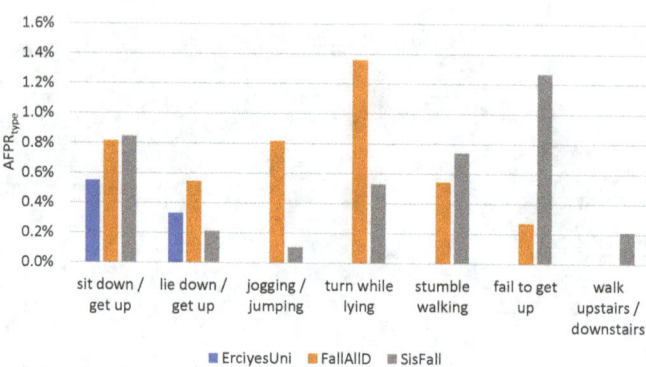

Figure 8. Percentage of all ADL misclassified as fall, grouped by ADL types ($AFPR_{type}$).

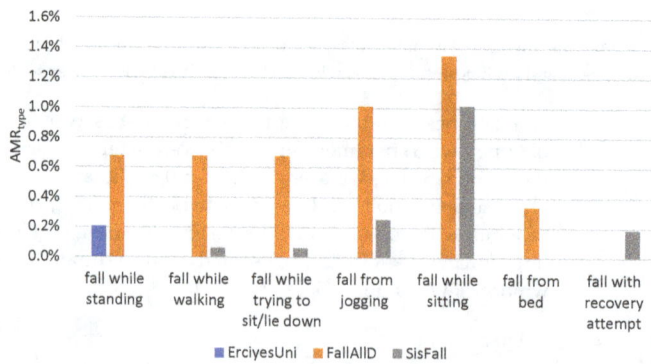

Figure 9. Percentage of all falls misclassified as ADL, grouped by fall types (AMR_{type}).

Data segmentation approaches for fall detection have been explored in previous studies. In their study, Putra et al. [19] compared an event-centered data segmentation approach with sliding window segmentation. They found that event-centered data segmentation based on three windows outperformed segmentation with a single sliding window in terms of computational efficacy and detection accuracy. In [18], detection accuracy between a single window for event-centered data segmentation was compared to data segmentation with an overlapping sliding window. On the other hand, instead of comparing performance between the sliding window and the event-centered data segmentation approach, we focused on finding the best performing configuration of windows for the event-centered segmentation. To the best of our knowledge, our study is the first to compare the usage of one, two, and three windows in event-centered data segmentation.

Further, we analyzed the effect of window durations on the system's performance when a configuration of three windows for data segmentation is used. Figure 7 shows the F_{score} values achieved for parameter pairs that define each window: W1 (t_3, t_4), W2 (t_2, t_4), W3 (t_1, t_3). Thereby, the F_{score} value represents the average of the highest scores from all three datasets used in the study. As shown in the figure, for parameter t_3, better scores are achieved when using lower values (0.25 s and 0.5 s). This is the parameter that defines the duration of window W1 in the period before a potential fall event and therefore incudes the impact peak. For parameter t_1, the best results were achieved with longer values (maximal tested value of 4 s). This means that longer durations of W2 that capture activity before the fall are favored (short t_3 and long t_1 values). As with t_1, longer values of t_2, close to 4 s, performed best. With parameter t_4, similar scores are achieved in a range of values lower that approximately 2.5 s. This parameter defines the amount of post-impact data included in window W1 as well as the starting point and duration of window W3. In one way, lower values of t_4 reduce the amount of post-impact data to interfere with impact focused window W1 and enable a longer duration of W2 for gathering data during rest after the fall. On the other hand, longer values of t_4 provide a time offset for the beginning of window W2 after the impact, so that less intermediate post-impact data is included in the rest analysis. The choice of the value of the parameter t_4 is therefore a compromise. Nevertheless, lower values for t_4 (less than 0.5 s) provided slightly better results.

To summarize, in our study, the best results were obtained when parameters t_{1-4} were set to values listed in the first row of Table 5. Because these parameters define the duration of segmentation windows, as described in Section 2.4, we can also express our results in terms of window durations. Hence, when three sequential windows for event-centered data segmentation are used, we recommend a shorter duration of impact window W1 (0.5 s or 1 s) and longer durations of pre- and post-impact windows W2 and W3 (3.5 s or 3.75 s).

Table 5. Duration of data segmentation windows used in previous research compared to the ranges recommended in this work.

Study	t_1 (s)	t_2 (s)	t_3 (s)	t_4 (s)
our study	4	4	0.25 or 0.5	0.25 or 0.5
Putra et al. [19]	1	2	0	1
Hsieh et al. [24]	0.3281	2.5	0.07815	0.0781 or 0.156 [1]
Zurbuchen et al. [25]	rest of the record [2]	rest of the record [2]	1.5	0.25

[1] depends on the event peak amplitude; longer duration is used for peak amplitudes < 6 g. [2] value of t_1 and t_2 depends on the duration of the record after the window around the event is formed.

Event-centered data segmentation with three windows has been utilized in previous studies with different window durations. In [19], pre-impact, impact, and post-impact windows of 1 s were used around the impact peak. Hsieh et al. [24] presented an adaptive approach where the duration of the impact window depended on the amplitude of the largest acceleration peak on record. In [25], an impact window of 1.5 s before and a window of 0.5 s after the largest acceleration magnitude was taken. Two additional windows were then placed before and after the impact window. In Table 5, the durations of the windows used in the aforementioned studies are expressed with parameters t_{1-4} for easier comparison to our results.

An analysis of the effect of the size of windows on fall detection accuracy was previously performed by [18]. They measured performance of a fall detection system with event-centered data segmentation using a single window of varying duration. The best results were achieved when they used a window of 3 s centered around the potential fall event. On the contrary, the focus of our study was in finding the best performing durations of each of three windows, because they showed better detection accuracy compared to using a single window.

For the purpose of this study, we employed three publicly available datasets with acceleration data from young subjects performing simulated falls and ADL. That is a limitation of our research because fall detection systems are aimed at assisting the elderly population. Some of the research indicates that the patterns of falls experienced by elderly people is similar to simulated falls from young subjects [45,46]. Acquiring data from elderly people that experience falls in real life situations is challenging, and only a few researchers have worked to acquire them [26,34,47–49]. Those acquired datasets are not publicly available.

Another limitation of this study is that we had to restrict our analysis of window durations to 4 s due to the length of data available in each fall or ADL record. The best results for window lengths of t_1 and t_2 were found to be at the maximal explored value of 4 s. In our future work, we plan to create a database of simulated falls and ADL activities with data records of sufficient duration to analyze longer ranges of window sizes.

Based on our findings for the parameter t_4 value, we plan to explore a more complex model of windows for data segmentation. With that model, two additional parameters will be introduced so that configurations with overlapping or separated windows can be investigated as well.

5. Conclusions

Data segmentation is an important part of automatic fall detection systems because it affects the overall detection accuracy. In this work, we explored different window configurations that can be used with event-centered data segmentation. A fall detection system based on an SVM classifier was built, and three publicly available datasets with fall and ADL records were used for the test. We compared the fall detection classifier's performance in the case of implementation with either one, two, or three windows for event-centered data segmentation. We found that using three windows for data segmentation yields better fall detection performance than using one or two windows. Finally, we analyzed a range of window durations and found that the best results were obtained with a shorter duration of impact window, W1 (0.5 s or 1 s), and a longer durations of pre- and post-impact windows, W2 and W3 (3.5 s or 3.75 s). These findings can be used as a guideline for implementing event-centered data segmentation in fall detection systems.

Author Contributions: Conceptualization, G.Š. and R.M.; methodology, G.Š., L.P., and I.L.; investigation, G.Š. and D.D.; writing–original draft preparation, G.Š.; writing–review and editing, I.L. and R.M.; supervision, I.L. and R.M. All authors have read and agreed to the published version of the manuscript.

Funding: This research received no external funding.

Institutional Review Board Statement: Not applicable.

Informed Consent Statement: Not applicable.

Data Availability Statement: Not applicable.

Conflicts of Interest: The authors declare no conflict of interest.

References

1. WHO. Falls Fact Sheet. Available online: https://www.who.int/news-room/fact-sheets/detail/falls (accessed on 22 May 2021).
2. Casilari, E.; Santoyo-Ramón, J.A.; Cano-García, J.M. On the Heterogeneity of Existing Repositories of Movements Intended for the Evaluation of Fall Detection Systems. *J. Healthc. Eng.* **2020**, *2020*. [CrossRef]
3. Igual, R.; Medrano, C.; Plaza, I. Challenges, Issues and Trends in Fall Detection Systems. *Biomed. Eng. Online* **2013**, *12*, 1–24. [CrossRef]
4. Mauldin, T.R.; Canby, M.E.; Metsis, V.; Ngu, A.H.H.; Rivera, C.C. Smartfall: A Smartwatch-Based Fall Detection System Using Deep Learning. *Sensors* **2018**, *18*, 3363. [CrossRef]
5. Stavropoulos, T.G.; Papastergiou, A.; Mpaltadoros, L.; Nikolopoulos, S.; Kompatsiaris, I. Iot Wearable Sensors and Devices in Elderly Care: A Literature Review. *Sensors* **2020**, *20*, 2826. [CrossRef]
6. Singh, A.; Rehman, S.U.; Yongchareon, S.; Chong, P.H.J. Sensor Technologies for Fall Detection Systems: A Review. *IEEE Sens. J.* **2020**, *20*, 6889–6919. [CrossRef]
7. Pannurat, N.; Thiemjarus, S.; Nantajeewarawat, E. Automatic Fall Monitoring: A Review. *Sensors* **2014**, *14*, 12900–12936. [CrossRef] [PubMed]
8. Vallabh, P.; Malekian, R. Fall Detection Monitoring Systems: A Comprehensive Review. *J. Ambient Intell. Humaniz. Comput.* **2018**, *9*, 1809–1833. [CrossRef]
9. Razum, D.; Seketa, G.; Vugrin, J.; Lackovic, I. Optimal Threshold Selection for Threshold-Based Fall Detection Algorithms with Multiple Features. In Proceedings of the 2018 41st International Convention on Information and Communication Technology, Electronics and Microelectronics, MIPRO, Opatija, Croatia, 21–25 May 2018.
10. Šeketa, G.; Vugrin, J.; Lacković, I. Optimal Threshold Selection for Acceleration-Based Fall Detection. In Proceedings of the International Conference on Biomedical and Health Informatics, Las Vegas, NV, USA, 4–7 March 2018; Volume 66.
11. Zulj, S.; Seketa, G.; Lackovic, I.; Magjarevic, R. Accuracy Comparison of Ml-Based Fall Detection Algorithms Using Two Different Acceleration Derived Feature Vectors. In Proceedings of the World Congress on Medical Physics and Biomedical Engineering, Prague, Czech Republic, 3–8 June 2018; Volume 68.
12. Bulling, A.; Blanke, U.; Schiele, B. A Tutorial on Human Activity Recognition Using Body-Worn Inertial Sensors. *ACM Comput. Surv.* **2014**, *46*, 1–33. [CrossRef]

13. Banos, O.; Galvez, J.M.; Damas, M.; Pomares, H.; Rojas, I. Window Size Impact in Human Activity Recognition. *Sensors* **2014**, *14*, 6474–6499. [CrossRef]
14. Hussain, F.; Hussain, F.; Ehatisham-Ul-Haq, M.; Azam, M.A. Activity-Aware Fall Detection and Recognition Based on Wearable Sensors. *IEEE Sens. J.* **2019**, *19*, 4528–4536. [CrossRef]
15. Saleh, M.; Jeannes, R.L.B. Elderly Fall Detection Using Wearable Sensors: A Low Cost Highly Accurate Algorithm. *IEEE Sens. J.* **2019**, *19*, 3156–3164. [CrossRef]
16. Yacchirema, D.; de Puga, J.S.; Palau, C.; Esteve, M. Fall Detection System for Elderly People Using IoT and Ensemble Machine Learning Algorithm. *Pers. Ubiquitous Comput.* **2019**, *23*, 801–817. [CrossRef]
17. Özdemir, A.T.; Barshan, B. Detecting Falls with Wearable Sensors Using Machine Learning Techniques. *Sensors* **2014**, *14*, 10691–10708. [CrossRef] [PubMed]
18. Liu, K.C.; Hsieh, C.Y.; Huang, H.Y.; Hsu, S.J.P.; Chan, C.T. An Analysis of Segmentation Approaches and Window Sizes in Wearable-Based Critical Fall Detection Systems with Machine Learning Models. *IEEE Sens. J.* **2020**, *20*, 3303–3313. [CrossRef]
19. Putra, I.P.E.S.; Brusey, J.; Gaura, E.; Vesilo, R. An Event-Triggered Machine Learning Approach for Accelerometer-Based Fall Detection. *Sensors* **2018**, *18*, 20. [CrossRef]
20. Shahzad, A.; Kim, K. FallDroid: An Automated Smart-Phone-Based Fall Detection System Using Multiple Kernel Learning. *IEEE Trans. Ind. Inform.* **2019**, *15*, 35–44. [CrossRef]
21. Wang, G.; Li, Q.; Wang, L.; Zhang, Y.; Liu, Z. Elderly Fall Detection with an Accelerometer Using Lightweight Neural Networks. *Electronics* **2019**, *8*, 1354. [CrossRef]
22. Palmerini, L.; Bagalà, F.; Zanetti, A.; Klenk, J.; Becker, C.; Cappello, A. A Wavelet-Based Approach to Fall Detection. *Sensors* **2015**, *15*, 11575–11586. [CrossRef]
23. Palmerini, L.; Klenk, J.; Becker, C.; Chiari, L. Accelerometer-Based Fall Detection Using Machine Learning: Training and Testing on Real-World Falls. *Sensors* **2020**, *20*, 6479. [CrossRef] [PubMed]
24. Hsieh, C.Y.; Liu, K.C.; Huang, C.N.; Chu, W.C.; Chan, C.T. Novel Hierarchical Fall Detection Algorithm Using a Multiphase Fall Model. *Sensors* **2017**, *17*, 307. [CrossRef] [PubMed]
25. Zurbuchen, N.; Wilde, A.; Bruegger, P. A Machine Learning Multi-Class Approach for Fall Detection Systems Based on Wearable Sensors with a Study on Sampling Rates Selection. *Sensors* **2021**, *21*, 938. [CrossRef]
26. Scheurer, S.; Koch, J.; Kucera, M.; Bryn, H.; Bärtschi, M.; Meerstetter, T.; Nef, T.; Urwyler, P. Optimization and Technical Validation of the AIDE-MOI Fall Detection Algorithm in a Real-Life Setting with Older Adults. *Sensors* **2019**, *19*, 1357. [CrossRef]
27. Lamb, S.E.; Jørstad-Stein, E.C.; Hauer, K.; Becker, C. Development of a Common Outcome Data Set for Fall Injury Prevention Trials: The Prevention of Falls Network Europe Consensus. *J. Am. Geriatr. Soc.* **2005**, *53*, 1618–1622. [CrossRef] [PubMed]
28. Becker, C.; Schwickert, L.; Mellone, S.; Bagalà, F.; Chiari, L.; Helbostad, J.L.; Zijlstra, W.; Aminian, K.; Bourke, A.; Todd, C.; et al. Vorschlag Für Ein Mehrphasensturzmodell Auf Der Basis von Sturzdokumentationen Mit Am Körper Getragenen Sensor. *Z. Gerontol. Geriatr.* **2012**, *45*, 707–715. [CrossRef]
29. Noury, N.; Poujaud, J.; Cousin, P.; Poujaud, N. Biomechanical Analysis of a Fall: Velocities at Impact. In Proceedings of the 38th Annual International Conference of the IEEE Engineering in Medicine and Biology Society, EMBS, Orlando, FL, USA, 16–20 August 2016; Institute of Electrical and Electronics Engineers Inc.: Piscataway, NJ, USA, 2016; Volume 2016-October, pp. 561–565.
30. Pierleoni, P.; Belli, A.; Palma, L.; Pellegrini, M.; Pernini, L.; Valenti, S. A High Reliability Wearable Device for Elderly Fall Detection. *IEEE Sens. J.* **2015**, *15*, 4544–4553. [CrossRef]
31. Saleh, M.; Abbas, M.; le Jeannes, R.B. FallAllD: An Open Dataset of Human Falls and Activities of Daily Living for Classical and Deep Learning Applications. *IEEE Sens. J.* **2021**, *21*, 1849–1858. [CrossRef]
32. Sucerquia, A.; López, J.D.; Vargas-Bonilla, J.F. SisFall: A Fall and Movement Dataset. *Sensors* **2017**, *17*, 198. [CrossRef] [PubMed]
33. Broadley, R.W.; Klenk, J.; Thies, S.B.; Kenney, L.P.J.; Granat, M.H. Methods for the Real-World Evaluation of Fall Detection Technology: A Scoping Review. *Sensors* **2018**, *18*, 2060. [CrossRef]
34. Klenk, J.; Schwickert, L.; Palmerini, L.; Mellone, S.; Bourke, A.; Ihlen, E.A.F.; Kerse, N.; Hauer, K.; Pijnappels, M.; Synofzik, M.; et al. The FARSEEING Real-World Fall Repository: A Large-Scale Collaborative Database to Collect and Share Sensor Signals from Real-World Falls. *Eur. Rev. Aging Phys. Act.* **2016**, *13*, 1–7. [CrossRef]
35. Casilari, E.; Santoyo-Ramón, J.A.; Cano-García, J.M. Analysis of Public Datasets for Wearable Fall Detection Systems. *Sensors* **2017**, *17*, 1513. [CrossRef]
36. Bourke, A.K.; Klenk, J.; Schwickert, L.; Aminian, K.; Ihlen, E.A.F.; Helbostad, J.L.; Chiari, L.; Becker, C. Temporal and Kinematic Variables for Real-World Falls Harvested from Lumbar Sensors in the Elderly Population. In Proceedings of the 37th Annual International Conference of the IEEE Engineering in Medicine and Biology Society, EMBS, Milan, Italy, 25–29 August 2015; Institute of Electrical and Electronics Engineers Inc.: Piscataway, NJ, USA, 2015; Volume 2015-November, pp. 5183–5186.
37. Abbate, S.; Avvenuti, M.; Bonatesta, F.; Cola, G.; Corsini, P.; Vecchio, A. A Smartphone-Based Fall Detection System. *Pervasive Mob. Comput.* **2012**, *8*, 883–899. [CrossRef]
38. Villar, J.R.; de la Cal, E.; Fañez, M.; González, V.M.; Sedano, J. User-Centered Fall Detection Using Supervised, on-Line Learning and Transfer Learning. *Prog. Artif. Intell.* **2019**, *8*, 453–474. [CrossRef]
39. Aziz, O.; Musngi, M.; Park, E.J.; Mori, G.; Robinovitch, S.N. A Comparison of Accuracy of Fall Detection Algorithms (Threshold-Based vs. Machine Learning) Using Waist-Mounted Tri-Axial Accelerometer Signals from a Comprehensive Set of Falls and Non-Fall Trials. *Med. Biol. Eng. Comput.* **2017**, *55*, 45–55. [CrossRef] [PubMed]

40. Luna-Perejón, F.; Domínguez-Morales, M.J.; Civit-Balcells, A. Wearable Fall Detector Using Recurrent Neural Networks. *Sensors* **2019**, *19*, 4885. [CrossRef]
41. Althobaiti, T.; Katsigiannis, S.; Ramzan, N. Triaxial Accelerometer-Based Falls and Activities of Daily Life Detection Using Machine Learning. *Sensors* **2020**, *20*, 3777. [CrossRef] [PubMed]
42. Šeketa, G.; Pavlaković, L.; Žulj, S.; Džaja, D.; Lacković, I.; Magjarević, R. Comparison of Human Fall Acceleration Signals Among Different Datasets. In Proceedings of the International Conference on Biomedical and Health Informatics, Chicago, FL, USA, 19–22 May 2019; Volume 74.
43. Casilari, E.; Lora-rivera, R.; García-lagos, F. A Study on the Application of Convolutional Neural Networks to Fall Detection Evaluated with Multiple Public Datasets. *Sensors* **2020**, *20*, 1466. [CrossRef]
44. Igual, R.; Medrano, C.; Plaza, I. A Comparison of Public Datasets for Acceleration-Based Fall Detection. *Med. Eng. Phys.* **2015**, *37*, 870–878. [CrossRef]
45. Jämsä, T.; Kangas, M.; Vikman, I.; Nyberg, L.; Korpelainen, R. Fall Detection in the Older People: From Laboratory to Real-Life. *Proc. Est. Acad. Sci.* **2014**, *63*, 253. [CrossRef]
46. Kangas, M.; Vikman, I.; Nyberg, L.; Korpelainen, R.; Lindblom, J.; Jämsä, T. Comparison of Real-Life Accidental Falls in Older People with Experimental Falls in Middle-Aged Test Subjects. *Gait Posture* **2012**, *35*, 500–505. [CrossRef]
47. Kangas, M.; Korpelainen, R.; Vikman, I.; Nyberg, L.; Jämsä, T. Sensitivity and False Alarm Rate of a Fall Sensor in Long-Term Fall Detection in the Elderly. *Gerontology* **2015**, *61*, 61–68. [CrossRef]
48. Klenk, J.; Becker, C.; Lieken, F.; Nicolai, S.; Maetzler, W.; Alt, W.; Zijlstra, W.; Hausdorff, J.M.; van Lummel, R.C.; Chiari, L.; et al. Comparison of Acceleration Signals of Simulated and Real-World Backward Falls. *Med. Eng. Phys.* **2011**, *33*, 368–373. [CrossRef] [PubMed]
49. Mosquera-Lopez, C.; Wan, E.; Shastry, M.; Folsom, J.; Leitschuh, J.; Condon, J.; Rajhbeharrysingh, U.; Hildebrand, A.; Cameron, M.H.; Jacobs, P.G. Automated Detection of Real-World Falls: Modeled from People with Multiple Sclerosis. *IEEE J. Biomed. Health Inform.* **2020**. [CrossRef]

MDPI
St. Alban-Anlage 66
4052 Basel
Switzerland
Tel. +41 61 683 77 34
Fax +41 61 302 89 18
www.mdpi.com

Sensors Editorial Office
E-mail: sensors@mdpi.com
www.mdpi.com/journal/sensors

www.ingramcontent.com/pod-product-compliance
Lightning Source LLC
LaVergne TN
LVHW082008090526
838202LV00005B/254